PHANTOM FORMATIONS

PHANTOM FORMATIONS

MARC REDFIELD

CORNELL UNIVERSITY PRESS   ITHACA AND LONDON

Aesthetic Ideology
and the *Bildungsroman*

TAB. V.

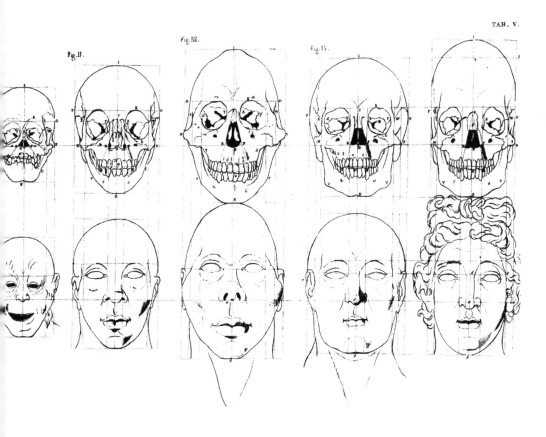

Open access edition funded by the National Endowment for the Humanities/ Andrew W. Mellon Foundation Humanities Open Book Program.

The illustration on the title page is from Peter Camper, *Dissertation sur les Variétés Naturelles qui caracterisent la physionomie des hommes des divers climats et des differens ages* (Paris: Francart, 1792). Reprinted by permission of the Bancroft Library of the University of California.

First published 1996 by Cornell University Press

Library of Congress Cataloging-in-Publication Data

Redfield, Marc, b. 1958
   Phantom formations : aesthetic ideology and the Bildungsroman / Marc Redfield.
     p. cm.
   Includes bibliographical references and index.
   ISBN-13: 978-0-8014-3236-1 (cloth) — ISBN-13: 978-1-5017-2316-2 (pbk.)
  1. Bildungsroman. 2. German fiction—19th century—History and criticism. 3. European fiction—19th century—History and criticism. 4. Aesthetics, Modern. I. Title.
PT747.E6R43   1996
809.3'0094—dc20   96-17186

Cover illustration: "The Sculptor Instructing Wilhelm," wood engraving from *Goethe's Works, Illustrated by the Best German Writers,* vol. 5. Ed. George Barrie. Philadelphia, 1885.

Contents

Preface

In a modest but ineluctable fashion, the specter of the *Bildungsroman* haunts literary criticism. This genre does not properly exist, and in a sense can be proved not to exist: one can take canonical definitions of *Bildung* (itself no simple term), go to the novels most frequently called *Bildungsromane*, and with greater or lesser difficulty show that they exceed, or fall short of, or call into question the process of *Bildung* which they purportedly serve. Even *Wilhelm Meisters Lehrjahre* can be (and has been) excluded from the genre it exemplifies. Nor does one need to be a postmodern literary theorist to encounter this paradox. Soundly humanistic Germanists have been doing so ever since the term *Bildungsroman* began to circulate in the early decades of the twentieth century (for another odd feature of this supposedly nineteenth-century genre is that its name barely appears in the literary record prior to the publication of Wilhelm Dilthey's *Experience and Poetry* [1906]: its currency is roughly coterminous with the professionalization of academic literary study). Yet despite, or because of, its referential complexity, the notion of the *Bildungsroman* is one of academic criticism's most overwhelmingly successful inventions. Few professional terms (let alone German ones) have achieved comparable dissemination in Western literary culture; and critics probably will go on talking about the *Bildungsroman* as long as the institutions of literary criticism as we know them survive. The *Bildungsroman* exemplifies the ideological construction of literature by criticism.

In consequence, the issues raised by this pseudo genre greatly surpass the literal terms of the debate over whether it exists or not. My central argument in this book is that the notion of the *Bildungsroman* brings into sharp focus the promises and pitfalls of aesthetics, and that aesthetics in turn exemplifies what we call ideology. As a result, this book is not in the ordinary sense a book about the *Bildungsroman*. It is certainly a work of literary criticism and offers as central to its self-justification readings of novels by Goethe, George Eliot, and Flaubert. But since my analyses discover in the rather minor professional embarrassment of the *Bildungs- roman* the infinitely inflatable question of the aesthetic, I am also writing about what we mean by culture, history, and humanity, what we do when we read or teach literature, and why the twentieth-century institutionali- zation of literature has generated the curious phenomenon of "literary theory." In an indirect fashion this book is about the literary institution and thus also about the political, technical, and cultural worlds which this in- stitution at once excludes and commemorates. This breadth of ambition stems from the peculiar difficulties of writing about aesthetic ideology.

Few narratives are more familiar to scholars of modern literature and culture than the story of the appearance of aesthetics, both as a new philo- sophical category and as a massively diffuse and influential discourse— one that provided the post-Romantic Western world with meanings for words such as "culture" and "art" that we now consider primary. The topic of beauty is as old as philosophy, but the notion of the aesthetic as a particu- lar sort of experience or judgment or class of objects does not begin to appear regularly until the eighteenth century. At the same time, large-scale historical developments were permitting, as is well known, the emergence of art and literature in their modern sense, and the transformation of the artist into the genius, the representative of universal humanity, whose pro- ductions transcend the system of commodity exchange which enables them. Aesthetics partakes of the emergence of the universal subject of bour- geois ideology.

Indeed, aesthetics enables and exemplifies the production of this subject. For though aesthetics has usually been subordinated to logic or ethics be- cause of its dependence on a sensory element, this very hybridity of the aesthetic makes it a privileged point of contact between the supersensible and the sensory worlds, and also grants it inherent pragmatic and ped- agogical force. Since its mission is to guarantee and promote spirit's artic- ulation with the world, the aesthetic establishes "disinterested" space in the service of a certain referential effectivity. In the harmonious free play of the faculties which results when Kant's subject performs a disinterested aes- thetic judgment, the judging subject becomes exemplary—capable, in its formality, of representing universal humanity. Thus in Schiller's influential *On the Aesthetic Education of Man* (1795), Kantian themes easily acquire political and historical dimensions. Because aesthetic education is at once the universal history "of man" and the specific history of the acculturation of certain groups and individuals, aesthetics provides a powerful self-validating mechanism for the representativeness of the social groups which can claim to have achieved and inherited this understanding of accultura-tion. The sheerly empirical qualities of being European, white, middle-class, male, and so on become either tacitly or overtly essentialized as privileged sites in the unfolding of an irreversible aesthetic history. Thus from the sober precincts of philosophy one is led with disconcerting speed to the large reaches of ideology; indeed, ideology then becomes a limit-term difficult to control. For this aesthetic logic of exemplarity subtends power-ful Western ideas and discourses of the self, the nation, race, historical process, the literary canon, and the function of criticism; it informs the role of the cultural sphere in modern Western societies, and the mission of the humanities in the modern university. And aesthetics not only structures crucial aspects of mainstream post-Romantic Western culture but also shapes this culture's internal nightmare, as Walter Benjamin indicated in his famous characterization of fascism as the "aestheticization of politics." A lurid but necessary task facing any genuine critique of aesthetics is that of engaging both the abyssal difference and the complex proximities between the humanist tradition and what Philippe Lacoue-Labarthe and Jean-Luc Nancy call "the Nazi myth"—a phrase coined to describe not the so-ciohistorical actuality of German fascism but rather the decisive turns of an ideology that transforms the representative subject of aesthetics into the exemplarity of a master race, and the humanistic, deferred promise of Schiller's Aesthetic State into the violent immediacy of a destiny.

Aesthetics thus poses the question of "ideology" itself in its vacillation between philosophy and politics, and between the languages and practices of high culture and those of modern propaganda. Furthermore, as a process of and discourse about formalization, aesthetics is always also prepared to function as a figure for the act of signification itself. The inflationary aes-thetic spiral generates the limit-term of ideology as "language." As a philo-sophical category, aesthetics is the place where the cognitive manifests itself in the phenomenal—where the essential structure of the sign, in other words, seems to unfold itself as an experience or intuition. Aesthetics trans-lates into psychological or phenomenal terms the unintuitable difference and repetition that allow a linguistic sign to mean and to refer. If Paul de Man asserted that "what we call ideology is precisely the confusion of linguistic with natural reality, of reference with phenomenalism," it was because he understood ideology as aesthetics. The full difficulty of such a claim becomes apparent once we realize that it is asking us to conceive of aesthetics as, paradoxically, at once structurally necessary, structurally in-coherent, and historically contingent—a ghostly event, haunted by its own inauthenticity, yet, despite its impossible and repressed dependence on linguistic difference, possessed of enormous social and political impact.

Polemical formulations are sometimes useful so long as one keeps in mind their limitations, and clearly the most polemical way to describe this book would be as an argument for the cognitive and ethical force of "deconstruction" as a critical activity. More specifically, as is perhaps already clear, this book situates itself in the tradition of rhetorical reading associated with the work of Paul de Man. I am certainly as aware as anyone that the profession has no great wish to hear more about this critic. Indeed, it may happen that even those who value de Man's project will feel a certain creeping lassitude at the invocation, yet once more, of this exhaustingly hypercathected proper name. Nonetheless I must ask readers to consider one more time the paradoxes of rhetorical reading: these paradoxes precisely and critically repeat those of aesthetics, and thereby allow us to begin measuring the true sociopolitical impact of aesthetic ideology. If my book has a single overriding purpose, it is to demonstrate that rhetorical reading *is* cultural critique and that, in the absence of a deconstructive or rhetorical analysis, cultural criticism will remain blind to the rationale and sometimes to the entire existence of the violent gestures with which aesthetic systems seek to exorcise their inability to ground their claims. Only by exposing aesthetics to the rhetorical predicament it both conceals and exacerbates is one able to explain the provenance, power, and instability of the aesthetic terminology—the language of type and stereotype, model and imitation, beauty and ugliness, prefiguration and exemplarity—that saturates the various discourses with which post-Enlightenment Western cultures have construed themselves as historical narrative, which is to say as aesthetic narratives of racial, sexual, and class identities and differences.

Both from cultural critics and Arnoldian humanists one frequently hears that the pursuit of political issues requires the sacrifice of literary concerns; yet the truth is the opposite: it is in its involuntary proximity to the self-reflexive and self-disruptive institution we now call "literature" that criticism comes into its own as ideology critique. The notion of literature, to be sure, forms part of the eighteenth-century emergence of aesthetics and may in fact be said to provide aesthetics with its most fully realized model. In the fully modern form it attains in the writings of the Jena Romantics, literature *is* criticism or theory: such is the full meaning (and the historical genesis) of the commonplace of the "self-conscious text" on which the scholarly and pedagogical edifice of modern criticism is built. Literature produces itself as the theory of itself, and it thereby becomes a "literary absolute," in Lacoue-Labarthe and Nancy's terms: a self-productive reflexivity that "aggravates and radicalizes the thinking of totality and the Subject." As a mirror and model for an autoproductive, proleptic, and synecdochic con-

sciousness, literature serves aesthetics and the institutions of aesthetic pedagogy, most visibly as the imaginary totality of the canon and its quite real
scholarly and pedagogical apparatuses.

But literature is also paradoxically incompatible with the institutions it
requires and sustains, precisely because it "aggravates and radicalizes"
aesthetics. In doing so, literature records the impossibility of the aesthetic
synthesis—which is why literary criticism and its institutions have always
inhabited a state of half-acknowledged crisis, and why any fundamental
critique of aesthetics has to pass through the space of literature. At this
point it is perhaps clear why I have focused this study on the *Bildungsroman*.
The notion of this genre functions as a pragmatic, aestheticized rendering
of the notion of the "literary absolute." It translates the literary absolute into
the empirical terms of human consciousness and action, proposing to confuse "reference with phenomenalism" directly and thoroughly by aestheticizing a life and thereby aestheticizing history. The *Bildungsroman* names a
faith in the congruence of literature and aesthetics (or, in other words, a
faith in the integrity of aesthetics per se) that criticism is neither able entirely to uphold or to do without. And since criticism depends on a model
of literature that is already its own criticism, further light on this paradox
may be obtained only from a reading of the literary texts themselves.

Given that the *Bildungsroman* exists only as a phantom, the choice of texts
to be read is in some ways an open one but in other ways comes burdened
with specific responsibilities. For any number of historical and theoretical
reasons, *Wilhelm Meisters Lehrjahre* lies at the heart of this spectral genre. It is
no coincidence that Schiller reacted with mixed enthusiasm and anxiety to
Goethe's novel when he read it in manuscript about the time he was finish-
ing *On the Aesthetic Education of Man,* or that Friedrich Schlegel's review of
the *Lehrjahre* contains his most concisely paradoxical formulation of the
relation between "literature" and "criticism." The issues I pursue here lead
directly and insistently back to this novel and its reception. And while it is
true that from *Wilhelm Meisters Lehrjahre* many possible routes of inquiry
spiral out, even at this point my choice of texts claims a certain rationale. I
have included a chapter on *Wilhelm Meisters Wanderjahre,* Goethe's curious
"sequel" to the *Lehrjahre,* not just because of Goethe's importance in discussions of the *Bildungsroman,* but because the *Wanderjahre* takes the plot of
Wilhelm's *Bildung* in directions that lead to a searching critique of aesthetics
as a political model. Subsequent chapters on George Eliot and Flaubert
partly record my wish to demonstrate that aesthetics is not simply a "German" problem, but more specifically seek to track major possibilities or
alternatives latent in aesthetic discourse. Eliot's *Middlemarch* represents the
culmination of a discourse of sympathy which originates with Shaftesbury
and eighteenth-century psychological aesthetics, whereas Flaubert's *L'Edu-*

cation sentimentale takes to the limit the aestheticization of irony as pure, impersonal form. Both texts, however, demonstrate the spectral origin and potentially violent destiny of aesthetics as a politico-pedagogical model, and both suggest the irreducibility of history to aesthetic narrative.

My discussions of Eliot and Flaubert thus claim to develop issues which my discussions of Goethe adumbrate; and all of the readings seek to document, elucidate, and develop the claims I set out in the opening chapters on aesthetic ideology and the *Bildungsroman*. Though it is not always the case with books built on close readings, *Phantom Formations* does intend its chapters to contribute more or less sequentially to an ongoing argument, and I can only hope that readers interested in this book's thesis will be willing to work through readings of three rather different, though of course also deeply related, nineteenth-century European oeuvres. With one exception the chapters are centered on canonical texts; and since *Wilhelm Meisters Wanderjahre* is no longer much read even in German departments, I have done my best to anchor my discussion of it in plot summary. Indeed, this book's purpose will be largely served if it manages to turn a few critical eyes, particularly in the English-speaking world, toward this last, strange, deeply political novel of Goethe's: a text that speaks with uncanny prescience to the disastrously pragmatic techno-aesthetics of our era. That literature cannot cure history has been a source of endless, sometimes comical frustration over the last two hundred years; yet texts of this sort can at least help explain why we have invested so much in literature's critical performance, and why it is neither simply erroneous to do so nor even a matter of choice. Literature may be a ghost, but the aesthetic machine that it discreetly haunts continues to play a major part in the production of norms of cultural identity. We can no more cease reading, or misreading, this predicament than we can cease being historical beings.

MARC REDFIELD

Claremont, California

Acknowledgments

Modified portions of chapter 1 have appeared as "Aesthetic Ideology and Literary Theory," *Centennial Review* 39.3 (1995); a compacted version of chapters 2 and 3 as "Ghostly *Bildung*: Gender, Genre, Aesthetic Ideology, and *Wilhelm Meisters Lehrjahre*," *Genre* 26.4 (1993 [1995]); another section from chapter 3 as "Gender, Aesthetics, and the *Bildungsroman*," *Wordsworth Circle* 25.1 (1994); a version of chapter 4 as "The Dissection of the State: *Wilhelm Meisters Wanderjahre* and the Politics of Aesthetics," *German Quarterly* 69.1 (1996); and a small piece of chapter 5 as part of "The Fictions of Telepathy," *Surfaces* 2.27 (1992). I am grateful for the editors' permission to reprint this material. The image on the title page of this book is taken from Peter Camper's *Dissertation sur les Variétés Naturelles qui caracterisent la physionomie des hommes des divers climats et des differens ages* (Paris: Francart, 1792), and shows a progression of skulls from monkey through various racial "types" to the Apollo Belvedere. It is reprinted courtesy of the Bancroft Library of the University of California.

Work on this book was aided by a Fletcher Jones Research Grant for the summer of 1992. The manuscript took final shape during a sabbatical year in France, while I was enjoying the support of the Borchard Foundation during the fall of 1993 and the Camargo Foundation during the spring of 1994. I am grateful to these foundations and their respective directors, W. A. Beling and Michael Pretina, and to Provost Murray Schwartz of the Claremont Graduate School, for making this year possible. The book's publication has been assisted by a grant from the CGS Provost's Office.

I thank Bernhard Kendler for his support for this project, and Teresa Jesionowski for her skillful editing of the manuscript. Cynthia Chase, Jonathan Culler, Neil Hertz, and J. Hillis Miller have given me invaluable advice and encouragement over many years, as have, more recently, Marshall Brown, David Clark, Constance Jordan, Wendy Martin, Gregory Polletta, Arden Reed, and my fellow Fellows at the Camargo Foundation. My sincere thanks as well to the students of the Claremont Graduate School's literature program; special thanks to Anita Bennett, Darcy Buerkle, Kimberley Cortner, Michael Ernest, Joel Lamore, and Daniel Scoggin, who provided crucial help with transatlantic requests for books, photocopies, and publication data; and to Kelly Douglass and Janet Retseck, who helped prepare the manuscript. Charles, Margaret, Peter, and Thomas Redfield provided constant intellectual and emotional support. My deepest debt is to Molly Ierulli; she has been part of this book since before it began. It is offered to the memory of Bill Readings, extraordinary scholar, colleague, and friend.

M. R.

PHANTOM FORMATIONS

1

Aesthetic Ideology

> If man is ever to solve that problem of politics in practice he will have to
> approach it through the problem of the aesthetic, because it is only through
> Beauty that man makes his way to Freedom.
> —Schiller, *On the Aesthetic Education of Man*

Critical accounts of contemporary Western literary culture invariably confront at some point the difficulty of explaining the vicissitudes of
literary theory. It is hard to account in rational or pragmatic terms for the
degree or kind of attention this rather forbidding academic discourse has
attracted, particularly in the United States, where the threat, and even to a
small extent the glamor of "theory" has achieved a certain sporadic recognition throughout higher middlebrow culture. One imagines that, somewhere, material interests must be involved: as Louis Althusser once remarked apropos of "Marxist theory," would there have been "the storms,
the denunciations, the passions which we have witnessed, if nothing had
been at stake except a simple quarrel over words?"[1] But though Althusser
can discern a historically efficacious specter—"Leninism"—behind the polemics he indicates, literary theory seems a specter without substance, a
phantom whose ability to scare or seduce resists easy translation into the
realities of power. Critics unsympathetic to theory have thus commonly
characterized it as, paradoxically, both awful and inconsequential.

But the puzzle of theory's popular reception does not lie simply in the
disproportion between a hysterical reaction and its occasion or referent.
Theory's representation has been far more ambiguous than, for instance,
Marxism's was in the U.S. media during the McCarthy era. It is perhaps
unsurprising that the hue and cry over theory has resulted in little one
would wish to call official repression or censorship, given how little appears to be at stake; but the mode of resistance which theory inspires seems
less tempered by tolerance than complicated by obsession. To be sure,

---

1. Louis Althusser, *Essays in Self-Criticism*, trans. Grahame Locke (London: New Left Books,
1976), 114; cited in Michael Sprinker, *Imaginary Relations: Aesthetics and Ideology in the Theory of
Historical Materialism* (London: Verso, 1987), 268.

opposition to theory can manifest itself in straightforwardly violent ways; but generally speaking a thread of fascination weaves through the texture of this resistance, as though theory were the object of a hysteria inseparable from a certain fetishism. Indeed, theory may be said to have profited from its demonization, against the backdrop of which it displays its glamorous cast of master theorists—figures in whom the fetishistic drift of theory finds embodiment. With the event of theory the culture industry's star system achieves manifestation in U.S. universities. And because theory may plausibly be said to have as its rationale the demystification of the kinds of illusions the star system exemplifies, theory has always also seemed at once radical and compromised, both from the perspectives of those practicing it and those opposed to it. The sort of hysteria that theory generates seems to encourage theory's relative success, but this success in turn immediately gets represented as theory's failure.[2]

Besides setting in motion contradictory hyperboles of power and impotence, representations of theory also entail certain obsessive associations. It is not prima facie obvious that theory should be so insistently qualifiable as "literary." Even if for argument's sake one assumes that something called theory was destined to enter the spotlight as the activity of a rather fictional "Yale School," one might have expected theory to assume a more philosophical or interdisciplinary public identity over the subsequent two decades, and to the extent that it has not, one remains faced with the question of theory's link to literature as a pedagogical institution. This problem leads to a related question, that of the popular media identification of "theory" with "deconstruction"—in one sense a wildly inaccurate equation, of course, but nonetheless not a straightforward case of bad reporting either, despite the unquestionable existence of a plurality of mutually hostile critical approaches with a claim to theoretical stature in the academy. Versions of the conflation of theory with deconstruction occur in professional as well as popular contexts, as does the further identification of the dyad theory/deconstruction with the proper names Jacques Derrida and, above all, Paul de Man. The fact that the actual influence exerted by these critics falls very short of their totemic stature offers us another version of the disproportion between theory and its hallucinatory projections. "The immense symptomatic significance of the *figure* of de Man," John Guillory notes, has been confirmed by the intensity of the furor accompanying the discovery of de Man's wartime journalism: "It would not have been necessary for so many theorists and anti-theorists, de Manians and anti-

---

2. See Barbara Johnson's chapter on this paradox, "Nothing Fails Like Success," in *A World of Difference* (Baltimore: Johns Hopkins University Press, 1987).

de Manians, to 'respond' to these revelations if *theory itself* were not per-ceived to be implicated in de Man. The easy condemnation in the media of theory along with de Man only confirmed a symbolic equation already present in the professional imaginary."[3] Theory is deconstruction and deconstruction is de Man: this fetishistic sequence may have no obvious link to institutional or discursive reality, but it goes into the making of the specter of literary theory.

And we may add at least one more term, or cluster of terms, to Guillory's equation. Mainstream journalistic and conservative academic portrayals of theory associate it with deconstruction on the one hand and "political" criticism on the other.[4] Once again, the actual debt that certain sorts of feminist, gay/lesbian, or Marxist critical practice might owe to (for in-stance) Derrida or de Man is hardly the issue. Anyone working seriously in the field knows the complexity of such filiations, and certainly also knows how few of the many critics presently engaged in some sort of cultural critique would term what they are doing "deconstruction." Even more rarely would one expect to hear de Manian deconstruction touted as the rationale for the gestures toward curricular expansion or reform that are often summed up under the rubric of "multiculturalism" —unless, that is, one is willing to listen to the ideological murmur that links these seemingly inappropriate things. When given full throttle, the resistance to theory ex-tends Guillory's "axis of imaginary identification" to achieve the sequence: theory-deconstruction-de Man-politics. Embodied and epitomized in the master critic, theory is the deconstruction of the canon, of aesthetic value, of "culture" itself. This in no way prevents theory from being charged with

3. John Guillory, *Cultural Capital: The Problem of Literary Canon Formation* (Chicago: University of Chicago Press, 1993), 178. For a particularly energetic instance of the equation of de Man with theory, see David Lehman, *Signs of the Times: Deconstruction and the Fall of Paul de Man* (New York: Poseidon, 1991). The popular success of Lehman's book reflects its ability to rework its story about theory into a story about a charismatic professor who embodies theory, but such personalizing gestures also crop up repeatedly in professional discourse on de Man: on the positive side, see the memorial writing collected in *The Lesson of Paul de Man, Yale French Studies* 69 (1985); on the negative, Frank Lentricchia's much-cited characterization of de Man as the "godfather" of the "Yale Mafia" in *After the New Criticism* (Chicago: University of Chicago Press, 1980), 282–83. I examine the imperative to humanize theory (and thus to some extent de Man) in this chapter; for more extensive accounts of de Man's totemic role in the organization of such questions in the contemporary critical scene, see my "Humanizing de Man," *Diacritics* 19.2 (1989): 35–53, and "De Man, Schiller, and the Politics of Reception," *Diacritics* 20.3 (1990): 50–70.
4. An example of this imaginary sequence unfolded in 1993 in the United States Senate, where, during his confirmation hearings, the candidate for the chair of the National Endowment for the Humanities announced his vehement opposition to "deconstruction," understood in this case as the theory that all enunciations are political. See Stephen J. Burd, "[Sheldon] Hackney Attacked and Praised for Criticizing Literary Theory," *Chronicle of Higher Education*, 14 June 1993, A21.

sterile inconsequentiality or aestheticism, since the "deconstruction" of value can always also be called a mere game of words. And we may add that if we press a little further into the political haunts of theory, we find ourselves once again traversing a Möbius-like surface in which accuser and accused tread each other's heels: the cultural critic or multiculturalist will more often than not share to some degree the conservative ideologue's suspicion of "theory" and echo back the sequence theory-deconstruction-de Man-politics, the only difference being that theory's politics will now be understood as nihilistic (and impotent) in a reactionary rather than a revolutionary mode. Between left- and right-wing political poles theory shuttles as a specter of the politics of the other. This pattern was observable well before the scandal of de Man's wartime journalism, which in one sense merely gave the screw one more turn by allowing the polemics surrounding theory to draw energy from our culture's rather suspect fascination with Nazism.

What are we to make of the phantasmatic paradoxes of literary theory? This book argues that they may be derived from those posed by the larger cultural and theoretical enigma of aesthetics. I shall eventually funnel the question of theory more narrowly into the puzzle of the *Bildungsroman*, a genre that my next chapter unpacks as the idea of a fully "aesthetic" literary genre. At that point I shall address head-on the question of theory's literariness; for the moment I propose to subordinate that question—without entirely forgetting it—to one concerning the relation between the specter of theory, as sketched, and a discursive entity called "aesthetics," which the rest of this chapter seeks to elucidate. I have already suggested ways in which this relation is at once well publicized and obscure. On the one hand, it seems the height of obviousness to say that theory represents aesthetics as ideology: indeed, scholars relatively indifferent to theoretical debate may well know that de Man's late work theorized something called aesthetic ideology, or may know about or even own Terry Eagleton's academic bestseller, *The Ideology of the Aesthetic*. The populist version of this knowledge, of course, casts theory as the assassin of aesthetic value. But on the other hand, as we have seen, theory is also persistently denounced as "aestheticism"—as though too large a helping of either aesthetics or theory turned it into its opposite. The hysteria coloring the topic of literary theory derives from this uncertain intrinsication of theory and aesthetics, which, as Fredric Jameson suggests in his dust-jacket blurb for Eagleton's book, has as its historical dimension the fact that theory originates "in the contradictions of philosophical aesthetics."[5] This indispensable genealogical insight

---

5. See Terry Eagleton, *The Ideology of the Aesthetic* (Oxford: Blackwell, 1990).

proposes aesthetics as a schizophrenic entity productive of the theory that critiques it—a theory, however, which then repeats within itself the self-consumption of aesthetics, turning away from itself as "aestheticism," which is to say, once again, "theory." Under such circumstances theory's demystification of aesthetics as ideology becomes an uncertain enterprise, though perhaps also an unavoidable one.

These considerations suggest some of the difficulties facing an analysis of aesthetics. We may add that in approaching aesthetics as ideology we are setting out to examine a vast and amorphous discursive disposition, in which the aesthetic lure wobbles between philosophy and politics, anthropology and psychology, and between the languages and practices of high culture and those of journalism, advertising, and propaganda. A critique of aesthetics, as we shall see, entails a critique of profoundly metaphysicial and efficaciously political notions of modernity, history, and human identity; it will be necessary to undertake an analysis that is at once wide-ranging and technically detailed, and this chapter returns to the problem of literary theory only at the end of a rather long trajectory. This last has been organized into four stages. The first section summarizes the development of aesthetics as a specific discourse in the eighteenth century, while also drawing attention to the peculiar difficulties raised by this discourse; the second looks closely at portions of Kant's *Critique of Judgment* which will help us confirm previous generalizations and locate certain sites of tension; the third rapidly surveys the post-Kantian development of aesthetics as a full-scale ideology and political model; the fourth returns laden with the fruits of a close reading of Kant to the late twentieth-century problem of "theory," and seeks to explain why theory functions as a name for persistent and disruptive difficulties in aesthetics. That these difficulties turn out to be representable in linguistic or rhetorical terms will allow us to understand why Paul de Man's work plays the role it does in contemporary debates about theory, and will prepare us for the claim, developed in chapter 2, that aesthetic education, or *Bildung*, finds its example, and its most intractable problem, in the idea of literature.

I

The question of art forms part of the inauguration of metaphysics with Plato and has played a prominent role throughout much of the tradition we construe as "Western." As is well known, however, the notion of the aesthetic as a specific sort of experience or category, and thus as a specific field of philosophical inquiry, belongs to the modern era. The term itself was coined in the mid eighteenth century by the Wolffian philosopher Alexander Baumgarten, in order to posit a "science of sensible cognition," as a subordinate complement to logic, the science of the higher faculty of reason.[6] Since for Baumgarten poetry is experienced as sensibility, the science of aesthetics comprehends the production and judgment of representations, and thus absorbs into its purview the faculties of imagination and taste. In Germany the term caught on rapidly. Baumgarten had many critics and imitators from the 1750s on, and by the 1820s Hegel could begin his lectures on fine art with the remark that despite the shortcomings of "the word Aesthetics, taken literally" (meaning as it does "the science of sensation" rather than the art of judgment), he will employ it anyway since it has "passed over into common speech."[7] In Britain the word did not achieve a comparable triumph until the end of the nineteenth century; however, the discourse we now call aesthetics knew a rich development in eighteenth-century Britain and with the Wolffian tradition in Germany formed the two wings of Enlightenment thought on sensibility and taste which Kant, in the *Critique of Judgment,* judged unphilosophical and sought to resolve.

The clarity with which one can delineate a history for philosophical aesthetics, however, is to some extent misleading, since even as a technical category it has proved deceptively volatile. Our understanding is not helped by epigrammatic claims such as Terry Eagleton's assertion that aesthetics is in some essential sense a "discourse of the body" (*Ideology of the Aesthetic,* 13): though aesthetics certainly has an irreducible commitment to phenomenal or sensory appearance, its entire rationale lies in the *articulation* of phenomenal appearance with the supersensible realm of cognition or spirit. Through the category of the aesthetic, philosophical systems seek to manifest and guarantee their own truth and coherence. Aesthetics consequently forms part of modern philosophy's effort to discover a ground for itself in the activity of the judging subject. With the post-medieval appearance of institutions and discourses invested in theories of the legislative subject—the subject, let us say, of an emergent capitalism—the topic of

---

6. Alexander Baumgarten, *Aesthetica* (Hildesheim: Georg Olms, 1961 [1750]), par. 1: "Aesthetica (theoria liberalium articum, gnoseologia inferior, ars pulcre cogitandi, ars analogi rationis) est scientia cognitionis sensitiuae."

7. G. W. F. Hegel, *Aesthetics: Lectures on Fine Art,* trans. T. M. Knox (Oxford: Clarendon Press, 1975), 1. Kant had registered more sustained misgivings: in the *Critique of Pure Reason* (1781), he rejected Baumgarten's neologism and insisted that, rather than signify a "critique of taste," aesthetics should obey etymology and name "that doctrine of sensibility which is true science"—the realm of *aistheta,* things perceivable, as opposed to that of *noeta,* things thinkable. See Immanuel Kant, *Critique of Pure Reason,* trans. Norman Kemp Smith (New York: St. Martin's Press, 1965), 66 (A21, B35/36). The shift from the aesthetic of the First *Critique* to that of the Third—from a sensory manifold always already subordinated to the concept, to a nonconceptual sensible instance carrying the mark of the supersensible—replays in miniature the itinerary of aesthetics in its modern exfoliation as philosophical category.

beauty became, as Howard Caygill suggests, "the crisis-point of judgment since it exceeded judgment."[8] Beauty at once names and conceals the problem of judging judgment—that is, of judging the production of the rules informing an act of judgment.

The eighteenth-century British debate about taste posits and elaborates a human ability to recognize and act according to what Shaftesbury called, in the teleological terms of the Cambridge Platonists, the "beautiful order" of the cosmos. Both natural beauty and the peculiarly disinterested activity of the artist communicate this divine order, which, in the Shaftesburean tradition of Hutcheson, Kames, and to some extent Burke, can be known only as aesthetic pleasure: "Though [the artist's] Intention be to please the World, he must nevertheless be, in a manner, *above it*; and fix his Eye upon that consummate *Grace*, that Beauty of *Nature*, and that *Perfection* of numbers, which the rest of Mankind, feeling only by the Effect, whilst ignorant of the Cause, term the *Je-ne-sçay-quoy*, the unintelligible, or the I know not what; and suppose to be a kind of *Charm*, or *Inchantment*, of which the Artist himself can give no account."[9] Taste cannot account for its own discriminative power, but this power confirms the harmony of individual interest or pleasure with universal law or moral end. Through intuition rather than through external law, the judging subject becomes integrated into the social and cosmic order. The discourse of taste thus not only generates our modern notions of artist and artwork but also forms part of the developing political discourses and institutions of post-1688 British civil society.[10]

8. Howard Caygill, *Art of Judgment* (Oxford: Blackwell, 1989), 37.

9. Anthony Ashley Cooper, Third Earl of Shaftesbury, *Characteristicks of Men, Manners, Opinions, Times*, 5th ed. (London, 1732 [1710]), vol. 1, "Advice to an Author," iii, 3 (332). A usefully concise definition of taste may be found in Hutcheson: "This superior Power of Perception is justly called a *Sense*, because of its Affinity to the other Senses in this, that the Pleasure is different from any *Knowledge* of Principles, Proportions, Causes, or of the Usefulness of the Object. . . ."; "[H]owever much we may *pursue* beautiful Objects from Self-love, with a View to obtain the Pleasures of Beauty . . . yet there must be a *Sense* of Beauty, antecedent to Prospects even of this Advantage, without which Sense these Objects would not be thus *advantageous*, nor excite in us this Pleasure which constitutes them advantageous." Francis Hutcheson, *An Inquiry into the Original of our Ideas of Beauty and Virtue*, 4th ed. (London, 1738 [1725]), I.xii, xiv (11, 12). For a historical survey of the notion of aesthetic disinterestedness in the British tradition, see Jerome Stolnitz, "On the Origins of 'Aesthetic Disinterestedness'," *Journal of Aesthetics and Art Criticism*, 20.2 (1961): 131–43.

10. For an important sociological account of aesthetics (as the commodification and compensatory glorification of the artist as representative of a "general common humanity"), see Raymond Williams, "The Romantic Artist," in *Culture and Society: 1780–1950* (New York: Columbia University Press, 1983 [1958]), 42. The political utility of aesthetics in a bourgeois society has been much remarked, and I offer my own further comments on this topic later in this chapter (and indeed, throughout this book); here we may note that the idea of aesthetic disinterestedness intersected with eighteenth-century (re)constructions of the "gentleman," whose reliably disinterested, "equal, wide survey" of society was frequently ascribed to his remove from active employment: see John Barrell, *English Literature in History, 1730–80: An Equal, Wide Survey* (London: Hutchinson, 1983). For a study of the tradition of civic humanism which forms

In the rather different political environment of Prussian absolutism, the seductions and difficulties of taste exerted pressure in ways that led, with Baumgarten, to the uneasy incorporation of "aesthetics" as a new science of sensibility within the Leibniz-Wolff system. Wolffian philosophy, which quite explicitly saw itself as the philosophical complement to the autocratic state, rested on a hierarchical distinction between reason and the senses, with the clarity of rational perception opposed to and, by rights, ordering and ruling the confusion of sensible perception. As the enlightened monarch of philosophy's domain, Wolffian reason could not easily tolerate the senses' claim to perceive unity or perfection in unmediated fashion, and this led to difficulties when the system was asked to provide a satisfactory account of judgments of taste. Caygill, tracing the compromises with Wolffianism effected by Gottsched, Bodmer and Breitinger, and Baumgarten, is willing to claim that "the apparently minor problem of pleasure in the beautiful brought down the whole Wolffian edifice" (*Art of Judgment*, 127). For though Baumgarten, like Gottsched, wrote as a Wolffian from a university chair, his work represents a turning point in pre-Kantian German philosophy: not only do the senses acquire a science, but sensible knowledge becomes the matrix of education and progress, because, according to the dogmatic categories which Baumgarten uses and displaces, the higher faculty of reason merely orders representations while the lower faculty, as imagination, produces them. Baumgarten's focus on the mind's productive power thus led naturally to a concern for this power's acculturation; and from these moorings Baumgarten's admirer, Herder, was able to launch a fully historical theory of culture—of culture, that is, as the historical self-production of humanity—in his prize-winning essay *The Origin of Language* (1771).[11]

The purpose of this whirlwind summary of eighteenth-century aesthetics is to prepare us to absorb and credit a few generalizations. First, we may note that, contrary to popular belief, aesthetics functions as a referential and political discourse. The "disinterestedness" it claims for its modes of manifestation serves to underwrite the coherence of even the most unnervingly complex social and epistemological orders: indeed, as Caygill points out, Adam Smith's *Theory of Moral Sentiments* identifies beauty—the perception of formal regularity in excess or in advance of utility—as the engine of economic production itself:

---

the context of the British discourse of taste, see J. G. A. Pocock, *The Machiavellian Moment: Florentine Political Thought and the Atlantic Republican Tradition* (Princeton: Princeton University Press, 1975).

11. For a full account of Baumgarten's system, its relation to Wolffianism and its (considerable) influence on Kant, see Caygill, *Art of Judgment*, 148–71.

If we consider the real satisfaction which all these things are capable of affording, by itself and separated from the beauty of that arrangement which is fitted to promote it, it will always appear in the highest degree contemptible and trifling. But we rarely view it in this abstract and philosophical light. We naturally confound it in our imagination with the order, the regular and harmonious movement of the system, the machine or oeconomy by means of which it is produced. The pleasures of wealth and greatness, when considered in this complex view, strike the imagination as something grand and beautiful and noble, of which the attainment is well worth all the toil and anxiety which we are so apt to bestow upon it.

And it is well that nature imposes upon us in this manner. It is this deception which rouses and keeps in continual motion the industry of mankind. It is this which first prompted them to cultivate the ground, to build houses, to found cities and commonwealths, and to invent and improve all the sciences and arts, which ennoble and embellish human life.[12]

Aimed toward beauty, desire becomes ruled by imagination and expresses itself as industry; and thus, through the "invisible hand" (184) of the providential trick of aesthetic pleasure, individual greed results in communal wealth and progress.[13] However much Smith's fable may seem consignable to a distant Enlightenment, we should at least keep in mind the larger point that, as a discourse, aesthetics intends to underwrite the origin and upkeep of material civilization, albeit by indirect or intangible means. The purpose of aesthetics is nothing more or less than to ensure *purposiveness*. Nineteenth-century theorists of "culture" make this point incessantly. Matthew Arnold's famous call for a disinterested criticism urges the critic to "keep out of the region of immediate practice in the political, social, humanitarian sphere" precisely in order to inculcate "that more free speculative treatment of things, which may perhaps one day make its benefits felt even in this sphere, but in a natural and thence irresistible manner."[14] Cardinal Newman distills the double gesture of aesthetics into a manifesto, asserting the moral necessity of the belief that

12. Adam Smith, *The Theory of Moral Sentiments* (Indianapolis: Liberty Classics, 1982), 183.
13. Caygill's remarkable intervention at this point is to observe that Smith's later *Wealth of Nations* needs to propose, as an analogue for taste, the harmony of natural value and market price: a harmony that can be guaranteed only by the invisible hand of "divinely established proportions," in this case proportions between production and consumption (*Art of Judgment*, 93). It is one of the less noticed paradoxes of modern history that economics may with as much justice be said to originate in aesthetics as the reverse. Or, more accurately put, both aesthetics and economics develop out of moral philosophy. For a fine discussion emphasizing this point, see the rendition of Caygill's argument in Guillory, *Cultural Capital*, 269–340.
14. Matthew Arnold, "The Function of Criticism at the Present Time," in *The Complete Prose Works of Matthew Arnold*, vol. 3: *Lectures and Essays in Criticism*, ed. R. H. Super (Ann Arbor: Michigan University Press, 1965), 275.

the process of imparting knowledge to the intellect in this philosophical way is its true culture; that such culture is a good in itself; that the knowledge which is both its instrument and result is called Liberal Knowledge; that such culture, together with the knowledge which effects it, may be fitly sought for its own sake; that it is, however, in addition, of great secular utility, as constituting the best and highest formation of the intellect for social and political life.[15]

Mutatis mutandis, similar formulations appear throughout the history of criticism from Coleridge to T. S. Eliot and the twentieth-century academic formalist tradition. The polished sides of the well-wrought urn mirror the providential order of the political itself.[16]

The second point, which may be considered a temporal projection of the first, is that aesthetics is a discourse or myth of history. The self-production of self which from Herder through Gadamer has been conceptualized in the German tradition as *Bildung* may without hyperbole be said to be *the* narrative of aesthetics, and we shall see that much of the ideological efficacity of aesthetic discourse derives from its temporal structure. At the heart of this story of self-production is the double bind which taste sets out to resolve through its figure of an unknowable but nonetheless intuitively "knowable" harmony. That is, the paradox of taste's having to "produce its own context, give itself law," as Caygill puts it (*Art of Judgment*, 38), unfolds into temporal narrative, as our excerpt from Smith's *Theory of Moral Sentiments* demonstrates. Aesthetics "rouses and keeps in continual motion the industry of mankind" because aesthetics is constitutionally in excess of itself as it asserts and reaffirms its own legitimacy. And it may be noted as a third general point about aesthetics that the paradoxes of taste cast a shadow of

15. John Henry Cardinal Newman, *The Idea of a University Defined and Illustrated*, ed. Martin J. Svaglic (New York: Holt, Rinehart and Winston, 1966 [1852–73]), 163. For an analysis of this passage, and of the politics of the "idea of the university" in nineteenth- and twentieth-century Britain—an idea positioned within an ongoing debate about the usefulness of useless knowledge—see Robert Young, "The Idea of a Chrestomathic University," in *Logomachia: The Conflict of the Faculties*, ed. Richard Rand (Lincoln: University of Nebraska Press, 1992), 97–126.
16. As Richard Ohmann comments, "[T]he pages of the New Critics are bound together with moral fiber, almost strident in urging a social mission for literature." *English in America* (New York: Oxford University Press, 1976), 71. As I note later in this chapter and discuss at greater length in chapter 4, the close-knit relation between the aesthetic and the political may in fact be said to mark the origins of Western political thought. We might note here that "art for art's sake," or aestheticism, in the negative sense that the term acquired in the late nineteenth century, has generally remained a marginalized mode of aesthetic discourse, linked to parody and to the construction of alternative middle-class sexual identities or styles. Much scholarship has recently focused on the development of homoerotic styles in fin-de-siècle literature, which is to be sure also the period in which medicalized typologies of "sexual identity" were being generated. The interplay between modern aesthetics and homoeroticism, however, goes back to Winckelmann and merits close analysis. For some remarks on the relation between aesthetics and gender see the concluding chapter.

illegitimacy, deceitfulness, or fictionality. Smith's nature "imposes on us" by practicing a benevolent "deception" on which civilization rests. Aesthetics occupies an ambiguous position—both foundational and marginal—in most post-Kantian philosophical systems for precisely this reason. Its very claim to produce the unity it discovers makes it vulnerable to the Platonic charge of lying.[17]

We may assimilate the referential and historical ambitions and anxieties of taste into a fourth general observation: unlike the classical tradition of poetics it displaces, aesthetics is in no way limited to being on or about the experience or object that it frames and specifies, but is always also a discourse on humanity and history, and the nature of representation itself. If aesthetics invents autonomy as the condition of the artwork, and disinterestedness as the condition of the perception of the artwork, it also defines art as the sign of the human, the human as the producer of itself, and history as the ongoing work of art that is humanity. Thus the philosophical category of aesthetics bleeds into the more general question of ideology, and into the paradox of a discourse which claims to be both historical (since it produces itself) and trans-historical (since it produces itself as universal form). It is not just that aesthetics is historically inseparable from the vastly complex developments one summarizes as the emergence of bourgeois hegemony—industrialization, capitalization, and the appearance of the modern bureaucratic state; mercantilist and imperialist expansion; the secularization of religious discourse; the reconfiguration of gender roles; the emergence of the culture industry; and so on. The point is that aesthetics intends, as it were, to be *about* all these things, to the extent that they form part of the "all" that is to be folded into aesthetic form. Because of its internal dynamics, the story of aesthetics inflates until one is telling stories of the largest sort of historical events (the consolidation of capitalism, or of the modern "subject"), events which compete in grandeur with the philosophical difficulties they contextualize (the self-production of judgment, the intuitive manifestation of unity). In consequence many stories of Romanticism move uneasily between historical and formal concerns, seeking to explain the history of their own representational possibility. Michel Foucault's famous claim that "man" is a late eighteenth-century "invention" derives its critical—and sensational—edge from its emphatic

17. Thus with relatively rare exceptions such as Schelling's *System of Transcendental Idealism*, nineteenth-century philosophies subordinate aesthetics to categories or modes more firmly grounded in reason or spirit. While art "points through and beyond itself," in Hegel's words, for instance, aesthetic truth must remain adequate to sensory experience and thus "neither in content nor in form is art the highest and absolute mode of bringing to our minds the true interests of the spirit" (*Aesthetics*, 9). In Kant, as we shall see, a hierarchy is even more sharply drawn, with the aesthetic serving as a propaedeutic for the ethical, though nonetheless also underwriting the coherence of the entire critical architectonic.

historicization of a transcendental term, but otherwise can hardly be said to deviate from a familiar paradigm in which the Romantic era serves to usher into existence a self-consciously historical modern world.[18] Modernity might plausibly be characterized as the reiterated retelling of the birth of the modern; and aesthetics is perhaps our culture's most suggestive name for this narrative. For in aesthetic narrative "man" is reinvented as nothing less than "culture," a word that replays the spiral of aesthetics by indicating at once the fine arts and all of civilization.[19]

II

In order to document these claims more fully and render the diagnosis more precise, I now turn to Kant's critical rewriting of eighteenth-century aesthetics in the *Critique of Judgment*. The problem of taste occupies a position in the critical architectonic which the above summary of pre-Kantian aesthetics will have rendered familiar. As Gilles Deleuze notes, aesthetic judgment in the Third *Critique* uncovers the "deepest" (though not the "highest") aspect of the soul, since it reveals under the parliamentary hierarchies of the Kantian faculties of mind "a deeper free and indeterminate accord of the faculties as the condition of the possibility of every determinate relationship."[20] In its speculative employment, reason operates under the rule of the understanding, as does the imagination; in its

18. Michel Foucault, *The Order of Things: An Archaeology of the Human Sciences* (New York: Vintage Books, 1973), 319, passim. Classic narratives that follow the aesthetic paradigm may be found in M. H. Abrams, *Natural Supernaturalism: Tradition and Revolution in Romantic Literature* (New York: Norton, 1971), and *The Mirror and the Lamp: Romantic Theory and the Critical Tradition* (New York: Oxford University Press, 1953). Romanticism is a charged locus of study precisely because it stages the historical appearance of the historicist humanism that directs the historical inquiry. Our understanding of historical periodization is itself Romantic, and more than one period constructed in this fashion is supposed to have witnessed the "invention of man": the Renaissance, for instance, particularly in the wake of Burckhardt's *Die Kultur der Renaissance in Italien* (1860), or "Ancient Greece."
19. A helpful guide to the emergence of the modern sense of the word "culture" and its relatives is Raymond Williams, *Keywords: A Vocabulary of Culture and Society*, rev. ed. (New York: Oxford University Press, 1985). See especially the entries "Aesthetic," "Art," and "Culture." (The latter, Williams tells us, is "the original difficult word" that inspired the project [14].) The word "culture" in its modern sense was not common until the late nineteenth century— Arnold's use of it in *Culture and Anarchy* (1867) was still controversial—but its appearance, as Williams's work among others has demonstrated, was overdetermined. For a complementary study focused on the fortunes of the term "civilisation" in France and "Zivilisation," "Kultur," and "Bildung" in Germany, see Norbert Elias, *The History of Manners: The Civilizing Process, vol. 1*, trans. Edmund Jephcott (New York: Pantheon Books, 1978 [1939]), 3–50. The modern notion of "art" or *Kunst* appears to be a late eighteenth- and early nineteenth-century development, and during this period a certain transition is particularly salient: Kant, in the *Critique of Judgment* (1790), for instance, is uncertain whether watchmaking is a fine art or a handicraft (sec. 43).
20. Gilles Deleuze, *Kant's Critical Philosophy: The Doctrine of the Faculties*, trans. Hugh Tomlinson and Barbara Habberjam (Minneapolis: University of Minnesota Press, 1984 [1963]), 68.

practical, moral employment, reason reigns supreme, and the two other active faculties assist in subordinate ways. In the *Critique of Judgment*, the imagination accedes to prominence in the rotating logic of the Kantian system, but with a difference: rather than legislate, the imagination engenders a free play of the faculties which testifies to the good health of the system. In aesthetic judgment the imagination and the understanding are "in free play" insofar as they "harmonize with each other as required for cognition in general."[21] (More specifically, "the imagination *in its freedom* harmonizes with the understanding *in its lawfulness*" [sec. 35]; the result is "lawfulness without a law.") Aesthetic pleasure is the feeling that accompanies and records this harmony, which is ultimately indicative of "nature's subjective purposiveness for our cognitive power" (sec. 57). Aesthetic judgment thus underwrites the validity of the cognitive processes, and in doing so it provides a bridge from cognitive to ethical judgment, for as we shall see, Kant also argues that "the beautiful is the symbol of the morally good" (sec. 59), the mark or sign of "the supersensible substrate of humanity" (sec. 57).

These remarkable accomplishments unfold from the act of formal reflection that composes what Kant, true to eighteenth-century tradition, calls taste. A pure aesthetic judgment, that is, a pure judgment of taste, refers a presentation to "the subject and his feeling of pleasure or displeasure" (sec. 1); however, judgments of taste distinguish themselves from the empiricism of judgments about the merely "agreeable" through their claim to universality. A judgment of taste is subjective, but it is also prescriptively universal in that it presupposes that all other judging subjects *ought* to agree with the judgment. The first half of the Third *Critique* is largely devoted to unpacking the logic and the implications of this universalizing demand, which occurs in the absence of any concept pertaining to the object, and emerges entirely from the formal disinterestedness of the judgment itself. In an aesthetic judgment the object is considered in its formality, which is to say, in Kantian terms, that the object is reflected in the imagination rather than enjoyed in sensation or cognized; and this disinterestedness—the absence, in other words, of any judgment as to the object's existence, meaning, or purpose—causes the judging subject to believe in the universal validity of the judgment (sec. 6). A "universal voice" of assent is postulated (sec. 8), which becomes the subjective principle of "common sense." Common sense is the ideal standard of universal communicability, and is "the effect arising from the free play of our cognitive powers" (sec. 20). The subjective

21. Immanuel Kant, *Critique of Judgment*, trans. Werner S. Pluhar (Indianapolis: Hackett Publishing Co., 1987), 62 (sec. 9). Since several translations are presently in circulation, in what follows I refer to citations by section number. References to the German are taken from *Kritik der Urteilskraft*, ed. Wilhelm Weischedel (Frankfurt: Suhrkamp, 1974).

necessity of the idea of a common sense is grounded not just in empirical fact ("That we do actually presuppose this indeterminate standard of a common sense is proved by the fact that we presume to make judgments" [sec. 22]), but also in systemic necessity:

> [I]f cognitions are to be communicated, then the mental state, i.e., the attunement of the cognitive powers that is required for cognition in general . . . must also be universally communicable. . . . [T]he only way this attunement can be determined is by feeling (rather than by concepts). Moreover, this attunement itself, and hence also the feeling of it (when a presentation is given) must be universally communicable, while the universal communicability of a feeling presupposes a common sense. Hence it would seem that we do have a basis for assuming such a sense, and for assuming it without relying on psychological observations, but as the necessary condition of the universal communicability of our cognition, which must be presupposed in any logic and any principle of cognitions that is not skeptical. (Sec. 21)

With the subjective universality of aesthetic judgment in place, the harmony of the faculties subsequently extends outward toward the world. Both empirical and rational interests can be indirectly attached to aesthetic disinterestedness: we deduce a fortuitous harmony between nature and our freely-playing faculties based on nature's willingness to supply the natural content (the colors, sounds, and so on) composing the object that is being judged formally. Aesthetic judgment thus paves the way for teleological and moral judgment: "Taste enables us, as it were, to make the transition from sensible charm to a habitual moral interest without making too violent a leap; for taste presents the imagination as admitting, even in its freedom, of determination that is purposive for the understanding, and it teaches us to like even objects of sense freely, even apart from sensible charm" (sec. 59).

This thumbnail sketch of Kant's argument suffices to suggest the considerable philosophical utility of aesthetic disinterest, as well as the makings of various complications and difficulties. For our purposes it will be useful briefly to examine the vexed status of empiricism in Kant's critical aesthetic. The main purpose of the analytic of taste is to establish non-empirical—and, of course, non-dogmatic—grounds for aesthetic judgment; but judgment nonetheless retains a complex proximity to the empirical in its dependence on the event of the judgment itself, which is always singular, and, even in the case of judgments about the sublime, occurs in a certain relation to objects of experience. In judgments about the beautiful the object is directly involved in its formality, with the twist that beauty is not a property or predicate of the object, but derives entirely from the nature of the judgment itself. But at the same time, like Adam Smith, Kant identifies aesthetic judgment with a certain systematic confusion or error: because aesthetic judgments "resemble" cognitive judgments in their universality, the judging subject "will talk about the beautiful as if beauty were a characteristic of the object and the judgment were logical (namely, a cognition of the object through concepts of it) even though the judgment is only aesthetic and refers the object's presentation merely to the subject" (sec. 6). In the analytic of the sublime Kant calls this act of reification "subreption": a displacement whereby "respect for the object is substituted for respect for the idea of humanity within ourselves as subjects" (sec. 27). Since, in Kant's system, the sublime engages "formless" objects and thus (unlike the beautiful) has no essential relation to the natural world, subreption appears as a more dramatic error in judgments about the sublime than in those about the beautiful. But a certain subreption infects, even enables, all aesthetic judgment. Aesthetic judgment would not provide the synthesis it does if it did not "resemble" ethical and logical judgments while remaining distinct from them. Yet this resemblance generates a constitutive instability: the purely subjective or formal nature of aesthetic judgment is constantly being effaced in and through its own production. The effacement is necessary if rational interest is to reassert itself at the close of the aesthetic trajectory; but this erasure of the formality of judgment must always have *already* occurred for the trajectory to be plotted in the first place.[22]

Furthermore, Kant appears to repeat the subreptive error himself, since a certain empirical objectivity of beauty recurs in his text as the difference between "free" and "adherent" beauty, and in the person of the "ideal" of beauty—"man." A pure judgment of taste occurs only when "free beauty" (*pulchritudo vaga*) is being judged: beauty that does not presuppose "a concept of what the object is meant to be" (sec. 16); otherwise the beauty is adherent or accessory (*pulchritudo adhaerens*). Thus, despite aesthetic judgment's purely subjective formality, the object being judged turns out to have a hand in determining the modality of the judgment. Certain objects presuppose the concept of their purpose; certain objects do not. Objects capable of

22. It is important to note that the predicament of the "always already" is not in itself an empirical one: empiricism is rather the *product* of this constitutive formal instability. My argument thus takes issue with Frances Ferguson's account of Kant, and deconstructive readings of Kant, in *Solitude and the Sublime: Romanticism and the Aesthetics of Individuation* (New York: Routledge, 1992). Ferguson's arguments are too complex to summarize here, particularly since I shall not be examining the *Critique of Judgment*'s sections on the sublime; but one may note Ferguson's tendency to translate structural fractures (here, the "always already" of subreption) into dialectical models of infinite or infinitesimal regress, which in turn allows her to recover, in sublime fashion, a transcendental subject (see, e.g., 1–32, passim).

occasioning a pure judgment of taste may occasion other sorts of judgments as well: "flowers are free natural beauties," but not to the botanist's eye; and a similar flexibility would hold for the other objects capable of free beauty making up Kant's rather curious list ("many birds (the parrot, the humming-bird, the bird of paradise) and a lot of crustaceans in the sea"; "designs à la grecque, the foliage on borders or on wallpapers, etc."; "all music not set to words").[23] But objects that presuppose their concept *cannot* be the object of a pure judgment of taste: "the beauty of a human being . . . or of a horse, or of a building" can only be "adherent beauty" (sec. 16).

The rationale of this second list has been unpacked by Jacques Derrida: a concept adheres to the horse because the horse adheres to man—that is, to man "no longer [considered] as a beautiful object (of adherent beauty) but as the subject of aesthetic and teleological judgments."[24] Certain objects require certain kinds of judgments because the field of conceptual and phenomenal discriminations is always already ordered around man. And because of his irreducible centrality within the field of judgment, man, "alone among all objects in the world," admits of an ideal of beauty (sec. 17). For since an ideal (that is, "the presentation of an individual being as adequate to an idea") is an idea of reason, ideal beauty is necessarily adherent ("An ideal of beautiful flowers, of beautiful furnishings, or a beautiful view, is unthinkable"). But ordinary adherent beauties ("a beautiful mansion, a beautiful tree, a beautiful garden, etc.") are equally incapable of ideality—"presumably," Kant writes, "because the purposes are not sufficiently determined and fixed by their concept, so that the purposiveness is nearly as free as in the case of *vague* beauty." Man is the only object so utterly defined by purpose that he "has the purpose of [his] existence within [him]self" (sec. 17). He is the empirical event as the closure of the ideal; he contains the free play of beauty within the self-reflexivity of embodied purpose, repeating taste's power to give itself its own law. Michel Foucault's story of the "invention of man," mentioned earlier, is anchored in such Kantian moments: "[T]he threshold of our modernity is situated not by the attempt to apply objective methods to the study of man, but rather by the constitution of an empirico-transcendental doublet which was called *man*" (*Order of Things*, 319). As the "being such that knowledge will be attained in him of what renders all knowledge possible," man is transcendental, and in providing a body for knowledge as transcendental critique, he provides knowledge's "empirical" ground (319). The invention of man is

23. All of these examples raise questions, but music plays a particularly ambivalent role in the *Critique of Judgment*'s various hierarchies and taxonomies: it is "situated in the gap between the beautiful and the agreeable, and confound[s] the distinction between form and content," as Arden Reed shows in "The Debt of Disinterest: Kant's Critique of Music," *MLN* 95 (1980): 569.
24. Jacques Derrida, "Parergon," in *The Truth in Painting*, trans. Geoffrey Bennington and Ian McLeod (Chicago: University of Chicago Press, 1987), 105.

the invention of a pragmatism indissociable from the transcendental space of the human.[25]

The empirico-transcendental doublet's relation to aesthetic judgment is, however, both fundamental and devious. For with the appearance of man as the ideal of beauty, a bifurcation occurs in the Third *Critique* between the pure and the ideal: as the ideal of beauty, "man" is also strictly speaking the only entity *in*capable of serving as an object of a pure judgment of taste. Man is the "impurity" necessary to provide taste with its ideal, even though the purity of the judgment of taste is what provides the system with its guarantee of internal and external harmony. Derrida captures this paradox in one of his evocative puns: man, the "paragon," seeks to enclose and annul the "parergon," or frame defining the formality of aesthetic judgment. The trope of the frame is Kant's, and the ambiguous status of the frame—neither of the artwork nor apart from it—sums up the difficulty of aesthetic formalism: "Even what we call *ornaments* (*parerga*), i.e., what does not belong to the whole presentation of the object as an intrinsic constituent, but [is] only an extrinsic addition, increases our taste's liking, and yet it too does so only by its form, as in the case of picture frames, or drapery on statues, or colonnades around magnificent buildings" (sec. 14). In giving shape to aesthetic space, the frame of form must cut itself off from interest, yet also mirror the finality it negates, effacing its own interruptive force. Constitutive and marginal, necessary and supplemental, neither intrinsic nor extrinsic, the parergon provides a figure for the undecidable, double bind of a "pure cut" of judgment that must also never entirely cut its links with perception and meaning. I take up the paradox of aesthetic formalization shortly in more specifically linguistic terms, but first let me prepare a more thorough understanding of the anthropological and political narratives which this paradox at once troubles and serves. The theories of history, society, and culture which arrange themselves around the parergon of aesthetics require for their understanding a closer look at the logic of aesthetic exemplarity.

III

The necessity of the universality of aesthetic judgment is *"exemplary,* i.e., a necessity of the assent of *everyone* to a judgment that is regarded as an

25. I discuss the pragmatic thrust of aesthetics throughout this book, but particularly in the next section of this chapter and in chapter 4 below. The relation between aesthetics and modern philosophical pragmatism would repay lengthy analysis, in lieu of which one may recall that in Dewey's *Art as Experience* (New York: Minton, Balch, 1934), aesthetic experience grounds and exemplifies experience itself: "[N]o experience of whatever sort is a unity unless it has esthetic quality" (40).

example of a universal rule that we are unable to state" (sec. 18). Exemplarity signifies an a priori presumption of a universal act of identification, yet it is the locus of an insistent subreption. Common sense tumbles into a "weak" empiricism "barely sufficient for a conjecture" just as the *Critique of Judgment* prepares to discover man's exemplarity as the ideal of beauty:

> The universal communicability of the sensation (of liking or disliking)—a universal communicability that is indeed not based on a concept—[I say that] the broadest possible agreement among all ages and peoples regarding this feeling that accompanies the presentation of certain objects is the empirical criterion [for what is beautiful]. This critierion, although weak and barely sufficient for a conjecture, [does suggest] that a taste so much confirmed by examples stems from [a] deeply hidden basis, common to all human beings, underlying their agreement in judging the forms under which objects are given them.
>
> That is why we regard some products of taste as *exemplary*. (Sec. 17)

In principle the example as sensuous particular does not determine the judgment, since the imagination is "productive and spontaneous" rather than reproductive in relation to the exemplary object.[26] And by the same token, as we have seen, the properly *aesthetic* example should not in itself perform an idealization, since in Kantian terms an ideal involves the rational idea of perfection.

But a certain subreption and idealization prove inseparable from the discovery of "man" and "common sense," two figures that intertwine in Kant's text in terms oddly reminiscent of empiricist accounts of taste as a process of abstraction (through which, as Hume puts it, "considering myself as a man in general, [I] forget, if possible, my individual being and my peculiar circumstances").[27] This empiricizing moment occurs when the example becomes the narrative of a movement from presentation to representation:

> [W]e compare our judgment not so much with the actual as rather with the merely possible judgments of others, and [thus] put ourselves in the position of everyone else, merely by abstracting from the limitations that [may] happen to attach to our own judging; and this in turn we accomplish by

26. The text is notably uneasy at this juncture: "Although in apprehending a given object of sense the imagination is tied to a determinate form of that object and to that extent does not have free play (as it does in poetry), it is still conceivable that the object may offer it just the sort of form in the combination of its manifold as the imagination, if it were left to itself [and] free, would design in harmony with the *understanding's lawfulness* in general" (Kant, "General Comment on the First Division of the Analytic," *Critique of Judgment*).

27. David Hume, "Of the Standard of Taste," in *Essays, Moral, Political, and Literary*, rev. ed., ed. Eugene F. Miller (Indianapolis: Liberty Classics, 1985), 239.

leaving out as much as possible whatever is matter, i.e., sensation, in the presentational state, and by paying attention solely to the formal features of our presentation or of our presentational state. (Sec. 40)

Sketched at such moments in the *Critique of Judgment* is the story of an ascent from the sensuous particular to the formal universal; and as David Lloyd has argued, this embryonic narrative composes the ideological matrix of aesthetics. The example unfolds into subreptive narrative because of the circular predicament of taste. The example is only an example thanks to the formalizing power of judgment, yet common sense depends on examples for its appearance and development: "The common sense that is the foundation of taste, precisely as a *sense,* cannot be deduced transcendentally or be supplied by universal rule: its exercise as its manifestation depends upon prior examples."[28] The a priori act of formalization that is exemplarity is thus always marked by a "prior" formalization: the exemplary is always belated with respect to itself. This paradox may be inverted: the exemplary is always ahead of itself, moving toward an ideal, precisely because of the lag or lapse inherent within the example. We have already encountered this paradox in the subreptive narrative movement from an empirical past (the exemplary as an accumulation of previous judgments) to an ideal futurity: "[T]he broadest possible agreement among all ages and peoples regarding this feeling that accompanies the presentation of certain objects is the empirical criterion [for what is beautiful]. . . . That is why we regard some products of taste as *exemplary*" (sec. 17). This self-confessedly "weak" empirico-transcendental narrative has been generated out of the non-empirical doubleness of an act of formalization which must always be behind or ahead of itself in order to be itself.

For the moment, however, let me focus attention on this narrative's inherently historical and political drift. Just as aesthetic judgment takes narrative shape as a movement from sensuous presentation to formal representation, civilization becomes the history of a passage from primitive sensuality to the universal communicability of aesthetic judgment proper—a narrative, however, that is always double: humanity must be at once an "original contract" and a latency, a product of its own history:

[A] concern for universal communication is something that everyone expects and demands from everyone else, on the basis, as it were, of an original contract dictated by [our] very humanity. Initially, it is true, only charms thus become important in society and become connected with great interest, e.g., the dyes people use to paint themselves (roucou among the Caribs and cinnabar among the Iroquois), or the flowers, sea shells,

28. David Lloyd, "Kant's Examples," *Representations* 28 (1989): 36–37.

beautifully colored feathers, but eventually also beautiful forms (as in canoes, clothes, etc.) that involve no gratification whatsoever, i.e., no liking of enjoyment. But in the end, when civilization has reached its peak, it makes this communication almost the principal activity of refined inclination, and sensations are valued only to the extent that they are universally communicable. (Sec. 41)

That the flowers and seashells of the sensually-minded primitive had earlier served Kant as the proper objects of pure judgments of taste suggests the persistently uncertain status of aesthetic formalization in this text.[29] The beautiful constantly threatens to degrade into the agreeable because it depends on the example (as sensuous priority). However, the example is also the only remedy against itself:

> Among all our abilities and talents, taste is the only one which, because its judgment cannot be determined by concepts and precepts, stands most in need of examples [Beispiele] of that which has enjoyed the longest-lasting approval [Beifall] over the progress of culture [Kultur], in order that it will not become uncouth [ungeschlacht] again and relapse into the crudeness of its first attempts. (Sec. 32, translation modified)

The rationale of the canon, of humanistic education, and of aesthetics generally as a political model unfolds from these passages with almost startling clarity. And we may now take a long step back from this rigorous, conflicted philosophical text, and survey briefly the far-flung ideological haunts of post-Kantian aesthetic narrative.

From such a bird's-eye perspective the *Critique of Judgment* acquires the patina of exemplary marginality proper to the category of "high" culture which Kant's work indirectly helped theorize. Yet we may begin riding out the inflationary spiral of aesthetics as ideology with the observation that aspects of Kant's project, and some of his formulations, underwent extremely effective popularization in the work of Friedrich Schiller, whose *Naive and Sentimental Poetry* (1795–96) and *On the Aesthetic Education of Man* (1795, 1802) distill the empirico-transcendental narrative of man into its canonical form. In Schiller the aesthetic becomes a supremely synthetic moment, an instant of freedom balanced between the binary oppositions of the empirical and the ideal—the "sensuous drive" and the "formal drive"

29. The possibility that a judgment about the beautiful might slip into an empirical judgment about the agreeable is one that Kant's text warns against repeatedly in ethico-political terms: "Any taste remains barbaric if its liking requires that *charms* and *emotions* be mingled in, let alone if it makes these the standard of approval" (*Critique of Judgment*, sec. 13). "[T]he view that the beauty we attribute to an object on account of its form is actually capable of being heightened by charm is a vulgar error that is very prejudicial to genuine, uncorrupted, solid [*gründlich*] taste" (sec. 14).

of the *Aesthetic Education*—a synthesis that provides man with "a complete intuition of his human nature" and "a symbol of his accomplished destiny."[30] The symmetrical chiasmus or "reciprocal action" (*Wechselwirkung*) of sensuous and formal drives also undergoes temporalization, however, such that the sensuous precedes and yields to the formal: man "begins by being nothing but life, in order to end by becoming form" (Schiller, *Aesthetic Education*, 20.2). History is the unfolding of this destiny as culture: that is, as the progress from a "naive," sensual aesthetic to a "sentimental" interiority, this last defined as the self-conscious quest for a return to the naive, and thus as the motion toward an ever-deferred "ideal" state of aesthetic synthesis. The evolution of poetry or aesthetic form is by definition also that of humanity. "This path taken by the modern poets is, moreover, that along which man in general, the individual as well as the race, must pass."[31]

Thus aesthetic, individual, and species formation all occur as an interdependent system of homologies, and as a progress in the form of a spiral or transumptive return, which is the only form of progress possible for a system of exemplarity. One could say that such a system always looks backward toward an exemplar and forward toward an ideal, except that the two gestures are inseparable: one goes backward to go forward, achieving the ideal through a return a higher naïveté: "We were nature . . . and our culture, by means of reason and freedom, should lead us back to nature" (Schiller, *Naive and Sentimental Poetry*, 85).[32] The double burden of repetition and self-production composes the paradox of identification as that of aesthetic education. On the one hand, the subject of aesthetics comes into existence by identifying with an exemplar, and the exemplar is exemplary because of its original spontaneity: what must be imitated is the inimitable. On the other hand, the exemplar is exemplary *for us*, as Hegel would say: an example cannot be exemplary except for a (fallen) subject, and in itself is a purely sensuous and unreflective spontaneity. Precisely because we have fallen from the example, are belated with respect to it, and exist as a reflection on our difference from it, we are oriented toward a yet higher synthesis

30. Friedrich Schiller, *On the Aesthetic Education of Man, in a Series of Letters*, bilingual edition, ed. and trans. Elizabeth M. Wilkinson and L. A. Willoughby (Oxford: Clarendon Press, 1967), 94/95 (letter 14, paragraph 2). Subsequent citations are referenced by letter and paragraph number.
31. Friedrich Schiller, *"Naive and Sentimental Poetry" and "On the Sublime,"* trans. Julius A. Elias (New York: F. Ungar, 1966), 112.
32. This circular, dialectical, or protodialectical return is a familiar topos in Romantic literature: e.g., "Paradise is locked and the cherubim behind us; we have to travel around the world to see if it is perhaps open again somewhere at the back," as one of Kleist's narrators puts it. "[W]e would have to eat again from the Tree of Knowledge in order to return to the state of innocence." Heinrich von Kleist, "On the Marionette Theatre," trans. Christian-Albrecht Gollub, in *German Romantic Criticism*, ed. A. Leslie Willson (New York: Continuum, 1982), 241–44.

as historical subjects. Schiller's Greeks, therefore—inherited from Winckelmann, and bequeathed to a properly *modern* nineteenth- and twentieth-century Hellenism—are at once exemplary and childish.[33]

As a narrative of subject-formation that is always also a narrative of universal history, aesthetics rapidly and easily becomes a political model. The inherently political character of aesthetics is already suggested in Kant's definition of aesthetic formalization as the hypothetical identification of the particular act of judgment with the universality of human judgment. In the *Critique of Judgment* this identification is purely formal and thus, properly speaking, identityless; but we saw that in aesthetic narrative a subreption—we might now wish to say, an excess of identification—is always already at work translating the hypothetical universal communality of judgment into the empirical manifestation of man. In Schiller's repetition and intensification of this gesture, the Aesthetic State becomes the idealized realization of humanity in its empirico-transcendental totality. This State, Schiller tells us at the end of the *Aesthetic Education of Man* exists "as a realized fact" only in "some few chosen circles," but exists as a "need" in every "fine-tuned," that is, fully human, soul (27.12). Scholars of English literature encounter Schiller's Aesthetic State most memorably in Matthew Arnold's assertion in *Culture and Anarchy* that "culture suggests the idea of *the State* . . . in our best self."[34] In a British context Arnold's statement was slightly eccentric; but the overtly authoritarian resonance of such formulations is finally less politically significant than the logic of their construction, which proposes the judging subject's identification with a hypothetical formal community as both the engine and the telos of history. In an entirely Arnoldian spirit one can replace the word "State" with "humanity," and obtain the tautology of "culture" out of which aesthetic narrative unfolds.

The production and consumption of culture, therefore, acquires a political destiny inseparable from its "disinterested" exemplariness, with the

33. On the subject of the fabrication of "ancient Greece" in the late eighteenth century, see Martin Bernal, *Black Athena: The Afroasiatic Roots of Classical Civilization*, vol. 1: *The Fabrication of Ancient Greece, 1785–1985* (New Brunswick: Rutgers University Press, 1987). See Lloyd, "Kant's Examples," for an analysis of a moment in Kant which comes closest to approximating Schiller's historical scheme. At the conclusion of the first part of the *Critique of Judgment*, Kant invokes a mythical, exemplary state in which the state itself required invention: "There were peoples during one age whose strong urge to have sociability *under laws*, through which a people becomes a lasting commonwealth, wrestled with the great problems that surround the difficult task of combining freedom (and hence also equality) with some constraint. . . . It is not likely that peoples of any future age will make those models dispensable" (sec. 60).

This is perhaps a good place to emphasize that the *Critique of Judgment* not only poses notorioius difficulties in its own right, but also forms part of a subtle and by no means monolithic philosophical corpus. The disruptive power of Kant's writing on history has been demonstrated by Peter Fenves in *A Peculiar Fate: Metaphysics and World-History in Kant* (Ithaca: Cornell University Press, 1991).

34. Matthew Arnold, *Culture and Anarchy*, in *The Complete Prose Works of Matthew Arnold*, 5:134.

result that the line between the artwork and the political, like that between the beautiful and the agreeable, is always being crossed and recrossed. Here the discourse of modern aesthetics opens very rapidly onto that of "Western culture" itself, for the State or City has been conceived in relation to the artwork since Plato. The political is a making or forming, a "fiction," in Philippe Lacoue-Labarthe's phrase: "The fact that the political is a form of plastic art in no way means that the *polis* is an artificial or conventional formation, but that the political belongs to the sphere of *technē* in the highest sense of the term: the sense in which *technē* is thought as the accomplishment and the revelation of *physis* itself."[35] The formation or fiction of the polis, in other words, is the mimesis and the fulfillment of nature. In the "modern" world of aesthetic exemplarity, this (self-)formation involves, as we have seen, the production and transumption of an "ancient" model—Athens, Sparta, Rome, Jerusalem; the points of reference can, of course, be multiple. Winckelmann's famous claim, at the beginning of his seminal *Reflections on the Imitation of Greek Works in Painting and Sculpture* (1755), that "the only way for us to become great or, if this be possible, inimitable, is to imitate the ancients," could doubtless only have been uttered in the particularly fragmented context of eighteenth-century Germany, but differently inflected versions of this paradox inform nationalist representations throughout post-Renaissance European history.[36] The nation is a fiction, not just in Benedict Anderson's sense of being an "imagined community," an entity superior to the possibility of empirical experience, but in the more turbulent sense of being a making, a *poiesis* that is always at once belated and proleptic with respect to the concept it presupposes.[37] Since the *technē* of the political must both mimic and exceed *physis*, the nation must be at once a "natural" movement of the people and an orchestrated, staged event; and in the course of this staging of the event of history, the artwork, for inherent rather than external or contingent reasons, will find its disinterestedness pressed into overtly political service.[38]

35. Philippe Lacoue-Labarthe, *Heidegger, Art, and Politics*, trans. Chris Turner (Oxford: Basil Blackwell, 1990), p. 66. For a fuller discussion of this point, see the opening pages of chapter 4.
36. J. J. Winckelmann, *Reflections on the Imitation of Greek Works in Painting and Sculpture*, bilingual edition, trans. Elfriede Heyer and Roger C. Norton (La Salle, Ill.: Open Court, 1987), 4/5.
37. See Benedict Anderson, *Imagined Communities: Reflections on the Origin and Spread of Nationalism* (London: Verso, 1983), and, for a subtle analysis of the temporality of national identification and identity, Homi Bhabba, "DissemiNation: time, narrative, and the margins of the modern nation," in *Nation and Narration* (London: Routledge, 1990), 291–322. It should be added that in the present context I am examining a *model* of the nation as constructed by aesthetic discourse. In specific contexts, particularly in postcolonial contexts, nationalisms will have specific overdeterminations. Nevertheless, the work of Bhabba, Lloyd, and others has demonstrated the considerable reach and force of aesthetic nationalism in concrete situations.
38. On the historical and theoretical imbrication of nation and spectacle, see Loren Kruger, *The National Stage: Theatre and Cultural Legitimation in England, France, and America* (Chicago: Uni-

The "aestheticization of politics" that Walter Benjamin diagnosed in early twentieth-century fascism thus represents no absolute break with the humanist tradition, for which fascism generally had little but scorn. Indeed, from the perspective of a critique of aesthetics it is no coincidence that in its National Socialist version fascist nationalism was first and foremost a racism. The development of normative models of racial difference in the late eighteenth century is inseparable from a neoclassicizing aesthetic of the body.[39] Aesthetics, of course, can hardly be charged with having invented European racism, which forms part of a shifting complex of discourses that has served visible and various economic and political interests from the discovery of the New World and the emergence of a modern slave-trade to the mid-twentieth-century production of a "Third" World. But in its specifically modern form as *racism*, racial discourse obtains a specifically aesthetic provenance and momentum as a version of aesthetic typology—in certain respects as typology's sharpest ideological expression: as, precisely, the instantiation of the *stereotype* as the mechanical reiteration of a caricature.[40] Precisely because of its aesthetic determination, however, the racial stereotype is not as simple a trope as its iterative, mass-produced nature might lead one to think. The racism that descends from Count Gobineau to Alfred Rosenberg does not simply fix essences in immutable corporeal signs, but identifies the type as self-formative: that is, as the (aesthetic) subject's self-

---

versity of Chicago Press, 1992). The model for the production of national spectacle, according to Kruger, is frequently Greek tragedy. Furthermore, the imperative to stage the nation cuts across political frontiers: from socialist writers who thought of theater as *Bildung*, as the coming-to-consciousness of a class through aesthetic education, to Wagner and the fascist spectacles of the twentieth century.

39. Indeed, in the nineteenth century Gobineau was forced to rely on Winckelmann's by then considerably outdated canon in order to construct the first fully modern racial theory. For a useful discussion of late eighteenth-century anthropology in relation to Winckelmannian classicism see George L. Mosse, *Toward the Final Solution* (New York: Howard Fertig, 1978). On Gobineau see in particular Françoise M. Taylor, "Esthétique et exclusion raciale: L'Argument du 'miracle grec' dans *L'Essai sur l'inégalité des races humaines* de Gobineau," *Nineteenth-Century French Studies* 17.3–4 (1989): 307–17. Seeking absolute racial distinctions, Gobineau found it necessary to appeal to a Winckelmannian "Greek miracle" that, as Taylor comments, required him to ignore numerous nineteenth-century developments in classical archaeology and art history: the discoveries of Minos and Mycenae in 1820; the growing scholarly certainty that it was the practice to paint statues in classical Greece; an increased interest in the archaic period, etc. Emphasizing the imitative structure of aesthetics and Gobineau's consequent need for an exemplary Greece, Taylor comments perceptively on the aesthetic humanism grounding modern racism: "[T]he works of art of this age of gold are doubly canonical: they represent perfection of the aesthetic act, but also and above all perfection of the human type being represented, which is proposed as the absolute ideal of beauty of the human figure" (309).

40. At the cost of considerable ambivalence, as Homi Bhabba shows in "The Other Question," *Screen* 24.6 (1983): 18–36: "[T]he stereotype must always be in *excess* of what can be empirically proved or logically constructed" (18). For a study emphasizing the role of racial discourse in the development of the institution of literary studies, see Franklin E. Court, *Institutionalizing English Literature: The Culture and Politics of Literary Study, 1750–1900* (Stanford: Stanford University Press, 1992).

determination in history *as* type, which is to say as race. "A race," Lacoue-Labarthe and Jean-Luc Nancy comment, referring to texts by Rosenberg and Hitler in an effort to diagnose a "Nazi myth," "is the identity of *a* formative power, of a singular type."[41] The individual subject's identification with the leader is an identification with the nation, but nation in the sense of race, and race in the sense of a power of self-formation, embodied in the naturalness of blood and soil. The manipulation of the masses through spectacle and symbol is at this point an end in itself. And the race that accomplishes itself in and through this spectacle would be, in Lacoue-Labarthe and Nancy's terms, "nothing more than the absolute, self-creating Subject" (310). In the terms we have elaborated here, this racial entity would be the hallucinogenic literalization of the "empirico-transcendental doublet," man, whom Kant proposed as the "visible expression of moral ideas" (*Critique of Judgment*, sec. 17), and whose universality has fallen casualty to a subreption so absolute as to destroy the human itself.

The fascist spectacle, however, can distract us from the hegemonic power of aesthetic narrative—a narrative which Schiller offers as an alternative to violent revolution and as a palliative for authoritarian rule. Here the principal ideological mechanism, as Lloyd observes of colonialist paternalism, is the transformation of "the stereotype into the type, allowing the fixed character . . . of the racial subject to become a letter into which a spirit can be breathed, the spirit, that is, of an evolving assimilation of the uncultivated, and therefore incomplete, to the civilized and complete."[42] The "type" functions in a rhetorical capacity as a prefiguration of its own fuller realization; and its insertion into the exemplary and developmental temporality of aesthetic history permits the "native" or, mutatis mutandis, the working-class or feminine subject to be represented as incomplete rather than different—with the unstated proviso that these "children" will also

41. Philippe Lacoue-Labarthe and Jean-Luc Nancy, "The Nazi Myth," trans. Brian Holmes, *Critical Inquiry* 16 (1990): 306. For another analysis of the National Socialist cult of immediacy and will, see Éric Michaud, "Nazisme et représentation," *Critique* 43.487 (1987): 1019–34. It is an interesting and to my knowledge unexamined fact that the Nazi racial theorist Alfred Rosenberg wrote a dissertation on *Longinus in England bis zum Ende des 18. Jahrhunderts* (Berlin: Mayer and Miller, 1917).
42. David Lloyd, "Arnold, Ferguson, Schiller: Aesthetic Culture and the Politics of Aesthetics," *Cultural Critique* 2 (Winter 1985/86): 153. Explicit experiments in domination through (aesthetic) culture compose an important chapter in nineteenth-century institutional history, as numerous studies have pointed out. See, e.g., Chris Baldick, *The Social Mission of English Criticism, 1848–1932* (Oxford: Clarendon Press, 1983), for an overview that stresses the class conflict shadowing middle-class theories of "culture" in the development of English studies; and see Gauri Viswanathan, *Masks of Conquest: Literary Study and British Rule in India* (New York: Columbia University Press, 1989), for an argument that "the discipline of English came into its own in an age of colonialism" (2). As Viswanathan demonstrates, "English literature" was being taught as an expression of national (and thus supra-national) character in the colonies as early as the 1820s, a good fifty years before "English" became a standard subject in the mainstream (that is, male and middle-class) British educational system.

never grow up: within the harmonious aesthetic universe they are *naturally* childish.[43] Yet the eschatological promise of history now moves to the foreground; and precisely because the instrument of reconciliation is culture, the politics of aesthetics derive from the seeming benevolence and normativity of a pedagogical model. Thus aesthetics achieves its most elaborate institutional manifestation in pedagogical contexts. The subject of aesthetics emerges through an identification with the exemplary texts and subjects that make up a tradition definitive of humanity itself (for taste, as we know from Kant, "stands most in need of examples of that which has enjoyed the longest-lasting approval over the progress of culture"). When institutionalized as pedagogical practice, aesthetics thus requires a canon and a scene of instruction in which this canon reiterates its own identity in forming that of the aesthetic subject. Whether any particular text or author "belongs" in the canon or not can always come into dispute; the important point is that there be an understanding, articulated or not, that the canonical text is representative and exemplary. The outlines of developmental and typological narrative can be nearly lost in the halo of aesthetic disinterestedness and representativeness; the canon can be "expanded" to incorporate representatives of previously marginalized groups without prejudice to its hegemonic function. Indeed, it is precisely in and through this expansion that aesthetics becomes properly hegemonic, by distributing its representative attentions over the widest possible social field, and internalizing as much as possible the terms of conflict. We are now in a position to appreciate why the idea of "multiculturalism" should meet resistance both within and without the present-day academy—but we are also prepared to understand the relative ease with which a certain multiculturalism is accommodated and promoted by scholarly, pedagogical, and other cultural institutions. As long as the multiplication of cultures remains inte-

---

43. The relation between aesthetics and gender is particularly complex, since aesthetic discourse so frequently relies on gender difference as a structuring device (i.e., not only is aesthetics itself relegated to a "feminine" position in relation to philosophy or science, but within aesthetics such differences as that between the beautiful and the sublime appeal to and reinforce ideological representations of sexual difference). My readings in the *Bildungsroman* will comment periodically on the gender politics of aesthetics, and my concluding chapter offers some general remarks on this matter. Here it will have to suffice to insist on the *difference* among the categories we so often invoke bundled together as "race-class-gender": though the racial, the working-class, and the feminine subject can (and do) all take up the position of the "child" in aesthetic narrative, they do so from different discursive and institutional sites. There result the complexities that cultural critique seeks to unpack (the racial or working-class male subject, for instance, can be figured as hyperbolically "male" within the childish, and often indirectly feminized, space of the "savage," etc.). For a study of the gender politics at work in the construction of eighteenth-century British aesthetics see Mary Poovey, "Aesthetics and Political Economy in the Eighteenth Century: The Place of Gender in the Social Constitution of Knowledge," in *Aesthetics and Ideology*, ed. George Levine (New Brunswick: Rutgers University Press, 1994), 79–105.

grated under the sign of the human (or, since the institutionalization of feminism is obviously also at stake here, that of "man"), and even as long as the noncanonical cultural objects studied are taken as *examples* of ethnic or national identity, an aesthetic logic controls the field of dispute, organizing ethnic identity upon the neutrally white background of "culture" itself, as the (Western, male, etc.) institution of aesthetics has defined it. The strenuous opposition to multiculturalism by conservative cultural groups, however, responds to the fact that all cultures are always multiple, and that even the imaginary totality of "Culture" is fragmented at its origin by its double task of producing what it affirms. The name of this instability within aesthetics is "theory," as I have already suggested, and shall now seek to elaborate.

I V

The preceding discussion has to some extent already launched us on yet one more of those dizzying leaps which the analysis of aesthetics as an ideology demands. If I now propose to shift attention from the panoramic unfolding of politico-aesthetic narrative to the strange but socioeconomically minute phenomenon of "theory" in late twentieth-century North America (and, mutatis mutandis, other major centers for the production of "Western" literary culture), it is on the strength of the observation that aesthetic pedagogy was fully institutionalized in the twentieth century, with the development of national literature studies in the modern, bureaucratic university. It must also be emphasized that the university has a relatively minor part to play in the diffusion of aesthetic narrative in the contemporary West—where, postmodern conditions notwithstanding, versions and fragments of the *grand récit* of aesthetics continue to circulate incessantly.[44] But the university serves our culture as, among other things, the museum of "culture" per se, which grants the humanities a symbolic role considerably in excess of their actual contribution to the school's explicit or implicit socioeconomic rationale. And within the humanities, the national literature department, based on the elucidation and dissemination

44. My allusion of course is to J.-F. Lyotard, *The Postmodern Condition: A Report on Knowledge*, trans. Geoffrey Bennington and Brian Massumi (Minneapolis: University of Minnesota Press, 1984). I have tried to suggest the persistence of aesthetic narrative in theories of the "postmodern" in "Pynchon's Postmodern Sublime," *PMLA* 104 (1989): 152–62. For a sociological study that turns up "Kantian" aesthetic notions throughout the middle and upper classes of a contemporary Western society (1960s France), see Pierre Bourdieu, *Distinction: A Social Critique of the Judgment of Taste*, trans. Richard Nice (Cambridge: Harvard University Press, 1984). I would situate aesthetics at the heart of the ideological double bind of the techno-bureaucratic university, as analyzed by Bill Readings in *The University in Ruins* (Cambridge: Harvard University Press, 1996); for further discussion of this point see chapter 7.

of an imaginary totality or "canon" of exemplary vernacular texts, provides aesthetic pedagogy with its most developed institutional elaboration. We have said enough about the difficulties and paradoxes besetting aesthetic discourse to suggest that the blend of symbolic importance and sociocultural marginality enjoyed by the university literature department is no accident. As we have seen, the aesthetic has never been conceived as an end in itself, despite—or because of—its formalism, its universalism, and its political ambition. The institutional site of aesthetics in the modern techno-scientific university is consequently the object of much rhetoric but little funding. Throughout this chapter I have been tracking versions of this fundamental contradiction, which all too often has been misrepresented or simplifed even in otherwise rigorous analyses of the politics of aesthetics.

It is necessary to qualify John Guillory's claim, for instance, that the "canon debate" and the emergence of "theory" record and react to the decreasing value of literature as cultural capital in an increasingly techno-bureaucratic society. The growing practical irrelevance of high literary culture may well be a fact, but it is also a fact that literary culture has *always* been constituted as marginal in relation to a popular culture against which "literature" gets defined. I take up the problem of literature more extensively in chapter 2; here it suffices to recall that the notion of literature, in the sense of imaginative fiction, emerged as part of the discourse of aesthetics—and, as the name for a self-reflexive linguistic form that speaks to the totality of the human condition, may in fact be understood as the discursive epitome of aesthetics.[45] With the invention of literature came the corresponding category of the "subliterary"; and critics seeking to demystify aesthetic discourse have frequently drawn attention to literature's troubled relation to the more overtly commodified forms of writing it excludes. All too often, however, this relation has been represented as unilaterally defensive, as though the marketplace success of sensation fiction represented a simple "reality" which Wordsworth or Goethe were seeking disingenuously to avoid.[46] The material and cultural processes that created the possibility of this marketplace, however, produced the possibility of literature as an integral dimension of it. The universalizing or homogenizing force of commodified "popular culture"—as well as much of its ideological content—is *aesthetic* in its rationale. The discourse of aesthetics, as the model of bourgeois ideology, registers this complication in its schizo-

45. Hence the claim of Philippe Lacoue-Labarthe and Jean-Luc Nancy which I examine in the next chapter: the literary as "absolute" "aggravates and radicalizes the thinking of totality and the Subject." *The Literary Absolute: The Theory of Literature in German Romanticism*, trans. Philip Barnard and Cheryl Lester (Albany: State University of New York Press, 1988 [1978]), 15.
46. I am exaggerating slightly, but such is the main thrust of, for instance, Martha Wood-mansee, *The Author, Art, and the Market: Rereading the History of Aesthetics* (New York: Columbia University Press, 1994).

phrenic ambition to be at once popular and elite, as our double sense of "culture" has come to imply. Thus, if the notion of literature cannot be fully extracted from the subliterary field it plunders and disdains, it is equally true—and not simply in a trivial sense—that the institution of "popular" culture presupposes and in a certain sense even reinforces that of "literature." Guillory discovers evidence of "the peculiar power of mass culture" in the fact that mass-cultural representations of literature rarely bother to deny literature's transcendental claims (*Cultural Capital*, 173); but his adversarial metaphors foreclose the logic governing mass culture's uncaring but consistent acceptance of its own putative inferiority. From the perspective of low as well as high culture the purpose of literature—or, more generally, the aesthetic per se—is precisely to be *both* marginal and fundamental. This contradictory role also communicates to high culture a flavor of ineffectuality, allowing mass culture to represent itself, when it so chooses, as after all more representative of essential humanity than its exemplary but bookish counterpart. The permutations of such a thoroughly symbiotic opposition are numerous; the point to note is that literature's decreasing value as cultural capital translates into a cultural crisis only insofar as "literature" remains a locus of investment (and crisis) *within the notion of "culture" itself*, in both its popular and elite manifestations. Put another way, as long as we continue to define a certain sort of activity as "cultural" or "aesthetic," we shall be lamenting (or celebrating) the endless death of literature.

The role of theory in this tragicomic scenario may be grasped even if we finesse, for the moment, the complex question of theory's relation to literature: it is merely necessary to grant the aesthetic foundations of literature as a pedagogical institution and to pursue a little further the linguistic character of the aesthetic aporia. The crucial role played by figurative language in aesthetic systems may be confirmed if we return once more to Kant, whose text has been presented here in enough detail to allow us access to at least one of its sites of rhetorical tension. We recall that rational interest can be indirectly attached to aesthetic disinterest, thus allowing judgments of taste to prepare the way for teleological judgments: this occurs thanks to the readmittance of semantic and referential content via "that cipher [*Chiffreschrift*] through which nature speaks to us figuratively [*figürlich*] in its beautiful forms" (*Critique of Judgment*, sec. 42). Figurative language mediates between form and meaning, disinterest and interest: "[T]he *sans* of the pure cut," Derrida comments, "is in truth a language that nature speaks to us."[47] In similar fashion the articulation between aesthetic judgment and ethical judgment depends on the figure of analogy. We judge the beautiful

---

47. Jacques Derrida, "Economimesis," in *Mimesis des articulations*, ed. Sylviane Agacinski et al. (Paris: Aubier-Flammarion, 1975), 78.

as if we were judging rationally or ethically: this moment of fiction, the analogical "as if," recuperates the errancy of *pulchritudo vaga* and allows aesthetic judgment to moor itself to interestedness.

The fictional "as if" of analogy, however, causes figurative language to become the locus of attention and anxiety as Kant defines the "symbol" in order to argue that beauty is a symbol of morality. Though the ideas of reason cannot be directly represented by intuitions, Kant argues that the sensory presentation or "hypotyposis" of a rational idea can occur "symbolically." The "symbol" thus takes up the task of aesthetic judgment itself in articulating pure with practical reason, the phenomenal with the noumenal realm:

> Symbolic exhibition uses an analogy [*Analogie*] (for which we use empirical intuitions as well), in which judgment performs a double function: it applies the concept to the object of a sensible intuition; and then it applies the mere rule by which it reflects on that intuition to an entirely different object, of which the former is only the symbol. Thus a monarchy ruled according to its own constitutional laws would be presented as an animate body, but a monarchy ruled by an individual absolute will would be presented as a mere machine (such as a hand mill); but in either case the presentation is only *symbolic.* For though there is no similarity between a despotic state and a hand mill, there certainly is one between the rules by which we reflect on the two and how they operate. This function [of judgment] has not been analyzed much so far, even though it very much deserves fuller investigation; but this is not the place to pursue it. Our language is replete with such indirect exhibitions according to an analogy, where the expression does not contain the actual schemata for the concept but contains merely a symbol for our reflection. Thus the word *foundation* (support, basis), to *depend* (to be held from above), to *flow* (instead of to follow) from something, *substance* (the support of accidents, as Locke puts it), and countless others are not schematic but symbolic hypotyposes; they express concepts not by means of a direct intuition but only according to an analogy with one, i.e., a transfer of our reflection on an object of intuition to an entirely different concept, to which perhaps no intuition can ever directly correspond. (*Critique of Judgment,* sec. 59)

In the wake of this discussion Kant ventures the crucial assertion that "the beautiful is the symbol of the morally good." The former depends on the imagination and is independent of concepts, while the latter depends on the freedom of the will and is grounded on concepts; however, the former becomes the symbol of the latter insofar as the "mere rule" by which judgment reflects on the beautiful is applied to the morally good. Kant's self-conscious digression on the figurative nature of key philosophical terms registers the magnitude of the stakes for which this passage plays.[48] For the analogy between the beautiful and the good is not an example among others: it is the condition of the possibility of the symbol as the articulation of the ethical and the phenomenal, and is thus exemplary *of* symbolism as the figure that will allow critical philosophy to unify itself. Beauty as a symbol for morality is the exemplary symbol, the symbol of symbols, and it is also radically problematic. For in aesthetic judgment a concept is not applied to an intuition such that the "mere rule" of this application could be abstracted and transferred. Aesthetic judgment is *already* an affair of "mere rule"; but even this is not quite accurate: aesthetic judgment is a free play that is harmonious with, or analogous to, mere rule. In aesthetic formalization the symbol or analogy is already at work prior to the concept of the symbol or analogy. Aesthetic judgment is always already analogous with the logical and the ethical, but for this very reason can never coincide with the analogical knowledge it enables. Aesthetic judgment may be said to "perform" the concept of the symbol, but the symbolic performance will always exceed or fall short of its own concept.[49]

The aporia of aesthetics thus becomes a disjunction within the figure of analogy; and this disjunction may in turn be described in a rhetorical vocabulary, as Roland Barthes once showed in a remarkable, brief meditation on "beauty" as that which "cannot assert itself save in the form of a citation," which is to say in the form of an enumerative referral ("lovely as . . ."): "There is only one way to stop the replication of beauty: hide it, return it to silence. . . . There is one rhetorical figure which fills this blank in the object of comparison whose existence is altogether transferred to the language of the object to which it is compared: catachresis (there is no other possible word to denote the 'wings' of a house or the 'arms' of a chair, and yet 'wings' and 'arms' are *instantly, already* metaphorical): a basic figure, more basic, perhaps, than metonymy, since it speaks around an empty

---

48. For a reading of this section that emphasizes the difficulty of distinguishing between "schemata" and "symbols," see Paul de Man, "The Epistemology of Metaphor," in *On Metaphor*, ed. Sheldon Sacks (Chicago: University of Chicago Press, 1979), 11–28.

49. For a study of the symbol in another part of Kant's critical system that would confirm and deepen the present analysis, see Cathy Caruth, "The Force of Example: Kant's Symbols," in *Empirical Truths and Critical Fictions: Locke, Wordsworth, Kant, Freud* (Baltimore: Johns Hopkins University Press, 1991), 58–85. With exemplary precision and rigor, Caruth traces the dependence of critical philosophy's project—the knowledge of its own limits—on the possibility of defining the "symbol"; and in a reading of Kant's *Prolegomena to Any Future Metaphysics* and other related texts she demonstrates that "what remains after the symbol has symbolized itself is always another term that is not contained within the symbolic structure" (82). The symbol's inability to close upon itself generates examples: "not 'empirical' examples, but examples in the argument, linguistic examples, which would always eventually take the form of a narrative" (83).

object of comparison: the figure of beauty."[50] Barthes's Kantian figure of beauty inspires an endless process of tropological displacement because, as a catachresis, it is always already metaphorical; furthermore, as an *absolute* transfer, the catachresis also incessantly interrupts the substitutive process it sets in motion and perpetuates. Beauty thus becomes a figure for the radical figurativeness of language.

And with that insight we encounter Paul de Man's project of rhetorical reading as precisely the critique which aesthetics enables and obscures. As a discourse and a philosophical system, aesthetics unfolds as the story of the construction of the symbol; but because of its unstable origin this narrative will always be doubled by the narrative of its undoing, which may be called "theory." The story of the symbol is not one with which aesthetics can dispense, because the aesthetic project of linking phenomenality to meaning and knowledge to action has to model itself on language. "Language" tropes the limit, the outer rind or shell which a total discourse must incorporate and know. And thus, if we call to mind the aesthetic narrative we extracted from the *Critique of Judgment*, we may observe that it is in fact composed of naturalized tropes. Man is the empirico-transcendental doublet because he is the symbol of symbols, the "visible expression of moral ideas" (sec. 17). Schiller's exaggeration of "man"'s empirical and transcendental poles has the paradoxical effect of making man's rhetorical construction more pronounced, since in the *Aesthetic Education* the judging subject borrows its powers from typology, claiming to prefigure the universal destiny of humanity with the concrete sensuality that Erich Auerbach, in an aestheticizing (and overtly Hegelian) gesture, ascribed to the medieval *figura*.[51] But where the historical reality of the *figura* could repose on divine foundations, that of aesthetics, as we have seen, must derive from the aesthetic synthesis itself. The subject of aesthetics is not only prefigurative and synecdochic of its own universality; it also *produces* itself as this subject in the act of judgment, modeling itself not just on tropes, but on the magical immediacy of a divine fiat, which is to say, in more prosaic terms, a performative. Since in the absence of God only language can claim to create *ex nihilo*, the linguistic model cannot be dispensed with; and thus, in naturaliz-

---

50. Roland Barthes, *S/Z*, trans. Richard Miller (New York: Hill and Wang, 1974), 33–34.
51. Erich Auerbach, "Figura" (1944), in *Scenes from the Drama of European Literature* (Minneapolis: University of Minnesota Press, 1984), 11–76. Auerbach's comment about Hegel is made in reference to an earlier study of Dante: "At that time I lacked a solid historical grounding for this view, which is already to be found in Hegel. . . . I believe that I have now found this historical grounding; it is precisely the figural interpretation of reality which, though in constant conflict with purely spiritualist and Neoplatonic tendencies, was the dominant view in the European Middle Ages: the idea that earthly life is thoroughly real, with the reality of the flesh into which the Logos entered, but that with all its reality it is only *umbra* and *figura* of the authentic, future, ultimate truth, the real reality that will unveil and preserve the *figura*" (72).

ing figurative structures and processes, the aesthetic subject inadvertently conjures up the specter of its own determination by language.

Language, however, is not an entity or subject, and cannot furnish a determinism. Its performative power appears fictional precisely to the extent that it appears effortlessly total: conjuring its worlds out of nothing, language can never escape the charge of being nothing itself: *ex nihilo nihil fit*. Whatever identity language has depends on an otherness to which it both points and fails to point, which means that a certain rupture within, or resistance to, self-effacement is the only specificity language "itself" can possess. When we say that a subject is modeled on linguistic structures, we have not made a positive claim but have merely pointed to a difficulty, a site of incomprehension—and in so doing have repeated the problem we diagnosed, for no personification could be more rhetorical than that which grants agency to "language." Yet a critique of aesthetics cannot avoid this gesture, which is scripted within aesthetics as the trace of its radical incoherence. De Man's definition of "theory" as "occur[ring] with the introduction of linguistic terminology into the metalanguage about literature" refers less to the development of twentieth-century linguistics per se than to the inextricability of theory from the aesthetics it deconstructs.[52]

Theory retells the story of aesthetics as the allegory of language which—in theory—aesthetics was all along. Theory identifies aesthetics as ideology by identifying ideology as a linguistic predicament: "What we call ideology is precisely the confusion of linguistic with natural reality, of reference with phenomenalism" (de Man, *Resistance to Theory*, 11). Aesthetics is thus the model of all ideology, since aesthetics builds its system out of linguistic functions that it treats as attributes of consciousness or spirit. In theory's aesthetic allegory, the disruptive free play of Kant's *pulchritudo vaga* becomes the figure for a potential randomness of the signifier, a randomness which can never appear without undergoing a "subreptive" ascription of meaning but which remains incoherently necessary if language is to occur. The subject of language, "man," becomes the subject of judgment and the "ideal of beauty," thanks to a play of the signifier which remains lodged at the heart of "man"'s possibility—the kernel of a trauma, rendered in Kant as the threatening, basilisk gaze of a pure judgment of taste.[53] And since

---

52. Paul de Man, *The Resistance to Theory* (Minneapolis: University of Minnesota Press, 1986), 8.
53. There is in fact a moment in the *Critique of Judgment* when a pure judgment of taste is leveled at the human body, in the context of a discussion of the disinteretsted, non-teleological orientation of aesthetic judgment: "[W]e must be able to view the ocean as poets do, merely in terms of what manifests itself to the eye [*was der Augenschein zeigt*]—e.g., if it is calm, as a clear mirror of water bounded only by the sky; or, if it is turbulent, as being like an abyss threatening to engulf everything—and yet find it sublime. The same applies to the sublime and beautiful in the human figure. Here, too, we must not have in mind, as bases determining our judgment, concepts of the purposes *for which* man has all his limbs [*wozu alle seine Gliedmassen da sind*]"

"man," in this narrative, reads his possibility—or has it read for him—in the signifier, the catachresis that establishes the signifier's legibility thereby also establishes the subject's interpellation by language, and insertion into the symbolic order. The catachresis is a prosopopoeia: a "giving face," as Cynthia Chase says, to something that may or may not be a sign, but which is taken as one in being *perceived*.[54] This illegible, radically external insistence making up the possibility of the sign's production is what theory calls materiality. We may recall that the term "ideology" originally signaled the attempt to derive ideas from the senses, and that in the wake of Marx and Engels's displacement of Destutt de Tracy's term, the critique of ideology became a troubled inquiry into the materiality of phenomenal form. If the notion of "ideology" preserves in its history an aesthetic ascent from the sensuous to the ideal, the critique of ideology becomes a critique of aesthetics in seeking to explain the effectivity of fiction, or, conversely, the fictionality of the real, since any materiality at the origin of ideology must be able to generate ideological illusion.[55] In a rigorous Marxism, materiality resists itself, and thereby generates history. Theory pursues this thought to its limit in locating the materiality and interpellative force of ideology in language's self-resistance.

The famous de Manian epigram that "theory is itself the resistance to

---

("General Comment on the Exposition of Aesthetic Reflective Judgments"). Under the pure aesthetic gaze, in other words, the body (of meaning) fragments into "limbs" [*Glieder*, which is also to say articulations] considered "in themselves," etc. The passage is discussed in Paul de Man, "Phenomenality and Materiality in Kant," in *Hermeneutics: Questions and Prospects*, ed. Gary Shapiro and Alan Sica (Amherst: University of Massachusetts Press, 1984), 121–44, and has become the object of frequent discussion by critics interested in de Man's work, since de Man presents this passage as an account of "formal materialism": the impossible, necessary inscription of form prior to its phenomenalization. My brief discussion of linguistic materialism in this paragraph will be supplemented periodically in later chapters. For a discussion of de Man's reading of Kant, see my "Humanizing de Man" and "De Man, Schiller, and the Politics of Reception," cited above, no. 3.

54. See Cynthia Chase's chapter "Giving a Face to a Name" in her *Decomposing Figures: Rhetorical Readings in the Romantic Tradition* (Baltimore: Johns Hopkins University Press, 1986). On ideology as interpellation see Louis Althusser, "Ideology and Ideological State Apparatuses," in *Lenin and Philosophy and Other Essays*, trans. Ben Brewster (New York: Monthly Review Press, 1971), 159–62. There are a number of tempting points of congruence between Althusser's theoretical writing and de Man's: an insistence on the irreducibility of ideology; an attempt to think history as "a process without a *telos* or a subject"; a refusal to confuse history with "'empirical' temporality" (*Reading Capital*, trans. Ben Brewster [London: New Left Books, 1970], p. 105). For a closely argued mediation between Althusser's and de Man's writings, see Sprinker, *Imaginary Relations*.

55. Étienne Balibar, "The Vacillation of Ideology," trans. Andrew Ross and Constance Penley, in *Marxism and the Interpretation of Culture*, ed. Cary Nelson and Lawrence Grossberg (Urbana: University of Illinois Press, 1988), 168. As Balibar points out, Marx's uneasy negotiation of the difficulty of "ideology" led to the disappearance of the term in his writings, and the brief appearance of the concept of "fetishism" in *Capital* as precisely another attempt to think "the real and the imaginary within ideology." I discuss the concept of fetishism in relation to aesthetics in chapter 6.

theory" falls into place at this point, and so do the paradoxes of theory's reception with which we began. In theory's allegory, the originary aesthetic-ideological error is both legible and irreducible. It is legible because aesthetics cannot do what it says, or say what it does: theory's narrative emerges out of this dissymmetry, and tells the story of its own emergence as the story of language's radical incoherence. Yet the aesthetic error is also irreducible, since theory, according to its own narrative, submits to the exigencies of the inflated, treacherous limit-term "language" itself: in accounting for its own production theory betrays the linguistic fracture it discovers. There results the spiral of dissatisfaction with which we are familiar. Theory is denounced as "aestheticism" because its critical purchase occurs in and through an aesthetics that, as Lacoue-Labarthe comments, "cannot be defined otherwise than as a theory of fiction . . . [as] the locus where fiction, the fictional in general, becomes worthy of theory."[56] I would reinflect this formulation slightly so as to emphasize that aesthetics is *both* a theory of fiction and (thus) a theory of fiction's occlusion, which is to say the production and occlusion of theory itself. Aesthetics is theory as the resistance to theory.[57] Or, put more patiently, aesthetics is the systematic resistance to the self-resisting theory it cannot help but generate.

The peculiarities of theory's dissemination and reception derive from the aesthetic character of literary culture in general and professional literary study in particular. In its specific manifestation as "de Manian deconstruction," theory is a discourse informed by the structures and exigencies of the research university and the history of literary study—let us say most generally, by the existence of an institutional apparatus in which critics, as part of their role within the academic bureaucracy, produce "interpretations" and teach students to produce them. This institutional focus on interpretation, nominally in the service of the literary text as aesthetic object, permits the very success of theory which both theory and theory's detractors decry. Indeed, deconstruction appears in such a context as a peculiarly "American" phenomenon precisely because it exploits and submits to the structure and productive mechanisms of the postwar U.S. research university. There is thus a limited truth to John Guillory's claim that, in its announced impersonality and its valorization of "rigor," de Manian deconstruction mirrors the routinized conditions of production in a scholarly bureaucracy. We may in fact say that the hyperbolic character of de Man's reception—his fetishization and ferocious abjection—derives to some extent quite directly from the commodified nature of U.S. scholarly production, which causes both

---

56. Philippe Lacoue-Labarthe, "The Unpresentable," in *The Subject of Philosophy*, ed. Thomas Trezise, trans. Thomas Trezise et al. (Minneapolis: University of Minnesota Press, 1993), 151.
57. This slight shift in emphasis will require an ongoing repositioning of Lacoue-Labarthe's claims, as the next chapter will show with respect to the "literary absolute."

the work and the name of de Man to become widely and repeatedly circulated irritants. If the de Manian critique occurs precisely where the internal coordinates of the cultural institution permit aesthetic ideology's systematic self-laceration, the culture of the commodity inflates this systematic process into a minor—but stubborn—public neurosis.

One should not conclude, however, that theory reduces to a local sociological symptom because it occurs as an institutional development. Guillory's shrewd account of the institutionality of "theory" misses its mark at precisely this point. While it is to some extent possible—though certainly also hastily reductive—to say that deconstruction "model[s] the work of theory on bureaucratic work" (*Cultural Capital*, 257), it is misleading to characterize this gesture as a blind reiteration of the ideology of professionalism—a cathexis of routine, that is, whereby "the charisma of the master theorist appears to constitute a realm of *absolute* autonomy" (254). Guillory has diagnosed the pathology of theory at the price of foreclosing the theoretical statement itself, which means that he has simply repeated a version of this statement without knowing it. Theory is *about* the charismatic effectivity of the bureaucratic—that is, the production of pathos out of "rigor," and of faces and names out of formal systems: a process exemplified in and as the story of aesthetics, which is to say, of course, as the story of the production of a certain illusion of "*absolute* autonomy." By way of a paradox which we have explored throughout this chapter, this aesthetic narrative (of "man") finds its sharpest and most visibly conflicted academic expression in the production of the master theorist ("de Man")—the pure subject of knowledge, who embodies theory's impersonal "rigor." In de Man's own terms one may speak of the hypostatization of "the deconstructive passion of a subject" into the illusory center of authority.[58] The fact that theory (as de Man) predicts the pattern of its own resistance does not prevent it from resisting its own insight. But in falling into error, theory, located as it is on the fault line of aesthetics, explains what Guillory's sociological reduction cannot: the fact that the master theorist's charisma recurs as, and within, a resistance to theory so widespread and conflicted that even critics without much sympathy for or interest in de Man's work have noted its peculiarity.[59]

58. Paul de Man, *Allegories of Reading: Figural Language in Rousseau, Nietzsche, Rilke, and Proust* (New Haven: Yale University Press, 1979), 199. Elsewhere this master-subject is characterized as being "as far beyond pleasure and pain as he is beyond good and evil, or, for that matter, beyond strength and weakness. His consciousness is neither happy nor unhappy, nor does he possess any power. He remains however a center of authority to the extent that the very destructiveness of his ascetic reading testifies to the validity of his interpretation" (173–74).
59. See, e.g., David Simpson's comments on the "abjection" of de Man in contemporary critical discourse, in *Romanticism, Nationalism, and the Revolt against Theory* (Chicago: University of Chicago Press, 1993), 181.

For good or ill, de Man's monumentalization is a symptom of a permanent crisis within the institutions of aesthetic culture. As long as the academic study of literature persists in anything like its present form, the death of theory will continue to be announced and predicted, analyzed and called for, while the theoretical critique will continue to circulate as an irrepressible irritant, a phantom repeatedly exorcised and rediscovered in the academic machine. The institution of literature is hardly invulnerable. It is at best two centuries old, and in its fully bureaucratized form is a twentieth-century phenomenon, which one day will no doubt pass from the earth. Yet in the meantime it forms an integral part of an ideology that informs the ensemble of disasters and opportunities we call modernity. Though literary study may continue to witness its own increasing marginalization within an increasingly techno-pragmatic educational apparatus, its future, in the short run at least, and despite appearances, is not really in danger. "Literature," in other words, is another name for the crisis of theory, as will become clear once we tunnel further into the literary institution and examine at close range the debate about the *Bildungsroman*.

2

The Phantom *Bildungsroman*

> For the being of *Geist* has an essential connection with the idea of *Bildung*.
> —Hans-Georg Gadamer, *Truth and Method*

Among the challenges the modern novel offers to genre theory, that of the *Bildungsroman* is remarkable on several counts. Few literary terms— let alone German ones—have enjoyed greater international success, both in the academy and in high culture generally. "If a person interested in literary matters commands as many as a dozen words of German," Jeffrey Sammons remarks, "one of them is likely to be: *Bildungsroman*."[1] If this person also commands the staples of Western literary history, she or he will also know that this subgenre is epitomized by *Wilhelm Meister's Apprenticeship*, is in some way deeply German, but represents nonetheless "one of the major fictional types of European realism."[2] At once international and national, a "major fictional type" embodied in the historical event of a particular novel, the *Bildungsroman* seems to have inherited the virtues of its nominal father, Goethe, the genius whose life captured for provincial Weimar the full radiance of human potentiality. One would be hard-pressed to find another instance of a genre in which particularity and generality appear to mesh so thoroughly. For since the *Bildungsroman* narrates the acculturation of a self—the integration of a particular "I" into the general subjectivity of a community, and thus, finally, into the universal subjectivity of humanity—the genre can be said to repeat, as its identity or content, its own synthesis of particular instance and general form. An equivalent repetition is audible in the German word "Bildungsroman" itself, which no doubt largely explains why it is more frequently borrowed than translated: even knowledge of only a dozen words of German suffices to hear an interplay of representation (*Bild*) and formation (*Bildung*), and

---

1. Jeffrey Sammons, "The Mystery of the Missing *Bildungsroman*; or, What Happened to Wilhelm Meister's Legacy?" *Genre* 14 (1981): 229.
2. Marianne Hirsch, "The Novel of Formation as Genre: Between *Great Expectations* and *Lost Illusions*," *Genre* 12 (1979): 300. See also Randolph P. Schaffner, *The Apprenticeship Novel: A Study in the "Bildungsroman" as a Regulative Type in Western Literature* (New York: Peter Lang, 1984).

thus the whisper of a profound homology between pedagogy and aesthetics, the education of a subject and the figuration of a text. The *Bildungsroman*, in short, is a trope for the aspirations of aesthetic humanism. Indeed, a stronger claim can be made: given its simultaneously self-reflexive and universalizing structure, this genre presents itself as a version—a humanist, and thus fully ideological version—of what Philippe Lacoue-Labarthe and Jean-Luc Nancy, in their study of German Romanticism, term "the literary absolute."[3]

The first of many paradoxes that one encounters in studying this genre is that this description of it probably surprises. I have done little more than unpack, in very abbreviated and literal-minded fashion, the assertions implicit in the notion of the *Bildungsroman*, yet the result no doubt seems at odds with the prosaic use to which the term is usually put. The very success of the term has made it part of the daily fare of educated discourse and has given it the aura of a well-worn literary tool. And besides the fact that one habitually employs this word to describe novels that may not display much literary value, the idea of the *Bildungsroman*, even considered abstractly as a form, appears compromised by a certain sordid wishfulness. It seems counterintuitive to expect high aesthetic ambition from a genre seemingly built around a hero who, in Hegel's ironic summary, "in the end usually gets his girl and some kind of position, marries and becomes a philistine just like the others."[4] We would certainly appear to be more than a little removed from the refined poetics of a Mallarmé, or the aestheticism of Pater or Wilde. Finally, even if this genre were not weighed down by bourgeois pettiness, it would still seem an illegitimate substitute for what Lacoue-Labarthe and Nancy call the "literary absolute," which, as "*the* genre of *literature*," no specific genre can embody (*Literary Absolute*, 11). I shall return to the question of the "literary" in short order; for the moment it will suffice to note that according to Lacoue-Labarthe and Nancy the Romantics inaugurate the thought of literature in its modern sense, with the "literary absolute" naming an emphatically new and self-transcending genre "beyond the divisions of classical (or modern) poetics" (11). Even if one recalls the Romantics' high claims for the novel as the genre that transcends genre, or Friedrich Schlegel's assertion that Fichte's philosophy, the

---

3. Philippe Lacoue-Labarthe and Jean-Luc Nancy, *The Literary Absolute: The Theory of Literature in German Romanticism*, trans. Philip Barnard and Cheryl Lester (Albany: State University of New York Press, 1988). Lacoue-Labarthe and Nancy's definition of the "literary" is highly nuanced, but for the moment their notion of the "absolu littéraire" can be taken in its proximity to idealist aesthetics: "[T]he literary Absolute aggravates and radicalizes the thinking of totality and the Subject" (15). I return shortly to the details, the implications, and finally the limitations of this claim.

4. G. W. F Hegel, *Aesthetics: Lectures on Fine Art*, trans. T. M. Knox (Oxford: Clarendon Press, 1975), 593, translation modified. The German text consulted is *Vorlesungen über die Ästhetik*, ed. Friedrich Bassenge (Berlin, 1955), 558.

French Revolution, and *Wilhelm Meister* are "the great tendencies of the age," the Romantic *absolu littéraire* will still at best halo the achievement of Goethe's novel, not the genre *Wilhelm Meister* presumably inspired.

But the tense interplay of meanings at work in the idea of the *Bildungsroman* is further complicated by a referential difficulty: it is uncertain whether this genre exists to be described in the first place. Scholarship in this area has turned up one complication after another. Problems begin, appropriately enough, on the level of the signifier itself, since the word "Bildungsroman," purportedly the name of a nineteenth-century genre, was nearly unknown before the early twentieth century—its widespread popularity is, in fact, largely a postwar phenomenon.[5] Generic terms are no doubt usually supposed to lag behind the phenomena to which they refer; but given the "Romantic" presuppositions that can be extracted from this particular term, its deferred occurrence raises questions about literary history which rapidly become complex and serious. One might begin to suspect that critics such as Lacoue-Labarthe and Nancy have good reason to claim that "a veritable romantic *unconscious* is discernable today, in the most central motifs of our modernity" (*Literary Absolute*, 15). At the same time, however, one might also wonder whether the term *Bildungsroman*, like the more notorious label "Romanticism," has at best an indirect relation to the texts it is supposed to describe. And indeed, unsurprisingly, scholars in German studies have been casting doubt on this word's referential purchase for nearly as long as it has been in wide circulation. As soon as one takes a serious look at the notion of the *Bildungsroman*, it begins to unfold such extravagant aesthetic promises that few if any novels can be said to achieve the right to be so defined—possibly not even the five or six German-language novels that, in postwar German studies, have constantly

---

5. On the history of the term *Bildungsroman* see Fritz Martini's classic study, "Der Bildungsroman: Zur Geschichte des Wortes und der Theorie," *Deutsche Vierteljahrsschrift für Literaturwissenschaft und Geistesgeschichte* 35 (1961): 44–63. The term, according to Martini, makes its earliest appearance around 1819–20 in essays by Karl Morgenstern, a professor at the Universität Dorpat. It then seems to have sunk into oblivion until, fifty years later, Wilhelm Dilthey rather offhandedly introduced it in *Das Leben Schleiermachers* (1870) to describe "those novels which make up the school of *Wilhelm Meister*," a definition he later elaborated in a famous passage in *Das Erlebnis und die Dichtung* (1906): "A regular development is observed in the life of the individual: each of the stages has its own intrinsic value and is at the same time the basis for a higher stage. The dissonances and conflicts of life appear as the necessary points of passage [*Durchgangspunkte*] through which the individual must pass on his way to maturity and harmony." *Das Erlebnis und die Dichtung: Lessing Goethe Novalis Hölderlin* (Leipzig: Teubner, 1913), 394. The idea of a *Bildungsroman* subsequently caught on, though scholarly studies of it did not begin to appear with great regularity in Germany until the postwar era. Morgenstern's, Dilthey's, and Martini's texts, among others, are conveniently collected in Rolf Selbmann, ed., *Zur Geschichte des deutschen Bildungsromans* (Darmstadt: Wissenschaftliche Buchgesellschaft, 1988).

been put forward as this genre's main (and not infrequently its only) representatives.[6] Sammons's well-known article, by no means the first of its sort,[7] concludes by wondering whether, among the "legends of literary history," there is one "so lacking in foundation and so misleading as the phantom of the nineteenth-century *Bildungsroman*" (Sammons, "Mystery," 243). Frederick Amrine writes more forgivingly of a "critical fiction"— though like Sammons, Amrine has hard words for members of English departments who appropriate the authority of the term *Bildungsroman* without investigating its history or, consequently, its referential difficulties.[8]

But the *Bildungsroman* seems to constitute one of those quagmires of literary study in which increased rigor produces nothing more tangible than increased confusion. On the one hand it is certainly true that under the lens of scholarship this genre rapidly shrinks until, like a figure in Wonderland, it threatens to disappear altogether. Even *Wilhelm Meister* has proved resistant to being subsumed under the definition it supposedly inspired: critics with little else in common have registered their sense that at the end of Goethe's novel, Wilhelm "is still a long way from Schiller's theoretically postulated 'beautiful moral freedom'."[9] As Sammons remarks, "[I]f the status of the model text is problematic, then *a fortiori* the genre itself must certainly be insecure" ("Mystery," 237). But on the other hand, Germanists seem all the more ideologically committed to the truth of this "critical fiction" for having examined it and found it ontologically wanting. Monographs on the *Bildungsroman* appear regularly; without exception they possess introductory chapters in which the genre is characterized as a problem,

---

6. The only novel consistently cited is, of course, *Wilhelm Meisters Lehrjahre*, though as noted below even this novel has been denied entry into the genre it is usually supposed to have founded or exemplified. Apart from *Wilhelm Meister*, the novels most frequently granted chapters in books on the *Bildungsroman* include Wieland's *Agathon* (1767); Novalis's *Heinrich von Ofterdingen* (1800); Stifter's *Der Nachsommer* (1857); Raabe's *Der Hungerpastor* (1864); Keller's *Der grüne Heinrich* (1854/55; 1879/80); and, in the twentieth century, the novels of Hesse and Mann.

7. See for instance Walter Pabst, "Literatur zur Theorie des Romans," *Deutsche Vierteljahrsschrift für Literaturwissenschaft und Geistesgeschichte* 34 (1960): 264–89.

8. Frederick Amrine, "Rethinking the *Bildungsroman*," *Michigan Germanic Studies* 13.2 (1987): 126, 127; Sammons, "Mystery," 232. The principal target of both critics is Jerome H. Buckley's *Season of Youth: The Bildungsroman from Dickens to Golding* (Cambridge: Harvard University Press, 1974).

9. Klaus F. Gille, "*Wilhelm Meister*" im *Urteil der Zeitgenossen: Ein Beitrag zur Wirkungsgeschichte Goethes* (Assen: Van Gorcum, 1971), 17. Cited by Amrine, "Rethinking," 125–26. (All translations in this chapter, as in other chapters, are mine unless otherwise noted.) See also Kurt May, "'Wilhelm Meisters Lehrjahre,' ein Bildungsroman?" *Deutsche Vierteljahrsschrift für Literaturwissenschaft und Geistesgeschichte* 31 (1957): 1–37. The title's question is answered negatively: "In the *Lehrjahre*, Goethe has written a novel around the belief that the modern humanistic ideal of harmonious 'Bildung' has to be abandoned" (34).

but as one that the critic, for one reason or another, plans either to solve or ignore;[10] and despite the variety of solutions proffered, the definition of the *Bildungsroman* that emerges in study after study usually repeats, in ways and for reasons that I seek to elaborate here, the self-referential structure of the aesthetic synthesis sketched at the beginning of this chapter—which returns one to the beginning of the cycle and necessitates, of course, another book or essay on the *Bildungsroman*. The more this genre is cast into question, the more it flourishes. And though it is certainly poor scholarship to reduce *Bildung* to a vague idea of individual "growth," as common parlance generally does, a more historically and philosophically precise understanding of *Bildung* does not appear either to keep the *Bildungsroman* healthy and alive, or to prevent its corpse from rising with renewed vigor each time it is slain. The popular success of vulgarized notions of the *Bildungsroman* simply repeats, on a grander scale, this genre's indestructibility within the specialized literature.

I shall be tracking the rationale of this vacillation at some length in what follows; but with a glance back to the preceding chapter's discussion of aesthetic ideology, we may note that the *Bildungsroman*'s paradox derives from that of aesthetics. The "content" of the *Bildungsroman* instantly becomes a question of form, precisely because the content is the forming-of-content, "Bildung" —the formation of the human as the producer of itself as form. Wilhelm Dilthey's seemingly content-oriented definition of the *Bildungsroman* as a "regular development . . . in the life of the individual," in which each stage of development "has its own intrinsic value and is at the same time the basis for a higher stage," is animated by a formal principle that undermines the content's specificity, as shown clearly in a remark by Robert Musil:

> When one says "*Bildungsroman*," [Wilhelm] Meister comes to mind. The development of a personal *Bildung*. There is, however, also *Bildung* in what is at once a narrower and a more extensive sense: with every true experience a cultured man educates himself [*bildet sich ein geistiger Mensch*]. This is the organic plasticity of man. In this sense every novel worthy of the name is a *Bildungsroman*. . . . The *Bildungsroman* of a person is a type

---

10. This remark may seem cavalier, but is meant seriously and could be justified with many examples, Todd Kontje's remarks at the close of the introductory chapter to his *Private Lives in the Public Sphere: The German Bildungsroman as Metafiction* (University Park: Pennsylvania State University Press, 1992) being simply more overt than most: "Thus I will not rehearse the tired debate as to whether or not particular texts examined here 'count' as *Bildungsromane*. Obviously I think they do" (17).

[*Typus*] of novel. The *Bildungsroman* of an idea, that's quite simply the novel per se.[11]

The content is thus in an essential sense the form, and the principle of formation is the human: if every novel worthy of the name is a *Bildungsroman*, this is because every human being worthy of the name embodies an essential humanity, an "organic plasticity" that permits the "geistiger Mensch" to produce himself (*sich bilden*). And yet, if the "person" immediately becomes a figure of the "idea"—and the novel a figure for the production of the novel itself—the ongoing debate about the *Bildungsroman* suggests that this power of formalization is less stable than Musil's comments imply. The idea of this genre persistently drives it in the direction of universality, but since its particularity is constantly in danger of disappearing, a "disturbing dialectic of everything and nothing," as Amrine puts it ("Rethinking," 124) comes to afflict the notion of the *Bildungsroman* as it vacillates between signifying in vague fashion a narrative in which a protagonist matures (such that "precious few novels would *not* qualify as '*Bildungsromane*'" [122]) and signifying in more rigorous fashion an aesthetic synthesis that threatens to disappear into sheer illusion. At once too referential and not referential enough, the *Bildungsroman* appears ineradicable from literary criticism. In its nonexistence it is so efficaciously present that Sammons is led to speak more than once of a "phantom genre" ("Mystery," 239, 243). And since a tension within the procedures of institutionalized literary studies has generated this ghost, one can hope to learn something about the nature of literary reception by keeping it in view.

A closer look at what Lacoue-Labarthe and Nancy call the "literary absolute" is in order here, since their study attempts to capture the presuppositions on which the institution of literary criticism is based. We may first dilate on a topic that surfaced intermittently in the preceding chapter: the appearance of the notion and institution of "literature" as part of the development of modern aesthetics over the course of the eighteenth century. Though Lacoue-Labarthe and Nancy are no doubt being overpunctual in locating the irruption of literature in Jena Romanticism, they are certainly right to insist on literature's modernity. As is well known, throughout most of the eighteenth century texts were organized rhetorically, according to generic principles that had not changed substantially since the classical era. The notion of "fiction" did not begin to have its present classificatory power before the Romantic period, as every student of the eighteenth-century novel knows: Samuel Richardson's stubborn insistence that he was indeed

---

11. Robert Musil, *Tagebücher, Aphorismen, Essays und Reden*, in *Gesammelte Werke*, ed. A. Frisé (Hamburg: Rowohlt, 1955), 2, p. 572. For the Dilthey passage see note 5 above.

the "editor" rather than the "author" of the letters composing *Pamela*, for instance, only begins to make sense when one considers the ambiguous epistemological and ethical status of a text unprotected by prestigious generic conventions, and written several decades too early to profit from the category of "serious fiction," or literature. This category became available as part of the wholesale rearrangement of discourses marking the advent of what we generalized in the preceding chapter as aesthetics. Literature emerges with the developing commodification of cultural production, the concomitant development of the "author" as the producer of intellectual property, and the production of the category of the aesthetic as the guarantor of social and philosophical unity. The fictionality of the text, like the disinterestedness of aesthetic intuition, becomes the mark of identity and value by being recoded as the imaginative expression of an exemplary subject.[12]

The history of literature's appearance and institutional development, which has been the object of many recent critical studies, does not in itself, however, answer the ritualistically modernist question, "What is literature?" It is imperative to take this question seriously if one's historical account is to have any real purchase on its object; and the great accomplishment of Lacoue-Labarthe and Nancy's *Literary Absolute* is to have provided an uncompromisingly rigorous formulation of literature as an aesthetic ideal. Building on the work of Walter Benjamin and Maurice Blanchot, Lacoue-Labarthe and Nancy unpack the commonplace of the "self-conscious text" into the model of a text that generates its own theory: into "theory itself as literature, or, in other words, literature producing itself as it produces its own theory" (12). The literary text becomes what it is— "literary"—in reflecting on its own constitution, pursuing, in Blanchot's words, "the almost abstract demand made by poetry itself to reflect itself and to fulfill itself through *its* reflection."[13] Literature thereby inscribes within itself the infinite task of criticism, hollowing out a space for readers who, in engaging the text, repeat the production of the text as its own (and their own) self-understanding. This self-understanding always lies on the horizon, *à venir*, because each production of the text calls out in turn for a further moment of completion. Literature is thus inexhaustible; it is an

---

12. On the aesthetic as the guarantor of social and subjective unity, see chapter 1. The relatively recent emergence of our modern notion of the "author" is emphasized and narrated in Michel Foucault's famous essay, "What Is an Author?" in *The Foucault Reader*, ed. Paul Rabinow (New York: Pantheon, 1984). Recent scholarship has also drawn attention to the ways in which copyright law developed in the eighteenth century, thus providing juridical space for the proprietary and "original" author. See especially Mark Rose, *Authors and Owners: The Invention of Copyright* (Cambridge: Harvard University Press, 1993), and Martha Woodmansee, *The Author, Art, and the Market: Rereading the History of Aesthetics* (New York: Columbia University Press, 1994).
13. Maurice Blanchot, "The Athenaeum," *Studies in Romanticism* 22.2 (1983): 165.

infinite, reflective, fragmentary movement, Schlegel's "progressive universal poetry," or, in Blanchot's words, "a veritable conversion of writing: the power for the work to be and no longer to represent" ("Athenaeum," 165).

Lacoue-Labarthe and Nancy rightly insist that "we ourselves are implicated in all that determines both literature as auto-critique and criticism as literature" (*Literary Absolute*, 16), for this understanding of literature provides the rationale of criticism's scientific and pedagogical operations, whether criticism knows it or not. On the one hand, literature is the "all," as Blanchot points out: literature concerns everything, to the point of conveying Being itself in an intuitive, unmediated moment of insight. On the other hand, literature is what one approaches endlessly, through specialized, technical processes of mediation. The absolute character of the text's truth calls for editions and variorum editions, biographies, memoirs, and all the minutiae of scholarship, as well as for the reiterated acts of interpretation we call criticism proper. One may thus claim in the abstract what the historical record confirms: not only is there no literature without criticism, but the history of the idea of literature is the history of the *institutionalization* of literary study. It must also be noted, however, that a contradiction highly productive of discourse labors at this institution's heart. "Literature" is both infinitely populist and irreducibly elitist in its aspirations, and at once avant-gardist and archival in nature. The result is a persistent tension between academic and anti-academic discourse about literature (a literature that is always being "betrayed" by the scholarly reverence it elicits); between scholarship and criticism within the academy; and between poetics and hermeneutics within criticism. The critical endeavor, however, is as irreducible as it is conflicted, since it embodies the very self-consciousness of the "literary" text. Indeed, criticism has so thoroughly displaced philology in the twentieth-century academy partly because criticism's appeal to the "opacity" and "inexhaustibility" of the literary text results in the full integration of the literary absolute as an institutional rationale.[14]

14. Michael Warner, "Professionalization and the Rewards of Literature: 1875–1900," *Criticism* 27.1 (1985): 11, 16. I thank John Rieder for drawing my attention to this article. The classic account of the struggle between philologists and belletristic critics during the early years of literature's integration into the U.S. university is provided in Gerald Graff, *Professing Literature: An Institutional History* (Chicago: University of Chicago Press, 1987). For a history of English studies in Britain, see Chris Baldick, *The Social Mission of English Criticism, 1848–1932* (Oxford: Clarendon Press, 1983), and for the development of professional literary study in France, see Antoine Compagnon, *La Troisième République des lettres, de Flaubert à Proust* (Paris: Seuil, 1983). The institutionalization of literature as criticism in Germany is documented and analyzed by Peter Uwe Hohendahl in *The Institution of Criticism* (Ithaca: Cornell University Press, 1982), and *Building a National Literature: The Case of Germany, 1830–1870*, trans. Renate Baron Franciscono (Ithaca: Cornell University Press, 1994). The special case of Spain is addressed in Wlad Godzich and Nicholas Spadaccini, eds., *The Crisis of Institutionalized Literature in Spain* (Minneapolis: Prisma Institute, 1988).

The discussion of aesthetics in chapter 1 has prepared us to understand that the emergence of literature as theory involves the participation of larger metaphysical and political issues than the extremely modest world-historical destiny of academic literary criticism might lead one to conclude. In modeling the autoproduction of reflection, literature, Lacoue-Labarthe and Nancy insist, represents an absolute instance of "poiesy or, in other words, production":

> Romantic poetry sets out to penetrate the essence of poiesy, in which the literary thing produces the truth of production in itself, and thus, as will be evident in all that follows, the truth of the production *of itself*, of auto-poiesy. And if it is true (as Hegel will soon demonstrate, *entirely against* romanticism) that auto-production constitutes the ultimate instance and closure of the speculative absolute, then romantic thought involves not only the absolute of literature, but literature as the absolute. (*Literary Absolute*, 12)

The literary absolute "aggravates and radicalizes the thinking of totality and the Subject" (15), and thereby becomes the privileged other of philosophy, at once the object of philosophy's desire and an excess toward which philosophy must maintain a reserve. For our purposes two consequences bear emphasizing. (1) The Subject, in the full metaphysical sense of the term, remains in proximity to and possibly depends on a linguistic model, since the thought of "literature" provides the Subject with its most immediate self-image—though not necessarily with a fully reliable image: Hegel's hostility toward Romanticism is only one event in the well-known story of philosophy's profound ambivalence toward literature. I shall return to this ambivalence, which is arguably at play even in Lacoue-Labarthe and Nancy's analysis of it. (2) The Subject, in its historicity, comes into being as *Bildung*, "the putting-into-form of form" (*Literary Absolute*, 104), the elaboration of the Subject in the specifically *aesthetic* terms of phenomenal or sensory realization.

The complex itinerary of *Bildung* in German or, more broadly, in European intellectual history from Herder onward can only be suggested here; however, lest it be imagined that Lacoue-Labarthe and Nancy are overstating the metaphysical force of this concept, we may recall Hans-Georg Gadamer's authoritative description of *Bildung* at the beginning of *Truth and Method*. I quote at length, since Gadamer's synthesis brings clearly into view the synthetic power of the aesthetic tradition:

> The first important observation about the familar content of the word Bildung is that the earlier idea of a "natural shape" which refers to external

appearance (the shape of the limbs, the well-formed figure) and in general to the shapes created by nature (e.g., a mountain formation—Gebirgsbildung) was at that time detached almost entirely from the new idea. Now Bildung is intimately associated with the idea of culture and designates primarily the properly human way of developing one's natural talents and capacities. Between Kant and Hegel the form that Herder had given to the concept was perfected. . . . Wilhelm von Humboldt, with his sensitive ear, already detects a difference in meaning between Kultur and Bildung: "but if in our language we say Bildung, we mean something both higher and more inward, namely the attitude of mind which, from the knowledge and the feeling of the total intellectual and moral endeavor, flows harmoniously into sensibility and character." Bildung here no longer means "culture," i.e., the development of capacities or talents. The rise of the word Bildung calls rather on the ancient mystical tradition, according to which man carries in his soul the image [*Bild*] of God after whom he is fashioned and must cultivate it in himself. The Latin equivalent for Bildung is formatio, and accordingly in other languages, e.g., in English (in Shaftesbury), "form," and "formation." In German also the corresponding derivations of the idea of forma, e.g., Formierung and Formation, have long vied with the word Bildung. . . . Yet the victory of the word Bildung over "form" does not seem to be fortuitous. For in Bildung there is Bild. The idea of "form" lacks the mysterious ambiguity of Bild, which can mean both Nachbild ("image," "copy") and Vorbild ("model").

In accordance with the frequent carry-over from becoming to being, Bildung (as also the contemporary use of "formation") describes more the result of this process of becoming than the process itself. The carry-over is especially clear here because the result of Bildung is not achieved in the manner of a technical construction but grows out of the inner process of formation and cultivation, and therefore remains in a constant state of further continued Bildung. It is not accidental that in this the word Bildung resembles the Greek physis. Like nature, Bildung has no goals outside itself. . . . In this the concept of Bildung transcends that of the mere cultivation of given talents, from which concept it is derived. The cultivation of a talent is the development of something that is given, so that the practice and cultivation of it is a mere means to an end. Thus the educational content of a grammar-book is simply a means and not itself an end. Its assimilation simply improves one's linguistic ability. In Bildung, contrariwise, that by which and through which one is formed becomes completely one's own. To some extent everything that is received is absorbed, but in Bildung what is absorbed is not like a means that has lost its function. Rather in acquired Bildung nothing disappears, but everything is preserved. Bildung is a genuine historical idea, and because of this historical character of "preservation" is important for understanding in the human sciences.[15]

Since *Bildung* is grounded in a linguistic model—in the "literary absolute" as the autoproductivity of language—it is unsurprising that Gadamer finds in this concept's signifier a fusion of process, telos, and self-representation ("In Bildung there is Bild. The idea of 'form' lacks the mysterious ambiguity of Bild"). Signifying both *Nachbild* and *Vorbild*, *Bildung* encloses the structure of mimesis itself, which, through the temporalizing prefixes *nach* and *vor*, becomes the structure of typology: *Bildung* mirrors and prefigures its own fulfillment. Thus, as the representation of its own striving, *Bildung* "remains in a constant state of further continued Bildung" and achieves the autoproductivity of nature or *physis*, having "no goals outside itself." Its destiny is the universality of Hegel's Absolute Spirit, which later on in his discussion Gadamer specifically invokes: "It is the universal nature of human Bildung to constitute itself as a universal intellectual being" (13).

There are, of course, well-known historical reasons why speculative philosophy, the idea of *Bildung*, and a certain thought of literature emerge with particular intensity in late eighteenth-century Germany. But as we saw in chapter 1, analogous concepts, frequently, though by no means always, the result of the direct or indirect influence of German thought, saturate post-Romantic European cultural discourse, informing directly political as well as philosophical or belletristic contexts.[16] This should be the less surprising in that the idea of *Bildung* is an idea about the historical realization of *Bildung*. "Promotion to the universal," Gadamer writes, "is not something that is limited to theoretical Bildung" (13); it could not be: its logic renders it an essentially political process. Lacoue-Labarthe has in fact argued that

15. Hans-Georg Gadamer, *Truth and Method* (New York: Crossroad, 1982), 11–12. To my knowledge no full historical study of the vicissitudes of the word and concept *Bildung* exists, though a useful overview, more concretely historical in orientation than Gadamer's meditation, is offered by W. H. Bruford, *The German Tradition of Self-Cultivation: Bildung from Humboldt to Thomas Mann* (Cambridge: Cambridge University Press, 1975).
16. The peculiar situation of the German bourgeoisie is often remarked in this context. Economically weak, politically fragmented, but intellectually advanced, and necessary to the construction of the bureaucratic state, the middle classes plausibly required more elaborate theoretical compensations in "Germany" (a still nonexistent "Germany," of course) than elsewhere. Aesthetic discourse, however, pervades European cultural history of the period, as we have sought to indicate: usefully general overviews may be obtained in Norbert Elias, *The History of Manners: The Civilizing Process*, Vol. 1, trans. Edmund Jephcott (New York: Pantheon Books, 1978 [1939]), 3–50, and the entries "Aesthetic," "Art," and "Culture" in Raymond Williams, *Keywords: A Vocabulary of Culture and Society*, rev. ed. (New York: Oxford University Press, 1985). For a more specific study of the (massive) influence of German thought on British writers, see Rosemary Ashton, *The German Idea: Four English Writers and the Reception of German Thought, 1800–1860* (Cambridge: Cambridge University Press, 1980). And, for searching analyses of the political role of aesthetics in post-Romantic Western culture, see in particular the work of David Lloyd, cited and noted below, no. 21.

Bildung summarizes *the* thought of politics in Western culture, insofar as "the political (the City) belongs to a form of *plastic art*, formation and information, *fiction* in the strict sense. This is a deep theme which derives from Plato's politico-pedagogical writings . . . and reappears in the guise of such concepts as *Gestaltung* (configuration, fashioning) or *Bildung*, a term with a revealingly polysemic character (formation, constitution, organization, education, culture, etc.)."[17] The ambitious analyses that Lacoue-Labarthe and Nancy derive from this insight are not our immediate concern here, but *Bildung*'s practical orientation holds sufficient relevance for the more humdrum problem of the *Bildungsroman* in the modern academy that it is worth pausing to recompose the preceding chapter's analysis of aesthetic narrative around the question of aesthetic pedagogy.[18]

The autoproduction of the literary or speculative absolute lies in its representing-itself-to-itself, its identifying with itself. Its process or historicity consists in its ongoing identification with an identity that is its own. However, in making overt the aesthetic or speculative absolute's pragmatic claim to realize itself in the phenomenal world, *Bildung* brings into play the figurative and temporal complications of exemplarity. An identity must be formed through identification with an example: a model that on the one hand is the true identity of the identity-to-be-formed, but on the other hand is separated from the ephebe by the temporality or process of *Bildung* itself. *Bildung*'s engine thus runs on the double bind of identification: the subject must identify with the model in order to become what the subject already is; however, this also means that the subject must *not* identify with anything—particularly not a master or exemplar—that is not always already the subject itself. Aesthetic history, in its rigorous manifestations, thereby becomes a dialectical story of pain—of "the seriousness, the suffering, the patience, and the labor of the negative" that Hegel elaborates very much in opposition to, though not, as we see, simply in contradiction with, the Romantic "literary absolute." Though Schiller's *On the Aesthetic Education of Man* does not work out a fully dialectical argument in Hegel's sense, it is arguably the most influential text on the notion of aesthetic pedagogy to come out of Germany during this period; so we may usefully extract and

---

17. Philippe Lacoue-Labarthe, *Heidegger, Art, and Politics: The Fiction of the Political*, trans. Chris Turner (London: Blackwell, 1990), 66.

18. The question of the aestheticization of politics was touched on in chapter 1; see also chapter 4 below. Of Lacoue-Labarthe and Nancy's texts, see in particular "The Nazi Myth," trans. Brian Holmes, *Critical Inquiry* 16 (1990): 291–312, for an analysis of the degradation of *Bildung* as fascism, where the "double trait of the mimetic will-to-identity and the self-fulfillment of form," which is "the fundamental tendency of the *subject*" (312), is exacerbated and naturalized as the putative immediacy of blood and race. The argument is a careful and nuanced one: "Nazism does not sum up the West, nor represent its necessary finality. But neither is it possible to simply push it aside as an aberration, still less as a past aberration," drawing as it does on ideological structures that "belong profoundly to the mood or character of the West" (ibid.).

examine its famous central claim, which we have already heard echoed in Gadamer's invocation of "the ancient mystical tradition, according to which man carries in his soul the image of God after whom he is fashioned and must cultivate it in himself":

> Every individual man, one may say, carries in himself, by predisposition and determination [*der Anlage und Bestimmung nach*], a pure ideal Man, with whose unchanging oneness it is the great task of his being, in all its changes, to correspond. This pure Man [*reine Mensch*], who makes himself known more or less clearly in every subject [*Subject*], is represented by the State, the objective and as it were canonical form in which the diversity of subjects seeks to unite itself.[19]

It would be difficult to find a more compact rendering of the essence and itinerary of *Bildung*, which appears here in its full anthropological determination as the aesthetic education of "man," a pragmatic process of autoproduction-as-identification that is both predestined and a "great task." The difference of history separates the subject from the Subject, and in the gap of this difference—which is an exacerbated version of the difference, at once annulled and maintained, which makes possible the self-identifying Subject—the political force of *Bildung* inheres. It is not simply that the subject discovers the objective form of its own ideality in the State, though this is certainly not without consequence for the political character of aesthetics. Even more crucial, however, as we saw in the previous chapter, is that the difference between subject and Subject allows the latter to reveal itself "more or less clearly" depending on the stage of development that the former occupies. Any particular subject, to the precise extent that it remains particular, will always remain underway toward full self-realization, just as every determinate State will remain "more or less" what Schiller calls a "dynamic state," underway toward the "moral" or Aesthetic State that forms the telos of *Bildung*. As an aesthetic event, however, *Bildung* demands phenomenal manifestation: this is to say that it requires a figure, a *Bild*, exemplifying and prefiguring the identity underlying *Bildung*'s difference and deferral. In the concordant discord of history, then, certain subjects and states can, indeed must, become exemplary. They will always fall short of their own exemplarity, but exemplarity inheres in this very shortfall: *Bildung*, as Gadamer says, "remains in a constant state of further continued *Bildung*." It is thus inherent in the logic of aesthetic education

19. Friedrich Schiller, *On the Aesthetic Education of Man: In a Series of Letters*, ed. and trans. Elizabeth M. Wilkinson and L. A. Willoughby (Oxford: Clarendon Press, 1967), letter 4, paragraph 2. Subsequent quotations from the *Aesthetic Education* are to this bilingual edition, and are indicated by letter and paragraph number.

that Schiller's treatise should regress from the universalist promise of its title to the less democratic model of history suggested in the text's conclusion: "[A]s a need, [the Aesthetic State] exists in every finely attuned soul; as a realized fact, we are likely to find it, like the pure Church and the pure Republic, only in some few chosen circles" (Schiller, *Aesthetic Education*, 27.12). These chosen few acquire the ability to identify with "pure ideal Man" by actualizing, through acculturation, their inherent human ability to perform an *aesthetic* judgment—a disinterested, formally universal judgment that enacts the individual subject's point of contact with the formal universality of humanity, thus providing the subject with what Schiller calls "the gift of humanity itself" (21.5).[20] And since the process of acculturation or *Bildung* that actualizes this potential will always in turn be found to have manifested itself most purely in a historically specific site (classical Greece; Germany, England, or, more generally, "Europe"; the educated classes; the male psyche; etc.), the narrative of *Bildung* clearly has enormous political utility and is in fact inseparable not just from the rhetoric of class struggle and colonial administration in the nineteenth century, but more generally from the very thought of history itself, as, in David Lloyd's words, the "individual narrative of self-formation is subsumed in the larger narrative of the civilizing process, the passage from savagery to civility, which is the master narrative of modernity."[21]

20. Exemplarity is consequently in need of unending renewal on the level of the individual subject: "True, he possesses this humanity *in potentia* before every determinate condition into which he can conceivably enter. But he loses it in practice with every determinate condition into which he does enter. And if he is to pass into a condition of an opposite nature, this humanity must be restored to him each time anew through the life of the aesthetic" (Schiller, *Aesthetic Education*, 21.5).

21. David Lloyd, "Violence and the Constitution of the Novel," in his *Anomalous States: Irish Writing and the Post-Colonial Movement* (Durham: Duke University Press, 1993), 134. A fuller discussion of the structure and politics of aesthetic exemplarity and of the aesthetic "narrative of modernity" may be found in chapter 1. It may be added that this "master narrative" weaves itself through the modern bureaucratic state in numerous ways, not least as the story of what Friedrich Kittler calls the "socialization," and Michel Foucault the "disciplining," of subjects. Exemplary or aesthetic pedagogy occurs not just as metanarrative, but as the concrete and microscopic practices we sum up as the civilization or socialization of a self. The institutions responsible for *Bildung* in this sense would include the nuclear family, the schools, and certain forms of mass media as well as the university; and, as Kittler suggests, the institution of literature has a central role to play in this scenario: not just as a discourse exemplary of national or ethnic identity, but as a pedagogical instrument central to the production of "individuals" on all levels of the socialization process. See Friedrich A. Kittler, *Discourse Networks, 1800/1900*, trans. Michael Metteer, with Chris Cullens (Stanford: Stanford University Press, 1990), 3–173, for a discussion of the newly prominent role of the mother in the discourse of primary education around 1800 (such that she becomes the *Bildnerin*, the erotic site of *Bildung*'s origins [50]), and an analysis of coeval developments in German educational bureaucracies, and in technologies of pedagogy and reading. Kittler's interpretation of the role of the *Bildungsroman* in this context is most fully laid out in his long essay "Über die Sozialisation Wilhelm Meisters," in Gerhard Kaiser and Friedrich A. Kittler, *Dichtung als Sozialisationsspiel: Studien zu Goethe und Gottfried Keller* (Göttingen: Vandenhoek und Ruprecht, 1978), 13–124. For Michel Foucault's

This account of *Bildung,* sketchy enough given that, as Lacoue-Labarthe and Nancy remark, this concept "brings together shaping and molding, art and culture, education and sociality, and ultimately history and figuration" (36), returns us to the task—mercifully limited in some respects, though far-reaching in others—of understanding what happens when *Bildung* acquires the suffix *Roman,* and the institution of criticism is forced to confront more directly its origins in the question of literature. The results, as we have seen, are mixed. It should at least be more obvious at this point why studies of the *Bildungsroman* generally display a deep investment in this genre's existence, since we are now able to establish that the *Bildungsroman* presents itself as a certain modality of the "literary absolute" in offering itself as the literary form of *Bildung.* This emerges most overtly in formalizing accounts such as Monika Schrader's, in which the *Bildungsroman* is defined as "the mimesis of poietical [*poietischer*] productivity";[22] but the aesthetic heritage is no less forcefully at work in seemingly more pragmatic definitions. If, as we are provisionally accepting, the literary absolute "aggravates and radicalizes the thinking of totality and the Subject," and if *Bildung* names the actualization of the Subject as pedagogy, which in turn generates the empirical determination both of the Subject (as "man") and of *Bildung* (as acculturation), then the notion of the *Bildungsroman* returns us to the literary armed with what Schiller would call "the determination [we] have received through sensation" (*Aesthetic Education,* 20.3): the literary will now be absolute as a mirror for the anthropological subject of *Bildung,* Musil's "organically plastic" Man.[23] This humanization of the literary helps explain certain vacillations that, as we noted earlier, seem inseparable from the *Bildungsroman.* The genre's definition inflates so easily into commonplaces of "progress" or "growth," for instance, because the pragmatic universalism of *Bildung* encourages it to. The case of the *Bildungsroman* confirms the generalization offered in the preceding chapter: "high" and "popular" culture are the two sides of a single coin, and an absolute aesthetic performance must be both at once. This double imperative accounts for the hint of crassness or vulgarity haunting the idea of a *Bildungsroman:* precisely because it is an aesthetic genre—the genre *of* the aesthetic—it will need to be a

---

account of the production of the disciplined modern subject, see *Discipline and Punish: The Birth of the Prison,* trans. Alan Sheridan (New York: Vintage Books, 1979). See also Dorothea von Mücke, *Virtue and the Veil of Illusion: Generic Innovation and the Pedagogical Project in Eighteenth-Century Literature* (Stanford: Stanford University Press, 1991), esp. 161–206.

22. Monika Schrader, *Mimesis und Poiesis: Poetologische Studien zum Bildungsroman* (Berlin: Walter de Gruyter, 1975), 21.

23. My citation from Schiller alludes to the *aesthetic* moment proper in his theory: the point at which the subject, having passed through sensuous determination and having developed the autonomous power of reason, must harmonize these faculties in a moment of disinterested free play: "[W]e must call this condition of real and active determinability the *aesthetic* [*den ästhetischen*]" (Schiller, *Aesthetic Education,* 20.4).

degradable form and address itself to what an acculturated class understands as the masses. In fascist or totalitarian Marxist narratives, the masses will, furthermore, become the protagonist of such a novel; the translation of the Subject into the fantastic immediacies of blood and race is a logical (though by no means a necessary) exacerbation of aesthetic ideology, as Lacoue-Labarthe and Nancy, among others, have shown.[24] The more banally sordid kind of upward mobility that drew Hegel's irony is for similar reasons an essential ambiguity within *Bildung*, which, though it manifests the universal disinterestedness of aesthetic culture, also (therefore) occurs as the accumulation of sensuous forms of this universality, and thus always remains exposed to its seeming opposite, philistinism—and more generally, in complex and far-reaching ways, to the commodity form and the ruses of capital.[25] Like aesthetics generally, the *Bildungsroman* will always risk the uneasy contempt of the philosopher. In short, as an aestheticized literary absolute, it will always risk falling short of itself as "literature."

Meanwhile, however, the genre will also demand to be understood in terms of internalization and negation, not just because it constantly risks tumbling into the world of economic exchange, but also because *Bildung*, as we have seen, constitutes the effacement of the difference between the ephebe and the exemplar: a task that, in presenting itself as infinite, becomes understandable as an ironic predicament and easily acquires the tonality of melancholy. The *Bildungsroman* is thus frequently characterized as the great genre of German inwardness; and numerous critics, faced with the paradoxes of this genre, have sought to define the *Bildungsroman* in ironic terms as the exemplary novelistic genre of failure or loss. I shall return to the concept of irony later in this chapter and in subsequent chapters; for the moment, we need simply note that so long as irony is understood as self-reflection or knowledge, the essential structure of *Bildung* is preserved: the subject "matures," either in a wry or a penseroso mode, by transforming loss into the knowledge of loss, thus acquiring representative

24. See Lacoue-Labarthe and Nancy, "The Nazi Myth," and see, e.g., Hans Heinrich Borcherdt's article, "Der deutsche Bildungsroman" (1941) (in Selbmann, *Zur Geschichte*, 182–238), which praises Hans Grimm's *Volk ohne Raum* as a novel in which "all of Germany [appears] as the hero of the work" (Selbmann, *Zur Geschichte*, 209; cited in Kontje, *Private Lives*, 14). Sammons provides shrewd observations on the nationalist ideology at work in the fabrication of "an *essentially* German tradition" in Germany from the early twentieth century through the National Socialist years. The production of the "phantom *Bildungsroman*," Sammons points out, is locatable to an era—the Wilhelminian period—that saw the formation of "the qualitative canon of German literature that we now recognize" ("Mystery," 239–40). (And one could add in this vein that the explosion of books and articles on the *Bildungsroman* since the Second World War responds to the need to reconstruct and reconfirm both a German and, more generally, a Western European identity.)
25. On the circulation of capital and its signs in this genre, see Jochen Hörisch, *Gott Geld und Glück: Zur Logik der Liebe in den Bildungsromanen Goethes, Kellers, und Thomas Manns* (Frankfurt am Main: Suhrkamp, 1983).

status as an entity capable of universalizing its own mortality. All of the dangers and opportunities sketched here return us to the predicament of aesthetic exemplarity. For it is, in short, because the *Bildungsroman*, as the literary form of *Bildung*, must be an *exemplary* genre that it must shoulder the compromises and contradictions that wait upon political efficacity.

If criticism depends on literature (as theory) to furnish it with the model of its own possibility, and if the *Bildungsroman* is the pragmatic, humanist rewriting of literature-as-theory, then it is certainly understandable that criticism as an institution, like Lacan's infant before its mirror, should perform a "jubilant assumption of its specular image" when faced with the notion of this genre—and should therefore find itself committed to a certain irreducible paranoia. Definitions of the *Bildungsroman* share a practically immovable deep structure for just this reason. Though the genre's instability forces its constant retheorization, the definition that results is always plotted around three interrelated qualities, which are those of a pragmatized *absolu littéraire*: self-reflexivity, self-productivity, and exemplarity. The frequency with which "self-reflexivity" is emphasized as the quality that makes the *Bildungsroman* different and distinct is perhaps the most glaring sign that something has gone wrong in the critical process and that whatever has gone wrong has something to do with the problem of literature. To define a literary genre as "self-reflexive" is to offer, in lieu of a definition, a supererogatory, paranoid assertion that the genre is indeed "literary."[26] One could make a similar point about "self-productivity," which is inseparable from self-reflexivity and is similarly literary in its generality, though here the pragmatic thrust of *Bildung* generates the appearance of greater specificity. Self-productivity, for *Bildung*, means the production of selves: in producing itself the genre produces—i.e., educates—readers. The *Bildungsroman*'s pedagogical power has thus constantly served as the focal point of its self-consciousness and exemplarity, as in the earliest recorded use of this term, by Karl Morgenstern in 1820: "It will justly bear the name *Bildungsroman* . . . because it portrays the *Bildung* of a hero . . . and also secondly because it is by virtue of this portrayal that it furthers the reader's *Bildung* to a much greater extent than any other kind of novel."[27] The full metaphysical system of *Bildung* rarely displays itself in contemporary criticism as overtly as it did in Gadamer's definition of the term; but a certain structure of assumptions generally remains intact, and remains capable of emerging as a recognizably aesthetic ideology. The

26. All writers on the *Bildungsroman* will at some point necessarily stress its self-reflexiveness, but for two particularly vivid examples, one from the period in which book-length studies of this subject were beginning to appear and one quite contemporary, see Schrader, *Mimesis und Poiesis*, and Kontje, *Private Lives*.
27. Karl Morgenstern, "Über das Wesen des Bildungsromans" (1820), in Selbmann, *Zur Geschichte*, 64.

pragmatics of *Bildung* inhere, for instance, even in the title of Michael Beddow's *The Fiction of Humanity* (1982): the human is the essence of fictionality because in being imagined it is produced; fictionality, however, is essentially human because the human is its referent and meaning. The *Bildungsroman*, consequently, is the exemplary genre of humanity's auto-production: "[T]he novels all testify to a conviction that there is something about imaginative fiction, and something about authentic humanity, which makes the former an especially suitable medium of insight into the latter."[28] If one turns to Martin Swales's influential *The German Bildungsroman*, one finds that once again the genre is exemplary of "the literary work" in its combination of self-consciousness and pragmatism, rendered here as a double attention to imagination and reality: "I want to suggest in my analysis of the Bildungsroman that, in general terms, the literary work is both referential and self-constituting, that, more specifically, the Bildungsroman is a novel genre which derives its very life from the awareness both of the given experiential framework of practical reality on the one hand and of the creative potential of the human imagination and reflectivity on the other."[29] The skeleton of the literary absolute remains visible in all these definitions. Reading is a process of *Bildung* inscribed in the text itself as the text's reflection on its own human essence; consequently, *Bildungsromane* are the most "realist" as well as the most "self-conscious" of novels, since their referent is the self-positing consciousness of the human. They are the most pedagogically efficient of novels, since they thematize and enact the very motion of aesthetic education.[30] In short, they are exemplary fictions, not least, as noted earlier, when they are characterized as the ironic knowledge of human finitude: such melancholy would in fact be the definitive manifestation of their realism, self-consciousness, and educative force.

It would be a mistake to imagine that more overtly skeptical readers or methodologies find it easy to avoid repeating these gestures. The Marxist tradition, for instance, while obviously committed to a critique of "German ideology," has nonetheless tended to accept uncritically the existence, and therefore the exemplarity, of the *Bildungsroman*. Ferenc Fehér writes that the *Bildungsroman* "differs from other novels only in so far as the educational

---

28. Michael Beddow, *The Fiction of Humanity: Studies in the Bildungsroman from Wieland to Thomas Mann* (Cambridge: Cambridge University Press, 1982), 5, 6.
29. Martin Swales, *The German Bildungsroman from Wieland to Hesse* (Princeton: Princeton University Press, 1978), 5.
30. This performative and referential power will always be found to coexist with the "inwardness" of *Bildung* or the *Bildungsroman*, precisely to the extent that the disinterestedness of the aesthetic serves the pure universality of the human. Swales's distinction between the *Bildungsroman* and the realist novel necessarily resolves itself through a tacit subsumption of the latter into the former, despite the "foreignness of the Bildungsroman tradition" to the European realist tradition (*German Bildungsroman*, ix).

process itself is purposely put forward as the goal of the action."[31] Franco Moretti, in a particularly emphatic profession of faith in this genre's uncomplicated existence, claims that it represents the "symbolic form" of modernity.[32] Even David Lloyd, whose critique of aesthetics informs much of my argument, seems unable to avoid making an overhasty investment in the existence of the *Bildungsroman*. Ironically, in Lloyd's case a political critique of *Bildung* leads to *Bildung*'s ghostly return: seeking firm differences between a "major" literary tradition laboring in the service of aesthetics and contestatory, "minor" literatures that prepare the way for political alternatives, Lloyd commits himself to a binary opposition in which the *Bildungsroman* becomes the other of otherness, the stable site of production of subjects whose claim to universality may be materially interested and bogus, but can be exposed as such only from the vantage of other cultural productions.[33]

If the *Bildungsroman* can figure so unproblematically in critical texts even when the critic's agenda and methodology oppose those of humanist aesthetics, one has reason to suspect that the persistent return of the problem of the *Bildungsroman* in recent scholarship is a symptom of an instability

31. Ferenc Fehér, "Is the Novel Problematic? A Contribution to the Theory of the Novel," in *Reconstructing Aesthetics: Writings of the Budapest School*, ed. Ferenc Fehér and Agnes Heller (Oxford: Blackwell, 1986), 47.

32. Franco Moretti, *The Way of the World: The Bildungsroman in European Culture* (London: Verso, 1987), 5, passim. Moretti's claim is particularly stark, but versions of this aesthetic of history are to be found throughout the critical literature—sometimes taking the reverse form, as in Beddow, for instance, where the *Bildungsroman*, notwithstanding its self-conscious fictionality and link to authentic humanity, is "more culturally remote" from modern readers "than they themselves realise," since it lies "outside the mainstream" of the European realist tradition (3, 4). The non-modern, in this case, turns out to be the authentic bedrock of the human: the self-conscious self-positing of fiction, or the imagination.

33. Thus one encounters claims such as the following: "In the typical *Bildungsroman*, from *Wilhelm Meister* through *Portrait of the Artist as a Young Man*, erotic and cultural or economic desires are mapped on one another so as to produce a certain coherence in the subject. For Mustafa Sa'eed [in Tayeb Salih's *Season of Migration*], on the contrary . . . ," and the analysis proceeds under the aegis of a binary opposition that is never entirely questioned. David Lloyd, "Race under Representation," *Oxford Literary Review* 13.1–2 (1991): 80. For a discussion of the *Bildungsroman* as the exemplary form of "major" literature, see Lloyd's *Nationalism and Minor Literature: James Clarence Mangan and the Emergence of Irish Cultural Nationalism* (Berkeley: University of California Press, 1987), 19–26 and passim. I should emphasize here that these are local, if symptomatic, gestures in texts of great theoretical sophistication and practical skill. When Lloyd grants real attention to canonical (but) powerful texts, interpretations of great complexity result; but for reasons of political as well as expository economy he is frequently drawn to binary oppositions that, for instance, pair *Jane Eyre* with *Wide Sargasso Sea* such that the latter "reverses Jane's attainment of ethical autonomy in Bronte's novel" (*Nationalism*, 21). The challenge of cultural critique, however—which Lloyd elsewhere meets in every respect—is to interrogate difference without relying on the canon's own account of its achievement. It is finally worth noting that these indirect affirmations of the *Bildungsroman* occur at moments in Lloyd's text when strongly ethical claims are being advanced, which suggests that the aesthetic's traditional role of mediating between understanding and ethics is still to some extent in force.

within criticism. The symptom, as a symptom of instability, is itself at once overdetermined and contingent: criticism obviously should be able to get along quite well in the absence of this recently invented *Bildungsroman*, which, however, as we have seen, is as saturated with meaning as if it were a metaphysical cornerstone. There is no secure way to decide whether the idea of this genre is either necessary with regard to aesthetics or referential with regard to literature, which means that criticism is threatened with an inability to know the status or control the production of its own knowledge. In response to this uncertainty, critics return obsessively to this phantom genre, usually in order to grant it human warmth and substance, and this frequently in the hyperbolic mode of naturalization. Moretti, for instance, not only idealizes the *Bildungsroman* into the "symbolic form" of modernity, but naturalizes it into a biological species that "emerged victorious from that veritable 'struggle for existence' between various narrative forms that took place at the turn of the century: historical novel and epistolary novel, lyric, allegorical, satirical, 'romantic' novel, *Künstlerroman*. . . . As in Darwin, the fate of these forms hung on their respective 'purity': that is to say, the more they remained bound to a rigid, original structure, the more difficult their survival" (Moretti, *Way of the World*, 10, Moretti's ellipsis).[34] Alternatively, one can seek to exorcise the problem through skepticism—a gesture all the easier to make if, like Sammons, one adopts the no-nonsense tone of an empiricist, and pretends to believe that a *Bildungsroman* would be very easy to recognize if only one could find one.[35] Such skepticism is thus in one sense no more than the negative face of a recuperative movement in which criticism's ability to account for its own error is reaffirmed. But even in its most naively empirical form, the skeptic's negative gesture has a critical force beyond its own limitations, because in seeking to recalibrate and remove the difference between criticism and literature, it reminds criticism that this difference exists. The entire debate about the *Bildungsroman* revolves around this difference, constantly suspected and repeatedly effaced, and since we have seen that the relation between criticism and

34. One encounters such language regularly in the literature on the *Bildungsroman*, from Dilthey to the present: see especially François Jost, "Variations of a Species: The *Bildungsroman*," *Symposium* (Summer 1983): 125–46. The recurrence of such nineteenth-century vitalism in a purportedly materialist study such as Moretti's, however, suggests the continuing power of aesthetics as ideology. Naturalization, as Lacoue-Labarthe and Nancy comment, is precisely the dream of auto-formation that art or *technē* locates in and seeks to borrow from *physis:* "the organic is essentially *auto*-formation, or the genuine form of the subject" (49).
35. In this context it is also worth pointing out that Sammons stops short of disbelief in his phantom: though he finds no evidence for a *Bildungsroman* in the nineteenth century, "the situation is obscured further by the fact that the *Bildungsroman* genre definitely occurs in modern German literature," specifically, in Hesse and Mann ("Mystery," 242). As noted below, however, Sammons's article possesses iconoclastic energy simply in being willing to deliver negative judgments, which in their negativity draw attention to the odd referential status of the notion of the *Bildungsroman*.

literature is one in which literature produces itself in and as criticism, the question of the *Bildungsroman* returns us to that of the "literary absolute," which is perhaps less absolute, or even more absolute, than Lacoue-Labarthe and Nancy are able to claim.

Lacoue-Labarthe and Nancy occasionally suggest literature's irreducibility to the Subject, but their pathbreaking study does tend to underplay or forget the most incisive gesture in Walter Benjamin's thesis: his contention that German romantic criticism understands "reflection in the absolute of art" to be in the strictest sense non-subjective, an "I-less reflection" (*Ich-freie Reflexion*).[36] "What is at stake in Benjamin's account," Samuel Weber affirms, "is nothing less unusual, idiosyncratic, or, if you prefer, original, than the effort to elaborate a notion or practice of 'reflexivity' that would not ultimately be rooted in the premise of a constitutive subject."[37] Weber's commentary elucidates non-subjective reflection in terms of what Benjamin calls "the irony of form," which Weber unpacks as "a practice of writing which, precisely by undermining the integrity of the individual form, at the same time allows the singular 'work' to 'survive'" ("Criticism Underway," 315). Rather than represent an internalization of reflection as subjectivity, this irony would reside in the excess of form over its own self-constitution *as* form: in the mechanical linguistic repetitions that destroy the singularity of the artwork while permitting it to emerge. This mechanical element in art is what Benjamin calls the "prosaic," and criticism, Benjamin writes, exists as a strange form of presentation [*Darstellung*] of this prosaic nucleus:

> Criticism is the presentation of the prosaic kernel in each work. The concept "presentation" is thereby to be understood in the chemical sense, as the generation of one substance [*Erzeugung eines Stoffes*] through a determinate process to which others are subjected [*unterworfen*]. This is what Schlegel meant when he said of Wilhelm Meister that the work "does not merely judge itself, it also presents itself [*stellt sich dar*]." (*Begriff der Kunstkritik*, 109)

Commenting on this difficult passage, Weber draws attention to its sacrificial logic: "The romantic idea of criticism thus turns out to consist in a process of 'subjection': 'others' are subjected so that something can *matter*." And then, tacitly reversing the poles of Benjamin's chemical analogy, he

36. Walter Benjamin, *Der Begriff der Kunstkritik in der deutschen Romantik*, in *Gesammelte Schriften*, ed. Rolf Tiedemann and Hermann Schweppenhäuser (Frankfurt: Suhrkamp, 1974), 40. The "strictest sense" in this context is Fichtean.
37. Samuel Weber, "Criticism Underway: Walter Benjamin's *Romantic Concept of Criticism*," in *Romantic Revolutions: Criticism and Theory*, ed. Kenneth R. Johnston et al. (Bloomington: Indiana University Press, 1990), 310.

continues: "As a result of this subjection to the other, criticism 'stellt sich dar,' *sets itself forth,* sets forth, departing from itself to become something else, something lacking a proper name and which Benjamin, and after him de Man, will call 'allegory'" ("Criticism Underway," 317). It is perhaps not immediately clear how or to what criticism subjects itself in this passage, but Weber's proposed reversal, though unexplained, is consequent: criticism is always the criticism or "Darstellung" of itself, and thus is a subjection of itself to an alterity which is itself. All of the terms in this sacrificial story can in fact be substituted for each other, as Benjamin's passive and paratactic syntax allows either "criticism" or the "prosaic kernel" to occupy the place either of "the one substance" or of the "others." It must be noted that this narrative is still essentially that of *Bildung,* when *Bildung* is unfolded into its full dialectical model and understood as the ironic understanding of its own impossibility. But another story shadows the sacrificial and substitutive one both in Benjamin's text and in Weber's, legible in the political term "subjection": the story of an *Unterwerfung,* a sub-jection or "throwing under" of a plural otherness. In this sense the anonymous "others" in Benjamin's sentence have no existence except as placeholders for the violence of the "determinate process" of *Darstellung:* they are thus irrecuperable, inaccessible to the substitutive process that, like syntax, they make possible. The sacrificial exchange, which leads back to the autoproductive world of natural production (*Erzeugung*) and *Bildung,* could not exist without this violent *Unterwerfung,* which nonetheless remains radically heterogeneous to it. The thrown-under others thus reiterate an alterity irrecuperable to yet constitutive of the *subject:* this is also to say that they mark the mechanical insistence that Benjamin, deliberately contesting the subjectivist model of irony, terms the "irony of form." Criticism, the "presentation" of this irony, is thus the figure of its own unwitting and unstoppable "subjection," an ongoing throwing-under of understanding that, as Weber reminds us, is what "Benjamin, and after him de Man, will call 'allegory'."[38]

What this might mean becomes clearer if we examine the passage to which Benjamin refers us in Friedrich Schlegel's famous essay on *Wilhelm Meister.* For Schlegel, this novel is so "thoroughly new and unique" that it can only be understood "in itself [*aus sich selbst*]."[39] When reading it we must perform a purely reflective judgment, deriving our generic concept (*Gattungsbegriff*) from the object in its particularity:

---

38. For a discussion of allegory as the figure of theory or criticism, see my "Humanizing de Man," *Diacritics* 19.2 (1989): 35–53.

39. Friedrich Schlegel, "Über Goethes Meister" (1798), in *Kritische Friedrich-Schlegel Ausgabe,* ed. Ernst Behler (Munich: Paderborn, 1967), 2:133. Subsequent references are to this edition.

Perhaps one should thus at once judge it and not judge it—which seems to be no easy task. Luckily it is one of those books that judge themselves, and so relieve the critic of all trouble. Indeed, it doesn't just judge itself; it also presents itself [*stellt sich auch selbst dar*]. (Schlegel, "Über Goethes Meister," 133–34)

Thus critical representations of the text would serve it badly, "apart from the fact that they would be superfluous [*überflüssig*]." But the strange order of *Darstellung* that Benjamin read in the formation of this "literary absolute" ensures that a certain reading, however superfluous, will be called for. A few sentences later we read that the novel "disappoints as often as it fulfills customary expectations of unity and coherence," and that it in fact fails to judge itself insofar as it fails to pass from the level of the particular to that of the general: a failure that signals the return of the formerly "superfluous" reader:

> If any book has genius, it is this one. If this genius had been able to characterize itself in general as well as in particular, no one would have been able to say anything further about the novel as a whole, and how one should take it. Here a small supplement [*Ergänzung*] remains possible, and a few explanations will not seem useless or superfluous [*kann nicht unnütz oder überflüssig scheinen*]. . . . [T]he beginning and the ending of the novel will generally be found peculiar and unsatisfactory, and this and that in the middle of the text will be found superfluous and incoherent [*überflüssig und unzusammenhängend*]. And even he who knows how to distinguish the godlike from artistic willfulness will feel something isolated in the first and last reading, as though in the deepest and most beautiful harmony and oneness the final knotting of thought and feeling were lacking. (134)

The text judges itself but does not judge itself; it accounts for its own particularity but fails to inscribe itself in a genre (*Gattung*). And the reader, initially suspended between judging and not judging, then made *überflüssig* by the text's self-reflexive power, finally becomes a supplement (*Ergänzung*) that is *nicht überflüssig*. This reader, a master reader who knows how to distinguish "the godlike from artistic willfulness," performs an aesthetic judgment and necessarily finds the text wanting—rather as Hegel, in the *Aesthetics*, was to find Schlegel's work of an "indefinite and vacillating character," "sometimes achiev[ing] too much, sometimes too little" (63). But nothing could be more suspect than this magisterial act of judgment, for it has been generated by the text's inability to account for itself—a predicament replayed in the lucid incoherence of Schlegel's own theoretical narrative.

Theory or criticism here is "literary" precisely to the extent that it is unable to know its own origin, and the literary is "absolute" only in the sense that it recedes from theory in the very act of constituting it. Theory becomes theory out of an irreducible self-resistance: a paradox nicely exemplified by Lacoue-Labarthe and Nancy's *The Literary Absolute*, which achieves its insight into the Subject's dependence on literature only by remaining blind to what Benjamin gives us to think as literature's disruptive *subjection*.[40] In meditating such "subjection" in terms of a fundamentally non-subjective, formal irony, Benjamin remains faithful to Schlegel's own much-misunderstood presentation of irony. In the passage just examined, for instance, irony must be thought precisely in Benjamin's terms, as an *excess* of exemplarity or of form, a surplus or remainder that produces the judging subject by disrupting the dialectical passage from particular to general. When Schlegel goes on to characterize *Wilhelm Meister* in terms of "the irony that hovers over the whole work" (137), he is referring to a textuality that, in this most exemplary of texts, is *überflüssig und unzusammenhängend*, "as though in the deepest and most beautiful harmony and oneness the final knotting of thought and feeling were lacking": irony here is the "permanent parabasis" of Schlegel's famous fragment 668, and is thus another word for literariness itself.[41] Irony, as Kevin Newmark comments, is therefore "a term that always marks the encounter and potential tension between literature and philosophy, or truth and tropes" ("*L'absolu littéraire*," 906). When Lacoue-Labarthe and Nancy tell us that irony is "the very power of reflection or infinite reflexivity—the other name of speculation" (*Literary Absolute*, 86), they are in a crucial sense very far from Schlegel, and paradoxically close to the formulations that Hegel directs against Schlegel in the name of speculative thought, when he defines irony as "the principle of absolute subjectivity" (Hegel, *Aesthetics*, 67), and condemns its "concentration of the ego into itself, for which all bonds are snapped and which can live only in the bliss of self-enjoyment. This irony

40. See the chapter 1 for a differently inflected discussion of theory as the resistance to theory. As we are now in a position to appreciate, it is no coincidence that de Man's work positions itself in proximity to that of Schlegel. For a reading of Schlegel that doubles as a de Manian critique of Lacoue-Labarthe and Nancy's *The Literary Absolute*, see Kevin Newmark, "*L'absolu littéraire*: Friedrich Schlegel and the Myth of Irony," *MLN* 107 (1992): 905–30. The present discussion would reconfirm the force of Newmark's claim that "irony might just turn out to be one of the most rigorous ways to name a 'readability' so resistant to theoretical formulation that it would necessarily remain hidden or dissimulated with respect to any properly philosophical understanding of Schlegel's text" (914).

41. See *Kritische Friedrich-Schlegel Ausgabe*, 18:85. Fragment 668 is famous in contemporary theoretical circles because of its prominent place in de Man's writing on irony. See especially "The Rhetoric of Temporality," in *Blindness and Insight: Essays in the Rhetoric of Contemporary Criticism*, 2d ed., rev. (Minneapolis: University of Minnesota Press, 1983), 187–228, and the closing pages of *Allegories of Reading: Figural Language in Rousseau, Nietzsche, Rilke, and Proust* (New Haven: Yale University Press, 1979), esp. 300.

was invented by Friedrich Schlegel, and many others have babbled about it or are now babbling about it again" (66).

In denouncing irony as a bad or parodic form of the Subject, and Schlegel as a bad or parodic version of the philosopher, Hegel draws a distinction between criticism and philosophy that is at once sharp and ambiguous:

> To touch briefly on the course of the further development of the subject, alongside the reawakening of the philosophical Idea, A. W. and Friedrich von Schlegel, greedy for novelty in the search for the distinctive and extraordinary, appropriated from the philosophical Idea as much as their completely non-philosophical, but essentially critical natures were capable of accepting. For neither of them can claim a reputation for speculative thought. Nevertheless it was they who, with their critical talent, put themselves near the standpoint of the Idea, and with great freedom of speech and boldness of invention, even with miserable philosophical ingredients, directed a spirited polemic against the views of their predecessors. [. . .] But since their criticism was not accompanied by a thoroughly philosophical knowledge of their standard, this standard retained a somewhat indefinite and vacillating character, so that they sometimes achieved too much, sometimes too little. (Hegel, *Aesthetics*, 63)

"Criticism" and the "critical," achieving at once too much and too little, fails the test of philosophy but in doing so attracts philosophy's anger, since in criticism's failure philosophy is confronted with a figure of its own demise. And if Hegel goes on to insist, again in raised tones, that "if irony is taken as the keynote of the representation, then the most inartistic of all principles is taken to be the principle of the work of art" (since "the result is to produce, in part, commonplace figures, in part, figures worthless and without bearing") (68), he is identifying criticism's failure as a failure to prevent irony from causing criticism to fail to become criticism. Literature would be another name for this failure, and the *Bildungsroman* would be an exemplary site in which criticism's failure and its failure to fail become legible as the simultaneous co-implication and incompatibility of literature and aesthetics, thanks to the illegibility of "the most inartistic of all principles," irony. Such reflections suggest that when the figure of *Bildung* survives to compel a reading—in other words, becomes a *Roman*—it survives as a phantom, built and unbuilt through *Bilder*, figures, which record in the excess of their formalism a historicity that aesthetics labors to conceal. The rest of this book will try to unpack that conundrum.

3

Ghostly *Bildung:*
Wilhelm Meisters Lehrjahre

Whoever could manage to interpret Goethe's *Meister* properly would have
expressed what is now happening in literature. He could, so far as literary
criticism is concerned, retire forever.
—Friedrich Schlegel, "Über Goethes Meister"

In the preceding chapter I argued that the notion of the *Bildungsroman* is a figure for the problem of reading, as this problem manifests itself
within a fully developed aesthetic ideology. Aesthetics, the discourse that
discovers in a certain formality of perception the sensuous appearance of
meaning's possibility, realizes its ideological potential when the artwork
becomes the model for human identity, the state, and, most generally, the
historical or phenomenal realization of the Subject. *Bildung* names the autoproduction of a subject that produces or forms itself in the very act of
coming to consciousness of itself. *Bildung* may thus be understood as a
figure for the accomplishment of absolute Spirit. However, as an *aesthetic*
principle, *Bildung* also remains a pragmatic program of sensuous realization, an "aesthetic education" that is always "of man," where "man" is
Spirit's empirical representative. Despite its inextricability from speculative
metaphysics, aesthetics is anthropological and ultimately political in orientation, and the *Bildungsroman* presents itself as the genre in which this
pragmatic grip of aesthetics displays itself as literature.

Indeed, we saw that "literature," which produces itself in the very act of
reflecting upon itself *as* literature, provides aesthetics with a mirror in
which to confirm its identity. Thus, as a literary genre defined by the aesthetic project of *Bildung*, the *Bildungsroman* may be said to symbolize the
possibility of aesthetics itself—the only problem being that literary criticism, as we have seen, is unable to guarantee the existence of a *Bildungsroman*. The status of this uncertainty is itself uncertain: this genre seems on
the one hand excessively available, since any narrative can be taken as some
sort of *Bildungsroman*, yet on the other hand hyperbolically absent, since

under inspection no literary text appears to meet the aesthetic expectations of the genre. Furthermore, criticism seems unable to cease affirming, as well as debunking, the existence of this phantom genre, which means that if we think of the *Bildungsroman* as a "purely theoretical" object, we confront an opacity within literary theory itself, a difficulty afflicting theory precisely to the extent that theory seeks to refer to and understand literature. This paradox is at once clarified and further obscured when one takes into account the theoretical definition of literature *as* theory: literature as the self-reflexive source of knowledge about literature. If criticism confronts itself as a persistent pattern of error, the error partakes of literature "itself," though what one then means by literature becomes all the more difficult to ascertain.

This resistance of literature to (its own) critical understanding may be thought in rhetorical terms as the problem of irony. Since the Romantics, irony has frequently been associated with the novel; and the *Bildungsroman*, as a novelistic genre that exceeds or falls short of itself, would seem in its very (non)existence to exemplify this association. The question then becomes how one reads the irony of this genre's failure. As a privileged form of disenchantment through narrative, the *Bildungsroman* could hope to recover some conceptual stability; and indeed, criticism has often explored this possibility, if only because instances of what Todd Kontje calls the "affirmative" *Bildungsroman* seem so hard to come by.[1] If the failure of *Bildung* can be transformed into the knowledge of failure, *Bildung* can rediscover itself as the production of an ironic consciousness and as the assumption of human finitude, while the *Bildungsroman* can become the narrative of its own inability to achieve self-definition. It is in this spirit that Georg Lukács calls the novel a genre that exists only "in the process of becoming," and writes that "irony, with intuitive double vision, can see where God is to be found in a world abandoned by God."[2] The difficulty we have encountered in our examination of the *Bildungsroman* thus far, however, is that the knowledge of failure seems unable to keep up with the *act* of failure, since criticism is persistently returning to the affirmations it disqualifies. This divergence between knowledge and performance suggests the need to consider the irony of the *Bildungsroman* as an effect of literary language that would include but would also be in some sense irreducible to criticism as knowledge. The texts examined at the end of the preceding chapter suggest both the pertinence and the difficulty of such a

---

1. Todd Kontje, *Private Lives in the Public Sphere: The German Bildungsroman as Metafiction* (University Park: Pennsylvania State University Press, 1992), 12–17.
2. Georg Lukács, *The Theory of the Novel*, trans. Anna Bostock (Cambridge: MIT Press, 1971), 73, 92.

claim. Since criticism's specificity—its particular crisis—consists in dwelling under an imperative to confront literary texts and since this imperative repeats the obscure self-confrontation of literature, the difference between philosophy and criticism that we saw Hegel seeking to enforce in the *Aesthetics* turns on the problem of irony. Reiterating one of the founding gestures of Western philosophy, Hegel expels a certain kind of imitative practice from the aesthetic state: by characterizing irony as a subjective structure, he subordinates irony to the Idea as a parody to its original. The violence with which Hegel sends this parody packing, however, suggests the defensive nature of the initial characterization, for if irony were indeed merely an incomplete attitude of the Idea, it would take its place in the dialectical system without difficulty. When Hegel uncompromisingly rejects irony as "the most inartistic of all principles," the trace of another irony appears in the interstices of his text's apotropaic gesture: an irony associated in the *Aesthetics* with criticism, and thus with the resistance of literature to the critical understanding for which it calls.[3]

Such reflections, however, do not yet fully respond to the question of the *Bildungsroman*, which as an aesthetic genre requires exemplification in a text. Ordinarily we do not think of genres as requiring a model, let alone a visible point of origin; but the *Bildungsroman* is not an ordinary genre: though all generic terms may be considered aesthetic categories, the *Bildungsroman* is the genre *of* aesthetics. In this it differs from a classical genre such as the lyric, for instance, which, for all the aesthetic and ideological investment it has occasioned, bears the traces of multiple and heterogenous histories. The notion of the *Bildungsroman*, however, has no existence apart from either the post-Romantic history of aesthetics, or the aesthetic formalization that this "genre" takes as its content—in the guise, of course, of the formation of a specific, anthropological subject.[4] As an aesthetic of genre, the *Bildungsroman* must find embodiment in an example; and the burden of such exemplarity has been assigned to *Wilhelm Meisters Lehrjahre* ever since Friedrich Schlegel nominated it, with Fichte's philosophy and the French Revolution, as one of the "greatest tendencies of the age," and asserted that it was "so thoroughly new and unique" that "only in itself [*aus sich selbst*] can one learn to understand it."[5] Schlegel emphasized the text's power to represent "nature or *Bildung* itself . . . in manifold examples" ("Über Goethes Meister," 143); at the same time, however, as we

3. G. W. F. Hegel, *Aesthetics: Lectures on Fine Art*, trans. T. M. Knox (Oxford: Clarendon Press, 1975), 68.
4. This is also what distinguishes the question of the *Bildungsroman* from that of other problematic genres such as the *récit* or *Novelle*—or, for that matter, from that of the novel itself.
5. Friedrich Schlegel, "Über Goethes Meister" (1798), in *Kritische Friedrich-Schlegel Ausgabe*, ed. Ernst Behler (Munich: Paderborn, 1967), 2:132.

saw, he wrote of "the irony that hovers over the whole work" (137), and told an uncanny story of a text that "judges itself" and "presents itself [*stellt sich selbst dar*]," yet strangely enough simultaneously fails to judge itself, generating a space for criticism precisely to the extent that its self-representation is "superfluous and incoherent" (134). The question of the *Bildungsroman* finally becomes that of how *Wilhelm Meister* figures the possibility of its own theorization, which is equally the question that any reading of this novel must pursue.

Since the reception of texts and more specifically the relation between aesthetics and reading is at issue, however, it will be useful at this point to work toward an encounter with *Wilhelm Meister* by examining the response it elicited in one of its first readers, Friedrich Schiller. In bending to critical purpose the terminology and presuppositions of his influential treatise, *On the Aesthetic Education of Man*, Schiller became in a certain sense the first critic to attempt to read *Wilhelm Meister* as a *Bildungsroman*. His remarks thus plot an interpretative path that much subsequent criticism has followed, but also provide a map of some of the more prominent difficulties encountered by the aestheticizing reading. Schiller's commentary has the additional merit of relating aesthetics to gender politics in ways that speak to the specific concerns of Goethe's novel, as well as to the more general question of the politics of aesthetics.[6]

I

The Schiller-Goethe correspondence from the period 1795–96 has become one of the sacred cows of the modern German canon, not least because it provides a bridge between *Wilhelm Meister* and *On the Aesthetic Education of Man*, allowing Goethe's novel to be understood as the "fictional counterpart" of one of the founding texts of aesthetic culture.[7] Schiller received installments of *Wilhelm Meister* while he was revising his treatise in

6. Like most other branches of criticism, mainstream Anglo-American feminist criticism seems to have found the term *Bildungsroman* remarkably congenial, as witnessed by the recent publication of a reference guide: Laura Sue Fuderer, *The Female Bildungsroman in English: An Annotated Bibliography of Criticism* (New York: MLA Publications, 1990). The arguments that follow do not address the politics of feminist criticism's appropriation of this term: all appropriations will, of course, be progressive or regressive in different contexts. The readings being presented here, however, do suggest the difficulty of extracting aesthetic ideology from phallocentric discourse.

7. See for instance the comments of Elizabeth M. Wilkinson and L. A. Willoughby: "We . . . would seek the most adequate fictional counterpart [to the *Aesthetic Education*] in the work that Schiller was receiving in installments while actually engaged on his treatise, namely *Wilhelm Meister*." In Friedrich Schiller, *On the Aesthetic Education of Man: In a Series of Letters*, ed. and trans. Elizabeth M. Wilkinson and L. A. Willoughby (Oxford: Clarendon Press, 1967), cxcv–cxcvi. Quotations from the *Aesthetic Education* are to this bilingual edition, and are indicated by letter and paragraph number.

1795, though his most interesting comments date from the following summer, when Goethe had finished the novel's last two books and Schiller was able to reflect on the text as a whole, ask himself what a "whole" is, and tentatively wonder out loud whether this text made up one. Much of the time the answer is affirmative, and at these moments the language of the *Aesthetic Education* moves squarely into view. "In him," Schiller writes at one point of the character Wilhelm, "dwells a pure and moral image of mankind,"[8] a phrase that recalls the typological system of the *Aesthetic Education*, according to which, as we saw in chapter 2, "every individual man . . . carries in himself, by predisposition and determination [*der Anlage und Bestimmung nach*], a pure ideal Man, with whose unchanging oneness it is the great task of his being, in all its changes, to correspond" (*Aesthetic Education*, 4.2, translation modified). Schiller thus implicitly presents Wilhelm here as the subject of aesthetics, representative of universal humanity. And since the State is "the objective and as it were canonical form in which the diversity of subjects seeks to unite itself," Schiller's scheme also easily accommodates the appearance of a secret society such as the pseudo-Masonic Society of the Tower (*Turmgesellschaft*) in Goethe's novel. For in the *Aesthetic Education*, we recall, the State remains underway toward the Aesthetic State, which is prefigured by the exemplary community: "[A]s a need, [the Aesthetic State] exists in every finely attuned soul; as a realized fact, we are likely to find it, like the pure Church and the pure Republic, only in some few chosen circles" (27.12). The Society of the Tower clearly presents itself as one such chosen circle; thus the story of the Society's interest in Wilhelm, its secret manipulation of his life, and eventual initiation of him into its ranks, appears as an exemplary representation of aesthetic pedagogy.

Schiller, accordingly, draws an ambitious link between the plot of Goethe's novel and the procedures of an aesthetic judgment. Since the Society of the Tower directs Wilhelm's life like a god or a force of destiny, its machinations are analogous to the machinery (*Maschinen*) of epic. But the Society's intervention is not a simple one, for it labors in the service of the "idea of mastery," and

> this idea of mastery [*Meisterschaft*], which is the work of ripened and whole experience, cannot itself guide the novel's hero; it cannot and must not stand *before* him as his purpose and goal, since as soon as he were to imagine the goal, he would have eo ipso already attained it. Rather, the idea of mastery must stand as a leader *behind* him. In this way, the whole obtains a beautiful purposiveness [*Zweckmäßigkeit*], without the hero

8. Siegfried Seidel, ed., *Der Briefwechsel zwischen Schiller und Goethe*, I, 1794–1797 (Munich: C. H. Beck, 1984), 189 (5 July 1796). Subsequent references are to this edition.

having a purpose [*Zweck*]. Thus the understanding finds a task fulfilled, while the imagination entirely asserts its freedom. (Seidel, *Briefwechsel*, 196)

A double bind composes the very essence of narrative as a teleological figure: the telos, the "idea of mastery" must "lead from behind," lest it stamp on the unfolding of *Bildung* the mark of an external force or goal. Narrative, in other words, must provide a temporal detour wholly subservient to the totalizing structure of a *Bild* that, as Gadamer insists, is at once *Vorbild* and *Nachbild*, prefiguration and model.[9] As always in the orbit of the *Bildungsroman*, and, more generally, in that of aesthetics per se, literary form and subjectivity are taken to be homologous, which means that Schiller can shift easily between the language of poetics and that of consciousness, and translate the structure of prefiguration into the paradox of Kantian disinterest. Pedagogue, pupil, and the narrative process itself must all intend and not intend, direct and not direct, the process of formation. For a subject or a text to be *exemplary*—a representation and prefiguration of the universal—its purposiveness must be purposeless. The use to which Schiller puts Kantian terminology in this passage is no doubt philosophically suspect; but here as elsewhere his vulgarization of critical philosophy has about it an inspired quality, compressing into a few sentences the ideological potential of Kant's notion of the aesthetic. Though the *Critique of Judgment* is vastly more cautious than *On the Aesthetic Education of Man* in its affirmation of the power of aesthetic judgment to underwrite and confirm the harmony of the faculties, the stability of the Kantian architectonic nonetheless does depend on a passage through the formal abstraction of "purposiveness without purpose": only in a truly free (purposeless) play of the faculties can the formal coherence (purposiveness) of the whole system of the faculties be ascertained.[10] In recalling this, Schiller not only emphasizes the central importance of the "subject" in aesthetics but also the importance of aesthetics for the subject. If history or narrative can be represented in the

9. Hans-Georg Gadamer, *Truth and Method* (New York: Crossroad, 1982): "In *Bildung* there is *Bild*. The idea of form lacks the mysterious ambiguity of *Bild*, which can mean both *Nachbild* ('image,' 'copy'), and *Vorbild* ('model')" (12). For further discussion see the preceding chapter.
10. For a compact and rigorous explication of the key role played by aesthetic judgment in Kant's system, see Gilles Deleuze, *Kant's Critical Philosophy: The Doctrine of the Faculties*, trans. Hugh Tomlinson and Barbara Habberjam (Minneapolis: University of Minnesota Press, 1984), 46–67. Though the notion of "form" in the *Critique of Judgment* is deeply disruptive, as Jacques Derrida has demonstrated in *The Truth in Painting* (Chicago: University of Chicago Press, 1987), it is also constitutive of its own ideological misunderstanding; and thus David Lloyd, in "Kant's Examples," *Representations* 28 (Fall 1989): 34–54, is able to make a strong case for the presence of a temporal narrative "from matter to form, from sense to commonality, from example to idea, from beauty to morality" implicit in the Third *Critique*'s account of aesthetic judgment (45), a narrative that Schiller, here and elsewhere, would simply be rendering more pragmatic and overt.

terminology of aesthetic judgment, this is because the historical model is a temporalized version of a subject that is deriving its coherence, which is to say its exemplarity, from an identification with aesthetic form. Much, as we shall see, will turn on the nature of this identification.

And precisely here problems develop: despite Schiller's enthusiasm for *Wilhelm Meister*, the novel will never fully satisfy him, and the shortcomings he perceives in it are, unsurprisingly, those commonly listed by twentieth-century critics who have trouble classing it as a *Bildungsroman*. Once again Schiller's response moves fluidly between the levels of character analysis and narrative form. Wilhelm's personal *Bildung* is suspect on Kantian grounds: he does not ever seem to learn how to perform a proper aesthetic judgment. At the end of the novel, gazing at aesthetic objects in the Hall of the Past, he is "still too much the old Wilhelm, who liked best to linger, in his grandfather's house, by the [portrait of the] sick king's son" (*Lehrjahre*, 208)—the Wilhelm of the novel's opening chapters, who consumes art narcissistically, identifying with its content rather than judging its form. And the *Bildung* of the text itself necessarily displays an analogous weakness, which Schiller again understands as an overly purposive relation to art: "Sometimes it seems as though you're writing *for* the actor, though you only wish to write *of* the actor" (Seidel, *Briefwechsel*, 82). Both character and text appear to fall short of the *Zweckmäßigkeit ohne Zweck* that was to guarantee the emplotment of *Bildung*, and the synthesis that Schiller had celebrated only a paragraph or so earlier suddenly threatens to fracture at all points. The meaning, *das Bedeutende*, of the aesthetic plot—the epic "machinery" provided by the Society of the Tower, as it manipulates Wilhelm along the road to *Meisterschaft*—does not demonstrate a "necessary relation to *inner* being" (Seidel, *Briefwechsel*, 197). Many readers will believe they have found in the "secret influence" of the Tower "merely a theatrical game and a trick [*Kunstgriff*]" (197). Earlier the imagination had asserted its freedom; now "the imagination seems to play too freely with the whole." This surplus of freedom is what Schiller has been calling and continues to call the "theatrical": the text suffers from "a more theatrical purpose [*Zweck*] and . . . a more theatrical medium, than is needful and proper in a novel" (197).

If, then, Goethe's novel falls short of the purposiveness without purpose of *Bildung*, this does not quite mean that the text is being overly instrumental in its treatment of its objects—rather, a different kind of "freedom," an excess of freedom, appears as the artwork (the novel) reflects on art (the theater), and thereby on "itself," but after a fashion that contaminates its own identity, exceeding the limits of what is "proper in a novel." Schiller formulates this threat more sharply in a subsequent paragraph, in which he returns to the tropes of narrative and telos (*Lehrjahre* and *Meisterschaft*), claims that Goethe's thematization of these concepts is too narrow, and questions the efficacity of what he sees as the novel's two symbolic encodings of *Bildung*—the "formula" of apprenticeship, and the story of Wilhelm's acknowledgment of his son Felix:

> Is everything made understandable through this formula? And can [Wilhelm] be freed [*losgesprochen*] from apprenticeship merely on the basis of the fact that his father-heart declares itself [*daß sich das Vaterherz bei ihm erklärt*] at the end of Book 7? Here I wish that the relation of all those particular parts [*Glieder*] of the novel to that philosophical concept [i.e., *Meisterschaft*] had been made clearer. I mean to say that the fable is perfectly true, and the moral of the fable is perfectly true—but the relation of the one to the other doesn't yet spring clearly enough into view. (Seidel, *Briefwechsel*, 200)

"The question touches on everything," Schiller affirms, for he has reached the point of questioning the possibility of reading itself, insofar as the relation between an understanding (the "*Moral*") and the process that enables it (the "*Fabel*") has become uncertain.

The textual pressures that have rendered the aesthetic plot so fragile remain obscure, and to advance further in our understanding of what occurs when *Wilhelm Meister* reflects on its own production we shall need to examine the novel itself. But a sketch of an answer is given in Schiller's worried recollection of the scene in which Wilhelm's "father-heart declares itself." Schiller may have had good reason to be taking fatherhood seriously as he wrote this letter—two days later his wife was to give birth to a son— but his allusion to Wilhelm's acknowledgment of Felix is responding to the language and structure of the novel, as well as to the momentum of his own discussion. For now we need only recall that by the end of book 7, Wilhelm has been informed by various authorities—first the duenna Barbara, whom he does not entirely believe; then the Abbé, whom he does—that Mariane, the actress he had abandoned in book 1, and who has since conveniently died, is Felix's mother and that he, Wilhelm, is the father. Having just received his *Lehrbrief* from the Tower and been "losgesprochen," in Schiller's phrase, from apprenticeship, Wilhelm accedes to his own over-determined patronymic—"Meister"—in acceding to fatherhood. "Yes, I feel it," he cries, embracing Felix, "you are mine!"[11] As always in Goethe,

---

11. Johann Wolfgang von Goethe, *Wilhelm Meisters Lehrjahre*, book 7, chap. 9. I quote from the fourteen-volume Hamburger Ausgabe, ed. Erich Trunz (Hamburg: Christian Wegner Verlag, 1950), 7:497. Since editions vary, and the novel's chapters are short, I have indicated subsequent quotations by book and chapter number. My translations follow but occasionally modify those

the scene is not without irony (Wilhelm subsequently asks Felix, "Where did you come from just this minute, my child?" and the Abbé replies, "Don't ask!"); but Schiller is right to assign the dramatic and thematic importance he does to this episode: if Wilhelm's *Bildung* is to occur at all, it will proceed, like Freud's famous "advance of civilization," under the affirmation that "paternity is a hypothesis, based on an inference and a premiss."[12] *Wilhelm Meister*'s version of this claim, as voiced by Friedrich near the end of the novel, is if anything more insistent than Freud's: "Fatherhood is based entirely and only on conviction; I'm convinced, and therefore I'm a father" (*Lehrjahre*, 8.6). Fatherhood, in other words, is not a neutral hypothesis: it is a speech act, a performative that imposes itself as truth through its own (always potentially illegitimate) act of persuasion. Schiller emphasizes this performative element by recalling that Wilhelm's "father-heart" must "declare itself" in order to exist. Fatherhood is a public act with legal consequences, no matter how private or internalized the paternal declaration, which is to say no more and no less than that fatherhood depends in its very essence upon language. Fatherhood is thus a privileged metaphor for the subject of *Bildung* but also a site of anxiety, since, figured as paternity, the self-positing subject becomes more overtly rhetorical in its constitution, more legibly dependent on the power of a performative to impose a meaning. And if *Moral* and *Fabel*, meaning and the means of meaning's *Erklärung* diverge, the *Vaterherz* can only declare itself (*sich erklären*), and thereby perform itself into existence, by risking its own irrecuperable loss.

Since the speech act of fatherhood grounds itself in its own perlocutionary effect ("I feel it"), the topic of fatherhood leads us to consider the role of pathos or affect in the itinerary of *Bildung*. Schiller reflects on pathos at several points in his commentary on *Wilhelm Meister*, usually in relation to Felix's ambivalent double in the novel, the character who was to capture the imagination of Goethe's reading public and become for the nineteenth century a virtual synecdoche for pathos, Mignon.[13] Schiller's investment in

---

of Eric Blackall, ed. and trans., *Wilhelm Meister's Apprenticeship* (New York: Suhrkamp Publishers, 1989). Subseqent references to other works by Goethe will be indicated by volume and page number to the Hamburger Ausgabe, abbreviated HA.

12. Sigmund Freud, *Moses and Monotheism*, in *Complete Psychological Works*, ed. James Strachey (London: Hogarth, 1953–74), 23:114.

13. As Hellmut Ammerlahn remarks, "No figure in *Wilhelm Meister* so spoke to the heart and imagination of Goethe's reading public as Mignon; over no other character was so much reflected, conjectured, and written; none has been so frequently imitated, and yet remained so mysterious." "Wilhelm Meisters Mignon—ein offenbares Rätsel: Name, Gestalt, Symbol, Wesen, und Werden," *Deutsche Vierteljahrsschrift für Literaturwissenschaft und Geistesgeschichte* 42 (1968): 89. See also Ammerlahn's, "Puppe—Tänzer—Dämon—Genius—Engel: Naturkind, Poesiekind und Kunstwerdung bei Goethe," *The German Quarterly* 54.1 (1981): 19–32. For a more recent study of the figure of Mignon in literary history, see Erika Tunner, "'L'Esprit de

Mignon is not unambiguous. She plays a curiously vivid role in his initial response to Goethe's novel: "I am restless and appeased; longing and peace are wonderfully mingled. Out of the mass of impressions that I receive, the figure of Mignon looms at the moment most strongly before me" (Seidel, *Briefwechsel*, 176). But in a long letter on *Wilhelm Meister* that Schiller sent Goethe three days later, the "fearfully pathetic element" of Mignon's destiny undergoes a curious metamorphosis:

> How well-thought it is, that you derive the practical monstrous [*das prak- tisch Ungeheure*]—the fearfully pathetic element in the destiny of Mignon and the Harper—from the theoretical monstrous—from the misbirths [*Mißgeburten*] of the understanding. Thus pure and healthy Nature has nothing imposed on her. These monstrous destinies that pursue Mignon and the Harper are hatched only out of the womb of stupid superstition. Even Aurelie is destroyed only through her unnaturalness [*Unnatur*], through her androgyny [*Mannweiblichkeit*]. Only in the case of Mariane would I accuse you of an act of poetic selfishness. I almost want to say that she becomes the novel's sacrificial victim, since in the natural course of things she would have been saved [*daß sie dem Roman zum Opfer geworden, da sie der Natur nach zu retten war*]. For *her* sake bitter tears will still fall, when in the case of the three other [characters] one has happily passed from the individual to the idea of the whole. (Seidel, *Briefwechsel*, 181)

Given the energy with which Schiller had focused on Mignon in his first response to the text, one is entitled to wonder what commerce obtains between his newfound composure with regard to Mignon's "fearfully pathetic" destiny and his intriguing characterization of Mariane as a victim [*Opfer*]. Goethe's killing off of Mariane, Schiller claims, is an unnatural act of poetic selfishness insofar as the novel is sacrificing one of its characters to itself, for its own sake, presumably in order to acquire supererogatory pathos. But since the text has had to act selfishly and violate nature in order to stimulate the "bitter tears" we weep for Mariane, Schiller is returning us to the haunting question of the legitimacy of pathos, with the result that his own analysis inevitably becomes caught up in the sacrificial economy he describes. For as soon as the origin of pathos becomes suspect, Mariane becomes as much Schiller's *Opfer* here as Goethe's, since one becomes free to speculate that Schiller is presenting her death as a violation of nature in

---

Mignon': Mignon-Bilder von der Klassik bis zur Gegenwart," *Goethe Jahrbuch* 106 (1989): 11–21. Like these essays—and Schiller's correspondence, and any number of other responses to *Wilhelm Meister*—the present chapter represents among other things an attempt to read the "riddle" of Mignon. For an important study that addresses itself in part to this question, see Jochen Hörisch, *Gott Geld und Glück: Zur Logik der Liebe in den Bildungsromanen Goethes, Kellers, und Thomas Manns* (Frankfurt am Main: Suhrkamp, 1983), esp. 30–99.

order to shore up the illusion that nature was whole enough to begin with to be able to undergo a subsequent violation.[14] Thus the "frighteningly pathetic element" of the destinies of Mignon, the Harper, and Aurelie can be more securely located in the realm of the monstrous ("das Ungeheure," "die Unnatur") and erased in an unimpeded progression to the "idea of the whole." Since the Harper and above all Mignon, as we shall see later, are figures associated with the illegitimacy of incest and the pathos of poetry, and since Aurelie is similarly associated with the false pathos of theater,[15] it is tempting to suppose that what Schiller is seeking to quarantine here is the "monstrous" possibility that *Bildung* depends on language's rhetorical power to generate effects, just as *Bildung*'s privileged trope, fatherhood, does. Schiller registers, naturalizes, and thus to some degree controls this possibility by representing it in a rigidly binary language of gender: the "misbirths of the understanding" and the "womb of superstition" figure a generative force that would be distinguishable from the causality of the aesthetic plot while still remaining within nature's purview. One sees that the final cost of this exorcism is an emphatic, if tactical, misogyny: the "womb" must bear away the threat of gender confusion (here, Aurelie's *Mannweiblichkeit*) because the (putatively natural) binary opposition of the sexes must exhaust the possibilities of figuration. Schiller thus sketches the outline of a violent, repetitive, and insistently misogynistic narrative, in which characters are "sacrificed" so that other characters—particularly Mignon—may be aestheticized and sentimentalized, thus diverting attention from the linguistic predicament they personify, and shoring up the (patriarchal) story of *Bildung* as a passage "from the individual to the idea

14. The "unnaturalness" of Mignon is frequently invoked in Goethe criticism when the "naturalness" of some other aspect of the novel is in peril: e.g., Michael Beddow, *The Fiction of Humanity: Studies in the Bildungsroman from Wieland to Thomas Mann* (Cambridge: Cambridge University Press, 1982): "Both Mignon and the Harper produce, in their solitary and secret predicaments, deeply moving poetry, but their creativity is not for them an experience of human freedom. . . . What little potential humanity they do manage to realise is embodied in the poetry which gives voice to their sense of separation from full humanity. . . . And so Mignon and the Harper take their place among the figures whose destinies develop so differently from Wilhelm's, reminding us that the course of his life, whilst eminently 'natural', is by no means to be taken as normal, in the sense of everyday" (146).
15. The itinerary we are taking through *Wilhelm Meisters Lehrjahre* will unfortunately make it impossible for us to examine the remarkable character of Aurelie, the actress who confuses *Schein* and *Sein* by carrying a real dagger and by mingling her real life with her role as Ophelia—a dark parody of Wilhelm's narcissistic investment in Hamlet. "Smile at me, laugh at my theatrical display of passion!" she cries at Wilhelm; but "the terrifying, half-natural and half-forced state of this woman tormented him too much for that." A moment later Aurelie cuts Wilhelm's hand with the dagger, striking a blow, perhaps, on behalf of the countless damaged and discarded female characters who litter the path of male *Bildung*: "One must mark [*zeichnen*] you men sharply!" (4.20). For a feminist reading of the *Lehrjahre* that discusses Aurelie see Jill Anne Kowalik, "Feminine Identity Formation in *Wilhelm Meisters Lehrjahre*," *Modern Language Quarterly* (June 1992): 149–72.

of the whole." More elaborate and far more disruptive versions of this theoretical narrative may be found in *Wilhelm Meister* itself.

II

Schiller's commentary may not possess a notably ironic tenor or tone, but it returns us to Goethe's novel with a sense of the textual landscape behind Friedrich Schlegel's affirmation of "the irony that hovers over the whole work" ("Über Goethes Meister," 137). In chapter 2 we briefly examined the dizzying paradoxes unleashed by Schlegelian irony: for Schlegel, we recall, *Wilhelm Meister* "doesn't just judge itself; it also presents itself [*stellt sich auch selbst dar*]"; yet at the same time that the text renders the reader "superfluous," it generates the necessity of a reader as a "supplement" (*Ergänzung*) to its own "superfluous and incoherent" self-presentation (134). Schiller's engagement with this text gives us a more concrete sense of how such irony would inscribe itself in the actual text of the novel. But we still do not know why the scenes, images, and structural elements that Schiller privileges—the theater, the portrait, the *Turmgesellschaft*, fatherhood, Mignon—convey the pressure of a divergence between meaning ("the moral") and the means of meaning ("the fable"), which is Schiller's version of Schlegel's perception of "something isolated in the first and last reading, as though in the deepest and most beautiful harmony and oneness the final knotting of thought and feeling were lacking" (134).

Taking a cue from Schiller's interest in the representations of art and aesthetic judgment in *Wilhelm Meister*, we might ask first after the relation between theater and portraiture in the unfolding of Wilhelm's *Bildung*. The two would initially seem to function in opposing ways. The theater is the (negative) locus of Wilhelm's education: he emerges from apprenticeship not just by assuming paternal responsibility to Felix, but by giving up his dream of becoming an actor. From his infant fascination with marionettes to his climactic assumption of the title role in *Hamlet* in book 5, Wilhelm plays out a dialectic of investment in and disillusionment with the theater that grants stature to his final renunciation (*Entsagung*) of it; though we shall need to ask what exactly is being renounced in the name of "theater," and why, the text would at least appear to be allowing its hero to acquire genuine self-knowledge, albeit in the negative mode of knowing what he is not. Meanwhile the recurrence of the painting of the sick king's son, as Schiller noted, seems to record a hitch in the works of *Bildung*. Though the painting is poorly executed, Wilhelm cheerfully affirms at the beginning of the novel that "the subject is what appeals to me in a painting, not the artistry" (*Lehrjahre*, 1.17), and near the end of the text he is still sticking to his guns: "He returned eagerly to the picture of the sick prince, still finding it as moving and affecting as ever" (8.3). Like the Beautiful Soul, the *schöne Seele*, Wilhelm remains vulnerable throughout his itinerary to the attractions of kitsch, unable to achieve the formal universality of the disinterested subject of aesthetic judgment. Indeed, in his attitude toward the painting Wilhelm would appear neurotically fixated, trapped in the defiles of a repetitive desire that the painting thematizes as oedipal impasse—the sick prince is dying for love of his father's bride. In the case of the theater Wilhelm can give up his narcissistic and oedipal investments, stop playing Hamlet, and start being a father; in the case of the painting he remains a son unable to give up forbidden desire.

Upon closer inspection, however, Wilhelm's failure to renounce the painting bears a certain relation to his ability to renounce the theater. The common denominator of both gestures is Wilhelm's inability to preserve aesthetic distance. He is only capable of responding to an aesthetic object when he can identify with its meaning or content; and, as he learns during the premiere of *Hamlet*, he is only capable of good acting when he can identify with the role to such an extent that he is not acting. In giving up the theater Wilhelm thus records his knowledge that he can never give up the particularity of self-interest. His response to the painting confirms this knowledge; and he can thus claim to have undergone a certain ironic *Bildung* insofar as he has learned that he will never truly become the universal subject of aesthetics, the "pure figure of mankind" that Schiller claimed to perceive in him. Since, as we saw in the preceding chapter, an aesthetic education is always underway toward its own occurrence, to a certain degree it accommodates being refigured as an impossibility, a refiguration that would be ironic in Lukács's sense of irony as compensatory knowledge. And indeed, Wilhelm's double gesture of renunciation and identification structures a complex dialectic in the course of which the text rigorously explores the possibility of *Bildung* as irony.

The Society of the Tower, it will be recalled, perversely lends its aid to Wilhelm's production of *Hamlet* by providing a Ghost capable of frightening Wilhelm into complete identification with his role. The Abbé justifies this intervention on the dialectical grounds that "error can only be cured through erring" (*Lehrjahre*, 8.5). The Society of the Tower helps in order to hinder and hinders in order to help; and Wilhelm, by acting well when he wasn't acting, learns that he isn't an actor. A genuinely dialectical sublation thus appears to occur, with knowledge emerging *within* error, as the truth of error. But the status of this knowledge is uncertain, as becomes clear when we examine more closely what it is that Wilhelm gives up in giving up the theater. Learning that he is not an actor, he learns that he cannot control the act of identification. Actors such as Serlo or Aurelie enter into their roles knowingly; one could say that, for them, identification is an intentional act. The "self" of an actor, qua actor, resides in his or her ability to intend identification. Wilhelm, the mildly talented amateur, however, identifies blindly with Hamlet because he is frightened by the Ghost: the aesthetic power of his performance is the result of an event over which he has no control. Identification occurs precisely where knowledge and intention are absent. It is therefore slightly misleading to say, as we did above, that Wilhelm cannot give up self-interest. His problem is not that he suffers from an excess or stubbornness of self that prevents him from acting well or judging aesthetically; rather, the opposite is the case: prefabricated roles seize him unpredictably and without encountering resistance. The actor is always an actor, but Wilhelm, experiencing "Hamlet's" fear, has no identity with which to structure this literary space: the sense of the uncanny that he feels belongs to no one and is in a sense experienced by "no one." We shall return to the interesting question of the status of literary pathos in this novel; for the moment the point to retain is that this uncanny moment is precisely the site of pedagogy or *Bildung*. A strange, radical self-loss, which from the "self"'s perspective arrives by accident, must be transformed into self-knowledge: the knowledge that the self cannot intend the occurrence, or construction, of the self—in other words, that the self is not an actor.

This transformation of loss into knowledge occurs as Wilhelm's renunciation, or *Entsagung*, of the theater, which consequently is a gesture of some complexity. In the first place, Wilhelm is not simply recognizing his own particular limitations: he is simultaneously renouncing an idealized image of the theater. Because acting consists in a power to control identification, the actor provides the illusion of being the aesthetic subject—the subject modeled on the artwork that knows what it does, or on the "literary absolute," in Lacoue-Labarthe and Nancy's sense, which performs itself into existence as the knowledge of its own performance. To the youthful Wilhelm, the stage had thus seemed to offer a middle-class route toward the *sprezzatura* of the aristocrat, and toward the nation as the Aesthetic State, the collective subject of aesthetics. In turning in disillusionment from the theater, Wilhelm recognizes the inessentiality of the theater's aesthetic synthesis: the actor intends identification, but only in the orbit of fiction. As Faust comments, "Welch Schauspiel! Aber ach! ein Schauspiel nur" (HA, 3: 22): when the act of self is known, it is a lie. This insight takes narrative shape as Wilhelm's gradual assessment of the fallibility, or indeed the vulgarity, of his professional colleagues, and as his turn toward the real-life theatrics of a company of genuine aristocrats, the Society of the Tower. The renunciation is thus also a substitution, and the coherence of renunciation depends on the nature of the Society of the Tower's difference from the acting company. The two communities intersect precisely at the point of *Bildung*—Wilhelm's uncanny thespian encounter with the Ghost. In taking up the role of the Ghost, the Society of the Tower acts in order to cure acting, enfolding the craft of the actor in a higher knowledge of a genuine act—the act of imparting knowledge to Wilhelm. Pedagogy thus replaces the theater as the matrix of aesthetics.

Whether Wilhelm has actually acquired knowledge rapidly becomes dubious, however, since the Society of the Tower is more fantastically theatrical than any of Wilhelm's acting companies. Actors at least know that their performance is fictional; the Society of the Tower, seducing Wilhelm with a parody of Masonic ritual, can either be seen as wiser than the actor, or vastly more naive and less genuine. It is for this reason that Schiller registered unhappiness with the idea of the *Turmgesellschaft*—as did another writer in the aesthetic tradition, the young Georg Lukács, who felt that the appearance of this "fantastic apparatus" introduces "a disruptive dissonance into the total unity of the whole," such that "the miraculous becomes a mystification without hidden meaning, a strongly emphasized narrative element without real importance, a playful ornament without decorative grace" (*Theory of the Novel*, 142). (All the same, "it is quite impossible to imagine *Wilhelm Meister* without this miraculous element.") On this account, the Society of the Tower is itself the aesthetic but inessential fiction that the actor performs. Pedagogy, therefore, would be not the negation but the redoubling of acting: the pedagogue, qua pedagogue, acts acting, and then, the day's work done, retires to the theatricality of a Society that, unlike the acting company, *intends* to prefigure the Aesthetic State. If Wilhelm has learned that he is incapable of the aesthetic synthesis of acting and that this synthesis is a sham, both he and his teachers would appear capable of attaining this insight only at the price of entering into a more absurd and literal-minded version of the original delusion. The teacher, in other words, knows how teaching occurs only to the extent that the teaching, like acting, is untrue: Wilhelm may acquire knowledge but cannot be said to *learn* anything.

The pedagogical plot thus assumes the aspect of a trick, a *Kunstgriff*, and the novel itself becomes the level on which the wise irony of *Bildung* would reside: the text "itself," as a *literary* text, can be said to know the event of itself as text, even if the characters it represents fall short of such aesthetic self-production. On this level too the novel follows out the skewed logic of Wilhelm's predicament by allowing the painting of the sick prince to dictate the terms of the text's closure. Wilhelm's recently acknowledged son Felix assumes the role of the sick prince: seeing a glass and a bottle of milk, he drinks, not knowing that there is a deadly amount of opium in the milk, since Augustin, the former Harper, has just discovered he is Mignon's incestuous father and is planning to commit suicide. However, the opium is only in the glass, not in the bottle, and the child's bad habit of drinking out of bottles rather than glasses saves him. The doctor speaks of "the luckiest chance [glücklichsten Zufall]" and subsequently of divine intervention: "a good spirit guided [Felix's] hand"; Nathalie offers the more dialectical comment that "he has been saved through his bad habit [Unart]" (Lehrjahre, 8.10). This revelation transforms into comedy two days of despair, since Felix, afraid of his father's anger, will not confess his poor table manners, and swears he drank from the glass; meanwhile he has been so frightened by the fear of the adults and so pumped full of medicine that for awhile he appears ill—and when, after a few hours, he appears well again, Wilhelm continues for some time to fear that his good health is merely appearance (Schein). Nathalie, meanwhile, swears privately to the Abbé that if Felix dies she will ask Wilhelm to marry her, an oath that Friedrich overhears and subsequently publicizes: "Now that the child lives, why should she change her mind? What one promises in that fashion, one holds to under any circumstance." And he embarrasses Wilhelm and Nathalie into confessing their love for each other by pointing to the painting of the sick prince, and mockingly asking for an unaesthetic, referential reading of it:

> "What was the king's name? . . . What's the name of the old goat-beard with the crown there, pining at the foot of the bed for his sick son? What's the name of the beauty who enters with both poison and antidote [Gift und Gegengift] in her demure eyes? What's the name of that bungler of a doctor who at this very moment is seeing the light, who for the first time in his life has the chance to order a rational prescription, a medicine that cures from the ground up [die aus dem Grunde kuriert], and is as tasty as it is wholesome?" (8.10)

Wilhelm, thus invited, moves from the position of the child to that of the father, whose illness, in this fantasy, is cured by the discovery that the sick child is not sick. Though the mother's promise of love had seemed to require the child's death, the promise holds without exacting its sacrifice: the child lives in the love that a father receives. These magic gestures of recovery and recompense culminate in Wilhelm's assumption of a unique happiness in the novel's closing words: "I don't know the wealth of a kingdom . . . but I know I have gained a fortune [Glück] that I haven't earned, and that I wouldn't exchange for anything in the world."

The novel itself thus "identifies" with the painting's content, as the text's closing tableau repeats and inverts the structure of Wilhelm's obsession, simultaneously replaying the pedagogical gesture of the Society of the Tower. Here Wilhelm is manipulated into post-oedipal love (for Nathalie) rather than oedipal fear (for Hamlet's father's ghost). In a final twist on the Abbé's attempt to "cure error through error," the text cures Wilhelm through his own neurotic fixation on the painting and its deadly oedipal content, a cure imaged in miniature in the text's construction of salvation for Felix through the child's own *Unart*. Given such intricacies of closure, it is hardly surprising that *Wilhelm Meisters Lehrjahre* should always have been regarded as a paradigmatically self-consious novel.[16] Nothing, indeed, could be more self-aware than the text's repetition of Wilhelm's act of identification; however, this is also to say that nothing could be more manifestly fictional than the closing tableau, the "fairy tale, or operetta-like character" of which, as Michael Beddow reminds us, is often remarked. The three promised marriages are all mésalliances between aristocrats (Nathalie, Lothario, Friedrich) and commoners (Wilhelm, Therese, Philine), and the novel refuses to offer the slightest indication that these liaisons cut across the grain of the social text[17]—which is fair enough, since the social text has been dissolved into a rush of stylized literary events: Mignon's death and burial, Augustin's multiple and finally successful attempts at suicide, Felix's false death, and what the novel ironically summarizes as "so many terrible and wonderful events coming one after another" as to put the community into a "feverish oscillation." The theatrics of the Society of the Tower are left behind by the text's own performance; and one could thus say that, in closing, the novel imitates not just Wilhelm (who imitates the painting), and not just the Society of the Tower (which imitates this imitation), but also the actor, who knows and controls the production of the self, but only does so in and as a fiction.

The *Lehrjahre*, in short, offers itself as a "literary absolute," and consequently as an ironic text in Lukács's sense. *Bildung*, the autoproduction of the self, is strictly speaking impossible, but this impossibility can be sublated into the self-knowledge of the *Roman* that is *Bildung*, the text that builds itself as a self-reflexive structure, a figure (*Bild*) of the fictionality of self-knowledge. This fictionality is figured as the symbolic sacrifice of aesthetics: as the text "identifies" with a poorly executed painting of its own invention, literature becomes literature in knowing and effecting its own

16. *Wilhelm Meister* in fact lent its "scènes de marionettes ou de fête au château" to André Gide's famous formulation of the *mise en abyme*: see *Journal 1889–1939* (Paris: Gallimard, 1948), 41. For a study of Gide's text that (briefly) engages *Wilhelm Meister*, see Lucien Dällenbach, *Le récit spéculaire: Essai sur la mise en abyme* (Paris: Seuil, 1977), 23–24.
17. "The utopian element here is not just that these marriages are proposed in the first place, but that they are envisaged without any issue being made of the socially outrageous character of the unions, even though the narrative has earlier drawn explicit attention to the 'vast gulf of birth and station' separating Wilhelm from the Countess, Nathalie's sister" (Beddow, *Fiction of Humanity*, 139). My reading will be indirectly questioning Beddow's assurance that the emphatic fictionality of the novel's ending "does not amount to a *radical* ironisation of Wilhelm's represented fulfilment" (139).

destruction.[18] The literary text's identification with kitsch is a renunciation that negates itself, transforming loss into the "fortune" invoked in the last words of the novel, the *Glück* that, Wilhelm insists, is beyond exchange and cannot be earned. The close of the text is an impossible, absolute gift, which emerges through a gesture of giving so absolute that the gift is precisely that of luck (*Glück*). Schillerian *Bildung* is negated and recuperated as the irony of luck: as the lucky chance that only fiction can reliably provide.[19]

But we have seen that readers of this novel have not always entirely shared its protagonist's happiness; and the grounds of Schiller's concern that the novel is written more "*for* the actor" than "*of* the actor" have become clearer. In itself, the "literary absolute," as the ironic knowledge of its own fictionality, is a demandingly ascetic form of aesthetic totalization; but the anxiety it inspires may be traced to the even less comforting status of the "fictional" in these scenes, which is always slipping away from its own knowledge. Fiction's power to posit is unlimited, but what is posited is fictional, bearing within it the insistent question of referential truth that reduces what is posited to "mere" fiction, and spurs the production of another fiction to compensate for the hollowness of the first. The falseness of the theater spurs Wilhelm's renunciation of it, but the result is an even more improbable theatricalization of his life and world; and though the self-conscious fictionality of the text thematizes and absorbs into itself the constant desire for an imperial referent ("What was the king's name?"), a residue of dissatisfaction will always potentially remain, "something isolated in the first and last reading," in Schlegel's words. The *Glück* of fiction at once exceeds the world of exchange and bears the trace of it—though

18. Goethe's writing about Wilhelm Meister and the theater, from the *Theatralische Sendung* (1777–85) to the *Wanderjahre* (1829), pursues a trajectory that ironically repeats Wilhelm's and his text's gestures of *Entsagung*—a reflexive turn typical of the *Bildungsroman* problematic, which at some point necessarily generates the referential question of the "author." If the hero of the *Theatralische Sendung* goes relatively unchastened in his ambition to build a national theater, and the Wilhelm of the *Lehrjahre* is brought to renounce that desire, the protagonist of the *Wanderjahre* will find that the theater has become the only artform to be banned in the Pedagogical Province—primarily because of its ability to attract crowds through "false and unsuitable emotions" (HA, 8:258). Lest we be tempted to confuse this apparent narrative of *Bildung*-through-*Entsagung* with these texts' (or Goethe's own) vastly complex relation to the theater, we are told that Wilhelm, after listening patiently to the pedagogues' lecture on the evils of drama, "was only half convinced and perhaps somewhat annoyed." Furthermore, "The editor of these pages might himself confess that he has allowed this strange passage [*wunderliche Stelle*] to slip by with some reluctance [*Unwillen*]; for has he not also in various ways expended more life and energy on the theatre than is proper? And is he now to be persuaded that this was an unforgivable error, a fruitless effort?" (ibid.). For further remarks on the *Wanderjahre*, see chapter 4.

19. For a fine reading of the figure of *Glück* and its relation to economic and libidinal exchange in this novel, see Hörisch, *Gott Geld und Glück*. The present analysis of fortune, luck, and fiction owes much to Jacques Derrida's remarkable analysis of these figures in *Donner le temps I: La fausse monnaie* (Paris: Galilée, 1991).

what one exchanges it for is always another fiction. *Entsagung* is thus not a true dialectical process, but rather an act haunted by being an "act," a fiction; and this fictionality cannot be renounced even by a fiction seeking to renounce fictionality via a renunciation of truth.

Consequently, as a figure of *Bildung*—of *Bildung* as the knowledge of the impossibility of *Bildung*—*Entsagung* becomes illegible. If the knowledge this figure conveys is that the self cannot posit itself, such knowledge can only emerge by annihilating itself: knowledge is knowingly renounced only through a posited homology between knowing and acting that is precisely what knowledge renounces. An ironic spiral results: the act of presupposition (of a homology between knowledge and act) contradicts the knowledge, which confirms the knowledge (of this contradiction), which contradicts it again, and so on. And this ironic spiral is not grounded in an inevitability of intention; rather, the homology between knowledge and act is precisely *fictional*, available only in and as a fiction. Fiction thus becomes (mis)understandable as an incoherent productive force lodged within intention, and within irony as an intentional structure. *Why* such a force should dominate the rhetoric and narrative of *Wilhelm Meisters Lehrjahre*, in the guise of *Bildung*, is not yet clear, and to advance further we shall need to look more closely at the text's analysis of the genesis of theatricality. But first we might briefly examine the novel's elaboration of the oedipal allegory that drew Schiller's attention, since the figure of fatherhood in the text provides a more lurid, and thus more manifestly unstable, version of the rhetorical difficulty we encounter in the trope of *Entsagung*.

III

The oedipal scenario, as psychoanalysis extracts it from literature, constitutes a dramatic version of the story of identification through the fiction of a renunciation: a story that Lacan captures memorably in his punning interweaving of the "Name" and the "No" of the Father.[20] The male subject becomes the father precisely by not becoming the father: by turning his desire elsewhere so as to desire what the father desires. Since the subject emerges under prohibition, desire is an endless process of substitution; and the psychological subject's successful negotiation of oedipal conflict occurs as the acceptance of loss, just as the ironic subject of aes-

20. Lacan's pun exploits the fact that "nom" (name) and "non" (no) are homophones in modern French: see in particular "The Function and Field of Speech and Language in Psychoanalysis," in *Ecrits: A Selection*, trans. Alan Sheridan (New York: Norton, 1977), 30–113. For a study of the *Bildungsroman* inspired by Hegel and Lacan, see John H. Smith, "Cultivating Gender: Sexual Difference, *Bildung*, and the *Bildungsroman*," *Michigan German Studies* 13.2 (1987): 206–25.

thetics accepts the endless deferral of aesthetic totalization. This analogy is prompted by the text itself: it is of course no accident that both the painting Wilhelm fetishizes and the play in which he acts feature oedipal narratives as the "content" with which he identifies. Borrowing Hamlet's fear of his ghostly father and the sick prince's deadly desire for his father's bride, Wilhelm engages himself in the errancy of family romance to the extent that, within the orbit of aesthetic judgment, he *fails* to perform one—thus, as we have seen, committing himself to the ironic recuperation of aesthetics through failure. The novel cooperates by negotiating a proper object-choice for him: in an often rambunctious parody of oedipal emplotment, Nathalie replaces the all-too-maternal Mariane, the "mother" of Wilhelm's child— Mariane who is implicitly paired with Wilhelm's own mother in the text's opening chapters, and is ultimately consigned in dream to Wilhelm's dead father ("[H]is father and Mariane seemed to be running away from him. . . . Impulse and desire impelled him to go to their assistance, but the Amazon's [Nathalie's] hand held him back—and how gladly he let himself be held!" [*Lehrjahre*, 7.1]). The accession to the Name of the Father ("Meister") involves the acceptance of a No that takes the form of a renunciation of the self and its desires: "Everything he planned was now to mature for the boy, and everything he built was to last for several generations. His apprenticeship was therefore completed in this sense, for along with the feeling of a father [*dem Gefühl des Vaters*] he had acquired the virtues of a solid citizen [*eines Bürgers*]" (8.1). Oedipal identification generates a social identity and a consciousness of historical temporality, and thus provides a model version of negative *Bildung*: though desire always points elsewhere, this lack can be transformed into an index of maturity.

The endlessness of desire, however, which is totalizable precisely *as* an endlessness, and hence as a loss or lack that can be mourned, derives from a less stable epistemological or rhetorical problematic: the transformation of doubt (whether Felix is really Wilhelm's son) into conviction (summarized, as we saw, in Friedrich's ironic *mot:* "I'm convinced, therefore I'm a father"). The uncertainty of fatherhood is certainly not simply subversive in its effects: it is a topos in Western culture that is regularly associated, as in Freud, with a passage from nature to culture, and from sense-certainty to cognition; if, in Stephen Dedalus's words in *Ulysses*, "paternity may be a legal fiction," this fiction, according to Stephen's parodic reading of *Hamlet*, underwrites theology itself.[21] Fatherhood is founded "upon incertitude,"

21. James Joyce, *Ulysses*, The Corrected Text (New York: Vintage Books, 1986), 170. The *Ulysses* episode in question ("Scylla and Charybdis") begins with an invocation of Goethe's novel ("And we have, have we not, those priceless pages of *Wilhelm Meister*. A great poet on a great brother poet" [151]). For an incisive analysis of the father as a metaphor for the supersensory, see Jonathan Culler, *The Pursuit of Signs: Semiotics, Literature, Deconstruction* (Ithaca: Cornell University Press, 1981), chapter 9.

but as a "mystical estate, an apostolic succession" (*Ulysses,* 170): thus, Stephen concludes, Shakespeare lives on in the ghost of Hamlet's father: "But, because loss is his gain, he passes on toward eternity in undiminished personality. . . . He is a ghost, a shadow now . . . a voice heard only in the heart of him who is the substance of his shadow, the son consubstantial with the father" (162). The tension in this narrative is between an initial "incertitude," on the one hand, and a dialectical passage from "loss" to "gain," on the other: uncertainty is not quite the same as loss, and though the dialectical narrative tells the story of the father's "undiminished" survival, the uncertain status of the father renders him "a ghost, a shadow," precisely because this uncertainty can never be entirely stabilized *as* a loss. Like *Ulysses, Wilhelm Meisters Lehrjahre* routes this tension through the figure of Hamlet's father's ghost. On the one hand, Wilhelm, terrified into his role as Hamlet by the mysterious Ghost, hears in its voice the power of an "undiminished personality": "The voice seemed familiar to everyone, and Wilhelm thought it sounded like that of his own father" (*Lehrjahre,* 5.11). On the other hand, when the Ghost reappears during Wilhelm's initiation into the Society of the Tower, Wilhelm is far less certain he has heard correctly: "[H]e thought he heard his father's voice, and yet not; so confused was he by present reality and past memories" (7.9). Doubt necessarily recurs within oedipal narrative, since this narrative is founded not on a referent but on uncertainty.

For this reason, fathers, for all their omnipresence in *Wilhelm Meister,* seem to have no more than a wraith-like grip on the world: Jarno is of uncertain parentage, and his name is strange (3.4); no one knows where the Abbé comes from (6); Lothario's name is a pseudonym (4.16); Nathalie's family is not in the genealogical books (4.11); and so on. If the Father is indeed a Hegelian "Geist der stets verneint," like Mephistopheles in *Faust* he manages to get very little accomplished. Even the identity of the actor playing the ghost of Hamlet's father is in doubt, since the Abbé turns out to have a mysterious twin brother who might or might not have taken the role. And because the father cannot guarantee his own promise to exist, the figure of the ghost drifts away from that of the father, becoming associated more generally with uncertainty itself. Thus, glimpsing the "shadow" of Norberg, the rival who helps bring uncertainty to the paternity of Felix, Wilhelm feels the "uneasiness" of a ghost-effect: "And like a ghost at midnight that scares the wits out of us, and when we regain our composure seems the product of our anxiety and leaves us with doubts whether in fact we ever saw it, a great uneasiness came over Wilhelm" (1.17). Unsure what woman visited him in the night after the production of *Hamlet,* Wilhelm is relieved at the end of the novel to be told that Philine, and not Mignon, had been the "lovely palpable ghost [*fühlbare Gespenst*]" in his bed (8.6). Similar ghostings proliferate, infecting the production of subjectivity at all levels in this novel.[22]

The duplicity of a ghost-effect that at once enables the Father to survive death and makes it impossible for him to come into existence is represented in *Wilhelm Meister* through counterpointed figures of portrait and mirror. The portrait, at least at first glance, represents a stable figurative structure, grounded in a particular referent that it sublimates into a meaning. When Wilhelm obtains his *Lehrbrief* and reads the *Turmgesellschaft*'s account of his life, "he saw a picture of himself, not like a second self in a mirror, but a different self, one outside of him, as in a portrait [*Porträt*]. One never approves of everything in a portrait, but one is always glad that a thoughtful mind has seen us thus and a superior talent enjoyed portraying us in such a way that a picture survives of what we were, and will survive longer than we will" (8.1). The subject of *Bildung*, brought to self-consciousness in the gaze of the Other, shoulders its oedipal discomforts ("one never approves of everything") for the sake of an identity that, portrait-like, would sublimate its referent into the historical temporality of a meaning. This, however, is what the text refuses to guarantee; and the "mirror," which Wilhelm distinguishes from the "portrait" in characterizing the narrative of his apprenticeship scroll, registers the volatile nature of all figural relations: the self can duplicate into the "second self" of the mirror because the first self is always possibly a figure masquerading as a referent.[23] In one of the novel's charged moments, Wilhelm, disguised as the count, sees "in the mirror" the real count entering his wife's bedroom: "He saw me in the mirror, as I did him, and before I knew whether it was a ghost or he himself, he went out again" (3.10). The shock of seeing himself redoubled drives the count to forsake the world for a Moravian community; and "you," Jarno tells Wilhelm later, "are the ghost who drove him into the arms of religion" (7.3).

22. The ontological uncertainty of identity repeats itself, within the terms of oedipal narrative, as a teasing ambiguity of gender identity: varying registers of *Mannweiblichkeit* inform nearly every female character in the novel. Schiller's emphatic insistence on Aurelie's gender ambiguity responds, perhaps, to the dagger she carries and the violent use to which she puts it when she cuts Wilhelm's hand, as well as to the ambiguous nature of theatrical affect, as discussed earlier. But the allocation of male attributes to female characters in the novel is remarkably pervasive. Wilhelm's education at the hands of "phallic women" begins with Mariane, who on the first page of the novel is dressed as a soldier; then, after the knife-wielding Aurelie, there is Therese, who becomes the perfect bourgeois housewife only by being mannishly independent; finally there is Nathalie, the "Amazon," who when we first meet her is dressed in a man's overcoat. Even the *schöne Seele* begins her career as a tomboy: she is called at one point an "errant son," and later, in becoming a Beautiful Soul against the wishes of her frivolous fiancé, demonstrates a "manly defiance." I discuss the special case of Mignon below.

23. This is one way to understand the frequent redoubling of characters in *Wilhelm Meister*. The Abbé's mysterious twin brother is only one instance of a more general narrative principle, according to which characters no sooner emerge than they divide and multiply: the countess generates a twin sister in Nathalie, Mignon is paired with Felix, and so on.

But to be or to see a ghost is precisely not to know whether or not one is or has seen a ghost. Even the "great uneasiness" one feels at such moments is "like a ghost" that "at midnight scares the wits out of us, and when we regain our composure seems the product of our anxiety and leaves us with doubts whether in fact we ever saw it" (1.17): the pathos of a haunting, as Schiller sensed, is itself spectral, infected with uncertain theatricality. It is significant that Wilhelm feels drawn to Hamlet's famous meditation on the fictional pathos of the actor ("What's Hecuba to him, or he to Hecuba / That he should weep for her?" [5.6]). The dignified suffering of the oedipal subject, the pathos of *Entsagung*, the labor and patience of the negative, emerge only at the risk of being exposed as fraudulent, just as the transcendental spiral of *Bildung* can occur only at the risk of being exposed as a trick, a *Kunstgriff*. And yet the production of *Bildung*, particularly in its oedipal form, relies upon affect: Wilhelm acquires "the feeling of a father [*Gefühl des Vaters*]" in passing out of apprenticeship. The father, as Schiller's commentary implicitly noted, is a rhetorical effect. And the structure of this rhetorical effect is double: on the one hand, it is uncertain, since it can always fail to convince; on the other hand, it can only exist as the obliteration of this uncertainty: unless one is convinced, one is not a father. Fatherhood exists as the repression of its own rhetoricity. Thus fatherhood repeats, more violently, the predicament of *Entsagung*: while the ironic subject of *Bildung* renounces self-knowledge but can only do so knowingly, the subject of paternity comes into being as a "knowledge" that, like Oedipus, blinds itself to itself. While the ironic spiral of knowledge culminates in the text's theatrical assumption of sheer fictionality, the paternal hoax recurs as the constant vacillation of an assertion that cannot know its own impossibility.

Implicitly linking Hamlet's ghost with the picture of the sick prince, Wilhelm insists that in the production of *Hamlet* there be a "life-size" portrait of Hamlet's father drawn and positioned "so that he looks exactly like the Ghost when it goes out the door. That will be very effective when Hamlet is looking at the Ghost and the queen at the portrait" (5.9). And, after the mysterious Ghost shows up at the opening performance, it is remarked that "he had looked exactly like the portrait, as if he had sat for it himself" (5.12). The portrait precedes its referent, which of course, as a "father," is not a referent but a ghost. Here, in other words, the portrait is revealed to be a trope, a metalepsis dependent for its referent on fiction's power to provide one, just as the father is only persuasive thanks to *Hamlet*'s, or the *Lehrjahre*'s, rhetorical force. And if we ask after the text's representation of the genesis of this problematic, we need to account for the remaining term in this oedipal scenario: the mother who gazes at the portrait, who is marginalized, half forgotten, and, in the person of Mariane, killed off, but who is also never entirely expelled from the narrative of *Bildung*.

IV

The figure of the mother presides over the opening of the novel, though not precisely over the origins of theatricality: Wilhelm cannot decide whether his love for Mariane caused him to love the theater, or vice-versa (4.19), and the reader similarly cannot decide whether Wilhelm loves Mariane or her masculine stage-costume, the "red uniform" and "white vest" that he embraces so eagerly (1.1). Via the language of erotic fetishism, the novel suggests that one can never be certain that desire has not already mimicked itself. And though we discover that a set of marionettes originally gave the child Wilhelm a "taste for the theater," this taste is uncertainly figurative: since the puppets are kept locked up in the maternal (and, of course, forbidden) space of the kitchen pantry, they literally acquire tastes and smells associated with maternal care (1.2).[24] On the one hand, the mother is paired with theatricality as the literal to the figurative; on the other hand, the difference between these two is precisely what cannot be established. This uncertainty means that the very relation between mother and theater, or literal and figurative meaning, is irreducibly theatrical or figurative, since no stabilizing ground of meaning presents itself. The drama of uncertainty confronting us here differs slightly, however, from that staged by the tropes of fatherhood or *Entsagung*. In keeping both with bourgeois gender roles and a metaphysical hierarchy that *Wilhelm Meister* at least pretends to respect, the mother represents a prelinguistic site of natural origin; and thus in her proximity the text allegorizes the impossible and contradictory referential drive of fiction as the condition of all language. Both fatherhood and renunciation represent the possibility that the referent can be recuperated through negation—that by turning from the father's desire one can become the father; that by giving up self-knowledge one can recover it; that by annihilating the referent in pure fictionality one can obtain the plenitude of *Glück*. The mother, however, represents not just

---

24. The young Wilhelm sneaks into the pantry and discovers the puppets there, and his mother ultimately rewards this mildly erotic transgression by giving the child the puppets, just as she gives the adult Wilhelm the key to the room where they have been stored (1.2, 1.5). The sexual dimension of the episode, obvious enough in the *Lehrjahre*, is made explicit in an equivalent scene in Goethe's first version of the novel, *Wilhelm Meisters theatralische Sendung*, where the young Wilhelm's lifting the curtain of the puppet theater is explicitly compared to falling into sexual knowledge: "Thus at certain times do children become conscious of the difference between the sexes, and their glances through the covers hiding these secrets bring forth wonderful movements in their nature." *Sämtliche Werke* (Zürich: Artemis Verlag, 1979), 8:532. In this early version of the story the puppets are in fact made by a maternal figure: the mother of Wilhelm's father, who uncovers them for *her* son's gaze on the first page or so of the novel, and in the following chapter organizes the puppet-play for Wilhelm, thus determining the course of her grandson's desire and inciting the anger of Wilhelm's mother, who sees in the grand-mother's act "a reproach to her unmotherliness [*Unmütterlichkeit*]." Wilhelm's thespian desire is thus, in this version, both maternal in origin and productive of "an alienation from his mother," who forbids him to play with the puppets.

a referent to be negated in oedipal narrative, but the site of referentiality itself; and the marks of maternal care—the tastes and smells of the pantry—figure the pressure of referentiality precisely as the *undecidability* of the sign.[25] Nourishment, belonging to what Lacan would term the realm of "need," is not language; yet as Cathy Caruth comments apropos of the "Blessed Babe" passage in Wordsworth's *Prelude*, "in order to nurse *his mother's* breast the babe first has to read it": gestures of care become maternal only when they are taken as signs.[26] There is thus no such thing as the "mother" outside of a signifying system, yet the mother marks the impossibility of closing this system. Language could be said to "prop" itself on nonlinguistic gestures, rather as Freud, in a famous passage, speaks of sexuality "attach[ing] itself to functions serving the purpose of self-preservation"—except that what is undecidable is precisely whether marks are nonlinguistic or not.[27] The mother, and the marionettes, figure a nonempirical *materiality* of the sign: the sign's dependence, or "propping," upon an illegibility rather than a presence.[28]

The sign is thus always already theatrical because it can only pretend to be unequivocally a sign. Its possibility entails a radical contingency which must be suppressed if the sign is to be taken *as* a sign, but which leaves its mark in the sign's excessive and insatiable need to refer. The puppets register the material condition of this predicament, which is that of signification as the *inscription*, the violent imposition, of the possibility of reading. As Wilhelm takes up the puppets, "he was transported [*versetzt*] back to the time when he thought they were alive [*wo sie ihm noch belebt schienen*], when

25. Of interest in this context would be the unstable place of smell and taste in Kantian aesthetics: see Jacques Derrida, "Economimesis," *Diacritics* 11.2 (1981): 3–25.
26. Cathy Caruth, "Past Recognition: Narrative Origins in Wordsworth and Freud," in her *Empirical Truths and Critical Fictions: Locke, Wordsworth, Kant, Freud* (Baltimore: Johns Hopkins University Press, 1991), 56.
27. Sigmund Freud, *Three Essays on Sexuality*, trans. James Strachey, *The Standard Edition of the Complete Psychological Works of Sigmund Freud* (London: Hogarth Press, 1953), 7:182. The translation of Freud's term *Anlehnung* as "propping" (in place of Strachey's "anaclisis") was originally suggested by Jeffrey Mehlman as a translation of Jean Laplanche's translation of Freud's term as "étayage": see Jean Laplanche, *Life and Death in Psychoanalysis*, trans. Jeffrey Mehlman (Baltimore: Johns Hopkins University Press, 1976). Caruth examines the rhetorical consequences of this moment in Freud's account of the origin of sexuality; see "Past Recognition," esp. 44–57. In this context it is worth noting that *anlehnen*, like the words Freud once represented as "primal," has two opposing meanings: "to lean against" but also "to leave ajar."
28. Cynthia Chase has brilliantly articulated Julia Kristeva's notion of the "abjection" of the mother with the allegory of meaning-production that a rhetorical reading uncovers: the uncertainty afflicting the sign aligns with the uncertain border between mother and infant, which is the uncertainty that the infant must expel as an "abject" in order to enter the linguistic world of subjects and objects. See in particular "The Witty Butcher's Wife: Freud, Lacan, and the Conversion of Resistance to Theory," *MLN* 102.5 (1987): 989–1013. The scenario Chase describes would clearly hold interest for the reader of *Wilhelm Meister*, given the narrative's reiterated expulsion of maternal figures (Mariane, Wilhelm's mother, Sperata, etc.; as suggested later in this chapter, Mignon is also in this sense a distorted figure of the "mother").

he thought he could bring them alive [*zu beleben glaubte*] by the liveliness [*Lebhaftigkeit*] of his voice and the movements of his hands" (1.2). The puppets, which as material objects are properly speaking neither dead nor alive, represent the "prop" necessary for the imposition of figure as *Schein* or *Bild:* in this sense they are not phenomenal or empirical objects, but rather indicative of an unguaranteed possibility of articulation. Like Mignon's corpse at the end of the novel they acquire a "Schein des Lebens" by virtue of a rhetorical event that Paul de Man's late work thematizes as catachretic prosopopoeia, the disruptive incoherence of which appears in the sentence above as the compressed conjunction of a false constative presupposition (*belebt schienen*) and a fictitious performative act (*zu beleben glaubte*).[29] Henceforth desire can vacillate between the binary oppositions of figurative and literal, life and death, appearance and reality, and so on: once the "appearance of life" has been posited, death can become negation.[30] This dialectic erects itself upon the *taking* of signs as such, figured here as the taking of *bodies*: the body is here the trope of the legible sign, and the marionettes register this body's material support, and hence its ongoing dismemberment. And as critics from Schiller onward have well understood, this predicament leaves its mark in the narrative through the figure of Mignon.

Mignon should indeed, as Eric Blackall claims, be understood as "the spirit of poetry" and the "guiding force of the book," though the consequences of such an insight are not necessarily positive.[31] Mignon, like

29. On catachresis and prosopopoeia, see in particular Paul de Man's essay "Hypogram and Inscription," in *The Resistance to Theory* (Minneapolis: University of Minnesota Press, 1986), 27–53. For a reading of Heinrich von Kleist's reading of *Wilhelm Meister*, "On the Marionettentheater" (1810), see de Man, "Aesthetic Formalization in Kleist," in *The Rhetoric of Romanticism* (New York: Columbia University Press, 1981), 263–90. Since this random element in signification is what lies concealed in the post-Kantian commonplace of the non-referentiality of aesthetic form, it is appropriate that the marionettes be complemented by an image of a scattered art collection: Wilhelm's grandfather's, which is broken up and sold around the same time that the puppets make their Christmas appearance in the Meister household.

30. Wilhelm, in other words, will be able to narrate a mini-*Bildungsroman:* the story of his internalization of the puppet theater's text, of how he reproduced its pathos (*pathetische Rede*) through his good memory (*gutes Gedächtnis*) (1.2). Mariane, appropriately, falls asleep during Wilhelm's story (1.8), for it bores (through) us, as the narrative of the disarticulation of narrative. Thus accounting, perhaps, for the addictive tonal blend of sentiment and lighthearted indifference that Goethe achieves in *Wilhelm Meister*—the blend that Schiller, acutely enough, found so disturbing. Pathos has an odd, theatrical status in a novel that, for instance, insists on Mariane's determinative emotional, erotic, and symbolic importance for Wilhelm's development, while granting her very little narrative or descriptive attention before ejecting her from the plot line at the end of book 1.

31. See Blackall's "Afterword" to his edition of *Wilhelm Meister*, 386. Blackall is invoking a topos in Goethe criticism that, as we have seen, informs the remarks of the novel's first critic, Schiller, and receives corroboration by countless nineteenth-century readers, from Friedrich Schlegel and Carlyle to Hegel, for whom Mignon's character is "wholly poetic [*schlechthin poetisch*]."

Wilhelm's grandfather's art collection (and its symbolic complement, the marionettes), comes from Italy, the land of art. Like her father the Harper, she provides the text with a mouthpiece for its famously haunting lyrics; as a corpse, she becomes herself a work of art at the end of the novel, lending her body to the "schöne Kunst" of the embalmer (8.5). As befits the "spirit" of poetry, she is deeply associated with the Father's Ghost, and implicated in every turn of Wilhelm's *Bildung*. Hers is the dead father of Hamlet and Wilhelm ("The big devil is dead" [2.4]); the Ghost, she has reason to add, is her "uncle" ("No one understood what she meant, except those who knew that she had called the man she thought was her father 'the big devil'" [5.12]). Knowing the secrets of the father, she knows that Felix, the child of light, whose oedipal determinants are so coercive that a father-figure actually threatens him with a knife (5.13), is Wilhelm's true son: "The ghost told it to me" (7.8). But this is also to say that Mignon is the "riddle" of the text: "Here is the riddle [*Rätsel*]," Philine says, introducing Mignon (2.4); and the legibility of this poetic riddle is never entirely certain. Though Wilhelm is finally told that Philine was the ghost, the *Gespenst*, who came to him in the night after his debut in *Hamlet*, the novel is curiously, even stagily, coy in its refusal to provide evidence: "His first guess was that it had been Philine, and yet the charming body he had clasped in his arms did not seem like hers" (5.13). Wilhelm is subsequently "frightened" by a new maturity he sees in Mignon—"she seemed to have grown taller during the night"—and though he persuades himself that his nocturnal visitor must have been Philine after all, the narrator adds, in an atypically theatrical aside, that "we too must share this opinion, because we are not able to reveal the reasons which had made him doubt this and had aroused other suspicions" (5.13). The rationale of this aside—the reason of these "reasons"—is never revealed; the *Rätsel* remains riddled. Mignon embodies a remainder of uncertainty within the transcendence of sense perception that is fatherhood. In relation to the gender difference that oedipal narratives seek to police, this means that Mignon, a product of the "Gespenst" of incest (8.9) must appear a "hermaphrodite creature" (3.11), the focal point for the text's interest in androgyny.

Thus, what must be expelled from the aesthetic plot, and reintegrated, however problematically, as a "corpse," is Mignon's body. A member of an acrobat's entourage when Wilhelm adopts her, Mignon is associated with bodily deformation as well as with poetic language. When she writes, her body interferes: "[T]he letters were uneven and the lines not straight. In this too her body seemed to contradict her mind [*dem Geiste zu widersprechen*]"

Hegel, *Aesthetics: Lectures on Fine Art*, trans. T. M. Knox (Oxford: Clarendon Press, 1975), 2:857.

(2.12). And if we examine the figurative resonance of this contradiction, we find that Mignon's crampings of the heart and epileptic seizures return us repeatedly to the puppet theater. Mignon prepares the ground of Wilhelm's *Vaterherz* in a series of curious scenes: accepting him as a surrogate parent, she performs an egg-dance for him like a mechanism (*Räderwerk*) or a clock (*wie ein Uhrwerk*), and Wilhelm, transported by this *Schauspiel*, desires to resuscitate her "with the love of a father" (2.8). A little later, Mignon has a seizure: her body convulses and she falls "as if every limb of her body were broken":

> It was a terrifying sight! "My child," he said, lifting her up and embracing her, "what is it?"—The convulsions persisted, spreading from the heart to the dangling limbs [*schlotternden Gliedern*]; she was just hanging in his arms. (2.14)

Then "all her limbs became alive again"; she clasps his neck "like a lock that springs shut," and when Wilhelm repeats "My child!" she responds "My father! . . . You will be my father!"

The dangling limbs and convulsive, mechanical motions recur later in a scene in which the puppets figure overtly. Wilhelm and his troupe are celebrating a successful premiere of *Hamlet*, and Mignon and Felix, sitting in a chair reserved for the mysterious Ghost, mimic the marionettes:

> The children, who, sitting in the big armchair, stuck out over the table like puppets out of their box, started to put on a little play [*Stück*] of this sort. Mignon imitated the rasping noise very nicely, and they finally banged their heads together and on the edge of the table, in such a manner as actually only wooden puppets can withstand. Mignon was almost frenetically excited . . . . she now began to rush around the table, tambourine in hand, hair flying, head thrown back and her limbs flung in the air like one of those maenads whose wild and well-nigh impossible postures still astonish us on ancient monuments. (5.12)

The final simile compresses and repeats, with a *frisson* of orphic dismemberment, the aesthetic trajectory that later in the novel Mignon will follow. And a deforming, disfiguring force will haunt that trajectory, wracking Mignon's body to the moment of death—when once again her "schlotternde Körper" will hang like a puppet's (8.5). Felix as well as Mignon must play out this *Stück*, sitting in the place of the father, for Felix's condition of possibility depends no less than Mignon's on an act of identification with a puppet—an impossible act that the text registers in one of its most astonishing turns of phrase ("banged their heads together . . . in such a manner as actually only wooden puppets can withstand").[32] The children are not puppets, but they do that which only puppets can do. It is impossible to identify with puppets, but this impossibility "occurs." The story of the child Wilhelm's projection of life onto the marionettes could be told with less manifest strain, since that act of *Belebung* could at least appear to originate in the plenitude of the child's living identity. But Mignon and Felix's grotesquely inverted repetition of Wilhelm's act underscores the violent, figurative origins of all identities and of all identifications. The children are actors, who intend the identity they posit, and in doing so they reveal the rhetorical precondition of all acting, and all aesthetics, which resides in a prosopopoeia irreducible to intentionality: the children, the actor, and the aesthetic text "are" puppets in the sense that they have, impossibly, been made possible by them; and the disruptive materiality of signification that the puppets record is one name for the deadly force inhabiting the body of the "spirit of poetry."[33] The expulsion of this foreign body takes, of course, the form of aestheticization as entombment: once dead, this body will be able to enter the meaningful universe of death and life *as* a body. Mignon thus becomes a beautiful object, a *Schein des Lebens*, through the *schöne Kunst* of the embalmer, as with great ceremony she is encrypted in an antique sarcophagus long devoid of its original inhabitant—a coffin become a commodified artwork, purchased in Italy, the land of art, by Nathalie's uncle. An artwork entombed in art, Mignon is a treasure (*Schatz*) and a portrait, a "beautiful picture of the past [*schöne Gebild der Ver-*

---

32. Eric Blackall's translation of this sentence is curiously elliptical: "[T]he children started a little game of their own, with Mignon making a rasping noise as puppets do. They banged their heads together as if these were made of wood. Mignon was almost frenetically excited. . . ." The translation of *Stück* ("play" in the sense of theater-piece) as "game," and the elision of Goethe's uncompromising equation of the act of the children with the being of puppets ("Mignon machte den schnarrenden Ton sehr artig nach, und sie stießen zuletzt die Köpfe dergestalt zusammen und auf die Tischkante, wie es eigentlich nur Holzpuppen aushalten können") relieves the scene of much of its figurative density. It is tempting to speculate that, once again, the reception of this "spirit of poetry" has exacted a sacrifice. The passage is accurately represented in Carlyle's translation: see *Wilhelm Meister's Apprenticeship* (London: Anthological Society, 1901), 292.

33. The figurative language attached to Mignon recurs in *Die Wahlverwandtschaften*, where Ottilie and her servant Nanni in some ways divide up Mignon's overdetermined role: Ottilie becomes an exquisite corpse, and Nanni, feeling the corpse beckon to her, falls out of a window and lands next to it: "[S]he seemed to be shattered in every limb [*es schien an allen Gliedern zerschmettert*]." Then "either by chance or providential dispensation" her "dangling limbs [*schlotternden Gliedern*]" touch the corpse and she is resuscitated (HA, 6:486). The place of these puppet metaphors in the rhetorical structure of *Die Wahlverwandtschaften* would require interpretation; for a reading that complements my reading of the *Lehrjahre* see J. Hillis Miller, "A 'Buchstäbliches' Reading of *The Elective Affinities*," *Glyph* 6 (1979): 1–23.

gangenheit]," and is ready to resurface in domesticated form as the senti-mental figure of melancholy, *Sehnsucht*, and *Heimweh* that literary history was to make of her.[34]

Death, however, does not lay the ghost to rest. Even before the funeral service has ended (the choir is still busy singing "Unconsumed, in marble it rests; in your hearts it lives and works"), the audience has stopped listen-ing: "no one heard the fortifying message," for everyone has been distracted by the appearance of a story about Mignon's origins. Once again Mignon must be encrypted; but this time, having exhausted other re-sources, the text can only tell the story of a false burial and a fictional body.[35] The story goes that Mignon, after disappearing from her Italian home, was presumed to have drowned in the local lake; her mother, Sper-ata, under the influence of a miraculous story, begins to comb the shore for her child's bones, believing that if she could only gather up the entire skeleton and take it to Rome, "the child would appear before the people, in its fresh white skin, on the steps of the high altar of St. Peter's" (8.9). Daily she gathers up animal bones, a deluded reader patiently and madly pursu-ing reading as the gathering (*legein*) of a body,[36] until public sympathy, in the hope of curing error through error, suggests that "the bones of a child's skeleton should gradually be intermingled with those she already had, to increase her hopes." Sperata experiences great joy as, thanks to yet another dead child, "the parts gradually fitted together." Only a few extremities remain missing when she has a vision of her child, embodied and thus transcendent: "It rose up, threw off the veil, its radiance filling the room, its

34. Mignon thus appears in the *Wanderjahre* fully aestheticized as a subject for sentimental exercises in painting by a young artist taken with her story (book 2, chap. 7; HA, 8: 226–41). See Tunner for a discussion of some of the many literary imitations and invocations of Mignon from Goethe's time to the mid-twentieth century.

35. Catriona MacLeod's article, "Pedagogy and Androgyny in *Wilhelm Meisters Lehrjahre*," *MLN* 108 (1993): 389–426, was published after a version of this chapter had gone to press as an article, so let me simply signal here my sense of the congruence between our readings. Though MacLeod understands the figure of androgyny in this text more positively than I do, her interpretation of Mignon's role in the novel is not dissimilar from mine: the arguments being advanced here may be taken as elaborations of MacLeod's claim that "the *Bildungsroman*, whose goal is the education of desire, declares itself as the agent of Mignon's death" (409), and that Mignon is "appropriated aesthetically by the *Turmgesellschaft*—after her elaborately the-atrical funeral, she is turned into narrative. The content of the Abbé's narrative is itself reveal-ing, in that it casts the child's story as an incest plot, the only form in which the androgynous Mignon can be rendered intelligible by these purveyors of bourgeois socialization" (411).

36. One thinks here of a well-known passage by Heidegger: "*legein*, being a laying, is also *legere*, that is, reading. We normally understand by reading only this, that we grasp and follow a script and written matter. But that is done by gathering the letters. Without this gathering, without a gleaning in the sense in which wheat or grapes are gleaned, we should never be able to read a single word, however keenly we observe the written signs." *What Is Called Thinking?* trans. J. Glenn Gray (New York: Harper and Row, 1968), 208.

beauty transfigured, its feet unable to touch the ground, even had they wished to. . . . I will follow my child." Sperata dies, and like Mignon, or Ottilie in the *The Elective Affinities*, her body miraculously resists corruption, and she becomes a religious icon: "There were several cures, which no attentive observer could explain or dismiss as false."

Sperata, the exotic, hoodwinked, and sentimentalized peasant mother, has been brought on stage by a fictional power that fiction is powerless to control. She is Schlegel's reader-as-supplement, a reader generated by the slippage of the text that is the production of the text: she is thus at once the figure of a reading, and the figure of the violence with which a text, or a reading, comes into existence—a blind force that is constantly, but always anxiously, misread as the exquisite corpse of a meaning. And if meaning here attains figuration as the body, meaning's materiality is that of scattered bones: minimal units of articulation that, like letters assembled into words, serve as the fragments of a fictional skeleton. This predicament is exemplary precisely to the degree that it is staged and suspect, and in a certain fundamental sense impossible—the impossible generation of identity or meaning out of a tangled pile of articulations, the fragments of marionettes or skeletons. If the *Bildungsroman* rises like a ghost from these scattered bones, this is because of, rather than despite, the impossibility of *Bildung*'s story: a story that can have no origin and no conclusion, since the aestheticization of texts, authors, and bodies must always be done over again to cover up the undoing that composes their possibility.

Thus the story of the puppets becomes the story of Mignon, which in turn becomes the story of a mad, mourning mother, whose incestuous production of her child is reiterated in her deluded labor to re-member or re-produce it. It is through the rigor of this figurative sequence that *Wilhelm Meister*, in deconstructing the Schillerian aesthetic, discredits the gender drama that we found sketched in Schiller's correspondence. The mother is neither a natural site of meaning nor a deviation from such a site, but is rather the mark of a linguistic predicament, the trace of a randomness within language that can neither be comprehended nor entirely effaced. This readable disjunction within signifying processes is the general condition for all tropes and figures, and can be termed irony. Irony, the "permanent parabasis" of language, disarticulates the aesthetic and naturalizing illusion that composes all ideologies, thus opening them to critique by accounting for their occurrence. *Wilhelm Meisters Lehrjahre*, in other words, in demystifying the Society of the Tower's "portentous words and signs" (8.5), registers the force, as well as the absurdity, of its corporate, multinational cultural ambition. For, as Jarno says, "since property is no longer safe anywhere," from our ancient Tower a Society [*Sozietät*] shall go forth, which will extend into every corner of the globe, and people from all over the world will be allowed to join it. (8.7)[37]

37. Since a version of this chapter had appeared as an article before I encountered Friedrich Kittler's remarkable essay, "Über die Sozialisation Wilhelm Meisters" (in Gerhard Kaiser and Friedrich A. Kittler, *Dichtung als Sozialisationsspiel: Studien zu Goethe und Gottfried Keller* [Göttingen: Vandenhoek und Ruprecht, 1978], 13–124), I shall simply try to suggest one or two ways in which Kittler's and my readings both complement and strain against each other. Kittler interprets the *Lehrjahre* as, among other things, the record of a historical shift from premodern pedagogical and social institutions to modern institutions of *Bildung* capable of producing an individualized, disciplined, sexualized, and psychologized subject. In contrast to such figures as Mariane or Mignon or Serlo ("fossils in the discourse of *Bildung*" [64]), Wilhelm treasures memories of his childhood, and this precisely because he has been socialized to *have* a childhood: a childhood complete with an oedipally triangulated theater of desire (i.e., the puppet theater) capable of launching him on a coherent narrative arc. Kittler usefully presents the nuclear family and the loving, eroticized mother as historical constructs, and argues strongly for their inseparability from the discourse of *Bildung*. He is more willing than I am to take the resultant "continuous life story" of the bourgeois subject at face value; in consequence he tends to equate *Bildung* with the institution of "literature" *tout court*, while I have argued that literature—as represented by the *Bildungsroman*—cannot be contained by the discourse of *Bildung* it stages. In both of our arguments, however, the discourses of literature and *Bildung* are mutually inextricable. Literature is an archivizing, personifying, and in Kittler's sense "socializing" discourse. In a fine interpretive move, Kittler reads the Society of the Tower as the *literary* institution per se: the Society embodies an aesthetic, disciplinary pedagogy, which operates by indirection, surveillance, and archival storage and retrieval (for the Society is above all an infinitely ambitious archive for the storage of paintings, bodies, and texts); and the textual system it sets in motion is "literary" in its valorization of individual experience, and in its production of the individual both as reader and as what Foucault calls the "author function." The Society of the Tower, in short, "is a literary bureaucracy and thus is the very institution of the *Bildungsroman*" (Kittler, Über die Sozialisation," 107). My own writing on literature, aesthetics, and the *Bildungsroman* has sought to link such an insight to the rhetorical instability that is legibly at work in the production of literature as an aesthetic institution. For further comments on bureaucracy and aesthetics, see chapter 7.

4

The Dissection of the State:
Wilhelm Meisters Wanderjahre
and the Politics of Aesthetics

Gestell is also the name for a skeleton.
—Martin Heidegger, *The Question concerning Technology*

One frequently encounters the claim that aesthetics is an essentially, and disingenuously, political discourse. The project of cultural critique, versions of which figure so visibly in the landscape of contemporary criticism, might be summed up as the attempt to demonstrate that aesthetics not only fails to transcend the purposeful machinations of power but also reinforces these machinations through its very pretense to transcend them. This demystification of aesthetics has enjoyed considerable success at least in part because aesthetics, as we have seen, is so clearly a historical phenomenon that can be incorporated into political narrative. The vehemence with which conservative journalists and critics parody and decry the "politicization" of aesthetics pays tribute to the force of the demystifying narrative: as soon as one considers with any care the historical emergence of the aesthetic sphere during the eighteenth century, it rapidly becomes obvious—particularly in the German contexts in which aesthetics was first and most elaborately theorized—that the idea, the funding, and the upkeep of a "cultural sphere" serves recognizable, and quite pressing, political and class interests. The disinterestedness of aesthetics thus provides as it were a detour or disguise for various and not necessarily complementary projects: the consolation and bureaucratization of a middle class within an absolutist state; the construction of an ideological base for an eventual middle-class hegemony; the diversion of revolutionary energies; and so on.[1]

1. For a sociological account of the emergence of aesthetics in eighteenth-century Germany, see Martha Woodmansee, *The Author, Art, and the Market: Rereading the History of Aesthetics* (New York: Columbia University Press, 1994). For an incisive definition of the project of cultural critique see Abdul JanMohammed and David Lloyd, "Toward a Theory of Minority Discourse:

95

Any attempt to recover a political mission for aesthetics, however, risks tendentiousness if it fails to recall and examine not just the unwitting external instrumentality of aesthetics but also its inherent and frequently overt political ambition. Schiller's assertion that one can approach the "problem of politics" only through the "problem of the aesthetic" ("because it is only through Beauty that man makes his way to Freedom") makes for a particularly dramatic moment in the early history of aesthetic thought, but it is hardly an eccentric claim.[2] As we have seen in the preceding chapters, Schiller's translation of Kantian themes into the narrative of an "aesthetic education of man" in a sense does no more than unleash the totalizing power implicit in the *Critique of Judgment*'s location of aesthetics in the process of formalization. Since, in Kant, the particular aesthetic experience, in its formality, claims subjective universality, aesthetic judgment easily comes to prefigure the universality of Schiller's "pure ideal Man" (*Aesthetic Education*, 4.2), whose full realization would take place as the emergence of the Aesthetic State, the "Staat des schönen Scheins" (27.12). The acculturation or *Bildung* of an individual by definition models a political process, however overtly apolitical or "inward" *Bildung*'s orientation, and despite the nonreferentiality of the aesthetic moment per se, since if this moment demonstrates the essential harmony and prescriptive universality of "man," aesthetic formalization is non-referential only so as to guarantee "man" as a transcendental referent. And since aesthetics presupposes sensory realization, aesthetics incipiently involves the political production of "man" in the world, whether as the education of an individual or the evolution of a community, nation, or race. Despite Heidegger's hostility to aesthetics, his elaboration of the ancient thought of *poiesis* as a mode of bringing-forth (*Her-vor-bringen*) does not finally run counter to the aesthetic tradition, insofar as aesthetics presupposes its own self-production. Indeed, aesthetics may be understood as a certain culmination of the notion of *poiesis*, though aesthetics may also, as we shall see, be linked to the "modern technology" that Heidegger opposes to *poiesis* as a "challenging [*Herausfordern*]" to a "bringing-forth."[3] It is one of the tasks of this chapter to suggest

---

What Is to be Done?" in *The Nature and Context of Minority Discourse* (New York: Oxford University Press, 1990).

2. Friedrich Schiller, *On the Aesthetic Education of Man, in a Series of Letters*, bilingual edition, ed. and trans. Elizabeth M. Wilkinson and L. A. Willoughby (Oxford: Clarendon Press, 1967); letter 2, par. 5. Subsequent references are to this edition and are indicated by letter and paragraph number.

3. Martin Heidegger, "The Question concerning Technology," in *The Question concerning Technology and Other Essays*, trans. and ed. William Lovitt (New York: Harper Torchbooks, 1977), 3–35. The German text referred to is in *Vorträge und Aufsätze* (Tübingen: Verlag Günther Neske, 1954), 13–44.

that the "politics of aesthetics" resides in the peculiar and fundamental relation of aesthetics to the technical.

At this point one needs to remark, however, that if aesthetics is a political model, the notion of "politics" has itself, since Plato, been conceptualized in relation to the mimetic arts, and, more generally, to *poiesis* as the production or formation of form. Tragedians are expelled from the city of philosophy because the polis itself is "a representation of the fairest and best life, which is in reality . . . the truest tragedy."[4] Thus, Philippe Lacoue-Labarthe insists,

> The political (the City) belongs to a form of *plastic art,* formation and information, *fiction* in the strict sense. . . . The fact that the political is a form of plastic art in no way means that the *polis* is an artificial or conventional formation, but that the political belongs to the sphere of *technē* in the highest sense of the term: the sense in which *technē* is thought as the accomplishment and the revelation of *physis* itself.[5]

As "fiction," the political is organic, as in the famous opening of Aristotle's *Politics,* in which "the state is a creation of nature and . . . man is by nature a political animal," precisely because "man is the only animal whom [nature] has endowed with the gift of speech."[6] One could say that, thanks to language, the political becomes the fulfillment of nature (*physis*) in the non-natural sphere of culture (*technē*). This not only means that the state is conceived as artwork but also that the community itself is organic in essence and discovers itself as such in the *technē* of art: "If *technē* can be defined as the sur-plus of *physis,* through which *physis* 'deciphers' and presents itself . . . political *organicity* is the *surplus* necessary for a nation to present and recognize itself. And such is the political function of art" (Lacoue-Labarthe, *Heidegger,* 69).

Mutatis mutandis, this constellation of assumptions can be traced through Renaissance humanism to the inverted Platonism of eighteenth-century aesthetics, and finally to the racial ideologies of the modern period.[7] Though as Lacoue-Labarthe comments, nothing requires aesthetic politics to become grounded in the pseudobiology of race, "it can very

4. Plato, *Laws* 7, 817b, trans. R. G. Bury (Cambridge: Harvard University Press Loeb Classical Library, 1961), 99.
5. Philippe Lacoue-Labarthe, *Heidegger, Art, and Politics,* trans. Chris Turner (Oxford: Basil Blackwell, 1990), 66.
6. Aristotle, *Politics* 1.2.1253a, trans. Benjamin Jowett, in *The Basic Works of Aristotle,* ed. Richard McKeon (New York: Random House, 1941), 1129.
7. For a useful history of the notion of the "aesthetic state," see Josef Chytry, *The Aesthetic State: A Quest in Modern German Thought* (Berkeley: University of California Press, 1989), esp. xxxi–lxxiv.

easily be taken in that direction once *physis* comes to be interpreted as *bios*," precisely because of the "*organic* interpretation of the political" (Lacoue-Labarthe, *Heidegger*, 69). Lacoue-Labarthe's point—that racism is "primarily, fundamentally, an aestheticism"—helps one appreciate the degree to which aesthetics, in the most general sense, shaped both the official culture and the ideological energy of Nazism, less in Hitler's or his party's relation—philistine at best—to the arts per se than in their understanding of politics as the community's autoproduction in and through the spectacle of a "natural" destiny. The political thus becomes the production of itself as the total work of art, and thus also becomes, as Lacoue-Labarthe and Jean-Luc Nancy have argued, a violent ideologization of "the absolute, self-creating Subject" of the metaphysical tradition, a subject that purports to embody itself in "an immediate and absolutely 'natural' essence: that of blood and race."[8] These claims represent an effort to discover nonreductive relations between twentieth-century fascism and a Western tradition for which the fascist regimes had, to be sure, utter contempt, but in the absence of which they are also inconceivable. Lacoue-Labarthe's specific project consists, of course, in the negotiation of a relation to Heidegger, and an assessment of the differences and complicities that Heidegger's thought and career offer in relation to National Socialism. This project has as its primary rationale not the weighing of personal or even philosophical guilt, but the examination of a thought that "can enlighten us as to the real, or profound, nature of Nazism" (*Heidegger*, 53), occasionally despite itself. As suggested in the citations above, Heidegger's meditations on *technē* thus take on considerable importance, offering as they do a reminder and an analysis of the intimacy between politics and aesthetics.[9]

I propose to return to the question of *technē*, and technology, as Heidegger asks it, via a route that at first glance may seem at best improbable. However, few texts address the interleaved questions of art, technics, and

8. Philippe Lacoue-Labarthe and Jean-Luc Nancy, "The Nazi Myth," trans. Brian Holmes, *Critical Inquiry* 16 (1990): 310. An understanding of the link between aesthetics and technology helps us understand the apparent paradox of what Jefrey Herf calls "reactionary modernism": the coexistence of technologism and organicism in fascist and protofascist ideologies. See Jeffrey Herf, *Reactionary Modernism: Technology, Culture, and Politics in Weimar and the Third Reich* (Cambridge: Cambridge University Press, 1984).

9. I offer a brief version of my understanding of the value of Heidegger's thinking about technology at the end of this chapter. Lacoue-Labarthe's somewhat different analysis sees significant continuities and differences between Heidegger's employment of *technē* as knowledge or science (*Wissen*) in the Rectoral Address and related texts of 1933, and as art in "The Origin of the Work of Art" in 1935. Heidegger's destruction of traditional aesthetics in favor of an understanding of art as *technē* allows one to understand the "essence" of Nazism as something at once proximate to and very different from historical Nazism: what Lacoue-Labarthe calls "national aestheticism," and which he analyzes as cited and described above. For a fuller discussion see Lacoue-Labarthe, *Heidegger*, 53–121.

politics more overtly, closely, and strangely than does the odd parody of a
sequel to the *Lehrjahre* that Goethe published, in two different versions, in
the 1820s as *Wilhelm Meisters Wanderjahre*.[10] Like much of Goethe's late
work, this text has until recently enjoyed a lukewarm reception even in
German contexts; it has been very nearly forgotten elsewhere, and my
discussion proceeds under the assumption that not all readers interested in
the theoretical issues being discussed will be familiar with the text being
read. It is certainly the case, though, that the *Wanderjahre* deserves to be
better known among critics of aesthetic culture. Like the second part of
Faust, this text has always been received as a social and political, if highly
symbolic, narrative, so much so that from the 1830s to the present readers
have frequently pressed it into the service of straightforwardly political
visions.[11] Thomas Mann, for instance, who in 1923 somewhat rashly
discerned in the *Meister* cycle a "wonderful anticipation of German progress from inwardness to the objective and political, to republicanism,"
summed up its plot in terms that distill the essence of *Bildung* as a political
principle: "It begins with individualistic self-development through mis-
cellaneous experiences and ends in a political utopia. In between stands the
idea of *education*."[12] The movement of "education" as a progression from
inwardness to action and from theory to praxis is the narrative of *Bildung*
that the *Wanderjahre* represents as the elaboration of a notion of art as *technē*,
in the course of which aesthetics emerges as a highly effective, and profoundly unstable, political force.

10. The first version of the *Wanderjahre* appeared in 1821; a longer and extensively rewritten
one appeared in 1829. The discussion presented here refers to the 1829 version; except where
noted, I quote from volume 8 of the Hamburger Ausgabe, ed. Erich Trunz (Hamburg: Christian
Wegner Verlag), abbreviated where necessary as HA. I have generally followed but sometimes
modified the translation of Krishna Winston, *Wilhelm Meister's Journeyman Years; or, The Renunciants*, ed. Jane K. Brown (New York: Suhrkamp, 1989). Double page numbers refer to the
German and English editions respectively.
    Two other editions of Goethe's works will be cited occasionally in what follows: the
Artemis-Ausgabe, *Sämtliche Werke* (Zürich: Artemis Verlag, 1950), abbreviated as AA followed
by volume and page number; and the Weimarer Ausgabe, *Goethes Werke* (Weimar: H. Böhlau,
1887–1919), abbreviated as WA followed by section, volume, and page numbers.
11. For a particularly emphatic association of this novel with Schiller's Aesthetic State, see
Chytry, *The Aesthetic State*, esp. 62. An account of the enthusiastic reception accorded the
Wanderjahre in certain Young Hegelian and Proudhonian circles of the 1830s and 1840s may be
found in Pierre-Paul Sagave, "*Les Années de voyage de Wilhelm Meister* et la critique socialiste
(1830–1848)," *Etudes Germaniques* 4 (Oct.–Dec. 1953): 241–51.
12. Thomas Mann, "Geist und Wesen der deutschen Republik" [1923], *Reden und Aufsätze*, in
Gesammelte Werke, 12 vols. (Oldenburg: S. Fischer, 1960), 11:855–56; cited in W. H. Bruford, *The
German Tradition of Self-Cultivation: "Bildung" from Humboldt to Thomas Mann* (Cambridge: Cambridge University Press, 1975), 88. For a discussion of the political context of Mann's essay, see
Bruford, *German Tradition*, 226–63. Mann refers only to *Wilhelm Meister* and would seem to have
both the *Lehrjahre* and the *Wanderjahre* in mind, with the latter, as Bruford notes, providing the
"political utopia."

I

Not many studies of the *Bildungsroman* examine *Wilhelm Meisters Wanderjahre*. Before one can broach the difficulties posed by that charged and questionable subgenre, one at least has to be willing to claim that the text in question is a *Roman*, a novel, and the *Wanderjahre*'s mélange of novellas, letters, speeches, journal entries, technical writing, poetry, and aphorisms, not to mention its overall symbolic density and narrative fragmentariness, make it difficult to assimilate to any generic standard, even one as capacious as that provided by the Romantic idea of the novel. The plot line involving the eponymous Wilhelm, though it forms the object of our attention here, is a shred of *Bildung* woven into a complex and not in any way obviously unified tapestry. It is not even certain what ought to count as *Wilhelm Meisters Wanderjahre* and what ought not, since, according to Eckermann, Goethe attached collections of maxims ("Reflections in the Spirit of the Wanderers" and "Out of Makarie's Archive") to the second and third of the text's three books simply in order to have more material to give the publisher, and then attached poems to the collections of maxims because this seemed a convenient way to dispose of two available and as yet unpublished poems. Where the *Wanderjahre* can be said to end is consequently such a vexed issue that the two most widely used scholarly editions of Goethe's works have decided the matter differently.[13] And if the border or frame of the text remains uncertain, the content, or what one chooses to count as "content," has proved impossible to pin down tonally or thematically. Hyperbolically symbolic characters, for instance, repeatedly interrupt seemingly realist narratives, as when Wilhelm encounters a matriarch whose soul contains "the entire solar system," and who is thus able to predict astral movements with scientific precision—a gift that the text both supports with a straight face and identifies as an "ethereal fiction" (HA, 8: 452/412). A similarly ambiguous irony colors the representations of political utopia to which the *Wanderjahre* has so often been reduced. Later in this chapter I examine more closely the "League" with which Wilhelm becomes involved in the text's third book; for the moment note that while on the one

13. I discuss the question of the *Wanderjahre*'s closure in some detail in the Postscript to this chapter. The editorial issue turns on whether or not to print the poems that Goethe attached to the maxim collections in the middle and at the end of the *Wanderjahre*: the Artemis-Ausgabe follows Goethe in printing them as part of the *Wanderjahre*, while the Hamburger Ausgabe, acting on different editorial principles for establishing Goethe's final intentions, prints them with the rest of Goethe's poetry in a separate volume (see, e.g., HA, 1:366–67).
    Since the *Wanderjahre* poses as a strange and belated "sequel" to the *Lehrjahre*, its beginning is of course in a sense as ambiguous as its ending; and its opening sentences suggest the violence and uncertainty of origins: "In the shadow of a mighty crag, Wilhelm was sitting at a gruesome, significant spot [*an grauser, bedeutender Stelle*]. . . ." Appropriately, he is engaged in writing ("Er bemerkte etwas in seine Schreibtafel . . .").

hand this organization's announced program offers the twentieth-century reader all the sinister touchstones of organicist politics (the League will "tolerate no Jews," since they "repudiate" the "origin and source" of "highest culture [*Kultur*]" [405/378]),[14] on the other hand the League's proposed legislation is so elastically cranky that at one point we are told by one of the group's two charismatic leaders that the new community will forbid the beating of drums and the ringing of bells (406/379). W. H. Bruford understandably comments that "it is hard to know how much of all this the author expects us to take seriously" (*German Tradition*, 103): there is a hint of Groucho Marx's Freedonia to a political vision that we also have every reason to handle with care.[15]

These large obstacles to interpretation have not prevented the emergence of a considerable body of secondary literature on *Wilhelm Meisters Wanderjahre*; and we may take a first step toward a reading of the role of aesthetics in this novel by noting the way in which the text's unruly shape and tone have tended to be aestheticized in the critical tradition, subsequent to the professionalization of literary studies and the hypercanonization of Goethe in the German academy. As in the case of the omnibus texts of the modernist period to which Goethe's late work is often compared, critics have frequently sought a unifying principle for the *Wanderjahre*'s heterogeneity in notions of "symbolic" narrative.[16] Appeal is often made to Goethe's famous definition of the symbol:

> The symbol transforms appearance [*Erscheinung*] into idea [*Idee*], idea into image [*Bild*], such that the idea remains effective and unreachable [*wirksam und unerreichbar*] in the image, and, though expressed in all languages, remains inexpressible. (HA, 12:470–71)

14. And, near the end of the *Wanderjahre*, the League members respond to a speech by one of their leaders with a song possessing the rather ominous refrain,"Heil dir Führer! Heil dir Band!" (413/385).

15. Similar questions of tone or representational mode afflict the *Wanderjahre*'s portrayal of other utopic communities, most notably the Pedagogical Province, a fiefdom-sized boarding school into which Felix, Wilhelm's son, is deposited much against his will, and where he suffers the attentions of an educational system too bizarre and complex for summary, though see note 25 below.

16. See, e.g., Eric Blackall, *Goethe and the Novel* (Ithaca: Cornell University Press, 1976), 236–69; Jane K. Brown, *Goethe's Cyclical Narratives: "Die Unterhaltung deutscher Ausgewanderten" and "Wilhelm Meisters Wanderjahre"* (Chapel Hill: University of North Carolina Press, 1975); Claude David, "Goethes *Wanderjahre* als symbolische Dichtung," *Sinn und Form* 8 (1956): 113–28; Volker Neuhaus, "Die Archivfiktion in *Wilhelm Meisters Wanderjahren*," *Euphorion* 62 (1968): 13–27. The generic issues raised by the *Wanderjahre* go far beyond the scope of this study. There has, for instance, been much discussion of the interpolated *Novellen*, which account for more than two thirds of the narrative—though some of these narrative digressions are not technically *Novellen*, while, to make matters worse, the main narrative line itself is at least as close in spirit to the *Novelle* as to the *Roman*, and so on.

Once identified as "symbolic," the *Wanderjahre*'s heterogeneity can be turned into a paradoxical ground of identity, to the extent that the gap between signifier and signified—the "unreachableness" of the idea—can become a transcendental signified, the signifier of the totality of an inexpressible world. Considerable support for such an interpretation may be found in Goethe's writings and recorded opinions, and one remark in particular has become well known among *Wanderjahre* aficionados:

> Now with such books, it's as with life itself: in the complex of the whole there is that which is necessary and aleatory [*Notwendiges und Zufälliges*], planned and unplanned, successful and flawed, whereby the book is endowed with a sort of endlessness [*eine Art von Unendlichkeit*] that cannot be entirely grasped or enclosed in comprehensible, rational language.[17]

Thanks to a transcendental meaning which, in hiding itself, projects its unity back onto the work, the text's "disparate elements," its accidents and contingencies, unite into the "endlessness" of a mystery—the unknowable "complex of the whole." The uncertain borders of the text can thus become a sign of this endlessness, and the ambiguous difference between seriousness and play in the text's tonal and thematic registers becomes the mark of an *obscuritas* that Ehrhard Bahr, in an influential study of Goethe's late style, calls irony.[18]

Over the course of the *Wanderjahre*'s aesthetic monumentalization in the critical tradition, the "endlessness" of the symbol-text reappears under various guises: as the idealization of the "author," for instance, into a sheerly formal principle of order, capable of serving as "the principle of thrift" for the most unruly "proliferation of meaning."[19] Thus in an impor-

17. Goethe to Johann Friedrich Rochlitz, 23 November 1829, WA, 4:46, 166. Comments of a similar nature appear in Goethe's correspondence in 1821 with regard to the first version of the *Wanderjahre*: see in particular letters to Sulpiz Boisserée, 23 July 1821 (WA, 4:35, 31–32) and to J. S. Zauper, 7 September 1821 (WA, 4:35, 73–77). It is worth noting, however, that Goethe's comments on the *Wanderjahre* include many of the sort critics usually cite only in order to ignore, as when he described the text as a "collective work seemingly undertaken only for the collection of the most disparate elements [*zu dem Verband der disparatesten Einzelheiten*]," (Goethe to Rochlitz, 28 July 1829, in WA, 4:46, 27). Variants of this phrase appear in other letters of this period: see Goethe's letter of 2 September 1829 to Boisserée, which discusses the second *Wanderjahre* as "this second attempt to unite such disparate elements [*disparate Elemente*]" (WA, 4:46, 66). In a similar spirit Goethe dismissed a friend's (Rochlitz's) "sentimental" attempt to "systematically construct and analyze the whole" as a "silly idea," since the book claims to be no more than an "aggregate" (Goethe to F. von Müller, 18 February 1830, AA, 23:667).
18. Ehrhard Bahr, *Die Ironie im Spätwerk Goethes* (Berlin: Erich Schmidt Verlag, 1972).
19. The phrase is Michel Foucault's, and the relevant passage in "What Is an Author?" is worth recalling: "The question then becomes: How can one reduce the great peril, the great danger with which fiction threatens the world? The answer is: one can reduce it with the author. The author allows a limitation of the cancerous and dangerous proliferations of significations within a world where one is thrifty not only with one's resources and riches, but also with one's

tant essay on the *Wanderjahre*'s formal organization, Volker Neuhaus concludes that none of the text's countless narrative styles and voices has any organizational or thematic privilege: "The single perspectives complement each other, strengthen each other or cancel each other out. The author speaks from all of them, and in none of his figures are we able to seize him and say: that is Goethe's opinion" ("Archivfiktion," 25). The author here becomes the human face of a monument which, like Shelley's Ozymandias, has no meaning except in its sheer claim to presence. Indeed, since no determinate interiority remains to limit his intentionality, this author does not even have to have "written" the text he masters: he can metamorphose into a *bricoleur* and take credit for such Shandean jokes as "Die pilgernde Törin," a novella introduced in the *Wanderjahre* as a "translation from the French," which indeed it was—Goethe having, in good eighteenth-century fashion, lifted it nearly unaltered from a French-language periodical.[20] The fully monumentalized author is himself "eine Art von Unendlichkeit," capable of assimilating anything to the transcendental silence of his identity. Since the content of his intention has been evacuated, it no longer matters whether or not he means what he says: he is the *obscuritas* of his text's irony, underwriting the "sehr ernsten Scherze," the "very serious jokes," of his art with the uninterpretable purity of a sheer gesture of arrangement.[21] In the terms that Jacques Derrida extracts from Kant's *Critique of Judgment*, the author is the paragon spun out of the parergon, or frame, that marks off and constitutes the text. He exists as the irreducible, ideal secret of textual form.

The slippage that occurs as one moves from form to the transcendental reserve of the author-ideal is recorded in Kant as a movement from an "entirely pure judgment of taste" to "a partly intellectual one," since a pure aesthetic judgment, being incapable of accommodating ideational content, cannot provide an "ideal of beauty."[22] A formalist aesthetic obtains ideality—and thus becomes an aesthetic—only by violating the purity of form; and this paradox suggests a potential incompatibility between the

---

discourses and their significations. The author is the principle of thrift in the proliferation of meaning." *The Foucault Reader*, ed. Paul Rabinow (New York: Random House, 1984), 118.

20. See Trunz's notes, HA, 8:568–69.

21. The phrase "diese sehr ernsten Scherze," which directs Bahr's study of irony, is Goethe's description of *Faust* in the last letter of his life, written to Humboldt on 17 March 1832. See WA, 4:49, 281–84 for the letter, and Bahr, *Die Ironie im Spätwerk Goethes*, 13–39 for discussion. Friedrich Kittler's account of the difference between the *Lehrjahre* and the *Wanderjahre* offers a darker irony: "[Wilhelm] stops being a hero of events, and becomes the chain-link of a machine that produces, distributes, and consumes discourse. Thus literature, which in the *Lehrjahre* is limited to an autoreferential point, becomes [in the *Wanderjahre*] the element in which the hero disappears." Friedrich A. Kittler "Über die Sozialisation Wilhelm Meisters," in Gerhard Kaiser and Friedrich A. Kittler, *Dichtung als Sozialisationsspiel: Studien zu Goethe und Gottfried Keller* (Göttingen: Vandenhoek und Ruprecht, 1978), 107.

22. Immanuel Kant, *Critique of Judgment*, trans. Werner S. Pluhar (Indianapolis: Hackett, 1987), 80–81 (part 1, par. 17).

symbol's transcendence and the figurative operation that produces it. We shall approach this question from a vantage adumbrated in the image of the idealized author as *bricoleur:* a figure suggestive of a relation between symbolic transcendence and technics. To readers of *Wilhelm Meisters Wanderjahre* the idea that transcendence and technics might be related will not come as a surprise. In various ways the text associates technics with unknowability, most memorably via the figure of a little casket discovered early in the narrative by Wilhelm's son, Felix. Since this *Kästchen* is initially described as being "no larger than a small octavo volume" (43/122) and since its contents remain unknown throughout the novel, critics have understandably tended to interpret it as a figure for the text itself as symbol. Associated with subterranean mystery—Felix discovers it in a cave—the casket is "meaningful" (458/416) precisely because it remains a "riddle" (*Rätsel*) or "secret" (*Geheimnis*), both for us and for the text's characters.[23] The narrative about the casket, furthermore, unfolds as an elaboration of the definition of symbol as the gathering of "disparate elements" into a unity. Early on in the novel, Wilhelm deposits the casket for safekeeping with a professional "collector," who warns him against forcing it open: "If you have been born lucky [*glücklich*], and if this casket means anything, the key will at some point have to show up, and precisely where you least expect it" (146/196). And the collector tells a parable of an ivory crucifix, a fragment when he first acquired it, for which he has been able to recover the missing pieces—the arms, a portion of the cross, and so on. (In this "lucky coming-together [*glückliches Zusammentreffen*]," he tells us, we recognize "the destiny of the Christian religion, which, so often dismembered and scattered [*zergliedert und zerstreut*], must always get itself together again [*sich zusammenfinden*] at the cross" (147/196).) As any reader of novels might expect, the key to the casket is eventually found. But when the impulsive Felix inserts it into the lock, it breaks into two pieces— literalizing the etymology of "symbol," and in the process reconfirming the *symbolon*'s transcendental resistance to decoding. The casket's contents thus remain a mystery, but we do shortly learn something else: first, that a skilled craftsman can in fact unlock a symbol, and, second, that one of the secrets to being a skilled craftsman is the skill of keeping secrets secret. In the wake of Felix's misguided attempt to possess the casket's meaning, a jeweler demonstrates that the two pieces of the key are "magnetically bound together," and "close only for the initiated"; then, rather as though the key were an electronic door-opener, he "steps a little ways away, the

---

23. See Birgit Baldwin, "*Wilhelm Meisters Wanderjahre* as an Allegory of Reading," *Goethe Yearbook* 5 (1990): 213–32, for a rigorous discussion of the rhetorical problems raised by the "symbolic" *Kästchen,* and a useful bibliography of the secondary criticism devoted to it.

casket springs open, he immediately closes it again: it isn't good to disturb such secrets, he believes" (458/416).

The symbol, by definition, is a gathering of itself unto itself, as exemplified by the recovery of the "dismembered and scattered" limbs of a holy body or icon. The role of the technician in this transcendental economy may be less obvious, but is certainly also of ancient provenance. Magic is a *technē*, and the jeweler a savant in the Masonic and hermetic tradition: a technician whose craft presents itself as both pragmatic and esoteric. As so often, the jeweler's antics are sufficiently exaggerated that one can never know "how much of this the author expects us to take seriously"; but this undecidably valorized scenario nonetheless dramatizes a relation between technics and renunciation central to the *Wanderjahre*. Technics is knowledge derived from the renunciation of knowledge, and this renunciation of knowledge links technical prowess to the transcendental unknowability of the symbol. The symbol turns out to be a pragmatic principle, as Goethe's definition of it as "effective and unreachable [*wirksam und unerreichbar*]" suggests. And as we shall see, the symbol's melange of secrecy, technics, and formal totalization acquires political clout through the valorization of a pragmatic aesthetic, which the text calls craft, *Handwerk*.

II

An emphasis on pragmatic knowledge characterizes the various utopic (or mock-utopic) communities which *Wilhelm Meisters Wanderjahre* either portrays or has its characters describe or theorize—perhaps most notably the League mentioned earlier. This League or *Bund*, an organization charged with the founding of utopic communities in both the new and the old worlds, is the new name and identity of the Society of the Tower of *Wilhelm Meisters Lehrjahre*. The transformation of the secretive, pseudo-Masonic Society of the previous novel into a colonizing venture marks an explicit politicization of the ends of *Bildung*: a politicization inseparable from the question concerning technology and technics. Generally, though not always, the League, in good Romantic-agrarian fashion, is opposed to technology but celebratory of *technē*, "less favorably disposed toward machinery [*Maschinenwesen*] than toward unmediated handwork [*unmittelbare Handarbeit*], where strength and feeling operate in unison" (337/332). The group's members, consequently, are idealized craftsmen [*Handwerker*], while its leaders—and its financial backing—are of aristocratic origin.

Thus consistently, if ironically, the text's characters and narrators propose handicraft, *Handwerk*, as a value.[24] Lenardo and Odoard's vision of their *Bund* gives overt political shape to an idealization of craft which we have already seen at work (or play) in the encounter of the jeweler and the casket, and which particularly marks the plot line featuring Wilhelm Meister. Within this narrative strand, *Handwerk* represents the effect or outcome of "renunciation," which in turn characterizes *Bildung*. When Wilhelm asks the Collector to whom he has consigned the mysterious casket to advise him where he might consign his son, the Collector recommends the Pedagogical Province as a place where students receive a limited, technical, and thus genuine education:

> "All living, all activity, all art must be preceded by technical skill [*Hand-werk*], which can be acquired only through limitation [*Beschränkung*]. To know one thing properly and be adept at it results in higher cultivation [*Bildung*] than half-competence in a hundred different fields. Where I am sending you, all the fields of endeavor have been divided up." (148/197)

And the father, like the son, will undergo *Bildung* under the aegis of technics: indeed, while Felix's training in the Pedagogical Province turns out to be considerably less focused and effective than the Collector's account might suggest,[25] Wilhelm's education will discover its ultimate rationale in his assumption of the manual trade of surgeon—a profession nearly as distant from the middle-class norms of the day as carpentry or weaving would be. In the *Lehrjahre* Wilhelm had had to renounce the possibilities for *Bildung* that the theater had seemed to represent—the proto-bohemian hope of capturing aristocratic well-roundedness through the protean grace of the actor; now, in the 1829 *Wanderjahre*, he must renounce not just aristocratic pretension but bourgeois dilettantism as well. In itself Wilhelm's renunciation of social prestige holds limited interest, since on this point the *Wanderjahre* is as cheerily unrealistic as the *Lehrjahre* had been in casually betrothing its middle-class hero to an aristocrat in its final chapters. In the

24. On Goethe's ironization of *Handwerk* see Bruce Armstrong, who in "An Idyll Sad and Strange: The St. Joseph the Second Section and the Presentation of Craft Work in Goethe's *Wilhelm Meisters Wanderjahre*," *Monatshefte für deutschen Unterricht, deutsche Sprache und Literatur* 77.4 (1985): 415–32, shows that handicraft is persistently shadowed by anachrony and absurdity, and is thus by no means the reliable value it appears.

25. As noted earlier, the Pedagogical Province is not an easy institution to summarize. It places emphasis on authoritarian communality and practical knowledge—the students sing in chorus while they work, are taught unquestioning respect for all forms of authority, learn languages while tending to agricultural chores, and so on. Poor Felix does not "adapt well to the quiet, toilsome farming life, against which he had protested in advance" (245/267), and does not appear to emerge from this educational utopia with any particular skills. For discussions of the intellectual heritage and (uncertain) symbolism of the Province, see Brown, *Goethe's Cyclical Narratives*, 87–97, and Bruford, *German Tradition*, 104–11.

symbolic universe of the Meister cycle, Wilhelm's *dérogation* is not an appreciably material sacrifice in anyone's eyes, least of all Wilhelm's. If, however, the "renunciation" at work in the "limitation" that is *Handwerk* lacks socioeconomic consequence, it nonetheless claims political relevance by serving as the founding principle of aesthetic pragmatism.

As we saw in the preceding chapter, the figure of renunciation, *Entsagung*, plays a central and complex role in the *Lehrjahre*'s account of *Bildung*—so central a role that in a sense the *Wanderjahre* can do no more than repeat the earlier text's thoroughgoing interrogation of the power of the negative. The *Lehrjahre* proposes itself as a *Bildungsroman* about the impossibility of *Bildung*, renouncing *Bildung* as a literal accomplishment so as to recuperate it as a pure fiction, the fiction of an impossibility. At the same time, as we saw, the text tells the disruptive story of the impossibility of this fiction, which is unable to refrain from positing its own (fictional) referentiality; and this blindly self-constituting and self-destroying gesture in turn becomes legible as the text's very condition of possibility. The *Wanderjahre* will retell this story, which is that of the predicament of reading. But it will tell it differently; and it is on this level of rhetorical self-presentation that this text can be taken in a non-trivial sense as a "sequel" to the *Lehrjahre*. In *Wilhelm Meisters Wanderjahre*, the story told is that of a pragmatic affirmation of the self-concealing arbitrariness of the sign. If the earlier novel tells the story of the uncontrollable production and deconstruction of aesthetic illusions, the later text narrates the attempt to aestheticize this linguistic volatility into a principle of political utility. The failure of aesthetics, in other words, can be reconfigured as pragmatism. If the articulation of meaningful form involves an irreducible violence, that violence can itself be rendered a discountable inevitability: all truth is arbitrary; therefore one can bracket the question of truth and pass on to practical matters. As Clark Muenzer writes in a fine study of the figure of *technē* in Goethe's thought, one can "reject self-presence as a delusion."[26] The gesture is a familiar one in post-Romantic thought, and frequently appears in both academic and popular circles in the form of arguments or manifestos "against theory."[27] *Wilhelm Meisters Wanderjahre*, however, demonstrates that such pragmatism is finally an exacerbated aestheticism.

If the aesthetic, in its post-Kantian formulation, brackets meaning in order to recuperate meaning as form, a pragmatized aesthetic reiterates this gesture to the second power. Meaning is bracketed (truth-systems have no ground that is not a "delusion"); meanings, however, nonetheless occur,

---

26. Clark S. Muenzer, *Figures of Identity: Goethe's Novels and the Enigmatic Self* (University Park: Penn State University Press, 1984), 141.
27. See in particular essays collected in W. J. T. Mitchell, ed., *Against Theory: Literary Studies and the New Pragmatism* (Chicago: University of Chicago Press, 1985).

and this occurrence can be erected into a value in its turn. Like Faust, aesthetic pragmatism valorizes the deed as the word. Meaning is sacrificed so as to be reborn as meaning-as-action, the "doing" of meaning. In terms of its negativity, pragmatism is thus dialectical insofar as its act of renunciation is ultimately intended to be self-canceling, so as to fulfill the Faustian hope of transforming nothingness into plenitude ("In deinem Nichts hoff' ich das All zu finden" [HA, 3:192]). Muenzer, writing of the "well-wrought deed" as "an adequate response to the challenge of pure communality" in the *Wanderjahre*, brings together many of the strands we have been following:

> "[D]oing" remains content to preserve the social ideal through an effort that acknowledges the significance of human bonding while renouncing its realization. . . . This ultimate techne-ology partakes of a putative order of things only by paradoxically transforming the circumspect products of work into symbolic testimonies of non-attainment. (Muenzer, *Figures of Identity*, 127)

"Doing" is thus a recuperation of meaning through meaning's renunciation, and Muenzer rightly calls this sacrificial economy "symbolic": the symbol, as Goethe theorized it, is the master-trope of this pragmatism. Technics and transcendental unknowability are the two faces of the symbol as *wirksam und unerreichbar*.

The aestheticism and the totalizing ambition of technical pragmatism is spelled out early in the *Wanderjahre* when Wilhelm's old friend Jarno delivers a speech on the virtues of specialization so eloquent that Wilhelm makes his decision to become a surgeon upon hearing it:

> "To restrict oneself [*sich beschränken*] to a craft [*Handwerk*] is the best. For the lesser man it will always be a craft, for the better one an art [*Kunst*], and for the best, if he does *one*, he does all, or, to be less paradoxical, in the one thing he does properly, he sees the likeness of all that is done properly." (37/118)

The seductive power of the trope of *Handwerk* as renunciation is both exemplified and analyzed in this passage: the figure is persuasive because it mingles the steely resolve of renunciation with the luxury of recompense. Art has not really been renounced at all, since it returns as the universality of that which has been "recht getan." In its very pragmatism, *Handwerk* is the truly totalizing term—which explains Wilhelm's otherwise puzzling assertion, made under curious circumstances that I shall examine later, that the passage from *Kunst* to *Handwerk* represents an imperative motion from the particular to the universal: "[W]hat is nowadays art must become handicraft, and what happens in individual cases must become universally possible [*was im Besonderen geschieht, muß im Allgemeinen möglich werden*]" (332/328). At the same time, the totalizing mirage of *Kunst* has been projected onto the world: Wilhelm will cut bodies instead of staging representations, and the Society of the Tower will build colonies instead of manipulating private lives, which is to say that any instability inherent in the aesthetic system will now work itself out on a political level. Thus the elements in the *Lehrjahre*'s narrative of renunciation undergo pragmatic intensification in the *Wanderjahre*'s. If, as I argued in the preceding chapter, the *Lehrjahre*'s closing scene figuratively renounces aesthetics in order to reclaim it, the *Wanderjahre* ironically allows its League to risk philistinism by literally renouncing art. The League's artists, we learn at one point, will be obtained from the Pedagogic Province—where they have been properly trained in the ethos of corporate art—but even so, the *Bund* will accept "very few": "[A]s salt is to food, so are the arts to technical science [*Technik*]. We want from art [*Kunst*] only enough to insure that our handicrafts will remain in good taste [*daß das Handwerk nicht abgeschmackt werde*]" (242/266).

We may now step back and begin to resurvey the terrain of aesthetics in the *Wanderjahre*, since, as these words of the Abbé suggest, the hyperaesthetic of pragmatism raises the specter of curiously specific aesthetic problems. As soon as *Handwerk* becomes the epitome of the aesthetic, another sort of epitome, *Kunst*, appears as a force needing to be controlled—but also as a homeopathic cure for a *Handwerk* inexplicably threatened with being "abgeschmackt." A sense of the tensions at play in the aesthetic of *Handwerk* emerges in Odoard's speech to the League late in the text. On the one hand, handicraft and art share a profound identity, and in the new colony *Handwerke* are to be declared *Künste*; on the other hand, the former are to be "set apart and distinguished from the 'free' arts by the term 'rigorous arts' [*strenge Künste*]" (411/383). And in fact, "the rigorous arts must set an example [*Muster*] for the free arts, and seek to put them to shame," since in *Handwerk* more is at stake:

> "If we examine the so-called free arts, which are to be understood and so named in a higher sense, it turns out to make no difference whether they are practiced well or badly. The worst statue stands on its feet with the best, a painted figure [*Figur*] with misdrawn feet still strides forward briskly, while its misshapen arms reach out powerfully [*kräftig*] enough; figures [*Figuren*] may not be standing in correct perspective [*stehen nicht auf dem richtigen Plan*], yet the ground [*Boden*] does not cave in on this account. With music it is even more striking: the screeching fiddle at the village tavern stirs stout limbs [*Glieder*] most powerfully [*aufs kräftigste*], and we have seen believers edified by the most abominable church music.

And if you wish to count poetry among the free arts, you will surely see that it, too, barely knows where it should find a limit [*Grenze*]. And yet every art has its internal laws [*innern Gesetze*], though disobeying them brings no harm to mankind; the rigorous arts, by contrast, can allow themselves no such liberties." (412/383–84)

If *Kunst* had earlier been seen as mere salt to the food of *Handwerk*, here the free arts are relegated to an even more tenuous supplementarity: inessential in comparison to the "rigorous arts," they have now also become the locus of a potential tastelessness, the status of which is somewhat peculiar. On the one hand, the "free arts" are subject to degeneracy precisely because they are referentially free: the ground does not cave in under the impact of misdrawn figures because they have no power to negate the real. On the other hand, art's irresponsibility does not in the least seem to preclude its having effects upon the real: the ugly statue stands; the misdrawn figure gestures; the screeching fiddle "stirs stout limbs most powerfully"; and the abominable church music "edifies" believers. Free art is not any less effective for being either non-referential or badly constructed. In fact, as the text's repeated invocations of force, *Kraft*, suggests, art's performative power might be all the greater for being indifferent to referential and formal constraints.[28]

And if the "free" and the "rigorous" arts are both tributaries of *Kunst*, the degeneracy of the former is possibly the visible sign of a disease hidden in the latter. The transcendental and pragmatic order of the symbol, in other words, might be animated by a referential force irreducible to the world of meaning it produces. In a well-known passage in *Dichtung und Wahrheit*, Goethe called this possibility that of the "demonic":

. . . something which manifests itself only in contradictions, and which therefore could not be comprehended under any idea, still less under a word. It was not godlike, for it seemed unreasonable; not human, for it had no understanding; not devilish, for it was beneficent; not angelic, for it often displayed malice [*Schadenfreude*]. It resembled chance, for it evolved no consequences; it was like providence, for it hinted at connection. It seemed to penetrate all that limits us, and to play willfully with the necessary elements of our existence; it compacted time and expanded space. It seemed to find pleasure only in the impossible, and to reject the possible with contempt. This being, which seemed to intervene among all others to separate and bind them, I called the demonic, after the example of the ancients and of those who had attested to something similar. Thus, in

---

28. The rhetoricians of the *Bund* speak a great deal of power [*Kraft*], and of solutions that are pragmatic [*tätig*] and practical [*praktisch*]; see, e.g., 405/378.

accordance with my habits, I sought to save myself from this terrible being by taking refuge behind an image [*Bild*]. (HA, 10:175–76)

In this text Goethe goes on to characterize the demonic as the "riddle" that all religion and philosophy have sought to solve; and when Johann Peter Eckermann later pressed him for more detail, he spoke of the demonic in terms that recall even more sharply the definition of the symbol. The demonic is the "inexpressible world- and life-riddle," a "secret problematic violence [*Gewalt*]" external to but determinative of intentionality and meaning: "It is not in my nature, but I am subjected to it [*ich bin ihm unterworfen*]."[29] The secret that the jeweler resecretes in the casket is perhaps best left undisturbed for this reason, but perhaps also for this reason is inhabited and constituted by disturbance. Neither the jeweler nor anyone else can allow the symbol to rest embalmed in its *Kästchen*, any more than a technologized criticism can entirely bracket, through monumentalization, the intentionality of authors or the meaning of texts, or than pragmatism can keep from reiterating the ambitions and difficulties of the metaphysics it abjures. *Wilhelm Meisters Wanderjahre* takes up this problem most visibly in the orbit of its master-trope of *Handwerk*, surgery.

III

If *Handwerk*, as limitation, is the privileged trope of *Entsagung*, surgery renders the essence of *Handwerk-as-Entsagung*, both in its etymology (the Greek root, *kheirourgia*, translates literally as "handwork" [*kheir + erg*]) and in its figure of the cut that heals.[30] Appropriately, a scene of surgery

29. Johann Peter Eckermann, *Gespräche mit Goethe in den letzten Jahren seines Lebens* (Munich: C. H. Beck, 1984), 402, 405 (28 February and 2 March 1831). For a fine discussion of the demonic in relation to the secret of the casket in the *Wanderjahre*, see Baldwin, "*Wilhelm Meisters Wanderjahre* as an Allegory of Reading," 220–23.

30. The metaphysics of the hand are elaborated by Odoard in the speech cited earlier on the distinction between "free" and "rigorous" arts: "He who devotes himself to one of the rigorous arts must be faithful to it for life. Previously they were called handicrafts [*Handwerk*], quite suitably and correctly. Their practitioners are supposed to work with their hands, and the hand that performs such work must be animated by a life of its own, must be a being [*Natur*] unto itself, with its own thoughts, its own will, and that cannot be spread over many skills" (412–13/384).

The question of the hand holds great interest for the question of technology in its Heideggerian inflection; and though I cannot develop this theme here, we might recall the importance Heidegger persistently grants the trope of *Handwerk*, particularly in *What Is Called Thinking?*: "Perhaps thinking, too, is just something like building a cabinet. At any rate it is a craft, a 'handicraft.' 'Craft' literally means the strength and skill in our hands. The hand is a peculiar thing. In the common view, the hand is part of our bodily organism. But the hand's essence can never be determined, or explained, by its being an organ which can grasp. Apes, too, have organs that can grasp, but they do not have hands. The hand is infinitely different from all

grants enough formal and metaphysical incisiveness to one of the *Wander-jahre*'s numerous formal borders that Eric Blackall unhesitatingly, and understandably, refers to it as "the real ending of the novel" (*Goethe and the Novel*, 259). In the last chapter before the epigram collection, Wilhelm, thanks to his surgical know-how, saves his son's life after Felix tumbles into a river. Wilhelm thus not only raises his son from apparent death ("no sign of life" remains when Felix is pulled out of the water) but also bandages the wound that created his desire to be a surgeon in the first place—for if we believe what Wilhelm tells his fiancée Nathalie at the end of book 2, he first acquired this desire after losing a childhood friend, whose death by drowning might have been averted if there had been a surgeon available to bleed the recovered body. In closing off the Meister plot, the *Wanderjahre* thus stages a therapeutic repetition: the father's knife heals the son, thereby healing the father. The religious and psychoanalytic intertexts that inevitably come to mind reinforce a figurative structure that the novel has built with considerable care. Surgery is the handwork of handwork, the renunciation of renunciation: its castrating cut seals the symbolic order, drawing the sting of time and death, healing past wounds in a present that excises all loss.

If surgery is the epitome of aesthetic *Handwerk*, however, it is also the locus of corruption; and a demonic, hyperbolically *abgeschmackte* version of Felix's resurrection unfolds in the third chapter of the *Wanderjahre*'s third book, as Wilhelm recounts the story of his surgical education to members of the League. We may note in passing that the chapter begins under the sign of technical pragmatism. It is preceded by a letter from Wilhelm's friend Hersilie to Wilhelm, in which Hersilie recounts finding the key to the mysterious *Kästchen:* Hersilie assumes Wilhelm will be interested in this event, but as the third chapter begins, we learn he isn't; his medical skills are much in demand among the League's rather accident-prone workers, and "at present he was much too busy with serious things to be in the least stimulated by curiosity as to what was in that casket" (322/321). Committed to surgery as the epitome of *Handwerk*, Wilhelm has renounced hermeneutics: the casket's mystery no longer moves him because the problem of meaning, formalized into transcendental obscurity, has in a sense ceased to be a mystery at all. Pragmatism, as we have seen, grounds itself in the symbol precisely by pretending indifference to the symbolic: paradoxically, the

---

grasping organs—paws, claws, or fangs—different by an abyss of essence. Only a being who can speak, that is, think, can have hands and be handy in achieving works of handicraft." *What Is Called Thinking?* trans. J. Glenn Gray (New York: Harper and Row, 1968), 16. For an important reading of this and other passages, see Jacques Derrida, "La main de Heidegger," *Psyche: Inventions de l'autre* (Paris: Galilée, 1987), 415–52.

technician fetishizes secrecy in order to abolish the secret as such.[31] If such pragmatism were genuinely possible, Wilhelm's story would come to an end here; instead, one evening he initiates what is to be a sequence of narratives in which the League members share with each other stories of experiences "that produced an education [*Bildung*]" (322/322).

Wilhelm's narrative, which occupies most of the chapter and is what Bernd Peschken has in mind when he calls this chapter one of "the most enigmatic [*rätselhaften*] of the novel,"[32] tells the tale of a problem and its solution, both of which possess an element of the bizarre. When Wilhelm begins surgical training, he discovers its fundamental component, its *Grundstudium*, to consist in the art of dissection (*Zergliederungskunst*), and he also finds out that the pragmatic bent of this paradoxical *Bildung*-through-*Zergliederung* has violent, even anarchic, consequences. The cadavers required by the medical school are in short enough supply to inspire both state-sponsored and individual acts of terror, which in turn generates tension between the people and the state:

> To provide as many as possible (if still not enough), harsh laws had been enacted, so that not only criminals, who had forfeited their individuality [*Individuum*] in every sense, but also those destroyed in body and soul were claimed for this use. Severity rose with need, and with severity rose the resistance of the people, who for moral and religious reasons cannot give up their own sense of personhood [*Persönlichkeit*], or that of a loved one. (323/322)

Simultaneously, grave-robbing flourishes, to the point that the body of the polis itself seems at the point of dismemberment: "The evil continued to spread. . . . [E]ven as the mourner walked away from the grave, he had to dread the possibility that the quiet, bejewelled limbs of the beloved person might be severed, dragged off, and dishonored" (323–24/322–23). Indeed, we learn later in Wilhelm's story that "murder has been committed in this city in order to provide the insistent, well-paying anatomist with an object" (333/329). The motive force of this legal and illegal industry is the pragmatic thrust of surgical *Bildung*: "[Y]oung men who had attentively followed the lectures felt the need to verify with hand and eye what had previously been seen and heard." Education thus generates an "unnatural" and socially disruptive cognitive desire: "In such moments there arises a sort of

31. The recent work of Jacques Derrida has explored the self-rupturing figure of the secret. See among other texts "Passions: 'An Oblique Offering,'" in *Derrida: A Critical Reader*, ed. David Wood (Oxford: Blackwell, 1992), 5–35.
32. Bernd Peschken, *Entsagung in "Wilhelm Meisters Wanderjahre"* (Bonn: H. Bouvier, 1968), 119.

unnatural scientific [*wissenschaftliche*] hunger which demands to be satis-
fied by fair means or foul" (324/323).

This phase in Wilhelm's story reaches a climax when "a very beautiful
girl," believing herself jilted by her lover, drowns herself; to the consterna-
tion of the city, she is handed over to the anatomists by the authorities,
"who had just increased the severity of the law" and therefore "could
permit no exceptions." Wilhelm is given her severed arm to dissect, and
though he is desirous of knowledge (*wissensbegierige*), he balks at the idea of
"further disfiguring [*entstellen*] this marvellous product of nature"
(325/323). A sculptor (*Bildhauer*), a mysterious figure whom the medical
students frequently see at their lectures, notices Wilhelm's moral dilemma
and invites him home to his studio, where, it turns out, the sculptor uses his
Kunst to teach the *Handwerk* of surgery by substituting wax and wooden
models for bodies. Despite the "enormous gulf [*Kluft*] between these aesthetic works [*künstlerischen Arbeiten*] and the scientific endeavors
[*wissenschaftlichen Bestrebungen*] from which they derived" (326/324),
Wilhelm is persuaded of their utility—and he finds out that in this the
League is ahead of him. Lothario and his colleagues have already made
plans to ship the sculptor's models to America: "It was considered particularly fitting, indeed, essential, for such a school to be founded in the growing colony, especially among naturally moral, high-minded people, to
whom actual dissection always has something cannibalistic about it"
(328/325–26).[33]

Thus far in our reading of the *Wanderjahre* we have traced an interplay
between *Handwerk* and *Kunst*, in which the latter occasionally acts as a
reservoir for difficulties needing to be expelled from the former. In
Wilhelm's narrative this pattern is complicated and displaced by the pressure of a newly prominent category: "science" in the sense of knowledge,
Wissenschaft, which appears here in demonic form as an uncontrollable
desire to analyze—literally, to dissect. The emergence of "science" as the
ground of *Handwerk* is not in itself surprising: as "rigorous art," *Handwerk*,
unlike "free art," *Kunst*, must be epistemologically reliable. But since this
reliability turns into a referential disease, free art stages a paradoxical return as "plastic anatomy," which offers to contain the referential drive of
Wissenschaft within the frame of the aesthetic while anchoring knowledge
to the world. The aesthetic is to heal the aesthetic in a homeopathic cure, as

33. And indeed, the *Bildhauer* might even be said to have sold his scheme to the author of the
Wanderjahre; Goethe promulgated the virtues of "plastic anatomy" on grounds similar to
Wilhelm's in an essay written a few months before he died, referring his reader back to the
"half-fiction [*Halbfiction*]" of Wilhelm's reportage: see "Plastische Anatomie"(WA, 2:49, 64). The
persuasive force of this curious narrative seems strangely excessive, capable of rupturing the
frame of "fiction" itself. Goethe dated the essay 4 February 1832, and mailed it to the Staatsrat
P. C. W. Beuth in Berlin, where it met with a polite but definitive rejection.

Kunst prevents *Handwerk* from becoming *abgeschmackt.* We may expect this solution to be a fragile one, since we have seen that *Kunst* is also possessed of unreliable referential power; and, indeed, complications emerge as the *Bildhauer* sums up the difference between old-fashioned dissection and his new plastic anatomy, in a phrase often taken to be the moral of the entire chapter: "[B]uilding up teaches more than tearing down, binding more than severing, giving life to the dead more than killing the slain even further [*Aufbauen mehr belehrt als Einreißen, Verbinden mehr als Trennen, Totes beleben mehr als das Getötete noch weiter töten]*" (326/324).[34] The maxim moves from the cleanly structured antonyms of building and destroying, binding and severing, to a counterintuitive opposition and semi-chiasmus: where one might have expected "giving life to the dead" to oppose "killing the living," the text rather insists that dissection be thought as "killing the dead even further." And since the opposition is between giving life to the dead and killing the dead, the word "dead" becomes a defaced residue within this tropological structure, inhabiting and enabling the opposition without being assimilable to it. To be dead, in this Gothic fiction, is not to be so dead that one cannot continue to die.

The disfiguring figure "killing the dead even further" (echoed when Wilhelm, confronted with the beautiful female arm, hesitates to "disfigure it even further [*noch weiter zu entstellen]*") sums up the essential (il)logic of dissection, as becomes clear when we examine more closely the political impact of this "unnatural scientific hunger." One will have noted, in Wilhelm's story, the peculiar influence that the needs of medical research seem to have on legislative procedure: "To provide as many [cadavers] as possible (if still not enough), harsh laws had been enacted. . . ." Even in authoritarian Germany one might not have expected such frenzied collusion between the state and its university, particularly since in this case the tail would seem to be wagging the dog—except, of course, that it has been clear from the beginning that dissection is no ordinary activity. As an approach to the question of what dissection is, we may ask what law is in this story. A negative definition emerges immediately: lawbreakers (*Verbrecher*) are those who have "forfeited their individuality [*Individuum*] in every sense." Law is the generality of a social contract within which individuality is defined; lawbreakers lose their individuality in the very act of breaking the law. Simultaneously, the law presents itself as a generality oriented toward the future possibility of particular application in the mode of violence: in this sense capital punishment would seem the essence of legal referentiality, because when the law refers, it does so by obliterating the

---

34. For a reading of the chapter that takes this phrase as its moral, see Peschken, *Entsagung,* 119–25.

particular *as* particular in relation to the whole. Law would thus essentially be the law of death. A closer look reveals that the truth is slightly more complex, however. Criminals, in becoming criminals, have "forfeited their individuality in every sense" through their own agency; in essence the criminal is a suicide, and capital punishment merely a literalization of the lawbreaker's self-annihilation. Thus the "harsh laws" that criminalize suicide are merely reflexive intensifications of ordinary laws. Criminals and suicides are the most extreme sort of renunciants or *Entsagenden* from a legal perspective; what the law punishes is in fact death itself—death, that is, understood as the self-consumption of the individual in an ultimate act of freedom. What the "harsh laws" reveal is that the law obtains no referential grip via capital punishment, and that in its referentiality law is finally the law of dissection. Suicides can kill themselves but cannot dissect themselves: only through *Zergliederung* can the law inscribe itself on the world.

According to the logic of the law, therefore, dissection "kills the dead even further." This deathless killing provides law with the referentiality that law must promise in order to come into being. The legal text is a text in which the referential dimension is paramount, and dissection thus becomes legible as a figure for language's need to refer.[35] The excessive death (as "dissection," as "killing the dead even further") inhabiting the binary opposition of death and life registers the symbol's inability to bracket reference and thus guarantee itself as a transcendental frame within which the pragmatic work of tropological exchange would occur. Referentiality can neither be bracketed nor made reliable: indeed, since laws are being generated in order to increase the supply of bodies to the medical school, the law opens itself to the suspicion that it exists simply in order to reconfirm its own referentiality. And only so fundamental a necessity as the need to refer could account for the insatiability of this "unnatural scientific hunger," or for the degree of havoc it wreaks, as the pragmatic need to "verify with hand and eye" generates both law and the violation of law, such that, as in the Chancellor's speech in *Faust*, "[I]llegality rules legally / And a world of error unfolds" ("Das Ungesetz gesetzlich überwaltet / Und eine Welt des Irrtums sich entfaltet" [HA, 3:151]).

If the referential drive of the linguistic system is excessively productive, however, it is also excessively formal: dissection is a mad end in itself, a mechanical iteration performed on body after body, an act of memorization rather than learning, but a memorization that endlessly memorizes the same thing. Dissection, as inscription, is a hypermemorization, a remembering that disremembers, and in effacing itself generates the madness of

---

35. Paul de Man writes in a not unrelated context that a law is "more like an actual text than a piece of property or a State." *Allegories of Reading: Figural Language in Rousseau, Nietzsche, Rilke, and Proust* (New Haven: Yale University Press, 1979), 268.

reference.[36] "Every doctor," Wilhelm sums up near the end of his narrative, "is nothing without the closest knowledge of the outer and inner articulations [*Glieder*] of men. . . . If he is serious, the doctor should refresh his knowledge daily, and seek out every opportunity to renew for eye and spirit the organization [*Zusammenhang*] of this living wonder, the body" (331/328). In the service of this constant need to re-member through dismemberment, doctors "who know what's good for them," Wilhelm continues, will hire anatomists ("in secret"); and this laudable need for precise knowledge will trigger the disaster of which we know:

> "The more this [need to know the body's articulation] is understood, the more busily, vehemently, passionately will the study of dissection be pursued. But the means [*Mittel*] will decrease precisely in proportion; the objects, the bodies, on which such studies are grounded, will be lacking, will become rarer and dearer, and a genuine conflict between living [*Lebendige*] and dead [*Toten*] will arise. . . . This conflict I foresee between the dead and the living [*Toten und Lebendigen*] will be a matter of life and death [*er wird auf Leben und Tod gehen*]; people will be terrified and will seek to make laws, but to no avail [*man wird untersuchen, Gesetze zu geben und nichts ausrichten*]." (332/328)

It is in the wake of these comments that Wilhelm delivers his memorable and much-quoted imperative that "what is nowadays art must become handicraft, and what happens in individual cases must become universally possible" (332/328). But we now see that this pragmaticist formalism emerges out of an unstoppable and violent proliferation of reference, which perhaps helps account for the difficulty of making sense out of the elisions and presuppositions structuring speeches like this one of Wilhelm's. The "laws," for instance, possibly the "harte Gesetze" we encountered earlier, designed to increase the supply of corpses, or possibly legislation such as England's 1832 Anatomy Act, designed to regulate the commodification of corpses, could in this paragraph as easily be laws of some other sort, promulgated, perhaps, by the "living" to protect themselves from the "dead," who have been inexplicably animated and put in charge of their own inter-

---

36. And the countermyth of mimesis, as represented by the *Handwerk* of plastic anatomy: "If you admit that most doctors and surgeons retain only a general impression of the diseased human body and believe that they can manage with that, then models like ours are sure to be sufficient to refresh their gradually fading mental images [*Bilder*] and keep alive what is essential for them. Yes, it requires but interest and inclination, and the most delicate results of the art of dissection can be reproduced [*nachbilden*]. This can be achieved with nothing more than pen, brush, and stylus" (328/326). The insistent pressure of metaphors of inscription in this and other passages on memory and dissection in this chapter returns us to Jacques Derrida's discussion of writing and memory in the *Phaedrus*. See "Plato's Pharmacy," in *Dissemination*, trans. Barbara Johnson (Chicago: University of Chicago Press, 1981), 61–171.

ests. If the lopsided chiasmus of "killing the dead even further" registered an excess of death, here there appears to be such an excess of life that the dead themselves cannot die. For whether one calls this endless residue "life" or "death" is indifferent, since as a trope for tropological residue either term is a catachresis.[37]

Since dissection is the *Bildung* of surgery, the transcendental and pragmatic secret of the symbol may be said to emerge out the referential predicament that dissection exemplifies. Thus, throughout Wilhelm's story, the *Bildhauer* will be associated with the symbol's secrecy—and its guilty conscience. At the end of his narrative Wilhelm recounts a story the *Bildhauer* has told him ("in greatest confidence") of the days when he, the *Bildhauer*, was an anatomy student engaged in dissection, and knowingly received a murdered corpse:

> "The reader of newspapers finds it interesting and almost funny, when he hears stories of resurrection men [*Auferstehungsmänner*]. First, in deepest secrecy, they steal the corpse; to prevent this, one hires watchmen: the resurrection men come with an armed multitude to obtain their booty through violence. And the worst of worst things will arise—I mustn't say it aloud, for I would be entangled in a most dangerous investigation, not indeed as an accomplice [*Mitschuldiger*] but nonetheless as someone who by chance knew about it [*Mitwisser*]. In any case one would have to punish me, since I did not instantly report the misdeed [*Untat*] to the authorities as soon as I had uncovered it. I confess it, my friend, murder has been committed in this city in order to provide the insistent, well-paying anatomist with an object. The lifeless body lay before us. I don't dare paint the scene. He discovered the crime [*Untat*], I did too: we looked at each other and both fell silent; we looked away and remained silent and went to work.— And this, my friend, is what has kept me between wax and plaster; this is what will certainly also hold you to art [*bei der Kunst festhalten*], which sooner or later will be praised above all else." (332–33/328–29)

Throughout Wilhelm's story, the *Bildhauer* is associated with secrecy—no one knows much about him except that he is a sculptor ("he was also considered an alchemist [*Goldmacher*]"); much of his house is closed to visitors, and so on—and the narrative never seriously tries to explain why. We learn that plastic anatomy must be pursued "in the deepest secrecy," yet for reasons slender enough to seem secretive themselves: "[Y]ou have cer-

---

37. This disarticulation composes the text itself, as suggested by the reception Wilhelm's story receives: Lenardo is "distracted" or "scattered" (*zerstreut*), "absent" (*abwesend*), despite "a certain animation [*Lebhaftigkeit*] in [Wilhelm's] voice and speech, which these days was not customary" (330).

tainly heard men in our field speak with contempt of this" (326/324). And not only are anatomical models to be distributed "in secrecy [*im stillen*]," but in a strange turn of phrase the *Bildhauer* sets forth the pedagogical ambitions of plastic anatomy in terms reminiscent of grave-robbing or worse: "There must be a school . . . one must seize and train the living, but in secret, or else one will be hindered [*das Lebendige muß man ergreifen und üben, aber im stillen . . .*]" (328/325). It is inevitable that the plastic anatomist as aesthetic educator come to resemble Burke and Hare: *Handwerk* is the excess of law which the law in part recuperates as guilt, secrecy, and the symbol.[38]

I V

Wilhelm's lurid and complex narrative, the story of aesthetic pragmatism, brings together the various threads we have followed through *Wilhelm Meisters Wanderjahre*—and, indeed, through the *Lehrjahre*, for it is here that we would need to locate the "reckoning with Mignon" that Eric Blackall shrewdly judges necessary "if Wilhelm was to find a firm place in society" (*Goethe and the Novel*, 248).[39] In chapter 3 we traced a repressed narrative of dismemberment at work in Mignon's epileptic body, and read this narrative as an allegory for textual production; in the surgeon's schoolroom this story reemerges—for if the tale of *Bildung* reveals itself to be the story of an endless repetition, the event of this story is itself a repetition. Logically enough, Wilhelm remarks at the outset of his account of his surgical education that he actually isn't learning anything: "In a curious way that

38. Goethe's interest in "plastic anatomy" was no doubt exacerbated, as he himself suggests in his essay, by the Burke and Hare case and the publicity and the imitative crimes it generated, but his interest in the medical utility of sculpture goes back to his earliest studies of anatomy in 1781, as Trunz remarks in his notes to the *Wanderjahre* chapter (HA, 8:646–47). Goethe's biographer, Nicholas Boyle, has drawn my attention to a reference to a "wooden surrogate" that appears in Goethe's diary for 1807 in the context of the early plans for the *Wanderjahre*, which would lend additional specificity to Trunz's claim that the chapter dramatizes long-standing concerns. There is also an undated schema for this chapter in the Weimar Edition apparatus (WA, 1:25.2, 255–60) which covers the essentials of the chapter's arguments for the necessity of plastic anatomy, but does not mention Burke and Hare. Dr. Boyle confirms that it is difficult to know whether the case influenced the composition of this chapter. Burke was executed on the 28th of January, 1829, and Goethe might easily have heard of the case through the French newspapers while he was writing or revising chapter 3, since book 3 of the *Wanderjahre* was largely composed between September 1828 and the end of February, 1829, and its first two-thirds were revised in January. "It is therefore possible that knowledge of the trial of Burke and Hare had some influence on the formulation of chapter 3, specifically on the reference near the end of the chapter to 'newspaper articles' about 'resurrection men,'" Dr. Boyle comments; however, "It strikes me as unlikely that the Burke and Hare affair was the sole inspiration for the idea of wax substitutes for cadavers," for the reasons given above (letter of 27 March, 1994). 39. Blackall's claim refers to an episode in which Wilhelm visits Mignon's homeland in the seventh chapter of book 2 of the *Wanderjahre*.

no one would guess, I had already come a long way in my knowledge of the human form during my theatrical career." On and behind the stage he has learned about the body's "outer parts," and for some unexplained reason has also even gained "a certain presentiment [*Vorgefühl*]" of the "inner parts" (323/322). Renunciation never quite works in the Meister cycle, and the *theatrum anatomicum* thus provides yet another version of the career that Wilhelm had had to give up in the *Lehrjahre*. The wooden bones and wax muscles with which the *Bildhauer* seeks to aestheticize dissection similarly recall the puppets that preside over the defaced origins of Wilhelm's *Bildung*, and form Mignon's deformed body.[40]

The recuperation of dissection's excess can be only partial and temporary for reasons we have elaborated: if both *Kunst* and *Handwerk* exploit, conceal, and suffer the effects of a referentially unreliable referential force, the homeopathic cure of the one through the other is doomed to fail. Plastic anatomy cannot halt the return of dissection: thus, as the *Bildhauer* explains to Wilhelm, the *Bund*'s New World colony will also be a state geared toward the production of corpses. Criminals will once again provide the raw material:

> "'So that no one will think,' said the master, 'that we are shutting ourselves off from nature and wish to disown her, we shall open a fresh prospect. Across the sea where certain humane views [*menschenwürdige Gesinnungen*] are steadily gaining strength, the abolition of the death penalty has made it necessary to build extensive citadels, walled-in precincts, to protect peaceable citizens against crime, and prevent crime from reigning and raging with impunity. There, my friend, in those sad precincts, let us build a chapel for Aesculapius; there, as sequestered as the punishment itself, let our knowledge be continually refreshed from such objects, whose dismemberment [*Zerstückelung*] will not wound our humane feelings [*menschliches Gefühl*], and whose sight will not, as happened to you with that lovely innocent arm, make the knife falter in our hand and extinguish all desire for knowledge in the face of humane feeling [*Gefühl der Menschlichkeit*].'" (330/327)

40. In Goethe's earliest version of the *Lehrjahre, Wilhelm Meisters theatralische Sendung,* a *Bildhauer* carves the "hands, feet, and faces" of puppets otherwise constructed (in this version) by Wilhelm's grandmother (HA, 8:489). The fetishistic role played by the dismembered female arm in Wilhelm's story in the *Wanderjahre* suggests the continuing pressure of gender as a code helping to structure these scenarios of potential structurelessness. The dismembered woman functions here as what Neil Hertz would call an "end of the line" figure, a lurid trope that serves to call a halt to potentially uncontrollable textual processes: see Neil Hertz, *The End of the Line: Essays in Psychoanalysis and the Sublime* (New York: Columbia University Press, 1985). The apotropaic violence of this figure is even more remarkable in Goethe's essay on "Plastic Anatomy," in which the limit of the tolerable is rendered as the anatomical rending of "fallen girls into a thousand pieces" (67).

Whether this carceral humanism represents an ethical advance over the *ancien régime's* Gothic cruelty is perhaps uncertain; nor does the *Wanderjahre's* ironic treatment of its "utopias" encourage easy answers. A political critique nonetheless emerges from the rhetorical critique to the extent that this latter uncovers and dissects the story of the aestheticization of the political. As the state becomes more absolute in its claim to mimic and complete nature's harmony, to absorb into its *technē* the self-sufficiency of *physis*, its violence must take unacknowledged and thus always potentially more violent form. The state's laws no longer deal death; yet since these laws nonetheless have inscriptive, dissective force, the objects of legal violence must be all the more obsessively effaced. Incarceration, like plastic anatomy, seeks to draw a frame around the uncontrollable proliferation of dissection; in no case can dissection be halted, but one can hope for various practical if always uncertain effects. Here, for instance, the state can hope that neither the *Volk* nor the occasional anatomist will rise to protest the obliteration of *Persönlichkeit*, since the objects of violence have been violently denied membership in the category of the "human" which imprisons and dissects them. They cannot die because they are not properly alive (that is, human) to begin with. The text has revealed this deathlessness to be a general predicament, that of language itself; but in the *Bildhauer's* brave new world this endless dying will be repressed and its recurrence quarantined.

It is thus as a rhetorical allegory that *Wilhelm Meisters Wanderjahre* offers a critique of the Aesthetic State. Though violence, and the violent effacement of violence, are certainly in no way specific to aesthetic humanism, the residue of a humanist universe takes deformed form as the *in-* or *non-*human, the human that is not human: more animal than human, but more inanimate than animal, since even animals are potentially alive and possibly even able to die. The criminals in the *Bildhauer's* fantasy are the defaced repetition of the anatomical models, which is to say, in the figurative vocabulary of the Meister cycle, that they are puppets, repeating humanism's repressed instability in the mode of inhumanity.[41] They are still being treated as useful pedagogical objects, rather than simply being "treated," like vermin or waste products, for this Aesthetic State is not yet an extermination camp. Yet without hyperbole, anachronism, or any notion of a German "destiny," one can and must read the operation of a certain exterminating logic in this narrative, a logic that the *Wanderjahre* critiques, or, in the figurative vocabulary of this text, dissects. The rationalist and utilitarian consumption of the in-human is a false ingestion, since these criminals are the excess of the very pragmatism that exploits them. In its extremity the

41. For an analysis of the figure of the puppet in *Wilhelm Meisters Lehrjahre*, see chapter 3.

Aesthetic State can only turn to more and more savagely displaced repetitions of its own disarticulation, and at the limit of its destructive course will need to obliterate its non-humans with the formal, mechanical violence of a purposeless, bureaucratic, technological operation—carried out "in secret," in "walled-in precincts." It should be emphasized that the ominousness of such tropes is in one sense profoundly false. The unspeakable of the Holocaust does not speak in this text; nor does the *Wanderjahre* "predict" Nazism. It is rather in destroying such aesthetic models of history as revelation and destination that this text offers a certain insight into the political aestheticism that Philippe Lacoue-Labarthe, at least, is willing to call the "real, or profound, nature of Nazism" (*Heidegger*, 53): an aestheticism that is always also a "humanism" to the extent that the "human" represents the Subject's self-productive incarnation.[42]

Lacoue-Labarthe achieves his reading of the Nazis' technical, bureaucratic program of extermination as "the useless residue of the Western idea of art, that is to say, of *technē*" (46) through a reading of Heidegger; and we can close our present attempt to think the politics of aesthetics by returning to the question of technology as Heidegger asks it, and as the *Wanderjahre* allows it to be read. Heidegger's well-known, though by no means unambiguous, distinction between *poiesis* and "modern technics" as different forms of revealing (*Entbergen, aletheia*) opposes the "bringing-forth" of *poiesis* (which occurs as nature, *physis*, which "is *poiesis* in the highest sense," or in less perfect form as *technē*, which requires for its bringing-forth the supplement of the craftsman [10]) to the "challenging" revealing of modern technology, which "puts to nature the unreasonable demand that it supply energy that can be extracted and stored as such" (14). The violence inherent in modern technology's mode of revealing lies not simply in its aggressive procedures of extraction, but in the fact that it extracts so as to store or stockpile: every technological action or object is for the sake of something else. Consequently there is no *object* in the technological universe, but only "standing-reserve," *Bestand*. Similarly there is no "subject" of technology; however, since technology conceals its own essence by concealing "revealing," *aletheia*, itself, humanity is led to imagine itself a subject in control of technology. Technology thus presents itself as metaphysics—

42. Because Nazism is a "humanism" in this sense, its violence takes place as a dehumanization, which is why the figure of the puppet occasionally appears in the rhetoric of extermination. Claude Lanzmann's *Shoah* records that the extermination camp guards at Chelmno forced the Jews to refer to corpses as *Dreck* ("filth") or *Figuren*, which can mean "puppets" as well as "shapes" or "figures of speech." And Hannah Arendt, speaking both of and against such dehumanization, writes at one point of the victims of the death camps as "ghastly marionettes with human faces" (*The Origins of Totalitarianism*, new ed. [New York: Harcourt, Brace, 1966], 455). For a discussion of this moment in Lanzmann's film, see Shoshana Felman, "The Return of the Voice: Claude Lanzmann's *Shoah*," in Shoshana Felman and Dori Laub, *Testimony: Crises of Witnessing in Literature, Psychoanalysis, and History* (London: Routledge, 1992), 204–83.

the metaphysics of the subject—at the same time that it threatens to transform everything, not excluding humanity, into "standing-reserve."

Heidegger calls the "challenging claim" that gathers man to modern technology *Ge-stell*, an untranslatable word conventionally rendered as "En-framing" in English, and which Heidegger proffers with a curious assertion of tresspass. "We dare to use this word in a sense that has been thoroughly unfamiliar up to now":

> According to ordinary usage, the word *Gestell* [frame] means some kind of apparatus, e.g., a bookrack [*Büchergestell*]. *Gestell* is also the name for a skeleton [*Knochengerippe*]. And the employment of the word *Ge-stell* [En-framing] that is now required of us seems equally eerie, not to speak of the arbitrariness with which words of a mature language are thus misused. Can anything be more strange? Surely not. Yet this strangeness is an old usage of thinking. (Heidegger, "The Question concerning Technology," 20)

Indeed, "compared with the demands that Plato makes on language and thought" in transforming the word for a thing's outward aspect, *eidos*, into a word for the thing's nonphenomenal essence, "the use of the word *Gestell* as the name for the essence of modern technology, which we now venture here, is almost harmless [*beinahe harmlos*]" (20). Heidegger says no more in this vein; but if his "unfamiliar," "eerie," "arbitrary," though also "required" "employment" or setting-to-work of the word "*Gestell*" is "almost harmless," which is also of course to assert that it might be nonetheless ever so slightly harmful, this is perhaps because what Heidegger has named as the essence of modern technology bears a resemblance to language as a general rhetoric. Language, in the Aristotelian tradition that Heidegger recalls and rewrites here, is *technē* in the highest sense—the essence of the human, and the completion of nature as *physis*—but the thought of *poiesis* cannot exhaust the problem of language, as *Wilhelm Meisters Wanderjahre* has confirmed. The violent slippage with which, according to Heidegger, "language and thought" occur, bears a greater resemblance to *Gestell* than to *poiesis*. *Wilhelm Meisters Wanderjahre* would lend support to Samuel Weber's claim that, contrary to what Heidegger most often or most obviously appears to be saying, "the unsettling effects of technics cannot be considered to be an exclusive aspect of its peculiarly modern form. Rather, the danger associated with *modern* technics is—as Heidegger explicitly asserts—a conseqence of the goings-on of technics as such and in general as a movement of unsecuring."[43] At the origin there is displacement and a

---

43. Samuel Weber, "Upsetting the Set Up: Remarks on Heidegger's Questing after Technics," *MLN* 104.5 (1989): 985. "Goings-on" is Weber's translation of *Wesen*, which is conventionally rendered "essence." Weber's essay employs many such carefully imaginative translations in

certain, violent "challenging," a *Ge-stell* which generates metaphysics yet remains the skeleton in its closet, a specter haunting the figure of the *eidos* and even that of *Gestell* itself, much as the force that Goethe called the "demonic" produces and haunts the image that disavows it.

In elaborating *Ge-stell* as an endless, mechanical dissection, *Wilhelm Meisters Wanderjahre* confirms the rhetorical character of Heidegger's insight. Dissection is a killing machine that is equally an animating machine, precisely because it can never finish killing what it kills.[44] It thereby figures an uncontrollable process of figuration that dismembers yet also produces the symbol's divine corpse, exceeding and ruining the instances of reference it enables. Dissection, in this allegory, is *Bildung* as the construction and deconstruction of the *Glieder* which make bodies possible, including textual and political bodies. Commenting on its own irreducibility to the symbolic totalities it encourages, *Wilhelm Meisters Wanderjahre* diagnoses the violence of the Aesthetic State as the effect of a technicity that proves all the more haunting when violence itself is aestheticized as pragmatism. And in consequence, the possibility of cultural critique becomes paradoxically inseparable from that of the rigorously technical linguistic performances we call literature.

---

order to convey the complexity and strangeness of Heidegger's writing on technology. Many elements in Heidegger's work, to be sure, move in the opposite direction: apart from the importance of *Handwerk* as a figure for thought in his texts, one might mention here the closing invocation in "The Question concerning Technology" of "the poetical" as a *technē*, which is to say a *poiesis*, offering "saving power" in the face of technology, by virtue of being "on the one hand akin to the essence of technology and, on the other, fundamentally different from it" (35)
44. Appropriately, in German, medical anatomical models are called "medizinische Phantome."

Postscript:
The Trouble with Schiller

I treat bones as a text, on which all life and all that is human can be said to
depend.

—Goethe to Lavater, 14 November 1781

When I find a scattered skeleton, I can gather it [*zusammenlesen*] and put it
together; for here eternal reason speaks through an analogue, even if the
skeleton be a giant sloth.

—Goethe, "Reflections in the Spirit of the Wanderers,"
Wilhelm Meisters Wanderjahre (307 / 311)

We have had occasion to note that it is a matter of some dispute
where *Wilhelm Meisters Wanderjahre* ends. After Wilhelm's resurrection of
Felix, which Eric Blackall understandably calls the "real ending of the
novel" (*Goethe and the Novel*, 259), there follow, if one's edition follows the
Ausgabe letzter Hand—the edition of Goethe's works that received the author's final corrections—a collection of maxims and a poem. The rationale
for their inclusion is a matter of anecdote and inference. According to
Eckermann, Goethe added the maxims because the second and third books
of the *Wanderjahre* were too short: he gave Eckermann "two large bundles
of manuscript" and instructed him to use them to "fill the gaps of the
'Wanderjahre,'" adding that "strictly speaking this material has nothing to
do with [the novel], but it can be justified by the fact that mention is made of
an archive at Makarie's place, in which such pieces [*Einzelheiten*] are to be
found."[1] At the same time, according to this account, Goethe decided to use
this opportunity to publish two poems he had written a few years earlier.
Eckermann, therefore, divided the maxims into two groups, entitled one
"Reflections in the Spirit of the Wanderers" and the other "Out of Makarie's
Archive," and appended them to the second and third books of the text
respectively, with a poem attached to the end of each collection of aphor-

1. Johann Peter Eckermann, *Gespräche mit Goethe in den letzten Jahren seines Lebens* (Munich:
C. H. Beck, 1984), 431–32 (15 May 1831).

isms.[2] The poem appended to the third book, and thus to the very end of the sequence of texts that the *Ausgabe letzter Hand* assembles as *Wilhelm Meisters Wanderjahre*, was never given an official title. Goethe referred to it in his journal only as "Terzinen" ("Terza rimas"), and once in a letter as "Schillers Reliquen."

Schiller had been buried in the cemetery of the Jakobskirche in Weimar, in the so-called *Kassengewölbe*: a common grave for citizens of distinction who did not own their own burial plots. In 1826, two decades after the poet's death, the cemetery was slated for destruction, and the Burgermeister, Carl Lebrecht Schwabe, undertook to rescue Schiller's remains. Schwabe collected twenty-three skulls, and was struck by the "noble, regular form" of one in particular;[3] he compared it to Schiller's death mask, consulted three Weimar doctors, and sought corroboration from everyone in the area who had known Schiller: opinion was unanimous that he had found the right skull. The jawbone was missing; it too was identified; and two anatomical experts from Jena subsequently pieced together the bones of Schiller's skeleton, listing the recovered and the missing bones in an official burial report. The skull spent a little while enshrined in the base of a bust of the poet in the ducal library at Weimar and was then kept by Goethe at his home; a year later, it and the other remains were "arranged in the shape of a skeleton" in a sarcophagus, and laid to rest in the Royal Crypt.[4]

2. Eckermann goes on to report that Goethe instructed him to put the supplemental material "where it belonged" in subsequent editions of his work, so that "without the maxims and the two poems, the *Wanderjahre* could be reduced to two books, as was originally the intention" (*Gespräche mit Goethe*, 432). Eckermann's account has been called into question; furthermore, early plans for the *Wanderjahre* include mention of some sort of collection of maxims: see Max Wundt, *Goethes Wilhelm Meister* (Berlin: Goschen, 1913), 493ff. Thus some scholarly editions of the *Wanderjahre*, such as the Hamburger Ausgabe, include the maxims but omit the poems.

3. Cited in Karl Viëtor, "Goethes Gedicht auf Schillers Schädel," *PMLA* 59 (1944): 142. The details of Schiller's exhumation and reburial being recounted here are taken from Viëtor's erudite study.

4. Whether this reconstruction was actually composed of Schiller's bones was a matter of so much subsequent dispute that in the early twentieth century a second skeleton, chosen through more scientific procedures, was installed in the crypt. For a full account, see Viëtor, "Goethes Gedicht" 146 n. 6, and Max Hecker, *Schillers Tod und Bestattung* (Leipzig: Insel Verlag, 1935). Hecker's book is also responding to an anti-Semitic pamphlet circulated in 1928 by Mathilde von Ludendorff—wife of the general, and the animating spirit of a far-right circle. The pamphlet, "Der ungesühnte Frevel" ("The unatoned crime"), ascribed Schiller's death—and Luther's, Lessing's, and Mozart's—to the machinations of "a combination of Jews, Jesuits, and Freemasons," and explained that Schiller had been secretly buried in a "mass grave" in order to avoid an autopsy. The pamphlet drew numerous responses apart from Hecker's: that of the physician Wolfgang Veil, "Schillers Krankheit" (1936), is now available in reprint, with an extract from von Ludendorff's pamphlet, in Rudolf A. Kühn, ed., *Schillers Tod* (Jena: Universitätsverlag Jena, 1992). In the wake of this pamphlet exchange, Goebbels banned all further discussion of Schiller's death and had the offending texts confiscated—including Mathilde von

Goethe's attitude toward these archeological-funerary endeavors displays an ambivalence similar to that dramatized in the stories of burial and disinterral which punctuate the *Wilhelm Meister* novels. He delegated his son to take his place at the ceremonials, and in various ways let it be known that he would have preferred to have had Schiller's remains reinterred without public display—as though the sleep of the dead were one of those secrets "best not disturbed," as the jeweler in the *Wanderjahre* says of the mysterious *Kästchen* (458/416). But skulls and skeletons form part of the plot of Goethe's destiny: this famous osteologue, the discoverer of the human intermaxillary bone, who had "treat[ed] bones as a text, on which all life and all that is human can be said to depend,"[5] was not able to remain entirely aloof from the project of recuperating Schiller: though he distanced himself from the public consecration of the remains, he attached enough importance to the skull to keep it in his study for a few months; and though he kept it in great privacy,[6] at some point during this period he wrote a poem that, as noted above, for no clear reason he included for publication with *Wilhelm Meisters Wanderjahre*. The poem, one of Goethe's rare experiments in terza rima, reenacts the gestures of quest, violation, and consecration that its author had shunned, as a first-person narrator repeats Burgermeister Schwabe's epiphany:

> Im ernsten Beinhaus wars, wo ich beschaute,
> Wie Schädel Schädeln angeordnet paßten;
> Die alte Zeit gedacht ich, die ergraute.
>
> Sie stehn in Reih geklemmt, die sonst sich haßten,
> Und derbe Knochen, die sich tödlich schlugen,
> Sie liegen kreuzweis, zahm allhier zu rasten.
>
> Entrenkte Schulterblätter! was sie trugen,
> Fragt niemand mehr, und zierlich tätge Glieder,
> Die Hand, der Fuß, zerstreut aus Lebensfugen.

Ludendorff's, which had always been something of an embarrassment because it had fingered Goethe, another national hero, as an acccessory to Schiller's murder. Georg Ruppelt has a useful account of the Ludendorff affair in his fascinating study, *Schiller im nationalsozialistischen Deutschland* (Stuttgart: J. B. Metzlersche Verlag, 1979), 20–23.

5. WA, 4:5, 217 (to Lavater, 14 November 1781); cited in Viëtor, "Goethes Gedicht," 157.

6. Wilhelm von Humboldt claimed to have been the only visitor allowed to see it, and also noted that Goethe asked him not to narrate the experience: "[E]r hat mich sehr gebeten, es hier nicht zu erzählen." Wilhelm to Caroline von Humboldt, 29 December 1826; cited in Viëtor, "Goethes Gedicht," 145.

Ihr Müden also lagt vergebens nieder,
Nicht Ruh im Grabe ließ man euch, vertrieben
Seid ihr herauf zum lichten Tage wieder,

Und niemand kann die dürre Schale lieben,
Welch herrlich edlen Kern sie auch bewahrte.
Doch mir Adepten war die Schrift geschrieben,

Die heiligen Sinn nicht jedem offenbarte,
Als ich inmitten solcher starren Menge
Unschätzbar herrlich ein Gebild gewahrte,

Daß in des Raumes Moderkält und Enge
Ich frei und wärmefühlend mich erquickte,
Als ob ein Lebensquell dem Tod entspränge.

Wie mich geheimnisvoll die Form entzückte!
Die gottgedachte Spur, die sich erhalten!
Ein Blick, der mich an jenes Meer entrückte,

Das flutend strömt gesteigerte Gestalten.
Geheim Gefäß! Orakelsprüche spendend,
Wie bin ich wert, dich in der Hand zu halten?

Dich höchsten Schatz aus Moder fromm entwendend
Und in die freie Luft, zu freiem Sinnen,
Zum Sonnenlicht andächtig hin mich wendend.

Was kann der Mensch im Leben mehr gewinnen,
Als daß sich Gott-Natur ihm offenbare?
Wie sie das Feste läßt zu Geist verrinnen
Wie sie das Geisterzeugte fest bewahre.[7]

It was in the solemn bonehouse, where I beheld
How skull arranged matched skull:
I thought of bygone time, turned gray.

Wedged in rows they stand, who each once hated each,
And sturdy bones, which fought in deadly struggle,
Lie crosswise, all tamely resting here.

7. Quoted from *Wilhelm Meisters Wanderjahre*, ed. Gerhard Küntzel, AA, 8:520–21. The pain-
fully literal translation that follows is mine.

Unjointed shoulder blades! what they bore
None now will ask, and delicate, active limbs,
Hand, foot, scattered out of life's joint.

You weary ones lay vainly down,
They leave you no peace in the grave: driven
You'll be, up to the light of day.

And no one can love these dry shells
That once a glorious, noble kernel held.
But for me, initiate, was the writing written,

The holy meaning not to all revealed,
As amid such a rigid crowd I saw
Inestimably glorious, a shape,

Such that in the chamber's moldy cold and cramp
I felt free and warmed, refreshed,
As though a life-spring sprang from death.

How this form, mysterious, delighted me!
The god-thought trace, which yet survived!
A glance, which took me to that sea,

Which, flooding, streams forth heightened shapes.
Mysterious vessel! Giving oracles,
How am I worthy to hold you in my hand?

Highest treasure, piously from mold purloining you
And into free air, to free sense,
To sunlight reverently making my way.

What more can man gain in life,
Than that God-Nature reveal herself to him?
How what is firm she has melt into spirit,
How what spirit creates she firmly preserves.

On the rare occasions when this poem has been read, it has been interpreted as a "natural philosophy poem," a celebration of the "mysteries of
nature's organization," in Karl Viëtor's phrase ("Goethes Gedicht," 173):
mysteries that, like the "idea" in the Goethean symbol, would remain
"effective and unreachable in the image." But the decent obscurity of an
encrypted body or meaning is precisely what the poem's narrator violates

in order to affirm, which is doubtless one reason why the symbolic interpretation has failed to elicit much satisfaction even in the critics who advance it.[8] We thus have an opportunity to advertise the utility of rhetorical reading: in the wake of our examination of the *Wilhem Meister* novels, the appearance of this poem was almost foreseeable. The *Meister* texts have figured their critique of Schillerian aesthetic ideology as a ceaseless disarticulation of the body's frame: from the stories of Wilhelm's puppets and of Mignon's epileptic body and, finally, her fictional corpse in the *Lehrjahre*, to the dismemberment staged by vocational *Bildung* in the *Wanderjahre*, the body as figure—as non-natural, non-organic, disarticulable aggregate—has provided an allegory of the radical incoherence of textual production. The terms of this allegory are certainly not without relation to Goethe's rich and lifelong interest in natural philosophy: these stories of dismemberment emerge precisely because the body—and particularly the body's frame, the skeleton—presents itself so forcefully in this oeuvre as "a text on which all life and all that is human can be said to depend." Over and over Goethe's literary texts have asked what it means for "life" and "humanity" to depend on a text, a bone-text that must be read (*lesen*) as a gathering (*zusammenlesen*) that depends not on nature but on the possibility, always uncertain, that rhetorical figures are animated by a logos: "When I find a scattered skeleton, I can gather it [*zusammenlesen*] and put it together; for here eternal reason speaks through an analogue [*Analogon*], even if the skeleton be a giant sloth" (307/311).[9] The allegories of reading that masquerade as Wilhelm Meister's *Bildungsromane* have told the story of reading as a gathering that scatters, a framing that disarticulates the meaning it ceaselessly disinters.

The poem is both a symptom and another text, another piece of this textual boneyard; as it distends the frame of the *Wanderjahre* it rehearses Mignon's story of dispersal and gathering once again. If one listens to Goethe's only known remarks about terza rima, communicated in a letter sent thirty years earlier to the then-living Schiller, the poem registers the pressure of deformation even in its form: terza rima, Goethe had written, "has no restfulness, and because of the continuous measures [*fortschrittenden Räume*] one can't close anywhere" (WA, 4:13, 71–72).[10] The poem, to

---

8. See Viëtor, "Goethes Gedicht," 173, and Blackall, *Goethe and the Novel*, 261.

9. Viëtor mentions in this connection Goethe's late poem "Typus," in which the skeleton figures the type, the ideal norm informing material form: "Es ist nichts in der Haut, / Was nicht im Knochen ist" (AA, 1:539; cited in Viëtor, "Goethes Gedicht," 163). The skeleton thus appears here as the equivalent of Schiller's "pure ideal man" in the *Aesthetic Education*: as a kernel of destiny or *Bildung*. The empty husks and scattered bones that we have encountered in Goethe's texts, however, would suggest that the trope of the skeleton be read with some caution even in idealizing contexts.

10. The terza rima form appears rarely in the German poetic tradition, and, as noted above,

be sure, finishes in conventional fashion with an extra line sealing off the stanza, and for that matter reinforces its closure with an aphorism structured as a chiasmus, as the text's language mirrors the exchange of properties that "Gott-Natur" dictates ("Wie sie das *Feste* läßt zu *Geist* verrinnen / Wie sie das *Geist*erzeugte *fest* bewahre").[11] But the conclusiveness of this conclusion is undermined by the uncertain rhetorical status of the question that frames it. The question, "Was kann der Mensch im Leben mehr gewinnen, / Als daß sich Gott-Natur ihm offenbare?" may be taken as literal or "rhetorical": it obtains a note of urgency as soon as one suspects the untrustworthiness of the poem's "I," a suspicion that then triggers an endless interpretative spiral, since the sincere urgency or literalness of the speaker's question is being generated by the difficulty of deciding whether or not to take this speaker seriously. For the speaker is an enthusiast, a *Schwärmer*, whose hunger for spiritual election forces a suspiciously abrupt revelation at the end of the fifth stanza: a revelation offered as a fact rather than a question, but as such a self-flattering fact that it becomes a questionable one: "Doch mir Adepten war die Schrift geschrieben, / Die heiligen Sinn nicht jedem offenbarte." As signaled by the reiterated verb, "offenbaren," Gott-Natur has implicitly revealed herself in the divine script that underwrites the identification of the skull, but in doing so has turned both herself and the "I" into a question.

Thus alerted, one might begin to find other things odd about the poem's miniature *Bildungsroman*: the fact, for instance, that the narrative begins not with a katabasis or descent but in the grave; or that, despite the overeager tone of the revelation in stanzas five and following, the "I" fades into gerunds and reflexives as it wends its way toward the solar universe of meaning ("zu freiem Sinnen, / Zum Sonnenlicht andächtig hin mich wendend"). There is a curiously ghostly quality to this narcissistic narrator; and if he begins his narrative among the dead rather than "nel mezzo del camin di nostra vita," this is because his "life" in fact depends on the revelation in stanzas five and six, at which point, at the sight of a shape [*Gebild*], the narrator "frei und wärmefühlend mich erquickte, / Als ob ein Lebensquell

---

Goethe's oeuvre in this respect affords no exception. Apart from the poem under consideration, there are translations from Dante, and, significantly, Faust's monologue in the opening scene of *Faust* II, in which Faust awakes from death-like sleep into a new life of striving, oriented toward and deflected from the blinding light of the sun: "Sie tritt hervor!—und leider schon geblendet, / Kehr' ich mich weg, vom Augenschmerz durchdrungen [. . .] Am farbigen Abglanz haben wir das Leben" (HA, 3:148–49). It is possible that "Im ernsten Beinhaus" and Faust's monologue were written around the same time as the translations from the *Inferno*, which Goethe attempted after an intensive reading of Dante in August and September of 1826. (Schiller's skull entered Goethe's possession at the end of that September.) See Trunz, HA, 3:584, and Viëtor, "Goethes Gedicht," 178–83.
11. See Franz H. Mautner, "'Ist fortzusetzen': Zu Goethes Gedicht auf Schillers Schädel," *PMLA* 59 (1944): 1156–62.

dem Tod entspränge." This life-giving revelation is identified, taut-
ologically, as an act of reading: "mir . . . war die Schrift geschrieben." The
enthusiastic narrator is thus as much a reading-effect as is the "heiligen
Sinn," "Form," or "gottgedachte Spur" that he discovers and bears forth. If
he is a suspiciously hyperbolic narrator, this is because rhetoric has animated him. The story of this possibility is that of the impossible encounter
of a minimal subject, an "I" who is in a certain sense neither alive nor dead,
with equally indeterminate objects. For what the "I" beholds in the poem's
opening lines is not precisely bones per se, but a grammar of bones:
". . . ich beschaute, / Wie Schädel Schädeln angeordnet paßten." The "I"
here transforms into a perception the unperceivable differences that make
language possible, summarized here in the untranslatable "passen" of skull
with skull:[12] the difference to be "seen" is the minimal mark of the dative,
the "n" that differentiates "Schädel" from "Schädeln," organizing a potential stutter into a grammatical structure.

Like the tangled pile of puppets at the beginning of the Lehrjahre, these
skulls and bones figure the material support of language as a system of
differences: they figure, in other words, the uncertainty that makes possible
all systems of articulation. This uncertainty is what the system at once
effaces and reiterates as it comes into being as a system, as the "I" apostro-
phizes the bones, granting meaning to fragments, joints, and body parts,
transforming the nonphenomenality of difference, the metonymy of skull-
on-skull, into the "gray time" of metaphor, in which skulls can function as
containers of lost meaning ("dürre Schale . . . / Welch herrlich edlen Kern
sie auch bewahrte"), a loss that can then be reversed into a plenitude. The
"I," however, is a product of this rhetorical process of animation rather than
its source; its apostrophes—and its climactic discovery and appropriation
of the "heiligen Sinn"—repeat an impersonal predicament: "They leave
you no peace in the grave: driven / You'll be, up to the light of day." The
motion upward toward meaning is endless, ungrounded, indifferent to the
subjects and meanings it generates, dependent only on the random order of
bones. "Lying crosswise," the bones are the skeleton truth of the poem's
closing, idealizing chiasmus; they are the condition for skeletons, but are
not skeletons; they are the frame, the Gestell, that makes the organic body
possible, but, "scattered out of life's joint," they reveal the dependence of
life, or meaning, on joints and articulations that are themselves meaning-
less, without pathos or interiority, alien to love ("Und niemand kann die
dürre Schale lieben"), to memory ("was sie trugen, / Fragt niemand

---

12. In modern German,"passen" used intransitively means "to fit," but Viëtor comments that
in eighteenth-century usage the word carried a temporal as well as a spatial meaning: the
narrator would thus be seeing "how skull awaits skull" ("Goethes Gedicht," 148 n. 7).

mehr"), and to the dialectical struggle of life and death ("die sich tödlich schlugen").

Such a material condition or "frame" should not, however, be mistaken for a foundation. The bones in this sense will always fail to form a true skeleton; they rather represent the very condition of being *zerstreut*, scattered or distracted, turned elsewhere, "driven / . . . up to the light of day." Thus, in the *Wanderjahre*—if we are still "in" it; if there is such a thing as a "text" we can delimit, name, and inhabit, which is precisely what is at stake, and which is no longer at all certain—there can be no rest for the dead. Like the title character in Hitchcock's macabre comedy "The Trouble with Harry," the dead must constantly be dug up so as to be reburied more legitimately. The bodies, whether Mignon's, Schiller's, or the anonymous cadavers of Wilhelm's story of surgical *Bildung*, cannot stay in their graves; and because the frame of the text of death, burial, and resurrection is an ongoing rupture, even the poem on Schiller's skull does not mark the end of *Wilhelm Meisters Wanderjahre*. Appended to the poem, in editions of the *Wanderjahre* that follow the format of the *Ausgabe letzter Hand*, is the phrase "Ist fortzusetzen" ("To be continued") in parentheses. Whether the phrase refers to the poem, to the novel, or to some other, less definite, textual articulation is impossible to ascertain.[13] As yet another scattered bone, another spur to meaning, another "sehr ernster Scherz" that resists being read, the phrase calls for interpretation and withdraws from comprehension, leaving us unable to decide whether its performative is a blessing or a curse. Nonetheless, the novel to which Goethe, perhaps arbitrarily, attached maxims, poems, and finally this dangling, fragmented phrase, narrates among other things the political violence attendant upon the nostalgic repression and aestheticization of such undecidability.

13. Since the phrase "Ist fortzusetzen" is set in the same typeface as the poem, most critics have tended to relate it to the poem; but since the poem's presence at the end of the novel also has to be explained, the question remains open. Blackall "find(s) no ready answer" (*Goethe and the Novel*, 261); Viëtor expresses uncertainty but suggests that the phrase refers not to the poem or the novel but to the "interpretation of the great world-mystery that becomes visible in the [poem's] closing formula" ("Goethes Gedicht," 183). For discussion see Viëtor, and the responses by Franz H. Mautner and Ernst Feise, and Viëtor's response to the responses, *PMLA* 59 (1944): 1156–72.

5

The Aesthetics of Sympathy: George Eliot's Telepathy Machine

> . . . for we all of us, grave or light, get our thoughts entangled in metaphors, and act fatally on the strength of them.
>
> —George Eliot, *Middlemarch*

The foregoing chapters have examined the rhetoric and politics of aesthetics from a vantage granting a narrower focus to our investigation than its conscience finally allows. Not that any other vantage presented itself; furthermore, the sequence of readings pursued up to this point has allowed for a satisfying degree of internal coherence. The problem of the *Bildungsroman*, which we established as an overdetermined locus of tension within literary studies, leads to the problem of reading *Wilhelm Meisters Lehrjahre*; and the linguistic, thematic, and historical proximities between this novel, on the one hand, and the theoretical writings of Kant, Schiller, Schlegel, and Hegel, on the other, allowed our reading of Goethe's text to engage and displace the discourse of aesthetics in ways visibly relevant to the conundrum of the *Bildungsroman*. The difficulty we then encounter springs from the peculiar nature of the object in question. Since the *Bildungsroman* is an aestheticized symptom of literature's uncertain manifestation of itself as criticism, it exists only as an exemplary instance of the ghostliness of aesthetics itself; and part of what we signal in these figures of ghosting and haunting is an ongoing process of framing that is also its own rupture. Aesthetics itself, as we saw in chapter 1, is a name for this paradox; and a critique of aesthetics is not only doomed to repeat the instability of its object, but furthermore obtains critical purchase only in and through this repetition. What this means in the case at hand is that our focus on the *Bildungsroman*'s exemplary text, *Wilhelm Meister*, is at once necessary, productive, and misleading to the extent that aesthetics thereby takes on the appearance of being a "German" problem. A specific constellation of problems may in all fairness be said to haunt both the culmination of the "metaphysics of the subject" in nineteenth-century German philosophy and the culmination of an aesthetic notion of politics in twentieth-century German fascist ideology. In terms of our more limited critical engagement here, the *Wanderjahre*'s deconstruction of pragmatized *Bildung* has particular force as a critique of the intensely aestheticized politics of the Nazi era. The very force of that critique, however, will at a certain point become profoundly misleading. As discussed in this book's opening chapter, aesthetic discourse inheres in the fabric of modern Western culture, which is in part why the notion of the *Bildungsroman* has proved so seductive and volatile.

Goethe's texts thus retain a legitimate exemplarity in this context while also needing to be abandoned at a certain point for other significant literary formulations of the possibility or impossibility of a *Bildungsroman*. Where one intervenes in such a complex, overdetermined, and phantasmatic history becomes a matter of strategy. The works of George Eliot provide us with a literary interrogation of aesthetics usefully distant and different from Goethe's, though still recognizably engaged with the Schillerian tradition that Matthew Arnold inherits and bequeaths to Anglo-American literary institutions.[1] It is a commonplace that Arnoldian humanism finds a close literary analogue in Eliot's novels; but it is equally a commonplace that Eliot anticipates Freud, whose earliest publications begin to appear only a decade after *Daniel Deronda* (1876): if her novels seek ethical and political ground in aesthetic pedagogy, they do so in a language of psychological and sociological nuance proper to their era of literary representation. Meanwhile, Eliot's thematization of the "sympathetic imagination" returns us to topics central to any study of aesthetic ideology. The link between pathos and poetics goes back, of course, to classical issues of mimesis, identification, and katharsis, but a more specific link emerges in post-Renaissance Europe with the development of a language of passion that, from Shaftesbury through Rousseau, Hume, Burke, and Kant, went into the making of the modern notion of "aesthetics" per se.

Sentimentalism, which here denotes not just the era of Sterne, Rousseau, and Klopstock, but also, more generally, a certain focus on and valorization of affect that remains a recognizable literary idiom until the First World

---

1. Eliot, of course, like Carlyle and Arnold, was immersed in German literature and culture, and is in fact the author of an essay titled "The Morality of Wilhelm Meister" (July 1855), in which she, like many critics before and since, registers unhappiness with the novel's flagrantly fictional ending: "Just as far from being really moral is the so-called moral *dénouement*, in which rewards and punishments are distributed according to those notions of justice on which the novel-writer would have recommended that the world should be governed if he had been consulted at the creation." *Essays of George Eliot*, ed. Thomas Pinney (London: Routledge and Kegan Paul, 1963), 145. Essays from this edition will be referred to by page number preceded by "Pinney."

War, may be distinguished from earlier discourses of the passions by its implicit or explicit claim to universality. As opposed to the melancholic, whom he may occasionally resemble, the man of feeling has a purposive structure bracing his sentiment: even on the occasions when he knows not why he is so sad, he knows, at least in theory, that he is in communication with essential humanity. The notion of aesthetic disinterestedness emerges in close relation with that of the universality of sentiment in the eighteenth century, and when Kant defines aesthetic judgment he does so by theorizing the formalization of affect itself: a judgment is "called aesthetic precisely because the basis determining it is not a concept but the feeling (of the inner sense) of that accordance in the play of the mental powers insofar as it can only be sensed."[2] Sentiment is pure communication, both between subjects and within the subject itself. It is the origin of language, and it is what remains when language fails. And thus sentiment is also, of course, senseless: a mute and irrational force of desire, at once effeminizing and a threat to official femininity, the stuff of Gothicism and romance, mob violence and revolution.

Furthermore, in becoming a dream of pure communication, sentiment not only vacillates between formal ideality and formless matter but becomes yet another figure for the linguistic processes it supposedly founds and transcends. On the one hand, sentiment registers as a somatic experience—and a certain equivocal valorization of the body traditionally marks sentimental discourse—but on the other hand, sentiment is never simply somatic. As an attitude of consciousness, it involves representation and identification: sentiment is sympathy. Irreducibly tied to the interplay of self and other, sentiment, as sympathy, is "always already an aesthetic experience," as David Marshall insists: one that can only "take place within the realm of fiction, mimesis, representation, and reproduction."[3] Despite its—usually explicit—hostility to poetics or rhetoric, the discourse of sentiment is necessarily also a discourse of tropes. Edmund Burke's definition of sympathy in the *Enquiry* may in this respect be taken as typical:

> For sympathy must be considered as a sort of substitution, by which we are put in the place of another man, and affected in many respects as he is affected. . . . It is by this principle chiefly that painting, and other affecting

2. Immanuel Kant, *Critique of Judgment*, trans. Werner S. Pluhar (Indianapolis: Hackett Publishing Co., 1987), 75 (sec. 15). Aesthetic affectivity, in other words, lies "not in a sensation of the object" but in subjectivity itself, which in turn guarantees taste as, precisely, a common *sense*. See Terry Eagleton, *The Ideology of the Aesthetic* (Oxford: Blackwell, 1990), 13–69, for a narrative of the origins of aesthetics that emphasizes the importance of sentimentalism.
3. David Marshall, *The Surprising Effects of Sympathy: Marivaux, Diderot, Rousseau, and Mary Shelley* (Chicago: University of Chicago Press, 1988), 21.

arts, transfuse their passions from one breast to another, and are often capable of grafting a delight on wretchedness, misery, and death itself.[4]

Pleasure is no longer the product of representation or mimesis per se, but of the occurrence of a "sympathy" structured *like* representation or, more precisely, like metaphor: "a sort of substitution, by which we are put in the place of another man." Even in this brief citation one recognizes some of the characteristic turns of sentimental writing: a Gothic idiom of rapture and displacement, complemented by figures at once organic and non-natural, as the arts "transfuse" passions and thus "graft" delight onto pain and death. By the very fact that it is a substitutive process, sympathy incorporates an unnatural, technical element into its naturalness, thereby ensuring that a certain violence will always qualify sympathy's occurrence. Sympathy seizes and dis-places: through an unnatural excess of naturalness—registered in the Burke passage as the supplemental activities of transfusion and grafting—sympathy destabilizes and threatens to destroy the subject it defines. Sentiment, a dramatic version of what Jacques Derrida has called the dream of self-presence as a "touching-touched," turns into the agent of the self's undoing, precisely because sentiment must always also be communication, even when reduced to the self-communion of subjectivity.[5]

Ethical and representational systems predicated on sympathy will consequently be precarious. Even before attending to their rhetorical complications, one encounters difficulties: sympathy's emphasis on empirical experience threatens to turn the self into an accumulation of accidents, while its reliance on representation and identification means that ethical judgment becomes flavored with voyeurism and sadomasochism, since sympathy requires for its existence the spectacle of an other's suffering. But the discourse of sympathy also possesses great resiliency and appeal; though sentimentalism per se is a recognizably historical phenomenon, the sentimental inheritance continues to manifest itself in the interstices of contem-

---

4. Edmund Burke, *A Philosophical Enquiry into the Origin of Our Ideas of the Sublime and the Beautiful*, ed. James T. Boulton (New York: Columbia University Press, 1958), 44.

5. Jacques Derrida, *Of Grammatology*, trans. Gayatri Spivak (Baltimore: Johns Hopkins University Press, 1976). In the British tradition, William Hazlitt's *Essay on the Principles of Human Action: Being an Argument in favour of the Natural Disinterestedness of the Human Mind* (1805) provides a particularly rich account of the paradoxes of sympathy. Individual identity, as Hazlitt sees it, for instance, depends on the self's proleptic identification with itself: "The imagination, by means of which alone I can anticipate future objects, or be interested in them, must carry me out of myself into the feelings of others by one and the same process by which I am thrown forward as it were into my future being, and interested in it." *The Complete Works of William Hazlitt*, ed. P. P. Howe (London: J. M. Dent, 1930), 1:1–2. I shall be examining versions of this paradox in Eliot's work.

porary culture and theory, most notably in what appears to be a persistent temptation to locate in the "body" a reservoir of affective meaning.[6] It is thus important to take this tradition seriously and follow, so far as possible, its unfolding. My reading of Goethe involved a brush with sentimental discourse in the orbit of Mignon—and it is certainly no accident that Mignon, the locus of sentimental investment, serves as the vehicle of semiotic stress. But it must also be said that the *Lehrjahre*'s disconcerting ironization of affect and denaturalization of the body takes place within a rather *ancien régime* blend of picaresque emplotment and sentimental tableaux. Despite the novel's baroque elaboration of oedipal structures, it has little of the Gothic chiaroscuro so prevalent in the English tradition from Richardson on. For any number of cultural, historical, and personal reasons—in this matter one clearly should not discount Goethe's post-*Werther* hostility to the sentimental tradition of Klopstock and the Jacobis—the *Lehrjahre* cannot really be said to be seeking to contribute to the construction of the richly psychologized "desiring subject" that the nineteenth-century realist novel was to be able to offer Freud.

George Eliot's work explores the strengths and instabilities of a sentimental aesthetic with a rigor and depth that owes much to a confluence of historical factors. The development of the life sciences allowed her to appeal to a complex organicism, while the resources of the high Gothic tradition provided her with the means to represent historical events or structures in psychological and protopsychoanalytic terms. In approaching these novels we enter what Eve Sedgwick has called the Victorian novel's "warm space of pathos and the personal," where the public dimensions of culture are translated into "the supposedly intrapsychic terms of desire and phobia," thereby composing the texture of the literary form that we rather misleadingly call realism.[7] At stake, however, in Eliot's text no less than in Goethe's, is the possibility of aesthetic history.

6. The Gothic and sentimental traditions not only continue to shape, mutatis mutandis, "popular" and mass-marketed culture but have also left their mark on more elite cultural activities. Eagleton's *The Ideology of the Aesthetic*, which begins with the claim that "aesthetics is born as a discourse of the body" (13) and closes with eudaemonic invocations of the body as the "natural" base for "creative self-making" (410), is deeply marked by the empiricist and sentimental tradition for all its putative Marxism, and its most successful chapters are those focused on British eighteenth-century material. One thinks too of Elaine Scarry's influential *The Body in Pain: The Making and Unmaking of the World* (New York: Oxford University Press, 1985). The body has also, given its various ideological charges, served as a locus for critical historicization and demystification: for a study that complements the concerns of the present chapter, see Mark Seltzer, *Bodies and Machines* (New York: Routledge, 1992) (see 101–3 and 205–6 n. 18, for a concise critique of Scarry). For a survey of current work on nineteenth-century discourses of the body, see the special issue of *Representations* 14 (1986), on "Sexuality and the Social Body in the Nineteenth Century," ed. Catherine Gallagher and Thomas Laqueur.

7. Eve Kosofsky Sedgwick, *Between Men: English Literature and Male Homosocial Desire* (New York: Columbia University Press, 1985), 67, 119. The much-disputed term "realism" has no particular privilege in the present discussion, but from the perspective of a critique of aesthet-

I

"The greatest benefit we owe to the artist, whether painter, poet, or novelist," Eliot wrote in "The Natural History of German Life," "is the extension of our sympathies" (Pinney, 170). The fiction she began writing in the wake of that assertion ceaselessly reflects on and reaffirms it; and by the time of her last, great novels, *Middlemarch* and *Daniel Deronda*, her aesthetic of sympathy had itself become exemplary of the extension it preached, drawing its metaphors to such telling effect from so many discourses that the gap between the domestic world of affective interchange and the public world of politics and history will often seem to have been at least provisionally overcome. The governing trope of the individual as psyche and organism is at once affirmed and subtly transcended, as in the famous passage in *Middlemarch* in which the text articulates the terms of Dorothea's sympathetic *Bildung:*

> We are all of us born in moral stupidity, taking the world as an udder to feed our supreme selves: Dorothea had early begun to emerge from that stupidity, but yet it had been easier to her to imagine how she would devote herself to Mr Casaubon, and become wise and strong in his strength and wisdom, than to conceive with that distinctness which is no longer reflection but feeling—an idea wrought back to the directness of sense, like the solidity of objects—that he had an equivalent centre of self, whence the lights and shadows must always fall with a certain difference.[8]

While the text emphasizes the self's privileged status throughout the educative process—a process leading from the stupidity of the "supreme self" of infantile narcissism to the recognition of difference as the other's "equivalent centre of self"—the trope of the udder suggests that even narcissism must nourish itself on otherness ("the world"). If *Middlemarch* has one overarching theme, it is the shaping of character, action, and destiny by environment. Dorothea, a Saint Theresa born too late, can accomplish only what the novel's final paragraph designates "unhistoric acts" (896): as a nineteenth-century woman she can find for herself "no epic life," being "helped by no coherent social faith and order which could perform the function of knowledge for the ardently willing soul" (25). Despite her inherent saintliness or heroism, she cannot help diverting her energies into a

---

ics, John Bender's definition of realism is suggestive: "a fine, observationally oriented, materially exhaustive grid of representation that accounts for behavior, in fact constructs it, in terms of sensory experience." John Bender, *Imagining the Penitentiary: Fiction and the Architecture of Mind in Eighteenth-Century England* (Chicago: University of Chicago Press, 1987), 11.
8. George Eliot, *Middlemarch: A Study of Provincial Life* (Harmondsworth: Penguin, 1965), 243. Subsequent references are to this edition.

romance plot, her range of motion being confined to the unhistoric act of marriage.

But though the novel emphasizes that historical constructions of gender (and genre) define the forms of being and doing open to Dorothea, the organic metaphors controlling *Middlemarch*'s official themes work to absorb her into a total historical process. Eliot's organicism has remained a potent influence in determining how her texts are read and taught thanks in large part to the subtlety with which her texts rework the classical figure of the text as body.[9] It is possible to argue, for instance, that in Eliot's novels, as in George Henry Lewes's *Problems of Life and Mind*, consciousness "is not an agent but a symptom," an element of the total "mind," which, according to Lewes, is the activity of the whole organism.[10] Actions and details lost to consciousness are grounded and stored in the body, or in the trope of the body: thus Bulstrode's ambiguous murder of Raffles emerges out of "misdeeds" that "were like the subtle muscular movements which are not taken account of in the consciousness, though they bring about the end that we fix our mind on and desire" (*Middlemarch*, 740). More dramatically and positively, Will seizes Dorothea's hand "with a spasmodic movement" under the external stimulus of a providential flash of lightning ("which lit each of them up for the other—and the light seemed to be the terror of a hopeless love" [868]); the body obeys a desire that consciousness evades or represses, or has not yet fully assimilated ("What she was least conscious of just then was her own body" [865]). Lewes's word "mind" is the appropriate term for the totality of this embodied self, since the body pursues ends dictated by an intention; however, thanks to its body, consciousness finds itself part of a larger entity capable of recording unperceived sensations, thinking "unconscious" thoughts, and acting out repressed truths or memories, as when Tito, in *Romola*, for instance, reacts involuntarily to the sight of his father, Baldassare, and thereby sets in motion the narrative sequence that will reveal and punish his own moral turpitude. The body is a reservoir of identity surpassing the conscious "self" while remaining controlled by

9. Interest in Eliot and science and bodies goes back to the publication of *Middlemarch*. One contemporary reviewer, Sidney Colvin, suggested a link between Eliot's "scientific consciousness" and her description of the bodies and bodily tics of characters; see David R. Carroll, ed., *George Eliot: The Critical Heritage* (London: Routledge, 1971), 331–38, esp. 334. Since the 1970s, criticism on Eliot's literary appropriations of science, medicine, and the body has proliferated, and the invocation of these categories not infrequently serves an effort to ground the textual complications offered by these novels. See in particular George Levine, "George Eliot's Hypothesis of Reality," *Nineteenth-Century Fiction* 35 (1980): 1–28, and Sally Shuttleworth, *George Eliot and Nineteenth-Century Science: The Make-Believe of a Beginning* (Cambridge: Cambridge University Press, 1984).
10. George Henry Lewes, *Problems of Life and Mind*, 3d series (London, 1879), 2:365; cited in Shuttleworth, *George Eliot and Nineteenth-Century Science*, 20.

the trope of selfhood; and thus the body tropes the insertion of the self into the larger intentional structure of history.

Consequently, from the point of view of the self, the body is a privileged trope for history or narrative. Lydgate's quest for the "primitive tissue" may be as doomed as Casaubon's for the "key to all mythologies"; but if Lydgate has frequently been taken as a figure representative of the kind of imagination that the narrator of *Middlemarch* valorizes, this is in part because his fascination with the body and its "tissues" returns us etymologically as well as thematically to the semantic field of *texere*, weave, and connects through Lydgate's mentor, Bichat, to histology and hence *histos*, web, the "particular web" of Eliot's organic, realist, non-Fieldingesque novel (170). To the guiding metaphor of the web, as J. Hillis Miller points out, "must be added the metaphor of the stream": "This figure is homogeneous with the figure of the web in that flowing water, for Eliot, is seen as made up of currents, filaments flowing side by side, intermingling and dividing. Flowing water is, so to speak, a temporalized web."[11] It is also a trope homologous with the body as a constantly growing or changing system of circulation. History, inscribing itself within bodies, is itself a body to the extent that the metaphors of web and current convey a promise of telos and form, and to the extent that "unhistoric acts" can be absorbed into history just as unperceived sensations or unacknowledged meanings are recorded by the embodied self. *Middlemarch*'s closing paragraph has the resonance it does because its dignified melancholy is compounded with affirmation:

> Her finely-touched spirit still had its fine issues, though they were not widely visible. Her full nature, like that river of which Cyrus broke the strength, spent itself in channels which had no great name on the earth. But the effect of her being on those around her was incalculably diffusive: for the growing good of the world is partly dependent on unhistoric acts; and that things are not so ill with you or me as they might have been, is half owing to the number who lived faithfully a hidden life, and rest in unvisited tombs. (896)

Dorothea's failure mingles with the anonymity of "the number" whose unhistoric acts help fuel history's melioristic movement, and she is taken up into the body of history through a death that assimilates her to an eschatology. The domestic sphere of sentiment, of narrative realism, and of unhistorical and feminine acts thus finds articulation with history through the "natural" medium of the textual body.

11. J. Hillis Miller, "Optic and Semiotic in *Middlemarch*," in *The Worlds of Victorian Fiction*, ed. Jerome H. Buckley (Cambridge: Harvard University Press, 1975), 132.

The subtlety of this figurative system becomes even more impressive when we examine its ethical correlative. If "the growing good of the world" partly depends on agents whose selfhood is effaced in the anonymity of the unhistoric, then this loss of self acquires a moral logic and can be attached to the ethical task of overcoming narcissism. As exemplified in Dorothea's effort to come to terms with Mr. Casaubon in Rome, the subject's education or *Bildung* consists in a movement from narcissism to sympathy, from a natural state ("taking the world as an udder") to a fully cultural one. Shocked into awareness of otherness by the other's desire, the self accedes to sympathy by sacrificing its narcissistic projections and recognizing the other's "equivalent centre of self"—that is, if the self is capable of this painful itinerary. Eliot's reformulation of the sentimental tradition is powerful in part because of her unsentimental focus on the difficulty of genuine sympathy. Sympathy requires energy, and Eliot's rhetoric here is usually quantitative: characters such as Romola or Dorothea are "ardent" enough to profit fully from the shocks they receive, while characters such as Mr. Casaubon have rather a "proud narrow sensitiveness which has not mass enough to spare for transformation into sympathy" (313). A sympathetic education thus consists in a check to the self resulting in a self-overcoming figured as growth or expansion. And the result is an unhistoric act that, contributing to the "growing good of the world," rejoins the greater current of history: thus the loss and gain of the sympathetic itinerary mirrors the loss and gain by means of which this itinerary is rendered historical.

We may step back for a moment and observe that this elegant and subtle figurative system constitutes an aesthetics in the sense we have given this term in previous chapters: that is to say, it is a historical and political model. The act of sympathy may be resolutely empirical, and is certainly by definition an interested act in Kantian terms; yet in performing it, the subject of sympathy nonetheless becomes representative of an essentially human potential. In theory, one might say, the subject of sympathy is ready to sympathize with anyone—or at least with anyone actually or potentially human. Sympathy is ultimately homologous with aesthetic judgment as the proleptic articulation of the individual subject with universal man. Consequently, art, or culture in an Arnoldian sense, proposes itself as the natural vehicle for the "extension of our sympathies." Culture is the public equivalent of private sympathetic acts. And thus the private itinerary from natural egoism to mature sympathy replays itself in historical form as the ascent from savagery to culture that we have seen to compose the narrative of aesthetic ideology. In "The Natural History of German Life," for instance, Eliot's self- and class-centered German peasant is bound to repetitive narrowness—not unlike Mr. Casaubon, paradoxically enough: "[C]ustom holds with him the place of sentiment, of theory, and in many cases of affection" (Pinney, 279). Untouched by the abstracting fires of culture, the peasant has no sense of universality and cannot perform the symbolic sacrifice of self that would grant him comprehension of "the rights of man" (283); like Felix Holt's working-men, he will need to grow slowly into entitlement through the diffusive effects of middle-class sympathy and the novels, poems, paintings, and middle-class politicians that transmit it. The organic model of history we find in *Middlemarch* thus remains a version of aesthetic history in all essential respects, which is to say that for all its putative modesty it remains a history of the subject, as the totalizing category of "Mind" in G. H. Lewes's terminology makes clear. Organicism, as Philippe Lacoue-Labarthe and Jean-Luc Nancy comment, is "essentially *auto*-formation, or the genuine form of the subject," which is also to say that an organic history will always eventually reveal itself, as J. Hillis Miller points out, to be a tributary of Hegel's claim that "at the bottom of history, and particularly of world history, there is a final aim."[12]

Precisely at this point, however, a certain degree of tension creeps into the organic-sympathetic aesthetic. If history is finally the self-disclosure of the Subject, then history should occur in and through a dialectic of recognition and internalization, as in the full Hegelian model: a dialectic that in fact has little in common with the temporal and ontological continuity ascribed to the natural world, just as and for the same reason that sympathy cannot be reduced to its somatic component. The painful shock and expansion of the sympathetic education ought in principle to be the engine of history, and here Eliot's texts may be said to retreat from the consequences of their own claims. A historical model as fraught with conflict, misunderstanding, and pain as a sympathetic education might still fall into an aesthetic paradigm, but would certainly involve more stress than one typically associates with the official version, at least, of George Eliot's meliorism. History, in *Middlemarch*, masquerades as a process of continuous, body-like growth only to the extent that the novel largely restricts its exploration of the drama of consciousness to the domestic sphere, confining the violence and discontinuity characteristic of stories of consciousness to the plane of the unhistoric. Texts of this sort consequently offer the Marxist critic a paradox that has not always been appreciated. If we ask what organic historicism finds difficult to assimilate, one answer, according to "The Natural History of German Life," is indeed the proletariat—"the sign and result of the decomposition which is commencing in the organic constitution of society"

---

12. Philippe Lacoue-Labarthe and Jean-Luc Nancy, *The Literary Absolute: The Theory of Literature in German Romanticism*, trans. Philip Barnard and Cheryl Lester (Albany: State University of New York Press, 1988), 49. Hegel's phrase is cited in J. Hillis Miller, "Narrative and History," *ELH* 41 (1974): 455; Miller is quoting Nietzsche quoting Hegel, "Die Weltgeschichte," *Enzyklopädie der philosophischen Wissenschaften im Grundrisse* (1830), para. 549.

(Pinney, 295). But a more general answer, with regard to the novels, would be the unhistoric field of the sentimental narrative itself. Terry Eagleton is certainly right to claim that *Middlemarch*, like many texts of its era and social provenance, casts "objective social relations into interpersonal terms," but it must be added that the latter thereby become the site of considerable tension. Rather than simply denounce the reduction of the historical to the intersubjective, we should consider the possibility that the intersubjective model might eventually, and in its own despite, find itself marked by a more genuine historicity than that offered either by the novel's periodizing detail or by its organic metaphors of historical development.[13]

The educative passage from narcissism to sympathy turns on a discontinuity, a gap between narcissistic illusion and the desire of the other; and this discontinuity manifests itself as a check or blow, which, as an intersubjective event, has a linguistic component. Not infrequently in Eliot's novels, blows are delivered verbally, their force sometimes figured in Gothic fashion as that of a brand or inscription: when Will Ladislaw lashes out at Rosamond, "what another nature felt in opposition to her own" is "burnt and bitten into her consciousness" (*Middlemarch*, 836).[14] What Will has to say—that his desire is other, directed at an other—is bound up with what his words do: their violence is their message. And though this particular scene has a satisfying ethical and structural simplicity to it—Rosamond has misread the signs of Will's desire, and her punishment consists in an accession to truth—the image of language burning and biting conveys a hint of deeper complications and suggests a less stable economy of representations and pleasures. We might briefly consider here a famous moment in *Daniel Deronda*: when Gwendolen tells Daniel that she "saw [her] wish outside [her]" while watching her terrible husband Grandcourt drown, she conveys the intensity of an event suspended between realist convention and Gothic allegory as the externalization of a desire.[15] The desiring self becomes the locus of uncertain agency (did Gwendolen's "murderous thought" have an "outward effect," causing her to hesitate to throw a rope?

13. Terry Eagleton, *Criticism and Ideology: A Study in Marxist Literary Theory* (London: Verso Press, 1978 [1976]), 121. See pp. 110–25 for a fine discussion of Eliot's ideological profile as a liberal urban intellectual; for a more recent and in-depth study, see Daniel Cottom, *Social Figures: George Eliot, Social History, and Literary Representation* (Minneapolis: University of Minnesota Press, 1987).

14. Neil Hertz comments on the "scenes of morally impeccable denunciation" that punctuate George Eliot's novels, "thoroughly gratifying scenes in which one character is licensed to verbally excoriate another" in "Some Words in George Eliot; Nullify, Neutral, Numb, Number," in *Languages of the Unsayable: The Play of Negativity in Literature and Literary Theory*, ed. Sanford Budick and Wolfgang Iser (New York: Columbia University Press, 1989), 280. I discuss this essay and the issues it raises in greater detail below.

15. George Eliot, *Daniel Deronda*, ed. Barbara Hardy (Harmondsworth: Penguin, 1967), 761. Subsequent references are to this edition.

[*Daniel Deronda*, 762]) and the text that has generated this self and its predicament thematizes itself as caught up in this uncertainty (is there a certain wishfulness at work in narratives in which characters such as Grandcourt or Casaubon come to grief, after serving as instruments of education or punishment?). The touch of sadism flavoring the image of Will's words burning and biting Rosamond's consciousness here becomes more systematically a part of the text's ethical texture. Meanwhile, the violence of sympathetic pedagogy spreads to the point that the pupil, Gwendolen, is educated only to the extent that she is ravaged by an event at once part of her and beyond her control, at once an occurrence and a recurrence—a symptomatic return of the "dead face" that has haunted her since the narrative began.

Such scenes, in other words, bring into focus the question of their own production. Reflecting on itself, the novel worries the status of its ethical categories even as it enforces them, and the question for the interpreter is whether or not the text's own ethical vocabulary can ultimately account for its operations. Critics have frequently noted the pressure of what F. R. Leavis disapprovingly calls "an emotional quality" that recurs in Eliot's prose, "something that strikes us as the direct (and sometimes embarrassing) presence of the author's own personal need."[16] Because Eliot's texts thematize imaginative activity in terms of egoism and sympathy, a comment such as Leavis's reaches further than it might otherwise: in a George Eliot novel, as Neil Hertz observes, "the play between imaginer and imagined, between author and character, and the possibility of a narcissistic confusion developing between the one and the other, has already been thematized and made available for interpretations."[17] The problem of whose wish, if any, is being realized when Grandcourt drowns derives from the terms of Eliot's imaginative project. But if, on the one hand, sympathy can always be reascribed to narcissism, on the other hand, the omnipotence of narcissism is nothing if not the essence of narcissistic fantasy—the very fantasy that Eliot's pedagogical fictions so patiently expose.

The question raised by Grandcourt's death—how and why can a wish be (or promise, or threaten to be) an act?—is a version of the question of how and why words burn or bite a consciousness, or more generally, how linguistic acts can be said to have a referential power that also feels like violence. An uneasy link among sympathy, fiction, and force surfaces repeatedly in Eliot's novels, and may be understood as a response to the problematic of fictional identification: an author, one might say a little

---

16. F. R. Leavis, *The Great Tradition* (London: Chatto and Windus, 1948), 32.
17. Neil Hertz, "Recognizing Casaubon," in *The End of the Line: Essays on Psychoanalysis and the Sublime* (New York: Columbia University Press, 1985), 82. Further references are indicated by page number prefixed when necessary by the abbreviation *EL*.

reductively, sees her wish outside her thanks to language's ability to refer to nothing at all, which means that the burden of authorial narcissism comes accompanied by the specter of the sign's irreducibility to self-presence. In *Middlemarch*, difficulties cluster around Dorothea's instrument of education, Mr. Casaubon, who, as Hertz has shown, is "made to seem not merely an especially sterile and egotistical person, but at moments like a quasi-allegorical figure, the personification of the dead letter, the written word" (*EL*, 78). His quest for the key to all mythologies has about it not just the mustiness of self-obsession, but the free play of an irresponsible fiction:

> Doubtless a vigorous error vigorously pursued has kept the embryos of truth a-breathing. . . . But Mr Casaubon's theory of the elements was not likely to bruise itself unawares against discoveries: it floated among flexible conjectures no more solid than those etymologies which seemed strong because of likeness in sound, until it was shown that likeness of sound made them impossible: it was a method of interpretation which was not tested by the necessity of forming anything which had sharper collisions than an elaborate notion of Gog and Magog: it was as free from interruption as a plan for threading the stars together. (520)

Casaubon collects these attributes in part because they compose the precipitate of a novelist's—George Eliot's—identification with a character—Dorothea—whose existence depends as much as Casaubon's on the "semicolons and parentheses" that, Mrs. Cadwallader jokes, circulate in Casaubon's body as a substitute for blood (Hertz, *EL*, 96). Similar symptoms of difficulty, as we shall see, plague the Lydgate half of the novel; but we may begin by examining Dorothea's aesthetic education, which forms the text's ethical centerpiece and negotiates both the possibility of a sympathetic aesthetic and that of aesthetic history.

II

The strengths of the sentimental tradition, the tensions at play in it, and the power and subtlety of Eliot's aesthetic and ethical project manifest themselves with clarity in the extraordinary scene in *Middlemarch* in which Dorothea, newly married to Mr. Casaubon, seeks to shoulder "the weight of unintelligible Rome":

> Ruins and basilicas, palaces and colossi, set in the midst of a sordid present, where all that was living and warm-blooded seemed sunk in the deep degeneracy of a superstition divorced from reverence; the dimmer and yet eager Titanic life gazing and struggling on walls and ceilings; the long

vistas of white forms whose marble eyes seemed to hold the monotonous light of an alien world: all this vast wreck of ambitious ideals, sensuous and spiritual, mixed confusedly with the signs of breathing forgetfulness and degradation, at first jarred her with an electric shock, and then urged themselves upon her with that ache belonging to a glut of confused ideas which check the flow of emotion. Forms both pale and glowing took possession of her young sense, and fixed themselves in her memory even when she was not thinking of them, preparing strange associations which remained through her after-years. Our moods are apt to bring with them images which succeed each other like the magic-lantern pictures of a doze; and in certain states of dull forlornness Dorothea all her life continued to see the vastness of St Peter's, the huge bronze canopy, the excited intention in the attitudes and garments of the prophets and evangelists in the mosaics above, and the red drapery which was being hung for Christmas spreading itself everywhere like a disease of the retina. (225–26)

To come to terms with Rome is to come to terms with Casaubon, whose "equivalent centre of self" it will be Dorothea's task to recognize; and as Hertz comments, that ethical task may be taken as "quite literally, a domestication" (*EL*, 92) of this overpowering encounter with the "city of visible history" (*Middlemarch*, 224).[18] Two other moments of resolution suggest themselves, Hertz adds: the darkly sublime evocation of Dorothea's haunted consciousness that closes this paragraph ("in certain states of dull forlornness Dorothea all her life continued to see . . ."); and the much-quoted lines that close a subsequent paragraph: "If we had a keen vision and feeling of all ordinary human life, it would be like hearing the grass grow and the squirrel's heart beat, and we should die of that roar which lies on the other side of silence" (226). These three responses to the "weight of unintelligible Rome" negotiate the necessity and the limits of an act of identification that is at once sympathetic and fictional.

We may add to this observation that Dorothea's sympathetic education—her progress toward the recognition of Casaubon—unfolds as a specifically aesthetic education and displays its discomforts in this idiom. It has already been pointed out in general terms that organicism is an aestheticism and that the act of sympathy implicitly mobilizes the formalizing power of aesthetic judgment; but to appreciate fully Dorothea's itinerary through Rome we should recall that, like Casaubon, Dorothea serves the narrative as a symbol as well as a character, and that what she symbol-

18. Jacqueline Rose has called Gwendolen, in *Daniel Deronda*, the "original literary hysteric," and probably had this passage in mind when she added that "the reference to hysteria was already present, albeit in a muted form, in Dorothea Brooke." See "George Eliot and the Spectacle of the Woman," in her *Sexuality in the Field of Vision* (London: Verso, 1986), 116. Rose also points out that "Saint Theresa was the patron saint of hysteria" (114).

izes is the insertion of symbolic value into realist narrative. Where *Daniel Deronda* begins with an aesthetic judgment aimed at a woman and turned into a question ("Was she beautiful or not beautiful?"), *Middlemarch* begins with the corresponding assertion ("Miss Brooke had that kind of beauty which seems to be thrown into relief by poor dress") and in fact draws attention to the particular aesthetic codes that Dorothea, a Puritan overwhelmed by Catholic Rome, will find exceptionally hard to understand ("Her hand and wrist were so finely formed that she could wear sleeves not less bare of style than those in which the Blessed Virgin appeared to Italian painters" [29]). Dorothea is the locus of aesthetic embodiment, and of the aesthetic irony with which this embodiment occurs. She will never entirely approve of the allegorical language of art that she nonetheless indirectly ratifies in specifically aesthetic fashion: that is, via the signs she provides of a potentially universal humanness. In no literal sense is she Saint Theresa or any of the numerous other saints that halo her presence in the novel; she is rather a figure for the eventual propriety of these figures. The balance is a delicate one, and the ironic nuances are worked out most clearly in their appropriate place—Naumann's studio in Rome, where the painter pretends to see Aquinas in Casaubon in order to paint Dorothea as Santa Clara. Casaubon is not "the idealistic in the real," and, crucially, neither is Dorothea. In aesthetic history the ideal is never entirely present; and when Naumann expatiates on Dorothea's beauty—to Will Ladislaw's irritation since "the ordinary phrases which might apply to mere bodily presences were not applicable to her"—the narrator provides the necessary parenthesis: "Certainly all Tipton," not to mention Dorothea herself, would have been surprised: "In that part of the world Miss Brooke had been only a 'fine young woman'" (250). The aesthetic can appear only as a promise of itself, and the *Middlemarch* narrator's wise and melancholy poise derives in part from the finely calibrated distance this narrative voice takes from affirmations that must also nonetheless be registered, and which are thus often routed through Will's proleptically Pateresque consciousness.[19]

19. "[T]he bow of a violin drawn near him cleverly, would at one stroke change the aspect of the world for him" (*Middlemarch*, 423). Will's commitment to what Mr. Casaubon describes as "the vague pursuit of what he calls culture" (106) is a little anachronistic in 1832, but plays an important role in the text's aesthetic system, not least because, as mentioned above, the narrator's irony can play off Will's aesthetic enthusiasm—as when he tells Dorothea "you *are* a poem" (256), finds her voice to resemble an "Aeolian harp" (105), and so on. Will Ladislaw is an interesting figure from the point of view of a study of aesthetics. Like Dorothea, he is a locus of aesthetic embodiment, with the emphasis cast more on the uncertain free play of aesthetic form: "a bright creature, abundant in uncertain promises" (512). He is linked through genealogy to the dead letter of Casaubon, on the one hand, and the sterile, hypercommodified world of Bulstrode, on the other; however, his grandmother had "not even a family likeness" to her sister, Casaubon's mother (101), and acts of disinheritance on both sides of the family frame him as aesthetic man. It is significant that, for all his associations with music, the stage, and a

Dorothea, in short, exemplifies the affirmative structure of the novel's ethical and representational system, which in all of its manifestations depends on aesthetic irony. In this system, signs mislead, but they do so in order to return themselves to their proper meaning at the far side of history's error. Bodies, in *Middlemarch*, do not always correspond reliably to interior states, but they promise eventual legibility: if the organic body is to be the self's unconscious historicity, the body must finally be an aesthetic body. Similarly, Middlemarchian common sense may be too common to judge Dorothea, Rosamond, or Fred and Mary accurately, but it at least knows that Dorothea is "too unusual and striking," that Bulstrode is essentially untrustworthy, and so on: in aesthetic history, *doxa* must be wrong only within the potential of its own truth. And aesthetic irony demands, and receives in the person of Dorothea, a ratification of the signs of irony's eventual demise. It is thus inevitable that the shock and trauma of her sympathetic education should unfold as a confrontation with art, and with history as the history of art. In encountering Rome, Dorothea provokes the text into an intense negotiation of fictional identification precisely because in this scene the stability of the aesthetic is at stake.

Consequently, the threat that Casaubon represents and domesticates inheres in the aesthetic itself, and Dorothea's relation to art remains a troubled one. Pictures, she tells Casaubon, after he has introduced her to Will, "are a language I do not understand. I suppose there is some relation between pictures and nature which I am too ignorant to feel—just as you see what a Greek sentence stands for which means nothing to me" (105). Her aesthetic education, which as we have seen, parallels her sympathetic education and in a deeper sense comprises it, enjoys indifferent success. It is true that the "Italian painters" whose Madonnas she resembles become less "monstrous" after she begins to learn art's language in Naumann's studio: "[S]ome things which had seemed monstrous to her were gathering intelligibility and even a natural meaning" (246).[20] But this ambivalent progress never takes her far from a specifically aesthetic trauma: "'At first when I enter a room where the walls are covered with frescoes or with rare

non-English bohemian levity, he will eventually go into politics: as aesthetic man he must finally be *representative*. Eliot's difficulty with this character is symptomatic of the tension *Middlemarch* puts on its own aesthetic.

20. And later in the text Dorothea will develop her ambivalence about art into a political critique: certain that much art is unsympathetic and cut off from the masses, she would prefer to "make life beautiful"—an activist stance that Will calls "the fanaticism of sympathy" (*Middlemarch*, 252). This theme climaxes in Dorothea's sharply political critique of the picturesque: after the completion of her aesthetic education (which includes the death of Casaubon), she comes to realize why she never liked the paintings in the well-traveled Mr. Brooke's collection: they sentimentalize real suffering and constitute "a wicked attempt to find delight in what is false" (424): a judgment the narrator echoes a little later when Brooke visits Freeman's End (429).

pictures, I feel a kind of awe—like a child present at great ceremonies where there are grand robes and processions; I feel myself in the presence of some higher life than my own. But when I begin to examine the pictures one by one, the life goes out of them, or else is something violent and strange to me'" (238). The "violent and strange" dimension of the aesthetic reappears in less central but more lurid fashion in the story of Lydgate's scientific education.

III

Lydgate's doomed quest for the "primitive tissue" orients him toward the figurative essence of the novel, and thereby makes him into an ethically and rhetorically complex character. In both its metaphorical and literal dimensions his project ensures that he will fall victim to the narrator's irony, which here is equally the irony of history: "What was the primitive tissue? In that way Lydgate put the question—not quite in the way required by the awaiting answer, but such missing of the right word befalls many seekers" (178). He will eventually betray this quest by betraying his professional ideal. Yet, like Dorothea, he testifies to the value of ardent error, since in his very choice of profession he is participating—unhistorically—in its historical development. Like Wilhelm Meister, Lydgate believes that medicine synthesizes theory and practice, calling forth the "highest intellectual strain" yet keeping the researcher "in good warm contact" with other human beings. And the high intellectual strain of medical research bears a remarkable resemblance to the imaginative gift of the mimetic artist, as critics have frequently remarked:

> Many men have been praised as vividly imaginative on the strength of their profuseness in indifferent drawing or cheap narration:—reports of very poor talk going on in distant orbs; or portraits of Lucifer coming down on his bad errands as a large ugly man with bat's wings and spurts of phosphorescence; or exaggerations of wantonness that seem to reflect life in a diseased dream. But these kinds of inspiration Lydgate regarded as rather vulgar and vinous compared with the imagination that reveals subtle actions inaccessible by any sort of lens, but tracked in that outer darkness through long pathways of necessary sequence by the inward light which is the last refinement of Energy, capable of bathing even the ethereal atoms in its ideally illuminated space. He . . . wanted to pierce the obscurity of those minute processes which prepare human misery and joy, those invisible thoroughfares which are the first lurking-places of anguish, mania, and crime, that delicate poise and transition which determine the growth of happy or unhappy consciousness. (194)

Particularly in its concluding sentence, this passage would seem to be describing the panoptic procedures of the novelist even more than those of the social scientist; and it has proved easy to discern in Lydgate's valorization of the scientific imagination "George Eliot's reflection on her own assumptions and beliefs."[21] Less frequently noted is the curious passion with which this passage invokes and discards a different kind of imagination, as though the "inward light" of the scientific mind instantly cast Gothic shadows, as it might in *Frankenstein* or *Faust*.

If Lydgate is an authorial surrogate, he is also persistently the locus of suspect sorts of literariness. It is he, not Casaubon, who is termed "a cluster of signs for his neighbors' false suppositions" (*Middlemarch*, 171); and while the suppositions may be legibly false, as when Mrs Dollop—her eye, perhaps, on *Wilhelm Meisters Wanderjahre*—suspects him of murder and grave-robbing, even this lurid bit of *doxa* acquires resonance when Lydgate finds it necessary to tell an unappreciative Rosamond of his admiration for the grave-robbing Vesalius (497). The origin of his "intellectual passion" has a Gothic feel to it, and entails an act of reading: on a rainy day the young Lydgate opens a volume of "an old Cyclopaedia" at random, and stumbles on a description of the valves of the heart: "He was not much acquainted with valves of any sort, but he knew that *valvae* were folding doors, and through this crevice came a sudden light startling him with his first vivid notion of finely adjusted mechanism in the human frame" (173). Not only does his career—his symbolically resonant search for the "primitive tissue"—unfold from the chance event of a signifier, but the "light" shining through its "crevice" has been made possible by a "liberal education," which (besides leaving him "free to read the indecent passages in the school classics") has enabled him to read *valvae* in valves, thus producing the "crevice" for the imagination's light. Everywhere in Lydgate's story one seems to encounter literature. He bears a poet's name; his "intellectual passion" resembles the love "sung by the Troubadours" (173); and "the primitive tissue" remains "his fair unknown" (305) until a more literal sort of love life generates too many obstacles.

It is in his erotic entanglements that Lydgate's literary ones become most visible, since his "spots of commonness" manifest themselves most strikingly in his relegation of women to the domain of cultured leisure. His

---

21. Shuttleworth, *George Eliot and Nineteenth-Century Science*, 143. Nearly all treatments of "*Middlemarch* and science" take Lydgate as representative of George Eliot's own imaginative procedures and ideals. One is reminded of Zola's "il me suffira de remplacer le mot 'medecin' par le mot 'romancier'." *Le roman expérimental*, in *Oeuvres Completes* (Paris: Bernouard, 1928), 41:11. The stress under which critics labor when they cast Eliot as a scientist is legible in the degree to which their formulations frequently work to efface the fictional altogether: e.g., "*Middlemarch* is a work of experimental science" (Shuttleworth, *George Eliot and Nineteenth-Century Science*, 143).

encounter with Madame Laure, which I shall consider at greater length in a moment, allows melodrama to erupt into his plot; and his courtship and marriage to Rosamond Vincy links his fate to that of a character described by Mary Garth as "just the sort of beautiful creature that is imprisoned with ogres in fairy tales" (166). Rosamond also functions as the locus of more systematic high literary allusion. Her bourgeois origins, romance-conditioned imagination, expensive habits, and marital dominance align her with the wife of another literary doctor; when the text has Rosamond and Lydgate's interest in each other begin when Lydgate gallantly hands her the whip for which she is reaching (144–45), the reference to *Madame Bovary* has all the signs of being purposeful.[22] In the course of time Rosamond will experiment in timid Victorian fashion with an Emma Bovary career: Captain Lydgate and Will are lightly sounded echos of Rodolphe and Léon. In meeting and marrying Rosamond, Lydgate has not just walked into a literary plot, but into the plot of a novel about the incessant and damaging novelization of life.

Consequently, in Lydgate's orbit the border between life and art, high and low literature, realism and romance, romance and melodrama, is strikingly permeable: "'Would *she* kill me because I wearied her?'" he wonders late in the novel (638), thinking of Rosamond but alluding of course to Laure, the actress who kills her husband by mistake on purpose during the performance of a Parisian melodrama, and who in turn serves as the cynosure of a variety of literary codes. Madame Laure earns her living by acting in plays that presumably "reflect life in a diseased dream," but she comes curiously adorned with tokens of high culture: she is a "Provençale," with a Petrarchan name and "dark eyes, a Greek profile, and rounded majestic form" (180). In certain respects Lydgate's encounter with her complements Dorothea's encounter with Rome: both scenes take place at an extreme remove from the middle-march of life in Middlemarch; both occasion self-conscious reflections on narrative procedure ("For those who want to be acquainted with Lydgate it will be good to know what was that case of impetuous folly. . . . The story can be told without many words"); and both appear to respond to non-dramatic necessities. The story of Madame Laure has elicited critical attention in recent years, but its oddity is still frequently underappreciated.[23] It is a story of mimetic contagion. After

---

22. Gustave Flaubert, *Madame Bovary: Moeurs de province*, 1.2: Charles, on his first visit to the Rouault home, is looking for his whip: "It had fallen to the ground, between the sacks and the wall. Mademoiselle Emma saw it, and bent over the flour sacks. Charles out of politeness made a dash also, and as he stretched out his arm, at the same moment felt his breast brush against the back of the young girl bending beneath him. She drew herself up, scarlet, and looked at him over her shoulder as she handed him his riding crop." *Madame Bovary*, ed. and trans. Paul de Man (New York: Norton, 1965), 12.
23. It is becoming a well-trodden topos, however. In addition to Simon During's essay cited in

Laure translates art into reality, really stabbing her husband instead of acting the mistaken stabbing of her lover disguised as the evil duke (and played by her real-life husband), Lydgate "really" falls in love with her and seeks her out in Avignon, causing even Laure to wonder at the infectiousness of melodrama: "You have come all the way from Paris to find me? . . . Are all Englishmen like that?" Their subsequent conversation is arguably the most bizarre in mainstream Victorian fiction. "My foot really slipped," Laure tells Lydgate. However, she continues, "*I meant to do it.*" Lydgate appeals to the possibility of complex hermeneutic and emotional depths: "There was a secret, then," he suggests. "You hated him." But Laure is Eliot's one truly existential killer: "No! he wearied me; he was too fond: he would live in Paris, and not in my country, and that was not agreeable to me." Finally she rules out premeditation: "I did not plan: it came to me in the play—*I meant to do it*" (182).

As Simon During has shown, this curious scene possibly alludes to a famous murder case in Paris in 1825.[24] More immediately, as feminist criticism from Gilbert and Gubar onward has noted, the episode gives melodramatic expression to the violence glinting in the turns of the realist text,

---

the subsequent note, see David Ferris's subtle and extensive discussions of the Laure episode in *Theory and the Evasion of History* (Baltimore: Johns Hopkins University Press, 1993); unfortunately I discovered this book too late to do more than signal the congruity I perceive between Ferris's approach and my own. Feminist criticism since the 1970s has drawn attention to *Middlemarch*'s Laure episode, often citing it as a particularly violent version of a connection between murder and marriage that Eliot's texts frequently make. See especially Sandra M. Gilbert and Susan Gubar, *The Madwoman in the Attic: The Woman Writer and the Nineteenth-Century Literary Imagination* (New Haven: Yale University Press, 1979), 499–520; Nina Auerbach, *Romantic Imprisonment: Women and Other Glorified Outcasts* (New York: Columbia University Press, 1986), 253–67; and Jacqueline Rose, "George Eliot and the Spectacle of the Woman."

24. Simon During, "The Strange Case of Monomania: Patriarchy in Literature, Murder in *Middlemarch*, Drowning in *Daniel Deronda*," *Representations* 23 (1988): 86–104. The murder inspired the production of a short-lived medical category called "monomania" in order to account for the perpetrator's apparent absence of motive. Monomania, During explains, "indicated a localized but profound break in the unity of the psyche. . . . At the most abstract level it operated on the classical divisions between the faculties: in monomania, will separated from emotion, reason from will, emotion from reason." Its peculiarity lay in its being a "pathology of structure rather than of content, so that the faculties themselves remained in order" (86). With the disappearance of faculty-psychology in the middle of the century, this classification was forgotten or ignored.

The term "monomania" seems to have circulated well beyond the medical and juridical contexts that During invokes, however. It appears in Edgar Allan Poe's short story "Berenice" (1835) to describe the narrator's "morbid attention" to objects that are "invariably frivolous," and at one point characterizes his habit of repeating "monotonously some common word, until the sound, by dint of frequent repetition, ceased to convey any idea whatever to the mind." *The Complete Edgar Allan Poe Tales* (London: Guild, 1984), 10. In the course of the story, the monomaniacal gaze fixes on Berenice's teeth: "Then came the full fury of my *monomania*," here taking the form of believing that these arbitrary signifiers are at once "ideas" and apotropaic fetishes ("I felt that their possession could alone ever restore us to peace, in giving me back to reason" [12]).

particularly when the story is of husbands and wives. When Dorothea, in her scene with Rosamond late in the novel, says that misdirected love "murders our marriage—and then the marriage stays with us like a murder" (855), the metaphor resonates in a web we have already sketched: Casaubon's death, like Grandcourt's in *Daniel Deronda*'s far more charged reworking of this topos, arrives with the convenience of a fiction, and leaves a residue that Eliot's texts represent in the figure of ambiguous murder. Murder is a crime of omission in George Eliot novels: if killing may be taken as action in its purest manifestation as violence, Eliot's texts worry the status of the act as a play of conflicting motives and circumstances— and not only when the death of a husband is in question: Bulstrode's murder of Raffles provides an elegant instance of such ethical discrimination.[25] But Casaubon's and Grandcourt's deaths provoke the supplemental and less stable question of what it means for an "author" to "act"—that is, in this idiom, to kill a fictional character, or identify with one, thereby seeing her wish outside her: murder, in other words, becomes the site for the staging of the question of what the act of fiction (as sympathy) is.

And with Madame Laure's murderous blow, agency becomes irreducible to intention or desire, let alone egoism. According to Laure, her blow, which annihilates the difference between representation and reality (or fictional character and "author"), is at once the expression of a pure intention ("I meant to do it"), a citation or quote ("It came to me in the play"), and an accident ("My foot really slipped"). Meaning (as the sheer form of intentionality) mimes perfectly an occurrence (the blow), but the articulation between these two dimensions loses its certainty: her blow is an intended accident and an accidental intention. Intention, here indistinguishable from a slip of the foot, can no longer guarantee a difference between its own pure occasion and the randomness of an event, and furthermore discovers its predicament only as a citation, as the mechanical reiteration of a text produced by "collaborating authors" (180).[26]

---

25. Particularly since Bulstrode's actions acquire their meaning from their context: the liquor he allows the housekeeper Mrs. Abel to give to Raffles was proscribed by Lydgate but would have been prescribed by the older medical school of Toller and Wrench (*Middlemarch*, 774). The complexity of the murderous act is discoverable even in violent scenes such as that in which Baldassare kills Tito in *Romola*. Tito appears already dead when Baldassare finds him; Baldassare kneels beside the body "watching the face," and when Tito's eyes open he begins strangling him: "Tito knew him; but he did not know whether it was life or death that had brought him into the presence of his injured father." *Romola*, ed. Andrew Sanders (Harmondsworth: Penguin, 1980), 638.

26. Simon During's interesting reading of this scene through the lens of "monomania" oversimplifies the conundrum of Laure's blow: "Without monomania two alternative readings are possible: either Laure is a liar who really did accidentally slip and is now frightening her persistent suitor off, or she is a criminal safely confessing at last. Monomania destroys this

Thus struck, Lydgate retreats into the error diagnosed in *Middlemarch*'s "Prelude": he resolves that henceforth he will "take a strictly scientific view of women" (183), and thereby consigns himself to a blind repetition of literary emplotment. For the "scientific" view of women is inseparable from their aestheticization—their relegation to what *Middlemarch*'s "Prelude" called "indefiniteness" (26). The Laure episode demonstrates what the rest of Lydgate's plot confirms: that the "intellectual passion" of the male scientific enterprise is permeable to, and possibly another version of, the "preconceived romance" into which Rosamond processes experience (195). Thus the novel that generates and weighs these categories and destinies has also told the story of the literariness of its own aestheticizing scientificity. The threat Dorothea is represented as perceiving in art inheres in the "primitive tissue" of the text that valorizes her. For Laure's blow constitutes the ultimately "unhistoric," domestic, female act, yet deprives the body of its reservoir of meaning and makes it the site of uncertain accident, an element in an undecidable textual process. Her blow performs the contagion of bad, anonymous art, the (non-)art of the crowd, and in this sense may be understood as a political blow precisely to the extent that it is uncertainly and uncontrollably literary. The blow's violence lies in its passage from figurative to literal status: it is precisely this slippage that is undecidably random or intentional. Yet the blow takes its origin in the domain of the figurative ("It came to me in the play"). Bad art, then, is a figure that does not know whether it is figurative or literal and cannot control the difference: hence the contagiousness of melodrama. The physician is at the center of this epidemic, aggravating it by trying to isolate and cure it. And Eliot's text, repeating the physician's predicament, quarantines this rhetorical plague within the ethical and aesthetic categories of melodrama and narcissism only at the cost of exposing organic history to

---

division by turning her wish for autonomy into a fiction that can make illusory sense of her motiveless act" ("The Strange Case of Monomania," 93). This way of stating the problem imposes alternatives that the text disallows: the scene holds interest precisely because a slip (of the body) and an intent (of the mind) become at once radically different and radically indistinguishable within the context of a mechanically reiterated text (the melodrama). During's analysis is in part set up to prepare a rebuttal of Paul de Man's reading of Rousseau's *Confessions* in *Allegories of Reading* (New Haven: Yale University Press, 1979). The difficulty of de Man's text prevents me from entering into that particular debate here; it will have to suffice to note that During needs to underplay the paradoxes of Laure's blow so as to allow a firmly historical category—"monomania"—to frame and explain the text. A fine reading of de Man's subtle and violent reading of Rousseau may be found in Ortwin de Graef, "Silence to Be Observed: A Trial for Paul de Man's Inexcusable Confessions," *Postmodern Studies 2: (Dis)continuities: Essays on Paul de Man*, ed. Luc Herman et al. (Amsterdam/Antwerp: Rodopi/Restant, 1989), 51–73.

disease, and raising the suspicion that a certain illegible, literary contagion infects and enables sympathy.

The further pursuit of these questions will take us past *Middlemarch*'s borders. We have seen that pockets of stress inhabit both the Dorothea and the Lydgate plots, yet *Middlemarch*'s aesthetic of sympathy remains relatively stable because the text leaves relatively unquestioned the homology between the sympathetic and the ardent. Characters such as Casaubon and Madame Laure are judged and exiled in vitalistic terms: they are morally deficient at least in part because they lack energy. They personify the error of the ardent soul; however, in the sheer generosity of its error the sympathetic soul remains a locus of value. Eliot's subsequent writing was to be more acutely haunted by the specter at work within the sympathetic aesthetic; and despite the bulk and complexity of *Daniel Deronda*, we may briefly consider here a set of passages to which Neil Hertz has drawn attention, in which this novel's themes of gambling and theatrical performance bring the sympathetic imagination into proximity with a certain mechanical, iterative passivity. Though the summary comments I offer over the next few pages make a poor substitute for Hertz's patient reading of *Deronda*, they will prepare us to trace continuities between *Middlemarch*'s organic fiction and a Gothic theme of telepathy which, as I hope to show in the final section of this chapter, haunts the extremities of George Eliot's oeuvre.

It is only a slight exaggeration to say that Madame Laure returns in Eliot's oeuvre as Daniel Deronda's mother, who is herself a minimally displaced representation of *Daniel Deronda*'s author. A world-famous, aging actress, the Princess Halm-Eberstein appears late in the novel in answer to Daniel's desire; and this "wish" that he, like Gwendolen, finally sees "outside him" poses a threatening resistance to his sympathy. The Princess is the last in a long series of female characters in Eliot's fiction whose egoism has murderous potential. When Daniel was two years old, the Princess had offered him to an old friend for adoption so as to pursue her career; during his interview with his mother Daniel melodramatically charges her with having "willed to annihilate" his identity as a Jew (*Daniel Deronda*, 727).[27] But the threat the Princess poses to the sympathetic imagination cannot be entirely translated into a dramatic and ethical vocabulary. The most ex-

---

27. His grandfather, he now learns, had been a "physician": a curious detail that reinforces the link between the Princess and Laure—though certainly Daniel's almost mythically patriarchal grandfather is in all other respects no Lydgate: "A man to be admired in a play—grand, with an iron will" (*Daniel Deronda*, 694).

traordinary passages in this somberly passionate scene are those in which Eliot seeks to render the Princess's consciousness:

> [T]his woman's nature was one in which all feeling—and all the more when it was tragic as well as real—immediately became matter of conscious representation: experience immediately passed into drama, and she acted her own emotions. In a minor degree this is nothing uncommon, but in the Princess the acting had a rare perfection of physiognomy, voice, and gesture. It would not be true to say that she felt less because of this double consciousness: she felt—that is, her mind went through—all the more, but with a difference: each nucleus of pain or pleasure had a deep atmosphere of the excitement or spiritual intoxication which at once exalts and deadens. But Deronda made no reflection of this kind. (691–92)

The sharp exclusion of Daniel from the common ground of the narrator's and the Princess's consciousness returns the novel to its dramatic register but also signals the extent to which the text has deviated from that register in seeking language for the Princess's interiority. The differences constitutive of consciousness—between feeling and its representation, emotion and acted emotion—are first elaborated into the comparative abstraction of a "double consciousness," and then "further dispersed," as Hertz comments, "into an indefinite number of nuclei, atoms of experience characterized in the abstract idiom of their most common denominators as units of pain or pleasure, each surrounded by its own ambivalently exalting and deadening aura" ("Some Words," 295). The Princess is Eliot's most resonant and ambitious self-portrait: a mimetic artist with the talent, the energy, and the hubris to "care for the wide world, and all that I could represent in it" (*Daniel Deronda*, 693), and with the authority to rebuke Daniel's imperial sympathy: "No. . . . You are not a woman. You may try—but you can never imagine what it is to have a man's force of genius in you, and yet to suffer the slavery of being a girl" (694).

The mother's appearance and (rapid) disappearance in this novel, as Hertz has shown, may be understood as a double gesture of affirmation and sacrifice: as George Eliot's "brief but intense experiment in writing herself into her text" (*EL*, 224), but also as a means of focusing and controlling the kinds of difficulties that we have been examining throughout this chapter. By embodying a certain linguistic opacity, the Princess, like Casaubon, and to a certain extent like Madame Laure, allows that opacity to be translated into an ethical idiom, and symbolically expelled from the novel. But the representational questions she raises haunt the narrative in other ways, and they cluster particularly thickly around a character who, like the Princess, appears briefly and exits under an ethical cloud: Lapidoth, the "undesirable father" of Mordecai-Ezra and Mirah (*Daniel Deronda*, 849). Undesirable on numerous counts—he is a "shabby, foreign-looking, eager, and gesticulating man," and a habitual gambler (807)—Lapidoth will be upbraided both by the narrator and by Mordecai: "That is," Hertz comments dryly, "the arrival of the father is the occasion for one more of those scenes of morally impeccable denunciation that have punctuated George Eliot's fiction from the first" ("Some Words," 280). Like Will lashing out at Rosamond, Mordecai-Ezra denounces Lapidoth with a force that leaves the son "exhausted by the shock of his own irrepressible utterance" and makes the father "cry like a woman":

> —and yet, strangely, while this hysterical crying was an inevitable reaction in [Lapidoth] under the stress of his son's words, it was also a conscious resource in a difficulty; just as in early life, when he was a bright-faced curly young man, he had been used to avail himself of this subtly-poised physical susceptibility to turn the edge of resentment or disapprobation. (*Daniel Deronda*, 847–48)

Lapidoth, like the Princess, "acts his own emotions," though not with the dignity of a great tragedian. His "hysterical" fit of crying is amenable to pragmatic exploitation, but as an occurrence, it is not under his control: the infection of life by art that the Princess embodies has now modulated into a grafting of intentionality, of "conscious resource," onto a "subtly-poised physical susceptibility." And the "poise" of Lapidoth's physical susceptibility is linked to the "poise" marking the consciousness of a gambler: "the habitual suspensive poise of the mind in actual or imaginary play" (843).

These passages prepare a final description of Lapidoth's consciousness, as he lies awake at night after his scene with Mordecai-Ezra, going "back over old Continental hours at *Roulette*, reproducing the method of his play, and the chances that had frustrated it":

> These were the stronger visions of the night with Lapidoth, and not the worn frame of his ireful son uttering a terrible judgment. Ezra did pass across the gaming-table, and his words were audible; but he passed like an insubstantial ghost, and his words had the heart eaten out of them by numbers and movements that seemed to make the very tissue of Lapidoth's consciousness. (849)

"If that last sentence is surprising," Hertz comments, "it may be because it seems to be composed of better language than Lapidoth is quite entitled to." The abstract, enigmatic metaphor of a "tissue" composed of "numbers and movements" that "eat out the heart" of morally significant words has the density, even the dignity of a figure that resists easy visualization: "[I]t is as if paper were both receiving and corroding print, or as if a ground could both accept and invalidate a figure" ("Some Words," 283). Like the Princess, Lapidoth marks a limit to the efficacity of the sympathetic imagination, and does so in ways that draw attention to a threat at once internal to sympathy itself and linked to *Daniel Deronda*'s running theme of gambling.

The "habitual suspensive poise" of the gambler, his compulsively repetitive representations of play, and the "numbers and movements" of his consciousness, recall other forms of mechanical behavior or states of mind in *Daniel Deronda*, such as Gwendolen's liability to hysteria, or Daniel's and Grandcourt's liability to different kinds of suspensive poise. Daniel's sympathy is so diffuse as to be paralyzing: his is a "reflectiveness that threatened to nullify all differences" (414). Grandcourt, Daniel's sinister double in many ways, but particularly in the matter of double consciousness, is frequently beset by a "languor of intention . . . like a fit of diseased numbness" (187): his will to thwart the expectations of others is so refined that it has trouble determining its object. The overlap between the "numbers" playing in the gambler's consciousness and the "numbness" afflicting sympathy on the one hand and a will to power on the other, occurs, Hertz suggests, "where motive is dispersed in equivocations, where agency is hard to distinguish from passivity, or from a poise that is at once suspensive and habitual" ("Some Words," 293). The mechanical, passive activity of the gambler summons these instances of ambiguous agency into a figure that to a certain extent allows for the reestablishment of ethical and thematic control.

But the body can no longer play the governing role it did in Eliot's earlier novel, and not simply because aesthetic power now explicitly involves mechanical prowess, as Klesmer tells Gwendolen: "Your muscles, your whole frame—must go like a watch, true, true, true, to a hair" (*Daniel Deronda*, 300). The body, framed as the body of sympathy, is also always a gambling body, and can no longer easily sacrifice itself to the construction of the organic historicity of a greater consciousness. Aesthetic embodiment has become a question ("Was she beautiful or not beautiful?"), asked by a male gaze of a female body ("She who raised these questions in Daniel Deronda's mind was gambling"): a body lodged in the inorganic architecture of a modern, historical, wearily literary consciousness ("not in the open air under a southern sky, tossing coppers on a ruined wall, with rags about her limbs, but in one of those splendid resorts which the enlightenment of ages has prepared for the same species of pleasure"). Jacqueline Rose rightly comments that in this novel "it is the degeneracy of the whole social body that is now in need of repair," and that Daniel's Zionist project rewrites in grand aesthetic-historical fashion Lydgate's search for the primitive tissue (Rose, *Sexuality*, 111). Yet in negotiating limits to its loss, *Daniel Deronda* not only splits into the two halves for which it is famous; it also offers up for sacrifice *Middlemarch*'s most privileged organic image, and constructs the figure of a "tissue" made of numbers and movements that devour words.

V

In an intriguing displacement of a phrase by Jacques Derrida, Nicholas Royle remarks that it is "difficult to imagine a theory of fiction, a theory of the novel, without a theory of telepathy."[28] The claim may seem melodramatic, but it is a peculiarly apt formulation of the predicament of a sentimental aesthetic, particularly in its nineteenth-century narrative manifestations. The formal developments that culminated in Eliot's omniscient narrators and James's crafted perspectives cast narrative conventions as paradoxes of consciousness. A narrator becomes the locus of a knowledge at once excessive and insufficient, since the telling of a story depends both on the knowledge of its end and the suppression or forgetting of this knowledge. This is also to say that the narrator knows and does not know the characters whose consciousnesses, in composing the story, compose the narrative consciousness of the story. These paradoxes emerge from the sentimental and Gothic tradition as the formal complement to this tradition's interest in the subject of desire. The Gothic, with its premonitory and oversignificant ambience, its doublings and redoublings of characters and desires, might be called the genre of telepathy; the genre's overt preoccupation with the occult would in this sense be the symptom of a more general interest in a more diffuse haunting.

Like the Brontës and other writers in the nineteenth-century high Gothic tradition, George Eliot allowed mind-reading and clairvoyance to take overtly supernatural form in her fiction, though in Eliot's case this occurred only once and under resolutely particular circumstances. *The Lifted Veil*, a short story she interrupted work on *The Mill on the Floss* to write, is in certain respects heavily framed as a *jeu de mélancolie* to be kept at a distance from the serious, ethical work of literary realism.[29] Yet the story is also

28. Nicholas Royle, *Telepathy and Literature: Essays on the Reading Mind* (London: Blackwell, 1990), 17. Cf. Jacques Derrida, "Telepathy," trans. Nicholas Royle, *Oxford Literary Review* 10 (1988): 3–41: "Difficult to imagine a theory of what they still call the unconscious without a theory of telepathy" (14): a phrase I discuss below.
29. "*Jeu de mélancolie*" is Eliot's phrase in a letter to Blackwood accompanying the manuscript; fourteen years after its publication she wrote to him to say that "[t]here are many things . . . [in *The Lifted Veil*] which I would willingly say over again, and I shall never put in any other form."

centered on the problematic of sympathy, and it has been widely recognized in recent years as a text that self-consciously "investigates and challenges two of [Eliot's] dearest values: sympathy and memory as the bases of moral action."[30] The telepathic, clairvoyant, first-person narrator, Latimer, presses the sympathetic imagination to its caricatural absolute before Eliot's fictional oeuvre is more than partly underway. He hears the "roar on the other side of silence"—for his power is "like a preternaturally heightened sense of hearing, making audible to one a roar of sound where others find perfect stillness"—and if he does not die of it, he admits into his consciousness a literary element that disturbs the difference between life and death, and disrupts the coherence of narcissism as an ethical category.[31]

For though Latimer is possessed of something like the "proud narrow sensitiveness" of a Mr. Casaubon, his assumption of the powers and burdens of an Eliotic narrator requires him to tell the story not just of his own life, but of his own death. As part of the text's self-conscious manipulation of narrative conventions and forms—one thinks of Moll Flanders' remark somewhat earlier in the history of the English novel that "no Body can write their own Life to the full End of it unless they can write it after they are dead"[32]—death becomes *The Lifted Veil*'s most prominent and complex narrative event. "The time of my end approaches," Latimer tells us in the text's opening sentence: "Just a month from this day, on the 20th of September 1850, I shall be sitting in this chair, in this study, at ten o'clock at night, longing to die, weary of incessant insight and foresight, without delusions and without hope." There follows a proleptic representation of the experience of death itself:

The George Eliot Letters, ed. G. S. Haight (New Haven: Yale University Press, 1954–56), 3:41, 5:380.

30. Charles Swann, "Déjà Vu, Déjà Lu: 'The Lifted Veil' as an Experiment in Art," *Literature and History* 5.1 (1979): 42. Until relatively recently *The Lifted Veil* was rarely discussed in Eliot scholarship, but since the mid-seventies it has elicited many fine critical readings: in addition to Swann, see Sandra Gilbert and Susan Gubar, *The Madwoman in the Attic*, 443–77; Gillian Beer, "Myth and the Single Consciousness: *Middlemarch* and *The Lifted Veil*," in *This Particular Web: Essays on Middlemarch*, ed. Ian Adam (Toronto: University of Toronto Press, 1975), 91–115; Terry Eagleton, "Power and Knowledge in 'The Lifted Veil,'" *Literature and History* 9.1 (1983): 52–61.
31. George Eliot, *The Lifted Veil* (Harmondsworth: Penguin, 1985), 26. Subsequent references are to this edition.
32. Daniel Defoe, *Moll Flanders*, ed. David Blewett (Harmondsworth: Penguin, 1989), 42. The temporality of Latimer's consciousness is far more complex than can be indicated here. At times, like the damned in Dante's *Inferno*, he will know the past and the future but not the present; he can foresee his death but not the death of his desire for the blond femme fatale of the story, Bertha, or her desire for his death. His powers disappear at a certain point and are displaced onto a bizarre scientific fantasy, as a character who knows Bertha's desire for Latimer's death is given a blood transfusion, brought back from death and enabled, like Poe's Mr. Valdemar—and of course like Latimer himself—to speak from beyond the grave. For a fine analysis of the text's narrative and rhetorical complications, see Swann, "Déjà Vu, Déjà Lu."

> Darkness—darkness—no pain—nothing but darkness: but I am pass-
> ing on and on through the darkness: my thought stays in the darkness, but
> always with a sense of moving onward. . . .
>   Before that time comes, I wish to use my last hours of ease and strength
> in telling the strange story of my experience. (2)

The experience of death reveals itself here as exemplary of the category of experience per se, representing the plenitude of reality that narrative form will betray: both the plenitude and the betrayal register in the ellipsis points qualifying "onward." Yet if death is the exemplary experience, in its excess of content over form or reality over representation, it is also of course the exemplary non-experience, available only as form, representation, or language. Death cannot be represented, and can only be represented. *The Lifted Veil* situates Latimer's consciousness at the intersection of this paradox. Since he is clairvoyant, no event in his narrative can be located definitively in space or time: the character Latimer can become the narrating Latimer at any point, since the story of his life—which is to say his death—can unroll for him without his having "experienced" it. Precisely *as* a narrator, he is neither dead nor alive. The "20th of September 1850" is undecidably past, present, and future at any "moment" or "point" in Latimer's narrative, as the story's closing sentences and final ellipsis points emphasize:

> It is the 20th of September 1850. I know these figures I have just written,
> as if they were a long familiar inscription. I have seen them on this page in
> my desk unnumbered times, when the scene of my dying struggle has
> opened upon me. . . . (66–67)

Latimer's death, the exemplary (non)event, has already occurred and has not yet occurred, which is to say that it has occurred as an inscription which opens the possibility of death and life, but remains irreducible to either. Telepathy in this sense is a "metaphor for reading" (Royle, *Telepathy and Literature*, 96), and is a particularly appropriate metaphor for an aesthetic of sympathy, grounded in a predicament of reading it must disavow. The numbness and numbers that devour sympathy in *Daniel Deronda* may be thought of as the pressure of telepathy as an irreducible difference and distance (*tele*) within *pathos*; and, as Latimer's predicament emphasizes, this difference and distance is that of language in its materiality, in its dependence on "arbitrary marks," in Hertz's phrase, "without which no investments of any sort—not just no bets—would be conceivable" ("Some Words," 295).

Only clairvoyantly would Latimer have called himself a telepath, since the first recorded use of the word "telepathy" dates from two years after

George Eliot's death.[33] We have said enough to suggest the term's eccentric but fundamental position within an Enlightenment discourse of sympathy; it should be added that this term and its cognates emerge at the fault line between the late nineteenth-century popularization of the occult, on the one hand, and the new psychological and social sciences, on the other. Much like the various theories and practices of hypnosis or suggestion current at the time, and in certain respects like those of hysteria, telepathy takes its place in the history of the production of the human sciences as another version of what one of the fathers of sociology, Gabriel Tarde, called the "contagion" of "imitation."[34] From our present perspective this is not without interest. The self-dispersion toward which the tropes of writing, theatricality, and gambling gesture in Eliot's novels may also be represented in the terms of the question Mikkel Borch-Jacobsen hears in Freud's texts: "Does primary sociality begin in the stage of transition toward the object, of the face-to-face encounter with others? Or does it precede the *positioning* of others, which means the positioning of the ego as well?"[35] Borch-Jacobsen's focus is on Freud's writings on mass psychology, but in the process he comments on the widespread interest in telepathy among turn-of-the-century scholars, from Bergson and William James to the sociologists and crowd-theorists whose texts had direct influence on Freud's. Tarde, for instance, defines "pure and absolute" sociality as "such an intense concentration of urban life that as soon as a good idea arose in one mind it would be instantaneously transmitted to all minds throughout the city" (*The Laws of Imitation*, 70). One finds a similar sense of primary, even magical, sociality in Le Bon's theory of crowds. For Le Bon, in Borch-Jacobsen's summary, the "unconscious . . . is indissolubly nonsubjectal and 'social'," since Le Bon "never designates anything but immediate communication with others . . . prior to any consciousness of self, and thus also prior to any consciousness of others. Taken to the extreme, it is thought transmission, telepathy. . . ."[36] As another name for the "contagion of

33. The *OED* lists "telepathy" as a coinage ventured in 1882 to "cover all cases of impression received at a distance without the normal operation of the recognized sense organs." See Frederick Myers et al., "First Report of the Literary Committee," *Proceedings of the Society for Psychical Research*, vol. 1, part 2 (London: Trübner, 1883), 147; cited in Royle, *Telepathy and Literature*, 2.

34. Gabriel Tarde, *The Laws of Imitation*, trans. Elsie Clews Parsons (New York: Henry Holt, 1903 [1895]), 11. Tarde's commitment to the principle of mimesis is so thoroughgoing that not only does society, in his text, begin "on the day when one man first copied another," but imitation itself turns out to be self-imitation, represented in psychological terms: "[E]very act of perception, in as much as it involves an act of memory, which it always does, implies a kind of habit, an unconscious imitation of self by self" (75).

35. Mikkel Borch-Jacobsen, *The Freudian Subject*, trans. Catherine Porter (Stanford: Stanford University Press, 1988), 133.

36. Borch-Jacobsen, *The Freudian Subject*, 140. From the viewpoint of a critique of aesthetic ideology as we elaborated it in chapter one, Le Bon's text and Borch-Jacobsen's discussion of it

imitation"—a phrase that Le Bon uses in imitation of Tarde—telepathy figures repeatedly in writings of this period as a fantastic shadow cast by the production of theories and practices of psychology and sociology, technologies of propaganda and marketing, and the various sciences of the self and its unconscious.

Freud's own conceptualization of the unconscious has a relation to telepathy sufficiently intimate that on at least one occasion he proposed the unconscious as the mediating element which might ultimately grant telepathy an organic base—though the first analogy that comes to Freud's mind, significantly enough, is that of a technical apparatus, the telephone:

> The analogy with other transformations, such as occur in speaking and hearing by telephone, would then be unmistakable. And only think if one could get hold of this physical equivalent of the psychical act! It would seem to me that psychoanalysis, by inserting the unconscious between what is physical and what was previously called "psychical," has paved the way for the assumption of such processes as telepathy. If only one accustoms oneself to the idea of telepathy, one can accomplish a great deal with it—for the time being, it is true, only in imagination. It is a familiar fact that we do not know how the common purpose comes about in the great insect communities: possibly it is done by means of a direct psychical transference of this kind. One is led to the suspicion that this is the original, archaic method of communication between individuals and that in the course of phylogenetic evolution it has been replaced by the better method of giving information with the help of signals which are picked up by the sense organs. But the older method might have persisted in the back-

---

would reward attention. For Le Bon the crowd embodies the "genius of a race," but also represents, as Borch-Jacobsen shows, "the hybrid and monstrous base" below race identity (136), and, furthermore, is associated with hysteria and femininity, since a crowd has no identity that does not come from an external "suggestion" or imitation. As in Tarde's text, a hyperinflation of mimesis besets this model. Borch-Jacobsen describes the leader of a Le Bon crowd as the incarnation of will-power and subjectivity that gives the crowd form; however, though this aesthetic and metaphysical model informs the tradition Le Bon inherited and forwarded, his text offers symptomatic complications: "The leader himself has most often started out as one of the led. He has himself been hypnotised by the idea, whose apostle he has become. It has taken possession of him to such a degree that everything outside it vanishes." Gustave Le Bon, *The Crowd: A Study of the Popular Mind* (London: Unwin Brothers, n.d.), 134. Also of interest is a passage in which language is imagined as emerging from the crowd's mimetic whirlpool, accompanied by a whiff of telepathy: "What, for instance, can be more complicated, more logical, than a language? Yet whence can this admirably organized production have arisen, except it be the outcome of the unconscious genius of crowds? . . . Even with respect to the ideas of great men are we certain that they are exclusively the offspring of their brains? No doubt such ideas are always created by solitary minds, but is it not the genius of crowds that has furnished the thousand grains of dust forming the soil in which they have sprung up?" (9).

ground and still be able to put itself into effect under certain conditions—
for instance, in passionately excited mobs.[37]

Freud's speculations on telepathy have struck many shrewd readers as
being speculations on the possibility of psychoanalysis itself: "That the
unconscious of the subject is the discourse of the other appears even more
clearly in the studies that Freud devoted to what he called telepathy," Lacan
comments.[38] Jacques Derrida's claim, which we earlier heard Royle imitat-
ing, is that it is "[d]ifficult to imagine a theory of what they still call the
unconscious without a theory of telepathy" ("Telepathy," 14). Borch-
Jacobsen will suggest in a similar spirit that "the analysis of the ego (psychoanalysis)" only occurs by surpassing itself and "identifying itself with
(and as) mass psychology" (*The Freudian Subject*, 133): a comment nicely
supported by Freud's implicit link, in the passage cited above, between the
unconscious and "passionately excited mobs." At the telepathic interface,
the trope of the unconscious overlaps with that of the crowd. The crowd
embodies a dream of direct communication, but a certain technicity, even
non-humanity, remains inscribed in this dream's production, and records
itself in Freud's phylogenetic and entomological speculations. As a locus of
excessive communicability, telepathy places psychoanalysis within the
thought of a pre-subjective, ineradicably social, and technically displaced
Dasein. Telepathy, in other words, is a figure for the radically fictional,
"literary" dimension of the political, and establishes undecidability as the
condition of the self. For whose pathos is it, once tele-pathy has begun?
And how would one ever even know whether it has begun or not?

The trope of the insect community appears to be lodged between telepathy and technics in late nineteenth-century discourse, and it surfaces with
surprising frequency in Eliot's oeuvre. "When George Eliot refers to insects
it is invariably in what we would call a telepathic atmosphere," Royle
comments (107), drawing attention to passages in *Daniel Deronda* (in which
ardent men of vision mold and feed "the more passive life which without
them would dwindle and shrivel into the narrow tenacity of insects, un-

37. Sigmund Freud, "Dreams and Occultism," in *New Introductory Lectures on Psycho-Analysis*,
vol. 22 of *The Complete Psychological Works of Sigmund Freud*, trans. and ed. James Strachey et al.
24 vols. (London: Hogarth, 1966–74), 22:55. Freud's principal other reflections on telepathy
may be found in "Psychoanalysis and Telepathy" (1941 [1921]), SE 18:177–93; and "Dreams and
Telepathy" (1925 [1921]), ibid., 197–220. On the overdetermined figure of the telephone see
Avital Ronell, *The Telephone Book: Technology — Schizophrenia — Electric Speech* (Lincoln: University of Nebraska Press, 1989).
38. Jacques Lacan, "The Function and Field of Speech and Language in Psychoanalysis," in
Ecrits: A Selection, trans. Alan Sheridan (New York: Norton, 1977), 55. For a study of the
interplay between psychoanalysis and telepathy (and more generally, suggestion and hypnosis, against which, of course, psychoanalysis rebelled in constituting itself), see François Rou-
stang, *Psychoanalysis Never Lets Go*, trans. Ned Lukacher (Baltimore: Johns Hopkins University
Press, 1983), 43–65.

shaken by thoughts beyond the reaches of their antennae" [749]) and *Mid-dlemarch* (in which Dorothea dilates with Mr. Farebrother "on the possible histories of creatures that converse compendiously with their antennae, and for aught we know may hold reformed parliaments" [843]). But Royle's examples do scant justice to the force of his observation: much more re-markable telepathic insects and machines populate texts that Eliot wrote before and after her novel-writing period. In an essay on "Women in France" (1854), reflecting on the changes mass literacy had brought to the conditions of literary production, Eliot observed that the intersubjectivity of the salon had yielded to the anonymity of print, the incessant labor of reading printed texts, and the possibility of being read by them. "It is no longer the coterie which acts on literature, but literature which acts on the coterie": "In fact, the evident tendency of things to contract personal com-munication within the narrowest limits makes us tremble lest some further development of electric telegraph should reduce us to a society of mutes, or to a sort of insects, communicating by ingenious antennae of our own invention" (Pinney, 90). The insect here acquires overlapping connotations of technics, telepathy, and mutilation—a mutilation of voice, consequent upon a "writing" in which the subject is lost in an excessive immediacy of communication. Two years later Eliot returned to a version of this microfan-tasy, substituting for the insect an animated machine. In the middle of a high-powered and affirmative discussion of tradition and language in "The Natural History of German Life," an imagined reader is suddenly warned of the evils of "a patent de-odorized and non resonant language, which effects the purpose of communication as perfectly and rapidly as algebraic signs": "With the anomalies and inconveniences of historical language, you will have parted with its music and its passion . . . and the next step in simplification will be the invention of a talking watch, which will achieve the utmost facility and dispatch in the communication of ideas by a gradu-ated adjustment of ticks, to be represented in writing by a corresponding arrangement of dots. A melancholy 'language of the future'!" (Pinney, 287–88). Here the Gothic possibilities of mutilation and prosthetic supplementa-tion remain unactualized, but the specifically linguistic nature of the threat attains sharper focus. Common both to this passage and to the one in "Women in France," furthermore, is a temporal scheme, one we saw inver-ted in Freud's phylogenetic speculations, but preserved right-side-up in his allusions to future posssibilities. In Eliot the emphasis is unidirectional: the mechanical overproduction of communication belongs to the future, as though for the sympathetic imagination, as for Latimer in *The Lifted Veil*, the end of history could only be its own death as telepathy.

  These visions may be little more than expository hiccoughs; but two decades later, after the novels, the telepathy machine was to make a more remarkable appearance in Eliot's oeuvre. The penultimate chapter of her last published text, *Impressions of Theophrastus Such*, is titled "Shadows of the Coming Race" in allusion to a science fiction story by Bulwer-Lytton, and it develops a pseudo-Darwinian hypothesis that, at the end of history, machines will supplant humanity. By evolving "conditions of self-supply, self-repair, and reproduction," technology will be able to "reproduce itself by some process of fission or budding," thus attaining the self-sufficiency of *physis* with parodic literalness.[39] The topic is a rather incongruous one for George Eliot, as the narrator's sourly mock-serious tone for the most part confirms—but, at the fantasy's climax, that tone shades into another key, as a final surge of energy illuminates Eliot's prose:

> Who—if our consciousness is, as I have been given to understand, a mere stumbling of our organisms on their way to unconscious perfection—who shall say that those fittest existences will not be found along the track of what we call inorganic combinations, which will carry on the most elaborate processes as mutely and painlessly as we are now told that the minerals are metamorphosing themselves continually in the dark laboratory of the earth's crust? Thus this planet may be filled with beings who will be blind and deaf as the inmost rock, yet will execute changes as delicate and complicated as those of human language and all the intricate web of what we call its effects, without sensitive impression, without sensitive impulse: there may be, let us say, mute orations, mute rhapsodies, mute discussions, and no consciousness there even to enjoy the silence. (*Theophrastus Such*, 254–55)

Without entirely losing its satiric edge, the text generates a moment of epistemological grappling worthy of those troubling the major turns of *Middlemarch* or *Daniel Deronda*: we hear in this paragraph something of the "rhythm of the sublime" that Hertz observes to be guiding Dorothea's attempt to internalize the alien codes of Rome (*EL*, 90). Even more remarkably, the anaphoric pulse of sublime language is attained by way of nothing less than the figure of "human language" itself. Something strange and plural, first called "processes," then "changes," is likened first to geological metamorphosis, then, more insistently, to language and its "effects," to

39. George Eliot, *Impressions of Theophrastus Such* (Edinburgh: Blackwood, n.d.), 250, 253; subsequent references are to this edition. The metaphysical inflection of technology has been discussed elsewhere, particularly in the previous chapter, but we may recall here Heidegger's definition of the contrast between *technē* and *physis:* the former involves an efficient cause—the artist or artisan—whereas that which is *physis* is "*poiesis* in the highest sense" because it "has the bursting open belonging to bringing-forth, e.g., the bursting of a blossom into bloom, in itself (*en heautoi*)." Martin Heidegger, *The Question concerning Technology and Other Essays*, trans. William Lovitt (New York: Harper and Row, 1977), 10.

language as trope and performance—the substitution of such technical terms would be entirely in the spirit of this passage. The most extraordinary representations barely suffice as Eliot's text seeks words for the strangeness of words. Here, at history's end, the telepathy machine has become sheer "tele," devoid of "pathos," an impossible trope-machine cut off from the phenomenal world but possessed of "effects" nonetheless. These uncannily neutral "processes" and "changes" are at once objectless and—since the machines lack all consciousness—subjectless: they describe the formality of a substitutive process apart from all meaning or intention. Radically a-referential in their formalized perfection, the machines might be said to act upon the world with the efficacity of a total technology, were it not for the loss of sense suffered by any notion of "action" in this scenario. The machines "execute changes" interpretable as linguistic "effects"; but in the absence of agent and object this effectivity becomes a paradoxical catechresis, legible only when we impute to it the meaning it disallows. However necessary it may be to conclude that "language" "acts," one cannot claim to have said anything meaningful in saying so—except by mistake.

Theophrastus Such is a strange text, one that Eliot's twentieth-century critics have largely preferred to ignore. It has, indeed, arguably proved the least welcome of all her works, lacking the vivid Gothicism of "The Lifted Veil," or the narrative and thematic interest of "Brother Jacob" and the poetry. Worst of all, it comes at the end of a career which can certainly be closed off in more satisfying fashion with the grander ambiguities of *Daniel Deronda;* one is instead presented with the spectacle of an author turning from her most courageously experimental novel to an atavistic genre and a tonality at once bitter and ponderous. But within the context of Eliot's oeuvre this text also presents itself as curiously overdetermined. The European revival of Theophrastus can be traced to Isaac Casaubon's publication of the Greek text with Latin translation and commentary in 1592; this, according to Gordon Haight, is in fact the edition that George Eliot used.[40] In her rewriting of it, Eliot touches most of the generic stops of the Theophrastan character sketch as it descends from La Bruyère and Addison and Steele: a didactic concern for decorum; a survey of the petty faults of an urban bourgeois class; a wide-ranging overview of society spun around the castigation of exemplary, allegorically named "characters." But in Eliot's hands these generic directives assemble a world saturated with conversation, writing, and publishing: nearly every sketch in *Theophrastus Such* concerns authorship, injury, and the dangerously volatile circulation of intellectual property. Eliot's own Mr. Casaubon had fought his ghostly textual

40. See Gordon Haight, "Poor Mr Casaubon," in *George Eliot's Originals and Contemporaries: Essays in Victorian Literary History and Biography,* ed. Hugh Witemeyer (Ann Arbor: University of Michigan Press, 1992), 31.

battles with critics bearing Theophrastan names (Carp, Pike, Tench); in *Theophrastus Such* Casaubon's anxious scholarly jousting inflates into the guiding principle of an urban, fin-de-siècle bachelor world in which quarter is rarely given or received.[41] Nearly every inhabitant of this world is a failed or failing author, suffers from the "disease of magnified self-importance belonging to small authorship" (*Theophrastus Such*, 224), and takes eager note of the shortcomings of everyone else: the first-person male narrator adds to these qualities that of slightly strident moralist, pronouncing in Juvenalian fashion on the debasement of the nation's "moral currency." In content and tone as well as in the conventions of its genre, the text turns away from or falls short of Eliotic sympathy; it is correspondingly hard to read.

But in a sense sympathy has withered under the weight of its own over-performance: it has shrunk thanks to its ungovernable inflation into a telepathic hypercirculation of signs. In the commodified and competitive world of *Theophrastus Such*, telepathy becomes the problem of plagiarism. One of the character sketches composing this strange, gloomy text stars a plagiarist who steals language from essays such as "The Natural History of German Life" as he expatiates on "that growing preparation for every epoch through which certain ideas or modes of view are said to be in the air, and, still more metaphorically speaking, to be inevitably absorbed, so that every one may be excused for not knowing how he got them" (158). In this sketch the narrator excoriates the plagiarist for his ethical levity; but curiously enough, after giving vent to his language-machine fantasy in "Shadows of the Coming Race," the narrator will plagiarize the plagiarist: the premises of his telepathy-fantasy, he says, "seem to be flying about in the air with other germs, and have found a sort of nidus among my melancholy fancies. Nobody really holds them" (249). This excuse, however, does not prove entirely airtight (even though "hardly any accusation is more difficult to prove, and more likely to be false, than that of a plagiarism" [163]). Like the narrator of the earlier sketch, Eliza Savage had no patience with such fudging; she wrote to Samuel Butler that "the only bit in the least bit readable [in *Theophrastus Such*] is a crib from *Erewhon*—a most barefaced

41. On the bachelor in nineteenth-century British narrative, see Eve Sedgwick, "The Beast in the Closet: James and the Writing of Homosexual Panic," in her *Epistemology of the Closet* (Berkeley: University of California Press, 1990), 182–212, especially 188–95: "Where the Gothic hero had been solipsistic, the bachelor hero is selfish. Where the Gothic hero had raged, the bachelor hero bitches. Where the Gothic hero had been suicidally inclined, the bachelor hero is a hypochondriac" (188–89). These comments capture at least part of the ambience of *Theophrastus Such*, as do Sedgwick's witty reflections on the "feline gratuitousness of aggression" in the bachelor world: "At odd moments one is apt to find kitty's unsheathed claws a millimeter from one's own eyes. . . . When one bachelor consults another bachelor about a third bachelor, nothing is left but ears and whiskers" (192).

crib."[42] Butler wrote in turn to his sister of the "compliment" Eliot had paid him in introducing "a certain chapter on machines": "I had the satisfaction that great minds had thought alike—that was all; but the resemblance is so close that there can be no doubt where she drew it from."[43] Eliot's biographer, Gordon Haight, suggests that "the idea had probably been discussed with friends like Spencer while Lewes was writing the section on 'Animal Automatism' in *Problems*";[44] and we are not likely to learn more about how this particular airborne germ blew into George Eliot's mind. It is, however, (nearly) indisputable that her title alludes to the text that Butler himself had been suspected of plagiarizing; he had gone to some pains in the preface to the second edition of *Erewhon* to prove that his novel had been written before "the first advertisement of [Bulwer-Lytton's] 'The Coming Race' appeared."[45] The ballooning question of plagiarism, within and without *Theophrastus Such*, enacts the predicament which embitters this text but which also made the novels possible. Sympathy's condition of possibility is its own destruction; or, put another way, sympathy's reiterated, fragile survival occurs thanks to a capacity for error which Eliot's texts at various times call writing, melodrama, gambling, plagiarism, or telepathy, and which, in the rhetorical terminology proper to a critique of aesthetics, may be called irony.

42. Geoffrey Keynes and Brian Hill, eds., *Letters Between Samuel Butler and Miss E. M. A. Savage (1871–1885)* (London: Jonathan Cape, 1935), 210.
43. Daniel F. Howard, ed., *The Correspondence of Samuel Butler with His Sister May* (Berkeley: University of California Press, 1962), 86.
44. Gordon S. Haight, *George Eliot: A Biography* (New York: Oxford University Press, 1968), 522.
45. "'Erewhon' was finished with the exception of the last twenty pages and a sentence or two inserted from time to time here and there throughout the book, before the first advertisement of 'The Coming Race' appeared. . . . [B]eing in an out of the way part of Italy, [I] never saw a single review of 'The Coming Race', nor a copy of the work. On my return, I purposely avoided looking into it until I had sent back my last revises to the printer." Samuel Butler, *Erewhon; or, Over the Range*, ed. Hans-Peter Breuer and Daniel F. Howard (Newark: University of Delaware Press, 1981), 41. *The Coming Race* had been published anonymously late in 1871, but was known to be by Bulwer-Lytton; *Erewhon* was also published anonymously, and its initial success, as Butler suspected, was mostly due to its being taken as a sequel to *The Coming Race*. When the *Athenaeum* of 25 May 1872 revealed Butler's authorship, sales dropped 90 percent.

6

Aesthetics and History:
L'Education sentimentale

I'm having a lot of trouble linking my characters to the political events of
1848; I'm afraid the background will devour the foreground.
—Gustave Flaubert to Jules Duplan

The foregoing chapters have emphasized that aesthetics is a theory
and an ideology of history, but so far the question of history has not
achieved centrality. We have seen that the notion of the *Bildungsroman* is
inherently historical insofar as it claims to represent or enact aesthetic pedagogy, since the temporal arc of the individual subject's *Bildung* always at
least potentially exemplifies that of humanity. We have also seen, however,
that the literary texts designated by the notion of the *Bildungsroman* destroy
the aesthetic narratives they provide. They do not simply cast doubt on the
rationale or the outcome of an aesthetic education; rather, they generate
within the narrative of aesthetics allegories of its incoherent and uncontrollable production. The disruptive figural narratives we have encountered in
variously innocent or sinister locales—a child's identification with marionettes in the *Lehrjahre*, a medical student's dissection of marionettes in the
Wanderjahre, Madame Laure's murderous blow in *Middlemarch*—suggest
that a "historicity" irreducible to representation inhabits aesthetic historicism, precisely because the latter ultimately has no choice but to seek to
ground itself on the potential arbitrariness—the "literariness"—of language.[1] It is now time to pursue that suggestion further by way of a text
more consistently focused on the matter of revolutionary history.

Flaubert's *L'Education sentimentale* is useful territory on which to plot a
conclusion to this study, since in addition to raising the question of the
historical event, the text mercilessly exacerbates the negative spiral that
seems to be the only condition of possibility of a *Bildungsroman*. Already in
the *Lehrjahre*, as we saw, *Bildung* is recuperable, if at all, only as its own

---

1. See chapter 1 for a full account of the paradox of aesthetic formalism.

negation; but in the case of Goethe's novel this insight required a degree of critical attention to obtain, while in that of *L'Education sentimentale* it would add up to little more than a critical commonplace. The *Bildungsroman* may or may not exist, but one can at least be sure that Flaubert's novel will participate in this generic conundrum only as "an *Unbildungsroman* of genius."[2] Such negative certainty has its own seductions, of course. Since Flaubert's irony is neither sympathetic nor olympian in tenor, the aesthetic promise of his texts is all the more extreme, for the rigor of such obviously undeluded irony purges aesthetics of any lingering traces of idealist naïveté. When one adds to this rigor the pathos of a life dedicated to it, the result is a potent brew. It is no accident that over the course of the last century Flaubert has become a more genuinely international figure than Eliot or Goethe. "Flaubert seems very much at the source of a conception of the artist which is still with us," Jonathan Culler comments;[3] and the historical success of this conception derives from its ability to link a valorization of the artwork's formal purity to a prurient obsession with the artist, or at the very least with the artist's self-sacrifice. The painful, sweaty, useless labor of writing; the blend of idealism, self-glamorization, and corrosive nihilism with which this labor is performed; the self-consumptive technologization of aesthetic composition such that writing becomes an endless askesis of rewriting, paring and deleting, asymptotically headed toward a "livre sur rien," or, in another famous formulation, toward a Book that "inasmuch as one separates oneself from it as author, does not require any approach by the reader"[4]—in short, the artist and the oeuvre of modernism find their image in Flaubert, the "true Penelope" of more than one twentieth-century literary destiny or desire. Flaubert's name has come to signify the production and ratification of literature itself.

As a result, Flaubert—particularly the Flaubert of *Madame Bovary*—has become the object of fascinated scrutiny in a way few other cultural icons have. There is probably no real equivalent to Sartre's massive *L'Idiot de la famille* elsewhere in mainstream literary-critical discourse, nor is it easy to think of a novel that has inspired more whimsical metafiction than *Madame Bovary*. The lure of impersonality partly lies in our urge to violate it: to

2. Stirling Haig, *Flaubert and the Gift of Speech: Dialog and Discourse in Four "Modern" Novels* (Cambridge: Cambridge University Press, 1986), 159. An older school of criticism emphasized more positive links between Flaubert and the putative father of the *Bildungsroman*. Flaubert admired Goethe and refers to him frequently in his correspondence: details may be obtained in Léon Degoumois, *Flaubert à l'école de Goethe* (Geneva: Sonor, 1925); see also René Dumesnil, *L'Education sentimentale de Gustave Flaubert* (Paris: Nizet, 1963), 80–82.
3. Jonathan Culler, *Flaubert: The Uses of Uncertainty*, rev. ed. (Ithaca: Cornell University Press, [1974] 1985), 12.
4. Stéphane Mallarmé, *Oeuvres complètes* (Paris: Gallimard, 1945), 372.

discover, whether in the name of existential analysis or metafictional play, a subject and a referential world behind the text's austere formal performance.[5] And in addition to aggravating our desire for biography, the formal opacity of the fiction inspires the telling of another sort of ætiological narrative: in becoming the signatory of "literature," Flaubert becomes the origin of various and conflicting literary-historical developments—realism, modernism, "postmodernism." In all cases these narratives are characterized by a double figure of preservation and destruction: a name and a story link themselves to a vision of literature's emergence through its own self-obliteration. Flaubert's excision of "any novelistic element," Zola tells us, produces realism; his self-reflexive practice of citation, Michel Foucault claims, produces modernism—"Joyce, Roussel, Kafka, Pound, Borges. The library is on fire."[6] Thus, at one point in the writings of the most prominent Sartrean in Anglo-American criticism, Fredric Jameson, Flaubert becomes "the privileged locus" of a modernity "which the term *reification* in its strictest sense designates": "[T]he depersonalization of the text, the laundering of authorial intention, but also the disappearance from the horizon of its readership, which will become the *public introuvable* of modernism, are all so many features on which the process of reification feeds, using Flaubert's aesthetic vocation as its vehicle and mode of realization."[7] Inherited from Lukács and Sartre, Jameson's model projects onto a historical axis the onto-theological patterns of the biographical and referential approach. At the origin, a closed communicative circuit returns meaning to a subject, while the fall into literature becomes an illegitimate descent into matter via the trope of "reification." Jameson's particular emphases in this passage are by no means determinative—at other points his dialectical model will valorize modernism differently—but Flaubert's appearance at this point in *The Political Unconscious* is not accidental and testifies to the ambivalence with which critics tend to express their fascination with the idea and practice of literature.

5. See Woody Allen's witty "The Kugelmass Episode," in *Side Effects* (New York: Random House, 1980), and Raymond Jean's less amusing *Mademoiselle Bovary* (Avignon: Actes Sud, 1991): both texts mobilize the conceit that Flaubert's novel is a world that can be entered, lived in, changed, and so on. An elegant and shrewd fictional meditation on Flaubert is Julian Barnes, *Flaubert's Parrot* (London: Jonathan Cape, 1984).

6. Emile Zola, *Les Romanciers naturalistes* (Paris: Charpentier, 1881), 125–26, cited in Jonathan Culler, "The Uses of *Madame Bovary*," in *Flaubert and Postmodernism*, ed. Naomi Schor and Henry F. Majewski (Lincoln: University of Nebraska Press, 1984), 1–12. For Flaubert as "postmodernist" see, of course, this collection. Michel Foucault's comments are directed at *La Tentation de Saint Antoine*: see "Fantasia of the Library," in *Language, Countermemory, Practice: Selected Essays and Interviews by Michel Foucault*, ed. Donald F. Bouchard, trans. Donald F. Bouchard and Sherry Simon (Ithaca: Cornell University Press, 1977), 92.

7. Fredric Jameson, *The Political Unconscious: Narrative as a Socially Symbolic Act* (Ithaca: Cornell University Press, 1981), 220–21.

No text by Flaubert has been more frequently celebrated for its formal virtuosity or mined for its biographical content than *L'Education senti-mentale*.[8] And as Jameson's comment makes clear, the question of Flaubert's formalism is bound up with the question of what history is. If history is the world's fall into capitalist reification, and if literature is a product and a mirror of that catastrophe, then the critic's recovery of a subject for the literary text—even the most negative, bored, self-hating subject—would function as a token of history's essential humanity. One may call such a hope "idealist," but it animates in covert fashion much of what counts as literary criticism, and it is not easy to avoid. *L'Educa-tion sentimentale* offers us the aesthetic in its most icily negative mode— as the humanization, universalization, and, thus, the historical recupera-tion of the petty destiny of Frédéric Moreau via the askesis of pure form. Yet as Culler remarks, a "curious indeterminacy" has also been felt to be exerting pressure on the seemingly clear theme of "a *Bildungsroman* gone sour" (*Flaubert*, 135–36). In what follows I hope to show that this novel allows us to read the irreducibility of history to narrative, even the narra-tive of a catastrophe. Not for nothing is Frédéric's story that of 1848, the revolution redux—the farcical reiteration of tragedy, as Marx famously put it, when "only the ghost [*Gespenst*] of the old revolution walked about."[9] Though *L'Education sentimentale* does narrate and scrutinize the story of reification that Jameson tells, the text also suggests the perti-nence of Marx's spectral trope by exploring the possibility that uncanny, non-organic and non-aesthetic patterns of repetition compose the events we call historical.

I

The peculiar difficulties Flaubert's texts pose to interpretation are well known. Although the forms and conventions of nineteenth-century narrative remain in place, particularly in the "realist" novels *Madame Bovary* and *L'Education sentimentale*, the meaning of these forms is program-matically compromised, and at times radically shaken. The characters in *L'Education sentimentale* are coherent entities, and Frédéric is a psychologi-cally nuanced one, but once we begin to read the text with care, the point of

8. For the canonical account of what used to be called "les protagonistes dans le roman et les personnages réels dans la vie," see Dumesnil's chapter of that title, in *L'Education sentimentale de Gustave Flaubert*, 15–78.
9. Karl Marx, *The Eighteenth Brumaire of Louis Bonaparte* (New York: International Publishers, 1963), 17. Subsequent quotations are to this edition; the translation has at times been silently modified with an eye to the German text in Karl Marx and Friedrich Engels, *Werke* (Berlin: Dietz Verlag, 1960), 8:115–207.

these representations rapidly becomes dubious. Not only is Frédéric's a boring and mediocre consciousness, but the novel's interest in portraying this consciousness is somewhat sporadic, as though the text itself felt as a burden the monotony of its own unfolding. The things that happen to Frédéric fall short of significance, despite the perfectly conventional—which is to say, reasonably Balzacian—assembly of coincidences moving him through a relatively circumscribed field of characters and events.[10] On the face of it—though of course this is the question with which we are here proposing to dwell—neither his "sentimental education" nor his encounter with history in 1848 appears to add up to much. The former interferes with his experience of the latter but, as we shall see, fails to provide any secure locus of value. Meanwhile, though Frédéric himself at various points feels he has missed out on history because of his overinvestment in a bourgeois romance plot, the text suggests the inadequacy and bad faith of this reading as well, since his participation in the assault on the Tuileries leaves him with no clear psychological or symbolic profit. Neither the public world of revolution nor the private world of love offers any immediate justification for novelistic representation.

Furthermore, no uncompromised symbolic meaning takes up the slack. In this respect the problem of historical representation is exemplary: the main articulations of Frédéric's private life echo those of the historical narrative, but never quite allow the hero's education, or the failure of his education, to acquire the full dignity of a symbol.[11] On the eve of the February uprisings, Frédéric fails to seduce Mme Arnoux but succeeds in getting her profane double, Rosanette, to take her place in his bed; on the eve of Louis Napoléon's coup d'état, witnessing the "vente de Mme Arnoux," Frédéric sees his ideal woman metaphorically dissolve into commodity exchange: these parallels—a second-best beginning; a sordid end—

10. The ways in which Flaubert mimes and undercuts the Balzacian novel have frequently been studied; for a recent analysis, see Peter Brooks, "Retrospective Lust, or Flaubert's Perversities," in *Reading for the Plot: Design and Intention in Narrative* (New York: Vintage, 1985), 171–215.

11. The parallels are elaborate and carefully plotted: see Maria Amalia Cajuero-Roggero, "Diner chez les Dambreuses: 'La réaction commençante'," in *Histoire et langage dans 'L'Education sentimentale' de Flaubert* (Paris: Société d'édition d'enseignement supérieur, 1981), 63–76, and Anne Herschberg-Pierrot, "Le travail des stéréotypes dans les brouillons de la 'prise des Tuileries'," 43–61, in the same collection. As Cajuero-Roggero shows, manuscript versions of *L'Education sentimentale* make clear that the dinner at the Dambreuses takes place on 2 July, which is when the forces of reaction gained visibility when Cavaignac reviewed his troops at the Concorde; similarly, Dussardier is killed on the day when, according to Flaubert's notes, popular resistance was definitively crushed. Flaubert suppressed or camouflaged his array of significant dates in the final version of the manuscript. Herschberg-Pierrot's study recovers several intriguing examples: the "prise des Tuileries" is carefully dated 24 February in an early manuscript; and Frédéric and Rosanette leave for Fontainebleau on the 20th of June.

offer the teasing possibility of a symbolic structure, but one is also left with a sense that the interpretation has succeeded only at the cost of missing the point. Textual elements that ought to be symbolic raise problems that nag at the reading mind: Rosanette's diseased and short-lived baby, for instance, should be an embodiment of historical decay, but the dates of its conception and birth do not quite match any date of political significance, and one is left either with a handful of loose ends or with the weaker and more gratuitous claim that the infant embodies belatedness, sterility, insignificance, and so on. The transformation of Arnoux's periodical and art gallery *L'Art industriel* into an earthenware factory and, finally, a trade in religious artefacts suggests, like the "vente" of Mme Arnoux, a certain degradation, an increasing triumph of the commodity; so does Frédéric's acquisition of a second mistress, the moneyed Mme Dambreuse, at the beginning of part 3; but the categories needed to organize these events into a meaningful pattern are sufficiently large and vague as to seem slightly otiose. Things get even worse if we abandon the historical dimension and begin portioning out the binary oppositions of literary and theological tradition. Mme Arnoux and Rosanette may be linked and opposed as the ideal and the actual, spirit and flesh, sacred and profane, and so on; with the arrival of Mme Dambreuse the lure of the profane becomes that of *avaritia* as well as *voluptas;* these and other allegories spin easily out of Frédéric's story, and in their overscripted facility announce themselves as received ideas, the hermeneutic equivalent of Arnoux's commodified icons. Anything can and must be interpreted in this textual world, but the resultant meanings come accompanied by a faint or glaring aura of *bêtise.*

Yet even that generalization is insufficiently guarded, for at times Flaubert's text will achieve a density such that one cannot be sure whether one is trapped within an ironic structure or not. In the great final scene between Frédéric and Mme Arnoux, for instance, the text blends ironic distance with dramatic intensity such that the status of phrases such as Mme Arnoux's famous future anterior "nous nous serons bien aimés" becomes impossible to decide.[12] The scene is genuinely moving, and draws on the memory of other moments of intensity in the history of Frédéric and Mme Arnoux's star-crossed love; yet the future anterior assertion—we will have loved: in a time not yet present, our love will be past; our love is fiction, the affirmation of an imagined memory—manages to be at once

12. Gustave Flaubert, *L'Education sentimentale*, in *Oeuvres complètes* (Paris: Club de l'Honnête Homme, 1971–75), 3:394. Subsequent references are to this edition; English translations have been taken from *Sentimental Education*, trans. Robert Baldick (Harmondsworth: Penguin, 1964), but have frequently had to be revised: Baldick's translation of Mme Arnoux's phrase, for instance, "we have loved each other well" (413), misses the whole point of the phrase by ignoring Flaubert's future anterior ("we will have loved"). Double page numbers refer to the French and English editions respectively.

delicately affirmative and naggingly deluded. The fragile and radical fictionality of love occurs as a citation that, in marking its fictional status, falls short of itself, while retaining its pathos:

> "Sometimes your words come back to me like a distant echo, like the sound of a bell carried by the wind; and I feel you are there, when I read about love in books."
>
> "Everything one criticizes as exaggerated in books, you have made me feel," said Frédéric. "I can understand Werther not being put off by Charlotte's bread and butter." (393–44/413)

Even the slightly comic reference to *Werther*, of all texts, does not strip the passage of its force; yet at the same time, if Frédéric and Mme Arnoux can express themselves only through literary language, the ethical and libidinal correlatives to this predicament create an uncertain hovering between authenticity and bad faith. Shocked by her age, Frédéric pours out his love "to conceal from her his disappointment," and falls into his own illusion: "She rapturously accepted this adoration of the woman she no longer was. Frédéric, drunk on his own words, began to believe what he was saying" (394/414). The scene builds toward an elegant and merciless paragraph:

> Frédéric suspected Madame Arnoux of having come to offer herself; and he was seized by a desire [*convoitise*] stronger than ever, frenzied, rabid. Yet he also felt something else, an indefinable feeling, a repulsion, like the dread of incest. Another fear stopped him, that of being disgusted later. Besides, what a nuisance it would be! And partly out of prudence and partly to avoid degrading his ideal, he turned on his heel and started rolling a cigarette. (395/415)

The slippage of love's literary language into the blend of passion and calculation of a "convoitise"; the careful splicing of motive such that Frédéric's archaic fear of incest becomes no more and no less compelling than his worry about an awkward entanglement; the coolly incisive summation of his turn away from Mme Arnoux, "tout à la fois par prudence et pour ne pas dégrader son idéal"—all this psychological fretwork shows Flaubert a master of literary realism and as such presents no difficulty; however, over the course of this scene the trope of "love" becomes illegibly poised between irony and affirmation. Read figuratively, as its own ironic negation, love provides a certain bleak knowledge: the sentimental education will at least have been able to confirm the essential falseness of love. Read literally, as an affirmation of itself, love offers us the delicate integrity of fiction ("nous nous serons bien aimés") but makes the sentimental education irrelevant, since the pure fictionality of this love's temporal structure has nothing to do with the accretive temporality of experience, being spun out of a grammatical subject's ability to be at once future and past.[13] Both of these alternatives have their seductions and drawbacks, but both exist only insofar as they destroy each other's possibility. It is impossible to say whether love should be read literally or as a self-consuming figure, and it is also impossible for the characters to remain suspended between these two alternatives, or securely ensconced in one of them. They know their fictionality yet they believe their own words, and in both cases they are at once justified and deluded.

At moments like these the text pushes to the limit our ability to read its irony. On the one hand, the novel has served us an illegible figure; on the other hand, in saying this we are also always saying that the text has *intended* to be illegible, and in Flaubert's case, of course, we can promptly beef up textual with authorial intent. His famous poetics of citationality has succeeded: *doxa* has been parroted with such elegant cunning that the reader cannot tell whether the performance is a parody or not.[14] Even as we state our uncertainty, we obliterate it by recanonizing text and author. When Roland Barthes, for instance, tells us that in Flaubert's case "one never knows if he is responsible for what he writes (if there is a subject behind his language)," he is also inevitably telling us that *Flaubert* has accomplished this uncertainty, and, indeed, should be given credit for having done so.[15] But the linguistic structures making possible *le Garçon*'s last and most subtle joke are indeed not necessarily under subjective control, for precisely the reasons Flaubert suggests in staging Frédéric and Mme Arnoux's last encounter. If we unmask fiction as merely fictional we thereby tumble into believing it; yet as soon as we start believing in it—by crediting Flaubert or Flaubert's text, for instance, with the knowledge of its own unknowability—we are as deluded as Frédéric, swept away by his own rhetoric of love. For whatever the historical Flaubert may have intended or known, the authoritative Flaubert one constructs while reading *L'Education sentimentale* is an irreducibly literary fantasy, projected onto a

13. A point made by Victor Brombert in "*L'Education sentimentale*: Articulations et polyvalence," in *La production du sens chez Flaubert: Colloque de Cerisy* (Paris: 10/18, 1975), 66–68, and by Culler, *Flaubert*, 151–56. Culler's emphasis falls on the "fragile romantic triumph" this scene provides, as well as on the fact that the detached fictionality of this romantic triumph "makes nonsense" out of "the explicit contrasts in terms of which the rest of the book appears to be constructed" (155).

14. There are many fine studies of Flaubert's techniques of citation and defamiliarization: the best is still Culler, *Flaubert*, esp. 75–156; see also Christopher Prendergast, "Flaubert and the Stupidity of Mimesis," in *The Order of Mimesis: Balzac, Stendhal, Nerval, Flaubert* (Cambridge: Cambridge University Press, 1986), 180–211. For a close study of Flaubert's subversive use of free indirect style (such that one cannot tell what degree of authority to grant utterances, etc.), see Claude Perruchot, "Le style indirect libre et la question du sujet dans *Madame Bovary*," in *La Production du sens chez Flaubert*, 253–74.

15. Roland Barthes, *S/Z*, trans. Richard Miller (New York: Hill and Wang, 1974), 140.

textual aporia. The result, as we have seen, is a highly successful, *because* profoundly ambivalent, canonization of Flaubert. We read an overabundance of meaning into his work in order to evade the difficulty of reading it—a difficulty that manifests itself in the preprofessional era of Flaubert studies as a condemnation of the textual nihilism one now so easily recuperates. "*L'Education,*" Thibaudet commented in the 1930s, "was immediately and is still today criticized for taking part itself, as a work of art, in this wastage, this emptiness, this bankruptcy."[16] One often speaks a little too easily of Flaubert's valorization of form. The "continual, monotonal, sad, indefinite procession" of his prose, as Proust famously described it, marks a habit of writing irreducible even to the negative aesthetics it propagates.[17]

It is no accident that in the closing pages of *L'Education* the figure of "love" should organize the text's resistance to understanding. Love not only stages the question of *Bildung* in this text, but the double-edged lure of literature itself. Nothing is more stereotyped than love, yet love alone has the power to forget its own banality. Love is the force of fiction, a force that, for all its power to shape lives and events, may only exist because we read about it in novels: this is the *idée reçue* providing what Michael Riffaterre would call the matrix or hypogram for the erotic destinies of Emma in *Madame Bovary* and Frédéric in *L'Education sentimentale.*[18] We may note in passing that one consequence of this literary problematic is the peculiarly atavistic forms that desire so frequently assumes in Flaubert—the odd slippage between realism and allegory, for instance, that causes Emma Bovary to be "burnt more fiercely by that intimate flame which her adultery kept feeding, panting and overcome with desire," as though the ancient figure of adultery, not the consciousness of a young bourgeoise, were desire's true subject.[19] The slightly archaic ring of Frédéric's "convoitise"

16. Albert Thibaudet, *Gustave Flaubert* (Paris: Gallimard, 1935), 150; cited in Culler, *Flaubert*, 149.
17. Marcel Proust, "A propos du 'style' de Flaubert," in *Chroniques* (Paris: Gallimard, 1927), 194.
18. See Michael Riffaterre, "Flaubert's Presuppositions," in *Flaubert and Postmodernism*, 177–91; for a more general elaboration of Riffaterre's terminology, see his *Text Production*, trans. Terese Lyons (New York: Columbia University Press, 1983).
19. Gustave Flaubert, *Madame Bovary*, ed. and trans. Paul de Man (New York: Norton, 1965), 210; for the French see *Madame Bovary: Moeurs de province* (Paris: Club de l'Honnête Homme, 1971–75): "brûlée plus fort par cette flamme intime que l'adultère avivait, haletante, émue, tout en désir . . ." (307). One of Flaubert's more remarkable descriptions of desire was excised from the final version of *Madame Bovary:* when Charles, after Emma's death, meets Rodolphe and pronounces his *grand mot* ("It was the fault of fate"), Rodolphe, who had had a hand in this fate, finds the remark "comic and slightly despicable": "For he understood nothing of that voracious love which hurls itself at random on things to slake itself, of that passion empty of pride, without human respect or consciousness, which plunges entirely into the loved object, seizes its sentiments, palpitates with them, and nearly attains the proportions of a pure idea, through its size and impersonality." *Madame Bovary, nouvelle version, précédée des scenarios inédits*, ed. J. Pommier and G. Leleu (Paris, Corti, 1949), 641.

serves in similar fashion to denaturalize his lust and attach it to a rhetoric of transgressive love that has no securable tie to the realist worlds in which he or Emma move. Love is literary to the extent that its power is undecidably that of myth or of cliché.

But the aporia of love does not exhaust the literary problematic staged by *L'Education sentimentale;* we have yet to approach the text's central crux, which is the relation between "love" and "history." The path I propose to follow at this point has been marked out by Flaubert's reception. Particularly in the wake of Sartre's *L'Idiot de la famille,* critics have frequently construed Flaubert's texts in terms of linguistic, libidinal, or socio-ideological fetishism.[20] To such construals the texts respond with such alacrity that a closer look at the notion of the fetish holds considerable promise. Our brief examination of the scene between Frédéric and Mme Arnoux has already made it obvious that in *L'Education* the conundrum of love is male; and besides marking the institution of sexual difference, the notion of fetishism will eventually help us sketch a relation between the aporetic figure of love and the revolutionary event it appears to foreclose.

II

What is a fetish? A dazzling apparition, self-originary and unique; a secret embodiment of sight itself:

It was like a vision [*Ce fut comme une apparition*]:
She was sitting in the middle of the bench, all alone; or at least he could not see anybody else in the dazzling light [*éblouissement*] which her eyes cast upon him. (*L'Education,* 50/18)

From the impersonal, gender-neutral demonstrative pronoun "ce," the passage fans out into the epiphanic primal scene of the male subject's love plot, as though both this subject and his fetish were simultaneously struck into existence—or indeed, as though the fetish emerged before the subject, rupturing the "sad indefinite procession" of Flaubertian prose in order to generate in its own ravishing gaze the possibility of the subject's. A hyperbolic, even hallucinogenic moment of privacy secretes this subject: the fetish exists only for *him,* and likewise he exists only for "her" ("or at least he could not see anybody else in the dazzling light which her eyes cast upon him").

20. Numerous studies of recent date touch on the question of fetishism in Flaubert; see in particular Charles Bernheimer's discussion of *Bouvard et Pécuchet* in *Flaubert and Kafka: Studies in Psychopoetic Structure* (New Haven: Yale University Press, 1982), 102–38, and above all Tony Tanner's discussion of *Madame Bovary* in *Adultery and the Novel: Contract and Transgression* (Baltimore: Johns Hopkins University Press, 1979), 233–367.

The wishfulness of this scenario shows up in the hint of uncertainty coloring the act of exclusion out of which male subject and female object emerge ("or at least . . ."); and the glory of the fetish resides in its ability to transform this uncertainty into the pleasurable pain of the sublime. "Her" gaze gives "him" sight as and through blindness (*éblouissement*), at the same time that she herself assumes the blindness of the object: her eyes cast light, but do not *see*. The oedipal threat, minimally registered here as the ideal object's power to blind, launches the subject of desire into its narrative of loss and substitution. Pushing further, one might venture the claim that the fetish's *éblouissement* provides a mythical, Medusa-esque origin for the story of the subject's eventual reification—an origin that we saw Fredric Jameson fetishistically locating in the event of Flaubert.

What, then, is a fetish? A dazzlingly overdetermined locus of speculation, knotting questions of language, religion, commerce, and desire. The word returns etymologically to artifice or representation (*facticius*) by way of the Portuguese *feitiço*. Originally signifying a token on which traders took oaths to ratify commercial treaties on the African coast, the word *feitiço* entered general European discourse at the end of the eighteenth century in association with the religious practices of the "primitive" cultures Europe was engaged in colonizing.[21] In its "origins," then, the fetish marks and guarantees the occurrence of discourse. It records the event of an oath or promise, underwriting the oath's performative force, and thereby securing commercial transactions. The fetish guarantees the promise that goods will circulate by recording the circulation of language and desire. It performs, as it were, the power of the performative and thereby draws on the arbitrary (and "primitive") force of the divine. This densely linguistic dimension of the fetish grants it great theoretical power. Though the Freudian and the Marxist appropriations of this term to some extent move in opposite directions—the former conceiving it as a palliative for loss, and the latter as an occlusion of labor—both draw on the fetish as a figure for illusory authority, and both elaborate this figure into a story of the production of a subject of desire.

Marx's brief discussion of commodity fetishism in *Capital* has frequently provided a springboard for sophisticated Marxist definitions of "ideology," because the fetishism Marx discovers in the commodity inheres in the process of production rather than in the deluded consciousness of the con-

21. For a history of the term "fetish" see William Pietz, "The Problem of the Fetish," parts 1, 2, and 3, in *Res* 9 (1985): 5–17, *Res* 13 (1987): 23–45, and *Res* 16 (1988): 105–23. See also Pietz, "Fetishism and Materialism: The Limits of Theory in Marx," in *Fetishism as Cultural Discourse*, ed. Emily Apter and William Pietz (Ithaca: Cornell University Press, 1993), 119–51, esp. 129–40, for a discussion of the term's appearance in late eighteenth-century theory and history of religion, its importance in Comte's positivist system (as the "first theological phase"), in nineteenth-century anthropological writing, and so on.

sumer. "A commodity," Marx writes, "appears at first sight an extremely obvious, trivial thing. But its analysis brings out that it is a very strange thing. . . . [A]s soon as it emerges as a commodity, it changes into a sensible suprasensible thing [*ein sinnlich übersinnliches Ding*]."[22] The commodity generates the fetishistic illusion that value inheres in it as an object of exchange: an illusion that Marx represents as a process of personification and reification. A piece of wood, turned into a table turned into a commodity, "evolves out of its wooden brain grotesque ideas," and this life of the commodity springs from the reifying dynamic of commodity production itself: "The mysterious character of the commodity-form consists therefore simply in the fact that the commodity reflects the social characteristics of men's own labour as objective characteristics of the products of labour themselves. . . . Through this substitution, the products of labour become commodities, sensuous things which are at the same time suprasensible or social" (Marx, *Capital*, 164–55). Crucial to Marx's insight, though occasionally overlooked in marxist theory, is his understanding of the commodity as both a rhetorical entity and an economic entity. Socially organized human labor produces it, but it becomes a *commodity*, a "sensible supersensible thing," only through the chiasmic exchange of properties between person and thing.[23] Self-obfuscation inheres in the production of the commodity. This excess of production also implies that in coming into existence the commodity generates a desire for itself over and above whatever attraction it might possess as a mere object. Commodity fetishism may thus be said to produce for capitalism a desiring subject—a subject that finds its epitome in the capitalist, whose unending desire to accumulate wealth derives from the personification of structural relations: "[I]t is only insofar as the appropriation of ever more wealth in the abstract is the sole driving force behind his operations that he functions as a capitalist, i.e., as

22. Karl Marx, *Capital* trans. Ben Fowkes (New York: Vintage, 1977), 1:163, translation modified; for the German, see *Das Kapital*, in Karl Marx and Friedrich Engels, *Werke*, 23:85.

23. This exchange of properties consequently poses a problem of reading: "Value, therefore, does not have its description branded on its forehead; it rather transforms every product of labour into a social hieroglyphic. Later on, men try to decipher the hieroglyphic" (Marx, *Capital*, 167). Close readings of *Capital* have drawn attention to the rhetorical complexity of the commodity form in Marx's analysis: see especially Thomas Keenan, "The Point Is to (Ex)Change It: Reading *Capital*, Rhetorically," in *Fetishism as Cultural Discourse*, ed. Apter and Pietz, 152–85. Keenan examines the figure of "abstraction" that transforms use value—which is always absolutely particular—into exchange value. This violent and impossible abstraction leaves as a "residue" a "ghostly objectivity [*gespenstige Gegenständlichkeit*]" (Marx, *Capital*, 128), the "residue of the abstraction itself" (Keenan, "The Point Is to (Ex)change It," 169). The play of ghosts in Marx's text has also been analyzed by Jacques Derrida, in his *Spectres de Marx: L'Etat de la dette, le travail du deuil et la nouvelle Internationale* (Paris: Galilée, 1993): see 246–79 for a discussion of Marx's example of the table. The difficult figure of "use value" in *Capital* is analyzed in Gayatri Chakravorty Spivak, "Scattered Speculations on the Question of Value," in her *In Other Worlds* (New York: Routledge, 1988), 154–75.

capital personified and endowed with consciousness and a will" (*Capital*, 254). The odd, impersonal quality of desire in Flaubert, a blend of passivity and insatiability that we earlier attached to allegorical language, may thus also be represented in terms of the personifying force of commodity exchange: capitalism is in this sense the ferocious accomplishment of allegory.

Freud's more systematic rewriting of the notion of fetishism overtly locates the fetish at the origin of the subject's production as a subject of desire, and thereby develops a complex understanding of the fetish's rhetorical character. As a substitute for the missing maternal phallus, the fetish in Freud is a radical fiction, and is compounded of seemingly contradictory qualities: it provides pleasure and consolation only and precisely to the extent that it memorializes a trauma. The (male) subject, reading its own possibility in the mirror of the mother's lack, papers over this absence with a substitute object; the subject's "interest" in this fictional penis then "suffers an extraordinary increase" precisely because "the horror of castration has set up a memorial [*Denkmal*] to itself in the creation of this substitute."[24] Freud's analysis of the Medusa's head is perhaps his most evocative account of the fetish's ability to eroticize trauma by representing it. Since "to decapitate" is "to castrate," the terror of Medusa is "a terror of castration that is linked to the sight of something"—the female genitals, and "essentially those of [the] mother."[25] The snakes on the Medusa's head symbolically threaten the male viewer since they recall the pubic hair surrounding the "castrated" maternal genitals; however, they also, simultaneously, "serve as a mitigation of the horror, for they replace the penis, the absence of which is the cause of the horror." Even the Medusa's power to petrify the male observer is paradoxically consoling: "For becoming stiff means an erection. Thus in the original situation it offers consolation to the spectator: he is still in possession of a penis, and the stiffening reassures him of the fact." The fetish is apotropaic because it represents the subject's annihilation to the subject, which can thereby persuade itself of its own existence.

Freud's schema yields a further refinement: as in Frédéric's first vision of Mme Arnoux, the fetish may be understood as the occlusion not of lack but of uncertainty. It requires an act of interpretation, after all, to see a lack, particularly a lack taken as the antonym—and the potential destiny, or deeper reality—of a penis's presence. The maternal phallus would thus be a fiction erected not over a void but over illegibility. Freud registered this dimension of the fetish in epistemological terms as the mechanism of

24. Sigmund Freud, "Fetishism," in *The Pelican Freud Library*, vol. 7: *On Sexuality: Three Essays on the Theory of Sexuality and Other Works*, ed. Angela Richards, trans. James Strachey (Harmondsworth: Penguin, 1977), 353.
25. Sigmund Freud, "Medusa's Head," in *Collected Papers*, ed. James Strachey (London: Hogarth Press, 1950), 5:105.

disavowal whereby the mother's "castration" is at once accepted and denied: the child believes and disbelieves, and the ego splits around this double bind. ("The whole process seems so strange to us," Freud comments dryly in a posthumous fragment, "because we take for granted the synthetic nature of the processes of the ego. But we are clearly at fault in this.")[26] Thus, despite its overwhelmingly visual ætiology in Freud, the fetish must in a sense be understood as prior to and productive of sight rather than the product of it. The terrifying "sight of something" has to be *read* as "something" to see before it can be "seen." One may thus speak of a fetishism at the origin of perception itself.

In *L'Education sentimentale* the dynamic of fetishism inheres in the production of subject and text, conditioning all forms of semiotic, economic, and libidinal circulation in the "capital of the nineteenth century" in which Frédéric loves and shops.[27] Desire is the desire of the commodity, and of the maternal and feminine as commodity; yet if desire and its representation express themselves through commodities, commodities, under the pressure of so much desire, become tokens of an inarticulate madness in the same way that Flaubert's text does. Whatever the cultural and socioeconomic codes mobilized, for instance, when Arnoux marches into the narrative line shod in "strange red boots, of Russian leather, decorated with blue patterns" (*L'Education*, 48/16), the objects in question—minuscule versions of Charles's cap in *Madame Bovary*—linger subtly past meaning, the occasion of an odd, empty astonishment and the product of a pointless and unstoppable fetishism. The self-annihilating aesthetic of the artwork, in this scenario, comes to coincide with the most degraded sort of sublimity—or vice versa: it would be equally accurate to say that Arnoux's boots or Charles's cap acquire the idiotic pointlessness of the artwork. The degradation of Arnoux's *L'Art industriel* into a ceramics factory and a trade in religious kitsch may be read as one of the many jokes the text makes at the expense of its own aestheticism, not to mention its future canonization.

As an essential part of its fetishistic project, Flaubert's text mirrors Frédéric's desire in funneling the polyvalent intensities and uncertainties of the fetish into the figure of Mme Arnoux. In her case we may indeed say that fetishism inheres in perception itself—so much so that Frédéric can construct memories of her that are more detailed than his initial perception

26. Sigmund Freud, "Splitting of the Ego in the Process of Defense," in *The Pelican Freud Library*, vol. 11: *On Metapsychology: The Theory of Psychoanalysis*, ed. Angela Richards, trans. James Strachey (Harmondsworth: Penguin, 1984), 462.

27. Walter Benjamin, "Paris: Capital of the Nineteenth Century," in *Reflections*, trans. Edmund Jephkott (New York: Schocken Books, 1978), 146–62: see in particular his comments on the erotics of "fashion": "It couples the living body to the inorganic world. Against the living it asserts the rights of the corpse. Fetishism, which is subject to the sex appeal of the inorganic, is its vital nerve" (153).

of her is: "[T]he whole of his journey on the boat came back to his mind so clearly that he could now remember fresh details, more intimate particulars: her foot, in a brown silk boot, peeping out under the lowest flounce of her dress, the drill awning forming a wide canopy over her head, and the little red tassles on the fringe trembling perpetually in the breeze" (53/22). As the fetish of fetishes, Mme Arnoux herself is unobtainable—in a Lacanian spirit one could say that she doesn't exist—and the objects that substitute for her meet Frédéric's desire with the arbitrary convenience of commodities in a shopping gallery. Though it is true that over the course of the narrative he pays particular homage to Mme Arnoux's feet, the other treasured objects of his gaze—her umbrella, her basket, pieces of clothing—are so numerous and so democratically invested with significance that the integrity of the fetish immediately finds itself compromised.[28] In fetishism, as Emily Apter observes, "a consistent displacing of reference occurs, paradoxically, as a result of so much *fixing*."[29] Mme Arnoux's dispersal inheres in her fetishization; only the pathos of repetition separates the beginning of the sentimental education from its end in the "vente de Mme Arnoux," when the fetish is scattered into memorials to be mourned in the sonorous rhythms of an extreme unction:

> In this way there vanished, one after another, the big blue carpet with its pattern of camellias which her dainty feet used to touch lightly as they came toward him; the little tapestry easy-chair in which he always used to sit facing her when they were alone; the two fire-screens, whose ivory had been made smoother by the touch of her hands; and a velvet pincushion, still bristling with pins. He felt as if a part of his heart were disappearing with each article; and the monotonous effect of the same voices accompanied by the same gestures numbed him with fatigue, afflicting him with a deathly torpor, a sense of disintegration. (387–88/407)[30]

The very force unifying Mme Arnoux into "the point of light on which all things converged" (53/22) scatters her into a litany of coveted detail; and the self that reads its identity in Mme Arnoux eventually finds itself

28. The arbitrary, metonymic quality of Frédéric's fetishism is examined in Maureen Jameson, "Métonymie et trahison dans *L'Education sentimentale*," *Nineteenth-Century French Studies* 19.4 (1991): 566–82; see also Michal Peled Ginsburg, *Flaubert Writing: A Study in Narrative Strategies* (Stanford: Stanford University Press, 1986), 132–53: "Dussardier and Madame Arnoux are indeed ideal mirror images, marked by purity, unity, and stability; but the qualities that make them into ideal mirror images are produced arbitrarily and contingently, and this fact undermines the very notion of ideal mirror image" (148).
29. Emily Apter, Introduction to *Fetishism as Cultural Discourse*, 3.
30. Brooks (*Reading for the Plot*, 205) notes and discusses the fact that these sentences echo those describing Emma Bovary's extreme unction: compare *Madame Bovary*, 335/237.

"numbed" by "the monotonous effect of the same voices accompanied by the same gestures." This numbness, fatigue, and disintegration recall the problems and seductions of literary language, since the "monotonous effect" of the auctioneers' gestures and voices is teasingly similar to the iterative splendor of the famous Flaubertian imperfect ("que ses pieds mignons frôlaient . . ."; "où il s'asseyait toujours . . .").[31] If Mme Arnoux "resemble[s] the women of romantic novels" (53/22), her lover, appropriately, resembles a frenzied connoisseur: "He knew the shape of each of her nails; he delighted in listening to the rustle of her silk dress when she passed through doors; he furtively sniffed at the scent on her handkerchief; her comb, her gloves, her rings were things of special significance to him, *as important as works of art, almost animated like people;* they all took possession of his heart and strengthened his passion" (92/66, emphasis added). The fetish of fetishes is the artwork and the woman as artwork: the "point lumineux" of Mme Arnoux that substitutes itself for the Virgin, the phallus, and the aesthetic symbol, and simultaneously disappears into the anonymity of exchange.

It is in this matrix of fetishism that the text's articulation of "love" and "history" will need to be sought. Yet first we may briefly observe that the very omnipresence of fetishism in this novel renders legibly arbitrary and overdetermined the text's repetition of Frédéric's fetishization of Mme Arnoux. Though *L'Education sentimentale* certainly leaves little space for any very satisfying feminine subject position,[32] the novel may at least be said to demonstrate the inextricability of aesthetic history, phallocentrism, and commodification, and to suggest that only the contingency of artifice, *facticius,* determines this tradition's erection of the maternal phallus as a figure for its fears and desires. A radical critique of this sort has its practical uses. Flaubert's texts at once predict and demystify the reactive gesture of a

31. More violent, punctual instances of the fetish's fragmenting power also occur in the text. After Rosanette's appearance at the beginning of the second part of the novel, Frédéric dreams of being raped and castrated by her, after seeing dismembered pieces of women pass back and forth: "[I]n the hallucination of his first sleep he saw passing to and fro before him the Fishwife's shoulders, the Stevedore's back, the Polish girl's calves, and the Savage Woman's hair. Then two big dark eyes [i.e., Mme Arnoux's], which were not at the ball, appeared; and light as butterflies, bright as torches, they darted here and there, quivered, flew up to the ceiling, then swooped down to his lips. Frédéric struggled to recognize those eyes, without success. But already a dream had taken hold of him; he thought he was harnessed side by side with Arnoux in the shafts of a cab, and the Marshal, sitting astride him, was tearing his belly open with her golden spurs" (*L'Education,* 152/134). The more irresolute passages we are focusing on may be read as counterweights to such aggressively focused, oedipal scenarios.
32. See L. Czyba, *Mythes et idéologie de la Femme dans les romans de Flaubert* (Lyon: Presses Universitaires de Lyon, 1983), for a study of the misogynistic stereotypes at work both in Flaubert's texts and in French culture from the July Monarchy and the 1848 Revolution through the 1870s. Czyba points out that *L'Education sentimentale* (mis)represents the 1848 Revolution as an exclusively male affair, barring figures of satire such as Mlle Vatnaz.

reader such as Jean-Paul Sartre, who, seeking to bring the "derealized" language of the Flaubertian text back to the certainties of experience, seizes upon a maternal scapegoat: "Flaubert's fetishism is the result and the summation of his sexual unrealizations, and these cannot be understood apart from the original derealization. His mother, male impersonator by imposture, woman by betrayal, constituted him such that he never stopped demanding from her a form of sexual retotalization that she had denied him from the cradle, and subsequently revealed herself incapable *by nature* of giving him."[33] Everything finally returns to nature, thanks to the mother—and it is her fault to boot: the mother represents at once "nature" and nature's lack or insufficiency. She is the ground of language, and her crime consists in ungrounding it. The fetishistic character of Sartre's argument is all the more striking in that he is basing it on a confessedly baseless fantasy: "The truth of this reconstruction cannot be proved; its likelihood is not measurable" (1:56); "This is a fabrication, I confess. I have no proof that it was so" (1:139). But soon enough the fantasy turns into fact: "It was his mother's pious and glacial zeal that *constituted* Gustave a passive agent; Mme Flaubert was the source of this 'nature' and the malaise through which it was expressed" (1:180). The energy with which Sartre repeats Frédéric's discovery of the oedipal radiance of a maternal Mme Arnoux responds to a literary insistence that exceeds and undermines the very fetish it composes. As always within the orbit of aesthetics, the uncertain status of language is a political issue, a matter for the paterfamilias, if not, indeed, for the police.[34]

33. Jean-Paul Sartre, *The Family Idiot: Gustave Flaubert, 1821–1857*, trans. Carol Cosman (Chicago: University of Chicago Press, 1981), 2:67. In the original French version the quotation comes from volume 1: see *L'Idiot de la famille: Gustave Flaubert de 1821 à 1857* (Paris: Gallimard, 1971), 1:719–20. The emphasis on "by nature" in this passage is Sartre's.

34. Flaubert's densely textured critique of the presuppositions at work in Sartre's fantasy is particularly visible early in the novel when Frédéric reads the words "Jacques Arnoux" on a marble plaque and thinks of "elle" (*L'Education*, 62–63/32)—Mme Arnoux, of course, though grammatically the pronoun also applies to the "plaque de marbre" on which the paternal name (which also here signifies the commercial entity *L'Art industriel)* is inscribed. A few pages later Frédéric's fetishization of this signifier becomes more pronounced: "The big letters spelling out the name of Arnoux on the marble plaque above the shop seemed to him to be unique and pregnant with meaning, like a sacred writing [*grosses de signification, comme une écriture sacrée*]" (77/49). The fetishization, which is to say the aestheticization, of the name of the father-capitalist occurs here through an assimilation of writing to a putatively natural power of (re)production ("pregnancy"). The mother thereby becomes the ground—the "plaque de marbre"—of meaning's inscription. Here, however, the arbitrariness and excess of Frédéric's gesture forms part of the text to be read, as does the relation of his idealizing and reifying focus on the maternal to the other dimensions of the fetish in *L'Education sentimentale:* the commodity, the artwork, and so on. A full study of gender and desire in *L'Education* would also want to examine desire's homoerotic circuits, visible here and elaborated elsewhere as Frédéric's charged relations with Arnoux and above all with Deslauriers. See Mary Orr, "Reading the Other: Flaubert's *L'Education sentimentale* Revisited," *French Studies* 46.4 (1992): 412–23.

III

The fetish, as we saw, includes in its makeup a historical dimension to the extent that it claims to commemorate an *event:* the event of a promise or contract in the mercantile model, or a trauma in the psychoanalytic one. This commemorative aspect, however, is also paradoxically mobile and uncertain, since the fixing and freezing energies of the fetish generate an equivalent displacement and disintegration. As representations, in other words, fetishes are always inauthentic, above all in their representation of "history." Flaubert famously constructed his "historical" scenes out of pre-processed data—memoirs, newspapaper reports, and so on—in order to tease into blank irony the stereotyped discourse that masquerades as historical truth. Indeed, in his representation of Frédéric's one sustained experience of a dramatic revolutionary event—the sack of the Tuileries on February 24—Flaubert not only draws heavily on "the 'one says' [*on dit*] of 1848, as represented in stereotypes," but draws attention to the fetishistic character of verbal stereotypes by recycling sexual ones.[35] The crowd's "frenzy" in the Tuileries ("An obscene curiosity caused everyone to ransack all the closets, search all the alcoves, and turn out all the drawers. Jailbirds thrust their arms into the princesses' bed, and rolled about on it as a consolation for not being able to rape them" [*L'Education*, 289/289]) recalls and parodies one of the best-known scenarios in Burke's *Reflections on the Revolution in France:* "A band of cruel ruffians and assassins . . . rushed into the chamber of the queen, and pierced with an hundred strokes of bayonets and poniards the bed, from whence this persecuted woman had but just time to flee almost naked."[36] Where Burke's rioters are bloodthirsty, Flaubert's jailbirds are always at least faintly ludicrous: in 1848 tragedy occurs as farce, and the revolution's symbols and archetypes—even that of the Medusa herself—have become commodities and clichés, and possess in consequence a ridiculous yet desperate power: "In the entrance hall, standing on a pile of clothes, a prostitute [*une fille pudique*] was posing as a statue of Liberty, motionless and terrifying, her eyes wide open" (289/290).[37] Such

35. Herschberg-Pierrot, "Le travail des stéréotypes," 45. As Françoise Gaillard comments, the stereotype may be conceptualized as a "fetishization of thought": see "L'En-signement du réel" in *La Production du sens chez Flaubert*, 198.
36. Edmund Burke, *Reflections on the Revolution in France* (Harmondsworth: Penguin, [1790] 1968), 164. The account continues to describe the king and queen being taken from a palace "swimming in blood, polluted by massacre, and strewn with scattered limbs and mutilated carcasses," and marched in a procession "amidst the horrid yells, and shrilling screams, and frantic dances, and infamous contumelies; and all the unutterable abominations of the furies of hell, in the abused shape of the vilest of women" (165).
37. According to P.-G. Casteux, *Flaubert: L'Education sentimentale* (Paris: Société d'Enseignement Supérieur, 1980), 183–84, Flaubert drew this image from a *Histoire de la révolution de 1848* (1850) by Daniel Stern (the pseudonym of Mme d'Agoult). The figure of the Medusa had in fact

visions are likely to strike us as historical only in the sense in which history can be understood as simply another discourse, another tissue of commonplaces and prescripted tropes, or outlet for ideological representations.

Yet the notion of the fetish as inscription or *Denkmal* nonetheless offers us the chance to think history in non-ontic fashion. To gain a better sense of this historicity we may, as it were, travel deeper into the heart of the fetish by looking closely at the two major instances in which Frédéric misses history while embroiled in the aporia of his love plot. The first occurs at the beginning of the 1848 Revolution: Frédéric refuses to join his friends in a demonstration on February 22, the first day of revolutionary activity, because of his rendezvous with Mme Arnoux; and because she stands him up, he spends February 23 courting Rosanette, and misses the day of rioting which led to the revolution itself. He thus experiences the "origin" of the revolution as an agony of waiting for the fetish-woman who never arrives, and as a compensatory lateral move in his sentimental education. Later in the year Frédéric misses the proletarian uprising in June—"the most colossal event [*Ereignis*] in the history of European civil wars" (Marx, *Eighteenth Brumaire*, 23)—because he and Rosanette have left Paris for a holiday in Fontainebleau. Let me begin by examining the Fontainebleau idyll, which overtly thematizes the fetish's power to romanticize and commodify history.

For the male and middle-class Frédéric, Fontainebleau provides history as erotic nostalgia. As he stands before the painting of Diana in the Banqueting Hall, the "point lumineux" of Mme Arnoux becomes the star-like radiance of Diane de Poitiers:

> The most beautiful of these legendary creatures was shown in a painting on the right, in the character of Diana the huntress, and indeed of Diana of the Underworld, no doubt to indicate the power she wielded even beyond the grave. All these symbols confirmed her fame; and something of her still remained there, a faint voice, a lingering splendour [*rayonnement*].

---

become a charged stereotype of the era: for an analysis of its functioning, see Neil Hertz, "Medusa's Head: Male Hysteria under Political Pressure," in *The End of the Line: Essays on Psychoanalysis and the Sublime* (New York: Columbia University Press, 1985), 161–215. Drawing on various accounts of 1848 and the Commune in order to comment on "a recurrent turn of mind: the representation of what would seem to be a political threat as if it were a sexual threat," Hertz, following Freud, suggests that the image of Medusa concentrates "a litany of nervous questions": "questions that give expression to epistemological anxiety (can I trust my eyes?), to narcissism (can I hold myself together?), to sexual anxiety (can I hold on to my penis?), to—beyond that—social and economic fears about property and status (can I hold on to anything, including representations of myself?)" (167). The tranformation of such uncertainty into a charged, specular confrontation with sexual difference works to buttress the fetishistic illusion "that one can see history as the features of a face, read it off a composed physiognomy" (179).

Frédéric was seized with an inexpressible feeling of retrospective lust [*concupiscence*]. (*L'Education*, 313–14/319–20)

This sharply focused fetishization of the past mutates into Frédéric and Rosanette's literary and touristic consumption of the Fontainebleau forest. Their guide takes them to the famous spots; the narrative voice pursues medieval fantasies in indirect free style ("on pense aux ermites, compagnons des grands cerfs . . ."); and the forest acquires the trappings of symbolic meaning: "Some [trees], astonishingly tall, bore themselves like patriarchs or emperors, or, touching each other at the tip, seemed to form triumphal arches with their long trunks; others, grown obliquely from the ground, seemed columns about to fall" (316/323). Arrived at this "forêt de symboles" we find ourselves at the locus of much interpretative or pseudo-interpretative activity, both in the text itself and in the criticism it has inspired. Here the trees are like triumphal arches and falling columns; a little further on they resemble a crowd [*foule*], while also possessing crowns [*couronnes*] like the ruler whom the crowd swept away in February. In short, the forest of Fontainebleau, symbol of royal, mystical France, offers itself as a symbolization and naturalization of history; yet as soon as one takes up its offer, of course, one repeats Frédéric's fetishism. History and the love plot entwine here precisely to the extent that one falls into the text's trap.[38]

Nonetheless, it will prove interesting to continue to follow Frédéric and Rosanette into the fetish-forest, since as their tour continues the text's language becomes excessive in a mode difficult—as so often in Flaubert—to pin down. From the unremarkably catachretic "crowns" of the beech trees we are moved through a descriptive catalogue that grows more and more baroque in its tropes: holly bushes seemingly "made of bronze"; birches bent in "elegiac attitudes"; pines "symmetrical as organ-pipes" that "seemed to sing as they swayed continuously to and fro"; finally, "huge

38. For a relatively straightforward reading of the Fontainebleau episode as a naturalization of history, see Brombert, "*L'Education sentimentale:* Articulations et polyvalence," and his *The Novels of Flaubert* (Princeton: Princeton University Press, 1966), 177–78; see Brooks for a similar reading, which concludes that the political message of Flaubert's text is quietism (*Reading for the Plot*, 203–4). Culler's discussion of Fontainebleau, directed against Brombert, emphasizes the text's ironic disqualification of the symbolic reading by noting that the natural analogy—trees that look like emperors or triumphal arches or columns about to fall—cuts two opposing ways: "Is political revolution an act of desecration like chopping down monarchical trees or destroying the Empire's monuments, or does the very posture of trees which look like columns about to fall offer a natural analogue which refutes the former suggestion?" From the first perspective, the natural analogy would underline the "tragic seriousness of political revolution" as an assault on a natural order; from the second, revolution would itself become a natural phenomenon, and the merely human sort would fade into "triviality and insignificance." The text gives us no means to privilege one option over the other: "It is clear that everything can be interpreted," Culler concludes, "but not what is the significance of such interpretations" (*Flaubert*, 102).

gnarled oaks" that "rose convulsively out of the ground, embraced one another, and solidly established on their torso-like trunks, threw out their bare arms in desperate appeals and furious threats, like a group of Titans struck motionless in their anger" (316–17/323). The passage hovers between reification and personification, since its tropological progression first swerves in an inanimate direction ("made of bronze"), then employs a technical rather than a natural anthropomorphic vehicle (organ-pipes) before leaping to an Ovidian idiom (the Titans). The twin tropes of fetishism collapse into each other and in doing so become hyperbolic, manifestly rhetorical fictions: it is as though these trees were registering the production of figurative language itself, prior to the establishment of the binary oppositions (animate/inanimate, person/thing) upon which the tropes of personification and reification draw.

It is precisely such an uncanny principle of textual production, I suggest, which drives Flaubert's paragraph toward a climax wickedly balanced between sublimity and irony:

> Then they crossed monotonous clearings, planted with saplings here and there. A sound of iron, hard and numerous blows rang out; it was a team of quarrymen striking the rocks on a hillside. These rocks became more and more numerous, finally filling the whole landscape; cube-shaped like houses, or flat like paving-stones, they propped each other up, overhung one another, and merged together like the monstrous, unrecognizable ruins of some vanished city. But the frenzied chaos in which they lay conjured up rather thoughts of volcanoes, floods, great unknown cataclysms. Frédéric said that they had been there since the beginning of the world and would stay like that until its end; Rosanette turned her head away, saying that "it would drive her mad," and went off to pick some heather. (317/323)

It is easy to interpret these apocalyptic rocks as signs of "the futility of [the revolution of 1848] in relation to geological revolutions" (Brombert, "*L'Education,*" 61), and also easy to cast suspicion on that sublime interpretation, which is specifically identified as Frédéric's both in this passage and again, more pointedly, a little later in the episode: "Sometimes they heard the roll of drums far away in the distance. . . . 'Why, of course! It's the insurrection!' Frédéric would say with a disdainful pity, for all that excitement struck him as trivial in comparison with their love and eternal Nature" (318/325). Yet this familiar Flaubertian paradox, whereby an interpretation is rendered at once silly and inevitable, does not entirely exhaust the passage's difficulty. We may begin with the simple observation that the scene does not appear to be describing "nature" at all. Prior to "conjuring up" thoughts of volcanoes and floods and inspiring Frédéric's sublime commonplace, the rocks are "houses" and "paving-stones" arranged in ways that resemble the "ruins of some vanished city"; whether or not they have gotten that way because "a team of quarrymen" is "striking" them, they record in their figurative shapes the expenditure of labor power. Should one then discover at work in this scene a "political unconscious"? Perhaps; so long as one does not imagine that either the proletarian uprising of the June days or labor in the abstract (i.e., the commodity) is the repressed truth of these rocks: such allegories would finally be as hasty and naturalizing as Frédéric's, if only because the activity of "striking the rocks" (*battant les roches*) is not even necessarily *labor*. If it is, it is labor in the sense that writing (in Flaubert's sense) is labor: hard work, no doubt, and productive of marks and sounds, and words and figures, yet work that is as useless as that of the prisoner, who in the French cliché that would be this passage's Riffaterrean hypogram if it had a hypogram, is condemned to break rocks, *casser les cailloux*. We risk misreading the figurative structure of the passage, however, if we seize too eagerly on the pathos that figures of social injustice provide. Like the prisoner, the "team of quarrymen striking the rocks on a hillside" is engaged in the redundancy of striking rocks so as to produce rocks—but these are not just any old rocks: "These rocks became more and more numerous, finally filling the whole landscape; cube-shaped like houses." This rock-striking produces the rocks upon which the fetish—the fetish of interpretation—stages itself. We may say without the slightest exaggeration that the text is figuring the possibility of its own coming into being.

This allegory of textual production intensifies as Frédéric and Rosanette's close encounter with rocks comes to a climax in the next paragraph, and the silent, solar logos of light itself "strikes" the fetish into phantasmatic life:

> One day they climbed half-way up a sand-hill. Its surface, untrodden [*vierge de pas*], was grooved with symmetrical undulations; here and there, like promontories on the dried-up bed of an ocean, rose rocks which bore a vague resemblance to animals, tortoises thrusting their heads forward, seals crawling along, hippopotamuses, and bears. Not a soul. Not a sound. The sand, struck by the sun, was dazzling [*éblouissant*]; and all of a sudden, in that quivering of the light, the animals seemed to move. They hurried away, fleeing vertigo [*fuyant le vertige*], almost panic-stricken. (317/324)

The *rochers de Fontainebleau* are famous for their shapes: we have certainly not left the circuit of the tourist, nor indeed the orbit of the ridiculous, as these tourists, after all, are running away from rocks.[39] But the text has also moved us into the denatured, erotic, oriental, and pointless world of Saint Antoine, and toward what Jonathan Culler calls Flaubert's notion of the "sacred": that is, "pure form" (*Flaubert*, 223), "the sentimental purified by irony, emptied of its content, so that it may come to represent in the allegory of interpretation the formal desire for connection and meaning" (226), which is to say a textuality built on "arbitrary meanings guaranteed not by man but by God" (227). We could almost agree with these shrewd characterizations, were it not for the persistent impurity of irony and formal closure in Flaubert. In the vocabulary developed here we may say that the sacred is always also a fetish. Yet Culler's comments respond to a predicament latent within fetishism: the fetish elicits as its condition of possibility a disruptive institution of the signifier which must occur "before" any meaning can guarantee this signifier's legibility. If the production of meaning is the production of the fetish, that institutive act of fetishism itself entails an impossible act of personification (or "reification") prior to the existence of persons or things. The rocks bearing a "vague resemblance" to the exotic animals of the Flaubertian imagination, which "seem to move" when struck by light—by the "éblouissement" that earlier shone out of the eyes of the "apparition" of Mme Arnoux—figure the production of meaning *as* personification, as the production of "figure" itself out of the uncertainty that is the condition of all signification, and which here leaves its mark as the image of ambiguous marks: a surface "vierge de pas," "rayée en ondulations symmétriques."

We encounter a similar pressure of the inscription within the fetishistic dilemma suffered by Frédéric a few pages earlier in the novel, and a few months earlier in the plot, as he waits for Mme Arnoux at the corner of the Rue Tronchet on February 22, while the first crowds of the revolution gather in the Place de la Concorde. As the hours pass, the strain of waiting causes him to "dissolve in despair":

> The echo of his footsteps jarred his brain.
> When he saw that his watch said four o'clock he felt a sort of dizziness and panic. He tried to recite some poetry to himself, to do a sum at random, to make up a story. It was impossible! he was obsessed by the image of Madame Arnoux. He longed to run and meet her. But which way should he go so as not to miss her? (277 / 277–78)

The subject of fetishism here suffers the fragmentation inherent in fetishistic unification, a crisis of the subject which is equally one of narrative—

39. I owe that last phrase to Susan Crane. This is perhaps a good place to thank my colleagues at the Camargo Foundation for their helpful responses to early portions of this chapter.

Frédéric cannot "make up a story [*histoire*]" any more than he can choose a direction to run in, for he is pinned by the fictionality of the fetish into the predicament of waiting endlessly for its arrival. The story of his waiting is brought to an end only retrospectively, when a few pages later we learn that "Frédéric had gone home": "He sank in to a kind of sleep; through his nightmare he heard the rain falling, and imagined all the time that he was still out there on the pavement" (279/281).

In between Frédéric's waiting and his dream of waiting, the text tells the story of why Mme Arnoux does not arrive: a story that itself begins as her own dream of waiting:

> The night before, she had dreamt that she had been standing for a long time on the pavement in the Rue Tronchet. She was waiting there for something indefinite yet important, and without knowing why, she was afraid of being seen. But a horrible little dog which had taken a dislike to her was worrying the hem of her dress. It kept coming back to her and barked louder and louder. Madame Arnoux awoke. The dog's barking went on. She strained her ears. The noise was coming from her son's bedroom. She rushed into the room in her bare feet. It was the child himself who was coughing. His hands were burning hot, his face red and his voice strangely hoarse. (278/278–79)

This barking or coughing will later be described as being "like the noise made by the crude devices that make cardboard dogs bark" (278/279): it resembles mechanically produced noises that resemble natural noises, and manifests itself as an impediment to speech: "[The child] seemed to be puffing out his words" (280) ("On aurait dit qu[e l'enfant] soufflait ses paroles" [279]). The cough interrupts Mme Arnoux's dream only to rewrite the dream as reality, transforming the suspension of waiting into a more agonizing vigil:

> The hours went by, heavy, dreary, interminable, heartbreaking; and she counted the minutes only by the progression of this death-agony. The spasms of his chest threw him forward as if they were going to break him up; finally he vomited something strange which resembled a tube of parchment. What was it? She supposed that he had thrown up a piece of his bowels. But he was breathing freely and regularly. This apparent improvement frightened her more than anything else; and she was standing there petrified [*petrifiée*], her arms dangling and her eyes fixed in a stare, when Monsieur Colot arrived. According to him, the child was out of danger. (279/280–81)

If the cough at once interrupts and causes Mme Arnoux's torment of waiting, the cessation of the cough might be said to produce Frédéric's, since
Mme Arnoux, interpreting her child's spontaneous cure as a sign from God,
offers up her love for Frédéric "as a sacrifice" (281). Flaubert's notes on
croup, taken from Trousseau's *Clinique médicale*, are more prosaic: "It sometimes happens, one time out of six or eight, that, through an act of vomiting
or coughing, the larynx clears itself all of a sudden, the child spitting out
strips of false membranes [*fausses membranes*] or membranal tissues coming
from the trachea and the glottis."[40] And an interpretation of this scene
adequate to its peculiarities will need to be more prosaic still, which is not
always to say more self-evident.

We have seen that the fetish is a visual affair: a double-edged gift of
blinding vision, brought into focus here as the figure—once again—of the
medusal mother, "petrified," "her eyes fixed in a stare." And we have also
seen that these paradoxes of vision negotiate a predicament that is not
visual but figural. Vision is a hypothesis that can never be guaranteed, no
matter how hard the fetish tries; and I suggest we understand the emergence of aural stimuli such as the "sound of iron" in the Fontainebleau
scene or little Eugène Arnoux's cough in this one as signals that relay the
non-phenomenal inscription of the fetish's phenomenality. Read in this
way, these sounds are not actually sounds at all; or, better, they are sounds
that record the uninsurable event whereby they are *taken* as sounds, just as
the fetish is taken as a vision ("une apparition"). Speculating on the privilege Freud grants to aural perception in the primal scene, Jean Laplanche
and J.-B. Pontalis suggest that "hearing, when it occurs, breaks the con-

---

40. The note continues: "—at that instant calm descends. The child falls asleep. But often
another false membrane forms itself and the sickness begins again." Flaubert's notes are reproduced in the Club de l'Honnête Homme edition, 452–53; they may also be found in Dumesnil,
L'Education sentimentale de Gustave Flaubert, 54. According to Dr. Chaume, who was in charge of
tracheotomies when Flaubert visited the Hôpital Sainte-Eugénie (now the Hôpital Trousseau)
in March of 1868, and who published an account of the visit in the *Chronique médicale* of 15
December 1900, Flaubert was too squeamish to attend an operation. Dumsenil draws from this
episode a rationale for Flaubert's decision to have Mme Arnoux's child cure itself spon-
taneously; we are seeking here the possibility of a less reductive explanation.

From Trousseau's study Flaubert also, for that matter, acquired the metaphor "a tube of
parchment" to describe the false membranes blocking the larynx: "What occurs there," Trousseau writes, "is what occurs if, between the reeds of a clarinet or bassoon, you interpose a bit of
wet parchment; and the comparison is all the more exact in that the false membrane can be
perfectly well compared to a bit of parchment swollen by humidity. The reed instrument
constituted by the larynx thus no longer works." A. Trousseau, *Clinique médicale de l'Hôtel-Dieu
de Paris*, 2 vols. (Paris: J.-B. Baillière et Fils, 1861), 1:320–21. Trousseau is drawn to the pathos of
the loss of voice engendered by the croup, and goes on at some length about the sound of the
cough, the tone of any surviving voice, and so on. Flaubert's notes are taken from pages 319–23
of this volume. Flaubert's comment that the relatively rare spontaneous cure for the croup often
results in the growth of more membranous tissue, however, runs slightly counter to his source:
Trousseau emphasizes that the spontaneous ejection of false membrane actually results in a
better rate of cure than the tracheotomy does (323).

tinuity of an undifferentiated perceptual field and at the same time is a sign (the noise waited for and heard in the night), which puts the subject in the position of having to answer to something."[41] Laplanche and Pontalis are working through the psychoanalytic version of the paradox of the constitutive event. The trauma of sexuality produces the subject, which must nonetheless preexist this event in order to experience it, and which consequently internalizes sexuality belatedly, as a repetition always already in place. The "sound" of the primal scene is the call of the signifier: an inaudible call which cannot be guaranteed by any intention, yet which is "heard" as intentional by the subject it constitutes or interpellates. This call echoes in Eugène's cough as a mechanical resistance to voice, and as a near-shattering force ("the spasms of his chest threw him forward as if they were going to break him up"); it inhabits the "striking" of the rocks at Fontainebleau as the doubleness of a sound at once singular ("un bruit de fer") and iterative ("des coups drus et nombreux").

One could thus say that Eugène coughs up the signifier's residue. The "something" which resembles "a tube of parchment" suggests the materiality of an event inaccessible to experience—a "sublime object of ideology," in Slavoj Žižek's phrase: that is, "a positive, material object elevated to the status of the impossible Thing."[42] Žižek's Lacanian terminology of the "real," however, lends a misleading substantiality to this diseased, vomited remainder, or excess of voice. As the residue of the signifier, these "false membranes" are neither real nor unreal, just as they are neither organic nor inorganic. The materiality of the signifier is the condition of the difference between dream and reality, or more generally between figure and ground. It is the blow of an event which has no singularity apart from its repetition, yet which is iterable only as the trauma of a radical, unanswerable singularity. And we may note at this juncture that the cough of the child continues to echo as the second volume of the novel closes. Wending their way back from a restaurant—the *Trois Frères provençaux*, where Flaubert and Maxime du Camp were also eating, that night of 23 February—Frédéric and Rosanette hear "a crackling noise behind them like the sound of a huge piece of silk being ripped in two. It was the fusillade on the Boulevard des Capucines." At the house in the Rue Tronchet which Frédéric had prepared for Mme Arnoux, and where he now takes Rosanette, the chapter closes with a final invocation of uncertain sounds: "About one

41. Jean Laplanche and J.-B. Pontalis, "Fantasy and the Origins of Sexuality," *The International Journal of Psycho-Analysis* 49.1 (1968): 10–11. At this point in Laplanche and Pontalis's argument the most immediate reference is to "A Case of Paranoia" (1915), in which Freud describes the case of a woman patient whose fears were at once visual and aural: she felt she was being watched and photographed while lying with her lover, and claimed to have heard a "noise," the click of a camera.
42. Slavoj Žižek, *The Sublime Object of Ideology* (London: Verso, 1989), 71.

o'clock [Rosanette] was awoken by distant rumblings; and she saw him
sobbing with his head buried in the pillow." To her query Frédéric explains
that he is crying out of an "excess of happiness": "I've been wanting you too
long!" (282/283). The blows on the rocks and distant roll of drums in the
Fontainebleau scene, the repercussion of Frédéric's waiting feet, the bark of
a dog, the cough of a child, the crackling of a fusillade, the "distant rumblings" and the gentleman's sob, mark the trace of a violence prior to and
yet *of* signification; and we may say that these marks inscribe an allegory of
history in the heart of the love-plot, at the point of love's non-
consummation.

IV

Why history? Because history remains the best name we can give to
the excess, the radical exteriority, of an event in relation to meaning, knowledge, or desire. The thought of history always appeals at a certain point to
referential force: we say, when pressed, that history is what happened, what
really happened—"what hurts," in Fredric Jameson's somewhat wishful
epigram, which hustles the referential difficulty of "what really happened"
a little too quickly into the subjective certainty of pain. But one could
venture the formulation that history is pain that cannot be *experienced*.
Flaubert's focus on trauma responds to the historical novel's conceit that
history can be captured as narrative, which is an ambition latent in all
aesthetic narrative. Indeed, the deepest motivation of aesthetics is discoverable in its attempt to gather the referential insistence of "history" into the
totality of consciousness or form. In its critical displacement of this project,
L'Education sentimentale rewrites *Bildung* as the making, *factio*, of a *feitiço*, a
fetish, and suggests that the subject "experiences" history as an inexplicable
interruption, or the fragmenting anguish of intolerable boredom. From the
subject's perspective, history can only be enountered as trauma: as the
"parole soufflée" of an occurrence that arrives too early or too late for the
consciousness it makes possible.[43]

43. See Jacques Derrida, "La parole soufflée," in *Writing and Difference*, trans. Alan Bass
(Chicago: University of Chicago Press, 1978), 169–95, for a meditation on the "parole
soufflée"—the word whispered, prompted, spirited away—of a "historicity long since elimi-
nated from thought" (170), the impossible "ground" of metaphysical differences (174): "Which
amounts to acknowledging the autonomy of the signifier as the letter's historicity; before me,
the signifier on its own says more than I believe that I meant to say, and in relation to it, my
meaning-to-say is submissive rather than active" (178). For an exploration of the relation
between history and trauma, see Cathy Caruth, "Unclaimed Experience: Trauma and the
Possibility of History," *Yale French Studies* 79 (1991): 181–92: "The historical power of the trauma
is not just that the experience is repeated after its forgetting, but that it is only in and through its
inherent forgetting that it is first experienced at all. . . . For history to be a history of trauma

Suspended between futurity and anteriority, the historical event, in *L'Education sentimentale*, becomes the aporetic narrative of love. Love tells the deconstructive story of its own inability to catch up with itself: it cannot know what it does, or do what it knows, precisely because its origins and mode of existence are historical. Love's literariness—that is, its dissymmetrical affirmation and destruction of itself as fiction—is in fact its historicity: love *occurs*, as an event that cannot be present to itself. The event of love manifests itself as fetishism, and the paradox of love plays itself out as a tension between the production and dispersal of identity and meaning in and as the fetish. And the subject that finds its possibility in the fetishization of love's aporia is indeed the subject "of history"—which means that it is in fact possible to think the scriptive force of history as "labor," so long as one specifies that the *historicity* of labor power resides not in labor's dialectical negation of the real, but in its opacity to its own intention, and its excess over any system of calculation and distribution.

We may say more generally that the lesson of *L'Education sentimentale* is that history is the production of a text. One should not rush toward the comfort of declaring such an insight idealist or bourgeois. Marx's comments at the beginning of the *Eighteenth Brumaire* refer us to a linguistic example precisely in order to declare history irreducible to consciousness:

> Men make their own history, but they do not make it just as they please; they do not make it under circumstances chosen by themselves, but under circumstances directly encountered, given and transmitted from the past. The tradition of all the dead generations weighs like a nightmare on the brain of the living. And just when they seem engaged in revolutionizing themselves and things, in creating something that has never yet existed, precisely in such periods of revolutionary crisis they anxiously conjure up the spirits [*Geister*] of the past to their service and borrow from them names, battle cries and costumes in order to present the new scene of world history in this time-honored disguise and this borrowed language. . . . In like manner a beginner who has learnt a new language always translates it back into his mother tongue, but he has assimilated the spirit [*Geist*] of the new language and can freely express himself in it only when he finds his way in it without recalling the old and forgets his native tongue in the use of the new. (*Eighteenth Brumaire*, 15–16)

Just when we think we are breaking with the past we are most haunted by it; we begin to speak the language of the new only insofar as we "forget" the

means that it is referential precisely to the extent that it is not fully perceived as it occurs; or to put it somewhat differently, that a history can be grasped only in the very inaccessibility of its occurrence" (187).

"mother tongue" of our own identity, which is to say that revolution occurs only in the eclipse of revolutionary consciousness. There is more empirical plausibility to such a paradox than might immediately meet the eye. It is not simply the complexity of causal relations that leads Franz Fanon to ascribe a certain randomness to the revolutionary event: "[I]n these circumstances the guns go off by themselves, for nerves are jangled, fear reigns and everyone is trigger-happy. . . . It must be remarked here that the political parties have not called for armed insurrection, and have made no preparations for such an insurrection. All these repressive measures, all those actions which are a result of fear are not within the leader's intentions: they are overtaken by events."[44] So far as we know, the massacre on the Boulevard des Capucines toward which Frédéric is so indifferent, which left some hundred or so dead and helped precipitate Louis Philippe's fall, occurred without any officer giving an order to fire; and the touch of personification in Fanon's figure of the guns "going off by themselves" resembles the tropes Flaubert scatters in his account of the February events: "[T]he insurrection organized itself powerfully, as if it were directed by a single hand" (*L'Education*, 285/286); "of itself, without upheaval, the monarchy was melting in a rapid dissolution" (286/286). The point is not that revolutions do not have causes; it is rather that as events they exceed causal explanation. As François Furet remarks of another, more revolutionary revolution, "[T]he mere fact that the [French] Revolution had causes does not mean that they are all there is to its history. . . . [T]he revolutionary event, *from the very outset*, totally transformed the existing situation and created a new mode of historical action that was not intrinsically a part of that situation."[45] Revolution, seemingly the moment in which history offers itself to experience, is in fact the moment of a rupture irreducible to causality or intentionality. If we understand literariness as a term for such constitutive moments of rupture, we arrive at the seeming paradox that history is literary history. The ideological or fetishistic recuperation of history in turn becomes understandable as the obsession with plot which Furet ascribes to "revolutionary consciousness" (53), and which Flaubert deploys as the literary conventions of the Balzacian novel.

We may observe in conclusion that to say that history is "literary" in this sense is to say that it is always potentially revolutionary. A certain sense of loss or wreckage clings to such insights: one thinks of Benjamin's assertion that allegory writes history "on the countenance of nature in the characters

---

44. Franz Fanon, *The Wretched of the Earth*, trans. Constance Farrington (New York: Grove Press, 1963), 56–57.
45. François Furet, *Interpreting the French Revolution*, trans. Elborg Forster (Cambridge: Cambridge University Press, 1981), 22. Furet also comments that "[t]he Revolution is the gap that opened between the language of the *Cahiers* [*de doléances*, the list of grievances submitted to Louis XVI] and that of [Marat's] *Ami du peuple* in the space of only a few months [in 1789]" (46).

of transience," and in the form of "ruin" and "irresistible decay."[46] But the loss which allegory mourns as history is not reducible to pathos. It bears a greater affinity to the "unanticipatable alterity" which Jacques Derrida affirms as the "democratic promise" of communism, for instance, than it does to the kinds of pain we are able to integrate as subjectivity or process as aesthetic pleasure.[47] Flaubert is not the sort of author one would normally want to think of as *engagé*; nor is *L'Education sentimentale* a text that offers much in the way of purchase for even the most nuanced utopianism. Yet this text's—and this author's—uncompromising literary vocation bears a curious similarity to the "rumeur continue" of the crowd which renders Frédéric fatigued and dizzy (100/75); and perhaps, if one bends one's ear far enough, it will become possible to hear in that impersonal murmur an affirmation of the event—always, necessarily, the revolutionary event—of the other: an affirmation indistinguishable from a loss which the phallocentric and aesthetic negativity of *Bildung* can only record and mourn without knowing it. If one were to win that interpretative gamble it would become possible to say that, in telling the story of the *Bildungsroman*'s ruin, Flaubert novelizes, betrays, and commemorates the irreplaceable alterity of the other as the apparition of love.

46. Walter Benjamin, *Origin of German Tragic Drama*, trans. John Osborne (London: New Left Books, 1977), 178. Though the melancholia Benjamin ascribes to allegory does not match the tone of Flaubert's denatured prose, Benjamin's formulations otherwise address the landscapes Flaubert constructs in the Fontainebleau episode; e.g.: "[I]n allegory the observer is confronted with the *facies hippocratica* of history as a petrified, primordial landscape" (166).

47. Derrida, *Spectres de Marx*, 111. In the context of a reading of *L'Education sentimentale* it is interesting to note the similarity between Marx's description of the non-revolution of 1848 ("when only the ghost [*Gespenst*] of the old revolution walked about [*ging um*]" [*Eighteenth Brumaire*, 17]) and Marx and Engels's famous claim that "[a] specter [*Gespenst*] walks about [*geht um*] in Europe—the specter of communism" (Karl Marx and Friedrich Engels, "Manifest der Kommunistischen Partei," in *Werke*, 4: 461). See Derrida, *Spectres de Marx*, for a study of the complex temporality and wide figurative range of the specter in Marx's writings.

For meditations on the promise of the communal similar in spirit to Derrida's, see Maurice Blanchot, *La Communauté inavouable* (Paris: Minuit, 1983), and Jean-Luc Nancy, "La Communauté désoeuvrée," in *Aléa* 4 (1983): 11–49. From this perspective it is possible to read Flaubert's comment that "the crowd has never pleased me except during the days of riot" as more than throwaway cynicism or misanthropic conservatism—attitudes Flaubert was obviously capable of striking both in his writing and his life, particularly the latter. See Flaubert to Louise Colet, 31 March 1853, in *Correspondance, 1850–1859* (Paris: Club de l'Honnête Homme, 1971–75), 8:320.

7

Conclusions

The symbol was force as a compass needle or a triangle was force, as the mechanist might prove by losing it, and nothing could be gained by ignoring their value. Symbol or energy, the Virgin had acted as the greatest force the Western world ever felt, and had drawn man's activities to herself more strongly than any other power, natural or supernatural, had ever done; the historian's business was to follow the track of that energy. . . . Thus far, no path had led anywhere. . . . The secret of education still hid itself somewhere behind ignorance, and one fumbled over it as feebly as ever. In such labyrinths, the staff is a force almost more necessary than the legs; the pen becomes a sort of blind-man's dog, to keep him from falling into the gutters. The pen works for itself, and acts like a hand, modelling the plastic material over and over again to the form that suits it best. The form is never arbitrary, but is a sort of growth like crystallization, as any artist knows too well; for often the pencil or pen runs into side-paths and shapelessness, loses its relations, stops or is bogged. . . . Compelled once more to lean heavily on this support, Adams covered more thousands of pages with figures as formal as though they were algebra.

—Henry Adams, *The Education of Henry Adams*

Any reader who has made it through the preceding six chapters has had ample exposure to the paradoxes and vicissitudes of aesthetics; nonetheless, it may be appropriate to recapitulate this book's principal claims. I began by noting the peculiarly hyperbolic reception literary theory has enjoyed, or suffered, over the past two decades, and I proposed that we understand "theory" as a shadow cast by our culture's deeply entrenched aesthetic ideology. The symptomatic equation of theory with "deconstruction" in general and Paul de Man in particular derives from the tense intimacy between theory and aesthetics: aesthetics depends on, exploits, and represses a linguistic predicament that de Man's rhetorical project both repeats and describes. Aesthetics seeks to discover in the sign's arbitrariness a disinterestedness that would guarantee signification itself—thereby guaranteeing the unity and health of the mind, the purposive structure of history, and the definition and destiny of humanity. Through a programmatic misrecognition of language, humanity and history become processes grounded in language, as the word *Bildung* so evocatively suggests. And we have seen that, on the one hand, this linguistic gambit grants aesthetics enormous practical force. As a system based on formalization per se, aesthetics is a model ideology that can be deployed wherever or whenever differences and identities need to be naturalized. Indeed, aesthetics succeeds precisely because of its radical incoherence: unable to guarantee its own production, it projects its possibility into the past and the future as the historical myth of *Bildung,* and thereby becomes a highly supple myth of history. But, on the other hand, the same incoherence that grants aesthetics totalizing power also renders it an uncertain enterprise, vulnerable to paranoid fantasies and perpetually open to a critique which it both forwards and forecloses. The seemingly modest and pedantic project of "theory" occurs as an exacerbation, and critical repetition, of this double bind within the institution of aesthetic pedagogy.

The link between theory and literature—such that theory (as "deconstruction") is always "literary" theory—stems from the fact that aesthetics discovers its most fully realized model in the idea of literature as an autoproductive and self-reflexive linguistic event. The literature department of the modern university draws its rationale more directly than any other academic institution from the ideology of the aesthetic, and for this reason has remained stubbornly identified with theory's production, despite the manifestly interdisciplinary reach of theoretical discourse. My analysis of aesthetics consequently discovered in the academic debate about the *Bildungsroman* an overdetermined site of aesthetic contradiction. As we saw, the paradoxes of the *Bildungsroman* repeat those of aesthetics generally. The genre expands to include any text that can be figured as a subject producing itself in history, which is to say any text whatsoever; it simultaneously shrinks to an elite, high-cultural coterie—the five or so novels, for instance, which German studies repeatedly nominates as *Bildungsromane*—and then, when those novels are examined more closely, disappears into the *degrée zéro de l'écriture* and becomes a mere fiction, discoverable everywhere only because it exists nowhere. The *Bildungsroman* is the pragmatic epitome of the "literary absolute," yet is also (therefore) suspiciously vulgar and perhaps even not truly literary. Its literariness, that is, consists in nothing more or less than the ongoing self-destruction of aesthetics.

Since the *Bildungsroman* as literary absolute founds itself on the obscure, exemplary self-knowledge of the literary text, the problem of this genre leads to that of reading specific novels. My interpretations of *Bildungsromane* by Goethe, Eliot, and Flaubert confirm the diagnoses that my first two chapters worked out in the more abstract terminology of theoretical or generic discourse. All of these texts explore, and ultimately exhaust, the resources of aesthetic or dialectical irony: that is, in various ways they are all anti-*Bildungsromane* which interrogate the possibility of recuperating *Bildung* through negation. At a certain point, however, this story of mourning is interrupted by another figural narrative telling the story of a trauma of signification which inspires the negative, dialectical tale of mourning but remains inaccessible to it. My reading of *L'Education sentimentale* elicited "history" as the name for this trauma. History is the inscription, the cut, or the rupture, through which an event occurs as an event *of* signification, which defines but remains radically external to the symbolic orders of consciousness and meaning. In retrospect we may think of such opaque, disruptive moments as Mignon's identification with puppets in the *Lehrjahre* or Madame Laure's murderous, unreadable blow in *Middlemarch* as these texts' allegories of the "historicity" of *Bildung*. The recuperation of this historicity as aesthetic historicism generates the symptomatic figure of a mechanized, deformed, or dismembered body. The ravages of *Bildung* express themselves as the puppet-like motions of Mignon's body in the *Lehrjahre*, as the trope of unstoppable disinterral and dissection in the *Wanderjahre*, as a widespread mechanization of bodies in Eliot's writings, and as the fetishization and symbolic dispersal of Madame Arnoux in *L'Education sentimentale*.

Futhermore, these texts all characterize the automutilative dimension of aesthetic organicism as simultaneously irreducible and contingent. If bodies acquire their identity—their illusion of unity—only by opening themselves to dissection and dispersal, these destructive processes represent or enact the body's historical contingency. This point holds obvious interest as regards the enormously complex question of the relation between aesthetics and gender. It will not have escaped notice that the bodies being mechanized and dismembered in these texts are almost always female, and frequently maternal. Historical reasons for the mother's prominence in these texts are not hard to come by. The construction, over the course of the seventeenth and eighteenth centuries, of middle-class domestic space around the erotic and tutelary figure of the mother, is a familiar story; and Friedrich Kittler has shown in great detail how pedagogical and aesthetic discourses in Germany around 1800 situated the mother at the origin *of* discourse.[1] My account of the rhetorical instability of aesthetics then permits an explanation for the symbolic violence wreaked on the mother, though in offering it I must blur Kittler's sharp historical focus. During my brief analyses of Schiller's comments on the *Lehrjahre* and Sartre's comments on Flaubert, I suggested in both cases that the commen-

---

1. Friedrich A. Kittler, *Discourse Networks, 1800/1900*, trans. Michael Metteer, with Chris Cullens (Stanford: Stanford University Press, 1990).

tator's use of maternal imagery worked to naturalize textual production and ground semiotic difference in a binary opposition between the sexes—with the result that the maternal figure was blamed for causing the linguistic ambiguity she had been brought in to cure.[2] A hundred and fifty years of history and any number of cultural differences separate Schiller from Sartre: in many contexts it would obviously make sense to claim that their notions of "nature" or the "maternal" are different, or that their texts stage different dramas of sexual difference. Yet it must also be said that it is not particularly surprising to discover a degree of overlap in their rhetorical vocabulary. "Europe," or the "West," in this context, is perhaps a useful category of analysis, and a hundred and fifty years a rather short amount of time. Both Flaubert and Sartre write within a modernity which, in this book, I have called the era of aesthetics. Nor, in such cases, can modernity be rendered a stable term, purged of historical sediments and scars. Feminist scholars have documented the Western tradition's long habit of identifying "woman" with whatever "nature" means, on the one hand, and with rhetorical deceit or inessentiality, on the other; on this level of generality the problem of aesthetics merges with that of "phallogocentrism" as our culture's heaviest historical burden.[3] A full study, if such a thing were possible,

---

2. In my discussion of the *Lehrjahre*'s displacement of oedipal narrative I also alluded to Cynthia Chase's remarkable recasting of Julia Kristeva's work on abjection. Kristeva's understanding of the maternal as a potential chaos that must be cast out or "abjected" if the infant is to enter the symbolic and imaginary orders provides a metapsychological narrative for gestures such as Sartre's or Schiller's. Chase's reading of Kristeva emphasizes that the infant's dilemma is that of *reading* indeterminate marks of maternal care: a crucial point, since as I am about to argue, it is the radically indeterminate predicament of reading which allows us to see the "maternal" element in Kristeva's scheme as historical rather than natural. Kristeva has frequently been accused of reducing woman to the maternal, and of constructing a theory which makes misogyny a necessary dimension of language acquisition; however, if one reads this theory rhetorically, as Chase suggests, its explanatory mechanisms become more supple. See Chase, "The Witty Butcher's Wife: Freud, Lacan, and the Conversion of Resistance to Theory," *MLN* 102.5 (1987): 989–1013. For similar speculations, see Neil Hertz's Afterword to his *The End of the Line: Essays on Psychoanalysis and the Sublime* (New York: Columbia University Press, 1985): a text of particular interest here since it offers an extended reading of the production and expulsion of Daniel's mother from the plot of *Daniel Deronda*. Kristeva's most succinct presentation of her theory of abjection may be found in "L'abjet d'amour," *Tel quel* 91 (1982): 17–32; see also *Powers of Horror: An Essay on Abjection*, trans. Leon S. Roudiez (New York: Columbia University Press, 1982).
3. For an interesting modern deployment of the classical (and ubiquitous) topos that "eloquence, like the fair sex," involves pleasurable deceit, see Locke's *An Essay concerning Human Understanding*, ed. Peter H. Niddich (Oxford: Clarendon Press, 1975), p. 508 (3.10.xxxiii–xxxiv: the chapter is titled "On the Use and Abuse of Words"). "Woman" similarly enters Hegel's monumental recasting of Western metaphysics as "the everlasting irony in the life of the community": see the *Phenomenology of Spirit*, trans. A. V. Miller (New York: Oxford University Press, 1977), 288 (para. 475). For a reading of Locke's text that examines scenes in which gender and maternity play odd and crucial roles, see Cathy Caruth, *Empirical Truths and Critical Fictions* (Baltimore: Johns Hopkins University Press, 1991). For an important rhetorical study of gender,

of the gender politics of aesthetics would require among other things a careful reading of the *Symposium*, in which Diotima defines love as a longing for "the procreation that the beautiful effects," and tropes this "procreation" as a male pregnancy and birth (*to kuoun*) effected by a female goddess, Beauty (*hē Kallonē*).[4] From the transcendental orbit of the *auto to kalon* to the empirico-idealism of bourgeois aesthetics, sexual difference and female generativity recur as figures—often highly ambivalent figures—for the figurativeness of language. However, a rhetorical critique allows—even forces—one to add that they are not *necessary* figures. That is, the readings collected in this book, while not focused on the complex question of gender, can at least help emphasize that the master-tropes of patriarchy are no less historically contingent for having participated in the history of metaphysics itself.

The point is an important one, and it may be helpful to take a moment here to follow the ancient link between rhetoric and the feminine through one of its postmodern spirals. With the Neoplatonic tradition in mind, Philippe Lacoue-Labarthe risks a counteridealist appropriation of the figure of "woman," claiming that "woman is at stake [in the aesthetic] because she represents, not as Hegel through Schiller would have liked, the sensuous itself in its opposition to the spiritual . . . but the sensuous in *its* 'truth,' which is the 'truth' of figure and the fictional."[5] This "other" Aphrodite would not be the goddess of male or metaphysical desire but rather "a figure figuring only the figure in its plasticity and thereby, in fact, the

---

see Barbara Johnson, *A World of Difference* (Baltimore: Johns Hopkins University Press, 1987), and for a classic account of the phallocentric structure of Western metaphysics see Luce Irigaray, *Speculum of the Other Woman* (Ithaca: Cornell University Press, 1985).

4. Plato, *Symposium*, in *Opera*, vol. 2, ed. John Burnet (Oxford: Clarendon Press, 1976); *Plato: The Collected Dialogues*, ed. Edith Hamilton and Huntington Cairns (Princeton: Princeton University Press, Bollingen Series, 1973). I thank Molly Ierulli for drawing my attention to this passage. Diotima goes on to explain that this longing for procreation is in fact the desire of a mortal being for immortality (207a): "Those whose procreancy is of the body turn to woman as the object of their love, and raise a family. . . . But those whose procreancy is of the spirit rather than of the flesh . . . conceive and bear the things of the spirit" (208e–209a). And thus the ideal seeker would approach the "final revelation" of an immortal beauty that "subsists of itself and by itself in an eternal oneness [*auto kath auto meth autou monoeides aei on*]" (211a–b). Clearly the figure of Diotima herself would repay close study in this context. A thematic reading that reduces her to the propositions she enunciates does not suffice, particularly since in this dialogue Socrates, the *eiron*, is ironically framed by Alcibiades as the greatest of all orators, whose philosophy "clings like an adder" (218a). Helpful readings of the question of gender in the *Symposium* may be found in David Halperin's chapter, "Why Is Diotima a Woman?" in *One Hundred Years of Homosexuality and Other Essays on Greek Love* (New York: Routledge, 1990), 113–51, and Luce Irigaray, "Sorcerer Love: A Reading of Plato, *Symposium*, 'Diotima's Speech'," in *An Ethics of Sexual Difference*, trans. Carolyn Burke and Gillian C. Gill (Ithaca: Cornell University Press, 1993), 5–33. I thank Teresa Jesionowski for bringing this latter text to my attention.

5. Philippe Lacoue-Labarthe, "The Unpresentable," in *The Subject of Philosophy*, ed. Thomas Trezise, trans. Thomas Trezise et al. (Minneapolis: University of Minnesota Press, 1993), 155.

tutelary goddess of aesthetics" (Lacoue-Labarthe, "The Unpresentable," 156). Lacoue-Labarthe's gamble replicates some of the problems and temptations of Jacques Lacan's subtle and notorious claim that "'the' woman does not exist."[6] It must at least be said that, precisely to the extent that aesthetics, as Lacoue-Labarthe claims, is "the locus where fiction, the fictional in general, becomes worthy of theory" (151), the sexual identity of its goddess perhaps ought to be slightly more dubious. Insofar as aesthetics destabilizes its own binary oppositions, it means gender trouble, in Judith Butler's phrase.[7] From Winckelmann to Baudelaire, Swinburne, and Wilde, modern aesthetics has provided a space for the production of alternative middle-class sexualities (alternative "male" ones, at any rate) at the same time (and for the same reason) that aesthetic theory has unfolded as an obsessive, and often obsessively binary and heterosexual, attention to gender difference. Lacoue-Labarthe's insight into the fictionality of aesthetics is crucial to retain, precisely because one is thereby able to remark the apo-

6. That is, woman in the abstract, *la* femme,"does not exist" because the symbolic order relegates her to the position of fantasy (hence the correlative claim, "there is no sexual relation"). See in particular Lacan's essay "God and the *Jouissance* of The Woman. A Love Letter," in *Feminine Sexuality: Jacques Lacan and the école freudienne*, ed. Juliet Mitchell and Jacqueline Rose (New York: Norton, 1985), 137–61. Even if restricted to texts rigorously attentive to the difficulties of Lacanian theory and the subtleties of its presentation, the bibliography on Lacan and "the woman" is massive and diverse: for two exemplary positions, see Stephen Heath, "Difference," *Screen* 19.3 (1978): 51–112, who argues that Lacan covertly naturalizes sexual difference and reiterates phallocentric ideology, and Jacqueline Rose, "Introduction II" in *Feminine Sexuality*, 27–57, who does not contest Lacan's participation in "the phallocentrism he described," but insists on the "symbolic and arbitrary nature" of the phallic order (56), and on the accuracy of the Lacanian diagnosis: "Lacan gives an account of how the status of the phallus in human sexuality enjoins on the woman a definition in which she is simultaneously symptom and myth. As long as we continue to feel the effects of that definition we cannot afford to ignore this description of the fundamental imposture which sustains it" (57).
7. Judith Butler, *Gender Trouble: Feminism and the Subversion of Identity* (New York: Routledge, 1990). Butler's uncompromising insistence on the constructedness of the body is particularly salutary insofar as much criticism—even quite rigorous criticism—shares with modern aesthetics the temptation to fall back on the naturalness of heterosexual difference, particularly when humanist models of "history" are in force. In an important essay, for instance, Mary Poovey notes that one of Shaftesbury's models for aesthetic harmony is the proportionality or fit between the sexes: "Thus," Poovey comments, after examining a similar moment in Burke's *Enquiry*, "sexual difference, which exists in nature, becomes the fundamental organizing dichotomy of a semantic system that produces distinctions—and therefore discriminations—in excess of the natural, originary difference." "Aesthetics and Political Economy in the Eighteenth Century: The Place of Gender in the Social Constitution of Knowledge," in *Aesthetics and Ideology*, ed. George Levine (New Brunswick: Rutgers University Press, 1994), 89–90. My concern here is to insist on the importance of refusing the temptation to think of sexual difference as "natural." Sexual difference *functions* as "natural" difference, but only because it has been constructed as such: on this point see Butler, *Gender Trouble*, 92 and passim. Elsewhere in the same essay Poovey describes modern aesthetics as involving "the enforcement of a set of truisms about gender" ("Aesthetics and Political Economy," 80), a claim with which I can agree; it is also plausible to describe aesthetics as participating in a modern "fetishization of sexual difference" (92), so long as one understands fetishism as a naturalizing activity rather than an activity grounded in nature.

tropaic potential of his deconstructive Venus, both as a gendered personification and a personification *of* gender. Gender, as a "subtle and politically
enforced performativity" (Butler, *Gender Trouble*, 146) may be said to be
grounded in the possibility of fiction, but fiction can only be gendered
fictionally. In other words, though the need to personify fiction in gendered
terms may be difficult or even impossible to avoid, the resulting gender will
never be entirely certain.[8]

The texts we have read suggest that anxieties and certainties of gender
saturate aesthetic discourse without, however, exhausting its problematic.
The *Lehrjahre's* focus on Mignon and on the maternal resonance of
Wilhelm's puppets, for instance, cedes in the *Wanderjahre* to a more general
spectacle of violence: though it is true that the latter novel's "plastic anatomy" finds its inspiration in Wilhelm's horror before the corpse of a female
suicide, the narrative also renders the process of dissection and disinterral
indifferent to the particular attributes of its object. In George Eliot's texts,
figures for figurative language migrate from Madame Laure and the
Princess Halm-Eberstein to Lapidoth and finally to *Theophrastus Such's* uncanny machines, while Flaubert's *L'Education sentimentale* plots the course
of its deconstruction of fetishism toward a sublimely inhuman spectacle of
rocks at Fontainebleau, on the one hand, and a domestic tragicomedy centered on Madame Arnoux's rather sexless and anonymous male child, on
the other. At the risk of overschematizing one could say that the question of
aesthetics cannot be translated as that of "woman" or "gender" without
residue, because its linguistic dilemma cannot be entirely contained within
the category of the "human," or even that of the "subject." The imagery of
machines and machine-like bodies which we have encountered so frequently in these novels records this excess of language over the subject. In a
post-Romantic idiom, the machine figures the divergence of process from
meaning, syntax from semantics: a predicament that can inspire a variety of
reactive gestures, as the *Wanderjahre's* dark parody of the Aesthetic State
demonstrates.

The *Wanderjahre's* political allegory is particularly lurid, and as we have
seen can easily be read as a demystification of the aesthetic statism of fascist

8. In this context it is worth noting that Winckelmann's ideal of beauty, in his frequently
strange and surprising *History of Ancient Art*, is hermaphroditic (and also, at certain points,
requires the blending of animal parts into the human: Jupiter's hair and brow, for instance,
derive from those of the king of the beasts, the lion). See *Geschichte der Kunst des Altertums*
(1764), ed. Wilhelm Senff (Weimar: Hermann Böhlaus, 1964), 127. Meanwhile, Burke's *A Philosophical Enquiry into the Origin of Our Ideas of the Sublime and the Beautiful*, ed. James T. Boulton
(New York: Columbia University Press, 1958), despite—or better, because of—its relentlessly
binary organization of its material, will also repeatedly register a certain unsteadiness at the
same moment that it enforces its identification of the beautiful with the female body: this latter,
for instance, will offer to the male gaze a "deceitful maze . . . about the neck and breasts . . .
through which the unsteady eye slides giddily" (115).

ideology; but it is possible to herd some of the consequences of that reading into less dramatic and distant environs. Readers familiar with the debates about fascism's relation to môdernism will perhaps not have been surprised to encounter the question of technology at the epicenter of the aesthetic state, though few may have predicted that this Heideggerian topic would snowball its way through a book on the *Bildungsroman*. No study of aesthetic ideology, however, can avoid becoming a question concerning technics. As we saw in chapter 4, Heidegger diagnoses modern technology as *Ge-stell*, "enframing," a process of extracting and stockpiling which transforms the natural world into *Bestand*, "standing-reserve"—a state in which objects per se no longer exist in or for themselves, but only in or for something else. This evacuation of content within the formality of a (seemingly) total process, however, generates and perpetuates the illusion of a *subject* of technology. Humanity comes to imagine itself as the will-to-power behind technics, while in fact becoming another element to be processed as standing-reserve. Heidegger's work needs to be approached carefully, but I think we can risk the following proposition: aesthetics sees both its own accomplishment and its own destruction in technics. From an aesthetic perspective, technics is formalization. That claim will seem less idiosyncratic if one thinks of Jacques Derrida's extensive, meticulous displacement of Heidegger's question of technics onto the problematic of "writing"—writing understood as the iterability which turns a mark into a sign and which unleashes effects of idealization and formalization that grant writing its enormous technical powers of storage and distribution. If for Aristotle language is the exemplary *technē*, the Derridean critique specifies that "all language is a tele-technology."[9] Technology may in this sense be said to leave its mark on the world thanks to a power of formalization which language exemplifies. While this insight certainly does not exhaust the purview of the question of technology, it may serve to explain the intimacy between aesthetics and technics, which is never more profound than when aesthetic systems tout their organicism—when, in other words, their *technē* pretends to the autoproductivity of *physis*. The limit-case of fascist ideology is usefully dramatic in this regard: its romantic organicism always also involves a glamorization of technical force and, as Walter Benjamin so clearly saw, finds its fulfillment in the phantasm of total, technologized, and apocalyptic war.[10]

9. Jacques Derrida, *Spectres de Marx: L'Etat de la dette, le travail du deuil et la nouvelle Internationale* (Paris: Galilée, 1993), 92. Derrida's classic text on writing, technology, and force is of course *Of Grammatology*, trans. Gayatri Chakravorty Spivak (Baltimore: Johns Hopkins University Press, 1976); see also, for Derrida's most famous, and compact, explication of iterability, "Signature Event Context," and related texts, in *Limited Inc*, ed. Gerald Graff (Evanston: Northwestern University Press, 1988).
10. See in particular Benjamin's remarks on Ernst Jünger's *Total Mobilization:* the condition

In its sober incarnation, however, the Aesthetic State is something more banally familiar: it is a bureaucracy. The modern individual is a bureaucratic product: a paradox captured nicely by Friedrich Kittler in his suggestion that the *Lehrjahre*'s Society of the Tower "is a literary bureaucracy and thus is the very institution of the *Bildungsroman*."[11] As a total artwork, which is to say a self-sustaining organic machine, the polis becomes representable as a Circumlocution Office. To be sure, such a state also either misrecognizes itself or hates itself, since its very aestheticism betrays its aesthetic principle: in fetishizing the arbitrary tautology of law, it predicates its rationale on the repression of its own arbitrariness. The *Wanderjahre*'s rhetorical critique of the Aesthetic State troped this paradox as that of the symbol, a figure which, in this particular text's allegory, transforms arbitrariness into a ground for meaning by valorizing the arbitrary as the unknowable. With reference thus bracketed, the symbol becomes a principle of technical force, and the subject of technology—that is, the subject as will-to-power—arises out of (or better, *as*) the transcendental reserve of the unknowable. From this perspective it becomes understandable that aesthetic bureaucracies valorize secrecy and secrete charismatic attachments, which at the limit collect into the fetish-figure of a national leader. For the same reason, aesthetic bureaucracies are as likely to denounce their own formality as they are to valorize it, since the valorization always involves a betrayal, shortcoming, or slippage. In this sense one would find in the excruciatingly literary vocation of Kafka the culmination of the aesthetic critique I have located in the *Bildungsroman*.

At this point, however, we also return to the vicinity of issues broached at the beginning of this book; and by way of conclusion I would like to focus once more on the academic and literary institution, since the understanding

---

described by the title is one in which, in Jünger's words, "there is no longer any movement whatsoever—be it that of the homeworker at her sewing machine—without at least indirect use for the battlefield." In this totality of movement the German "encounters himself" in the community as form (*Gestalt*). Benjamin diagnoses this theory as "an unrestrained transposition of the theses of *l'art pour l'art* to war": see *Gesammelte Schriften* (Frankfurt: Suhrkamp, 1972), 3:240. Hannah Arendt's analysis of totalitarian ideology as a law of "movement" would also make necessary reading here: see *The Origins of Totalitarianism* (New York: Harcourt, Brace, 1966), 460–79. On fascism, modernism, and technology, see Jeffrey Herf, *Reactionary Modernism: Technology, Culture, and Politics in Weimar and the Third Reich* (Cambridge: Cambridge University Press, 1984). Useful post-Heideggerian reflections on the philosophical ramifications of *technē* may be found in Bernard Stiegler, *La technique et le temps: La faute d'Épiméthée* (Paris: Galilée, 1994). See also, for a powerful and far-reaching analysis of ways in which de Man's work functions as a critique of fascist organicism and technologism, Cynthia Chase, "Trappings of an Education," in *Responses: On Paul de Man's Wartime Journalism*, ed. Werner Hamacher, Neil Hertz, and Thomas Keenan (Lincoln: University of Nebraska Press, 1989), 44–79.
11. Friedrich A. Kittler, "Über die Sozialisation Wilhelm Meisters" in Gerhard Kaiser and Friedrich A. Kittler, *Dichtung als Sozialisationsspiel: Studien zu Goethe und Gottfried Keller* (Göttingen: Vandenhoek und Ruprecht, 1978), 107.

of aesthetics we have achieved should allow us to mark an advance over the discussion I was able to offer in my opening chapter. We may begin by pointing out that the arguments presented here clearly weigh against those of the so-called "new pragmatism," or of the sort of unapologetic professionalism advanced in recent years by critics such as Stanley Fish. If aesthetics is the ideology of bureaucracy, pragmatism is this ideology's focused misrecognition and repetition of itself. When one valorizes as "professionalism" the arbitrariness of procedure, one debunks metaphysics only to recover the Subject as will-to-power, whether as an "interpretative community" or as the "steadfastness of purpose" and "core sense of the enterprise" which "makes a field a field."[12] Typical of the double bind of aesthetics, though, is the fact that overt professionalism never fails to elicit a certain degree of resistance within the aesthetic-pedagogic insitution. Formalism never satisfies, even when disguised as pragmatism, with the result that antitheoretical pragmatism regularly encounters a mild version of the resistance to theory, and—as Fish's work demonstrates—finds itself mechanically repeating the same arguments in essay after essay, chasing the shadow of what is in fact its own resistance to its own unacknowledged act of formalization. Academic humanists, and particularly literary critics, experience this predicament as a vacillation between the professionalism Fish champions and the "antiprofessionalism" or "self-loathing" he condemns. This vacillation is ultimately institutional rather than personal in origin: if "literature" comes into existence as the formalized procedures of an archive and a scene of instruction, it also comes into existence as a refusal of its own institutionality. The history of the institution of literature records this tension as the well-known opposition between humanists and philologists, or critics and scholars.[13] The bureaucratization of aesthetic pegagogy as literature began as—and to some extent remains—a productive but often fractious compromise between professionalism and bellettrism: both the fetishization and the denigration of professionalism are scripted within the literary institution.

12. Stanley Fish, *There's No Such Thing as Free Speech and It's a Good Thing Too* (New York: Oxford University Press, 1993), 220. It may be noted that Fish's announced "antiformalism" in fact relies on a tacit formalism through which the ungroundedness of discourse is totalized into a pragmatic principle. In the so-called new pragmatism of Steven Knapp and Walter Benn Michaels, the irreducibility of authorial "intention" substitutes for the disciplinary intentionalism Fish invokes here: see Knapp and Michaels, "Against Theory," in *Against Theory: Literary Studies and the New Pragmatism*, ed. W. J. T. Mitchell (Chicago: University of Chicago Press, 1985), 11–30. For a rigorous critique of Knapp and Michaels, see Peggy Kamuf, "Floating Authorship," *Diacritics* 16.4 (1986): 3–13.
13. I discuss the double character of literature—as the immediate or "all," on the one hand, and as the infinitely mediated, archival object, on the other—in chapter 2; see that chapter as well for a brief list of recent secondary work on the history of the academic literary institution.

These comments intend to reinforce as well as complicate John Guillory's suggestion that "professionalism is . . . lodged within bureaucracy as the affirmation of the principle antithetical to bureaucracy itself, the principle Weber called 'charisma.'"[14] As I noted in chapter 1, Guillory sees bureaucratic charisma exemplified in the "theory canon" and personified in the figure of Paul de Man. De Man, that is, acquires charisma by seeming to embody an impersonal "rigor"; and Guillory, in a brilliant tour de force, interprets this fetishization of rigor as a blind, defensive repetition of the bureaucratization of the university and of society generally. I proposed then, and can propose with more authority now, that we accept a qualified version of this claim. In the wake of our rhetorical readings in aesthetics it should be clear that the "rigor" of rhetorical reading is a technical formalism very much at the heart of whatever charismatic force de Man, or "de Manian reading," commands; however, by the same token it is clear that in describing what theory (aberrantly) does, Guillory forgets and to a certain extent unwittingly repeats what theory itself *says*. A similar qualification needs to be attached to Guillory's larger argument that "the moment of theory is determined . . . by a certain defunctioning of the literary curriculum, a crisis in the market value of its cultural capital occasioned by the emergence of a professional-managerial class which no longer requires the (primarily literary) cultural capital of the old bourgeoisie" (xii). "A certain defunctioning" is built into the literary institution, which is to say—and this is not exactly a surprising discovery—that the "moment of theory" is *over*determined. Theory's emergence in professionalized form as de Manian rhetorical reading cannot be isolated from the unprecedented technopragmatic restructuring of the university in the twentieth century, but the technologization of education draws its rationale from the ideology which theory critiques.

Wlad Godzich has recently pondered a version of this question by drawing attention to the fact that the high-cultural debates about "theory" in the United States in the 1980s coincided with a massive "redistribution of money and personnel away from the teaching of literature and criticism and toward the teaching of writing and composition."[15] While the teaching of writing and composition is obviously in itself a very desirable thing, Godzich perceives this development—correctly, in my view—as less egalitarian than it looks, to the extent that the new programs can be said to be

---

14. John Guillory, *Cultural Capital: The Problem of Literary Canon Formation* (Chicago: University of Chicago Press, 1993), 254.
15. Wlad Godzich, *The Culture of Literacy* (Cambridge, Mass.: Harvard University Press, 1994), 1. On the "post-historical university," see also Bill Readings, *The University in Ruins* (Cambridge: Harvard University Press, 1996).

fundamentally vocationalist in their orientation and rationale. Specific codes such as technical writing, pre-law compositional skills, and so on are taught within the context of a global marketplace in which knowledge is the premier commodity and the university an increasingly rationalized site for the production of knowledge. In linguistic terms one may understand the intimacy between globalism and the teaching of specialized skills as the assumption, or demand, that all codes be universally translatable— translatable into the transparency of a universal equivalent, "language." At the limit, Godzich suggests, this techno-universalism would herald the accomplishment of the Hegelian state of Absolute Knowledge, as the state's historical destiny withers into an "all-encompassing concern with effi- ciency and competence that takes the form of exclusive specialized practice and rejects as inefficient any broader concerns" (*The Culture of Literacy*, 14). In the terms we have worked out here, we may say that at such a point history cedes to the absolute technopragmatism of the accomplished Aes- thetic State. And in Godzich's view, the "growing hegemony" of universal- ist pragmatism "has only found literary theory in its path." Theory arises "out of the same ground as the new literacy," since both presuppose a post- Enlightenment ideology of a transparently universal language; "but whereas [the new literacy] has sought to accommodate, or even further, the emergence of the posthistorical state, theory has sought to oppose this emergence, frequently as blindly as literacy on its side of the divide" (14).

Those comments largely accord with the findings of this book, though when Godzich goes on to declare that "the gravest menace to theory today" is its "professionalized simulacrum, well ensconced in the system of knowl- edge, usurping the voice of the Other while silencing it and the practice of resistance that is genuine theory" (33), one needs to agree with Guillory that the problem has been misstated. Theory's "professionalism" is in a certain sense irreducible, and neither theory's resistances nor its complicities can be taken in isolation from the technopragmatics of aesthetic ideology. What one *can* say, of course, is that theory demystifies aesthetic ideology, explains how and why it works, and how and why it also at a certain point or in a certain fashion fails to work. If such insights have about them their own seductive sheen of professionalism, they nonetheless possess a critical, diagnostic force that the aesthetic tradition willingly or unwillingly con- firms. Theory renders predictable, for instance, Guillory's turn toward aes- thetics at the close of his antitheoretical project, as he invokes, first, the irreducibility of aesthetics ("there is no cultural product, then, which does not possess form, and therefore no way to experience cultural objects with- out having aesthetic experience" [*Cultural Capital*, 336]), and then goes on to imagine as a "thought experiment" what might happen if "a total democratization of access to cultural products" disarticulated "the formation of cultural capital from the class structure and from the markets" (337):

> The point is not to make judgment disappear but to reform the conditions of its practice. If there is no way out of the game of culture, then, even when cultural capital is the only kind of capital, there may be another kind of game, with less dire consequences for the losers, an *aesthetic* game. Socializing the means of production and consumption would be the condition of an aestheticism unbound, not its overcoming. But of course, this is only a thought experiment. (*Cultural Capital*, 340)

It is a thought experiment with a long pedigree. We have studied the history and the rationale of this Schillerian vision, and it remains only to comment that this book will have been grievously misread if its arguments are taken simply to oppose the values and ideals Guillory invokes. The more access to cultural products is democratized the better; however, it must be said that if "socializing the means of production and consumption" resulted in "an aestheticism unbound," Guillory's utopia would rapidly cease to be one. For better or worse, aesthetics is as conflicted as it is irreducible. Under the right circumstances its terminology remains perhaps our most effective counter to authoritarian or totalitarian or techno-functionalist ideologies, but only because these ideologies are themselves aesthetic in rationale. Certainly in the context of the contemporary debate about "culture" one can neither discard nor endorse aesthetics without slipping into highly scripted aesthetic roles and without losing the critical purchase which aesthetics, as theory, affords. In its mobile dependence on context, theory will thus always to some extent resemble pragmatism (which one might think of, in Godzich's phrase, as theory's "professionalized simulacrum"); but where pragmatism imagines for itself a hyper-aesthetic, technologized subjectivity (as "hands on" know-how, as intentionality, etc.), theory takes up the burden of contingency as that of reading. Reading, in this sense, can guarantee neither its own possibility nor the effects of its occurrence; and if there is a highly theoretical sense in which reading is as impossible as it is necessary, there is a more prosaic sense in which reading is frustrating, and leads immediately to the compensatory delusions of professionalism. The promise that thought will someday capture history and death remains an irreducible fiction, the hard kernel of what Marx and Engels called "German ideology." Aesthetics itself destroys this aesthetic lure; and though we can hardly help experiencing this destruction as a loss, we also experience it as literature, and inhabit it as history.

Index